Modernizing
Women

Women and Change in the Developing World

Series Editor
Mary H. Moran, Colgate University

Editorial Board

Modernizing Women

Gender and Social Change in the Middle East

Valentine M. Moghadam

Lynne Rienner Publishers · Boulder & London

Published in the United States of America in 1993 by
Lynne Rienner Publishers, Inc.
1800 30th Street, Boulder, Colorado 80301

and in the United Kingdom by
Lynne Rienner Publishers, Inc.
3 Henrietta Street, Covent Garden, London WC2E 8LU

Library of Congress Cataloging-in-Publication Data
Moghadam, Valentine M., 1952-
  Modernizing women : gender and social change in the Middle East /
by Valentine M. Moghadam.
    p. cm.—(Women and change in the developing world)
  Includes bibliographical references and index.
  ISBN 1-55587-346-4 (alk. paper)
  ISBN 1-55587-354-5 (pbk)(alk. paper)
    1. Women—Middle East—Social conditions. 2. Women, Muslim—
Middle East—Social conditions. 3. Women—Middle East—Economic
conditions. 4. Women, Muslim—Middle East—Economic conditions.
    I. Title. II. Series.
HQ1726.5.M64 1993
305.42'0956—dc20   92-37454
                                                               CIP

British Cataloguing in Publication Data
A Cataloguing in Publication record for this book
is available from the British Library.

Printed and bound in the United States of America

The paper used in this publication meets the requirements
of the American National Standard for Permanence of
Paper for Printed Library Materials Z39.48-1984.

5 4 3

▲
Contents

▲
Illustrations

▲ Photographs

▲ Figure

▲ Tables

▲

Acronyms and Abbreviations

ALN	Armée de Liberation Nationale (Algeria)
AWC	Afghan Women's Council
AWSA	Arab Women's Solidarity Association
CEDAW	Convention on the Elimination of All Forms of Discrimination Against Women (UN)
CIA	Central Intelligence Agency
DRA	Democratic Republic of Afghanistan
DOAW	Democratic Organization of Afghan Women
DYO	Democratic Youth Organization (Afghanistan)
EAP	Economically active population
EOI	Export-oriented industrialization
EPZ	Export processing zone
FIS	Front Islamique du Salut (Algeria)
FLN	Front de Liberation Nationale (Algeria)
GDP	Gross Domestic Product
GDR	German Democratic Republic
GNP	Gross National Product
ILO	International Labour Organisation
IMF	International Monetary Fund
INSTRAW	United Nations Research and Training Institute for the Advancement of Women
ISA	International Sociological Association
ISI	Import-substitution industrialization
NIC	Newly industrializing country
NIF	National Islamic Front (Sudan)
OPEC	Organization of Petroleum Exporting States
PDPA	People's Democratic Party of Afghanistan
PDRY	People's Democratic Republic of Yemen
PLO	Palestine Liberation Organization
RAWA	Revolutionary Association of Women of Afghanistan

TNC	Transnational corporation
UAE	United Arab Emirates
UNDP	United Nations Development Programme
UNESCO	United Nations Educational, Scientific, and Cultural Organization
UNFPA	United Nations Fund for Population Activities
UNFT	Union Nationale des Femmes Tunisiennes
UNHCR	United Nations High Commission for Refugees
UNICEF	United Nations Children's Fund
UNRISD	United Nations Research Institute for Social Development
UNU	United Nations University
WFS	World Fertility Survey
WID	Women-in-development
WIDER	World Institute for Development Economics Research

▲
Preface

The subject of this study is social change in the Middle East, North Africa, and Afghanistan, its impact on women's roles and status, and women's varied responses to, and involvement in, change processes. It also deals with constructions of gender during periods of social and political change. Social change is usually described in terms of modernization, revolution, cultural breakdown, and social movements. The standard literature on these topics does not examine women or gender, as feminist and women-in-development scholars have noted time and again. I hope this study will contribute to an appreciation of the significance of gender in the midst of change. Neither are there many sociological studies on the Middle East or studies on women in the Middle East from a sociological perspective. Myths and stereotypes abound regarding women, Islam, and the Middle East. This book is intended in part to "normalize" the Middle East by underscoring the salience of structural determinants other than religion. It focuses on the major social-change processes in the region to show how women's lives are shaped not only by "Islam" and "culture," but also by economic development, the state, class location, and the world system. Why the focus on women? It is my contention that middle-class women in the Middle East are consciously and unconsciously major agents of social change in the region, at the vanguard of the movement to modernity.

I have written this book for a wide audience: those who study gender and social change, students of the Middle East, women-in-development researchers, and those bureaucrats and policymakers with time to read. Thus, the book is descriptive, explanatory, and at times policy oriented. Policy implications are especially noticeable in the chapters on employment (Chapter 2) and the changing family (Chapter 4), as well as in the case study of Iran (Chapter 6).

The idea for the book originated in April 1990 over a delicious Moroccan meal at a restaurant in Paris with Moroccan sociologist and feminist Fatima Mernissi, author of the classic *Beyond the Veil: Male-Female*

Dynamics in Modern Muslim Society. She asked me why, despite all the journal articles I had published, I had not yet written a book on the subject of women and Islam. She then pushed aside plates, bowls, and glasses, brought out a notepad and pen, and proceeded to list the subjects of my various articles in one column and suggestions for chapter headings in another. Fatima even proposed a title for my future book; all I can recall of it now is that it included the word "Islam" and that I balked at that. But I did promise a sociological approach to women in the Middle East.

The next source of inspiration was Kumari Jayawardena, Sri Lankan political scientist, historian, and feminist. I had been asked by the Institute of Development Studies of the University of Helsinki to conduct a seminar series for the fall of 1990. Kumari wisely suggested that I organize the lectures around chapter themes for the book, adding that her own famous book, *Feminism and Nationalism in the Third World,* took shape in just this manner. I took her advice and began to write lectures with the book in mind, continuing to work on the project during 1991.

That year I received an announcement from Lynne Rienner Publishers that Mary Moran, whom I had met in 1988–1989, when I was a postdoctoral fellow at Brown University's Pembroke Center for Teaching and Research on Women, would be editing a series called "Women and Change in the Developing World." Coincidentally, my book's working title at that time was *Women and Social Change in the Middle East.* I took this coincidence to be a good sign, wrote to Mary, and sent her the first draft of the manuscript. After I received a challenging and very helpful external review, I was off and running with the second draft. I can only hope that I have not disappointed these friends and colleagues.

Various other associates have read chapters, shared their work, and discussed ideas with me. I am indebted to the participants of the first UNU/WIDER conference I organized, called "Identity Politics and Women," which convened in Helsinki in early October 1990. The papers prepared for that conference and the discussions that took place were enormously stimulating and helped shape my thinking about the gender dynamics of Islamist movements. Debra Kaufman has twice invited me to be on an ASA panel she has organized on gender and fundamentalism, and our discussions have helped refine my ideas about the unintended consequences of Islamization and women's activism. Margot Badran carefully read Chapter 5 and offered valuable suggestions for its improvement. For assistance during research travel in North Africa, I am grateful to Fatima Mernissi, Myriam Monkachi, M. Abdelhay Bouzoubaa, Cherifa Bouatta, Doria Cherifati-Merabtine, Nassera Merah, Alya Baffoun, and Alya Chérif Chamari.

Eric Hobsbawm, Sheila Rowbotham, Judith Lorber, John Foran, David Gibbs, and Wally Goldfrank read and commented on an early version of the chapter on revolutions; David Gibbs also read the chapter on Afghanistan.

The chapters on employment, the family, and Iran have benefited from materials and suggestions from Hooshang Amirahmadi, Azita Berar-Awad, Mounira Charrad, Shahin Gerami, Deniz Kandiyoti, Massoud Karshenas, Nabil Khoury, Victor Mirza-Moghadam (as always), Carla Makhlouf Obermeyer, Mohammad Razavi, Mohamad Tavakoli-Targhi, Nayereh Tohidi, and John Waterbury. I have also benefited from discussions with various visiting scholars at WIDER, especially Ajit Singh, Amiya Bagchi, Amartya Sen, and Martha Nussbaum, and with colleagues in Finland, especially M'hamed Sabour of the University of Joensuu and Tuomo Melasuo of the University of Tampere. Of course, I alone am responsible for any errors.

I am enormously indebted to my institution, UNU/WIDER, for providing an academic's dream of resources and facilities, including research travel, an excellent secretarial staff, and the most supportive and encouraging boss imaginable, Lal Jayawardena, the outgoing director of WIDER. Arja Jumpponen, research secretary, has worked with me on the project since its inception; I am most grateful for her diligence, perseverance, and good humor. In the summer of 1992, Anne Kirjavainen, a graduate student at the University of Turku who had an internship at WIDER, checked and updated the tables on employment and the demographic data. Such an environment allowed me to complete the present book while carrying out other responsibilities and research projects at WIDER. Finally, I am most grateful to the editors at Lynne Rienner Publishers for their careful attention to the manuscript.

This book is dedicated to two women who brilliantly combine scholarship, activism, and teaching: Fatima Mernissi and Kumari Jayawardena; and to Afghan women whose dreams of empowerment and equality have been deferred.

Val Moghadam

▲

Transliteration
and the Iranian Calendar

The system of transliteration adopted in this book is a modified version of that recommended by the *International Journal of Middle East Studies*. All the diacritical marks are deleted, with the exception of the *ayn* and the *hamza* when they appear in the middle of a word, denoted in this book by a prime mark. It is difficult to be consistent when transliteration involves Arabic, Dari, Persian, and Pushtu, but I finally settled on the following spellings: ayatollah, burqa, gharbzadegi, hezbollah, hijab, jihad, Khomeini, Mutahhari, Pushtunwali, qabila, qawm, Quran, Shari'a, walwar.

The Iranian solar (*shamsi*) calendar year starts on March 21. An Iranian year may be converted to the international year by adding 621. Thus the Iranian year 1367 refers to the period March 21, 1988, to March 20, 1989, or, as a shorthand, 1988. In 1992 the Iranian year was 1371.

▲ 1
Introduction and Overview: Recasting the Middle East

> *Men are the managers of the affairs of women*
> *for that God has preferred in bounty*
> *one of them over another. . . .*
> *And those you fear may be rebellious*
> *admonish; banish them to their couches,*
> *and beat them.* —Quran, Sura 4, verse 38

> *God . . . makes it the duty of the man to provide all economic means for [his wife]. . . . And in exchange for this heavy responsibility, that is, the financial burden of the woman and the family, what is he entitled to expect of the woman? Except for expecting her companionship and courtship, he cannot demand anything else from the woman. According to theological sources, he cannot even demand that she bring him a glass of water, much less expect her to clean and cook. . . .*
> —Fereshteh Hashemi, Iranian Islamist intellectual, 1980

The study of social change has tended to regard certain societal institutions and structures as central and then to examine how these change. Family structure, the organization of markets, the state, religious hierarchies, schools, the ways elites have exploited masses to extract surpluses from them, and the general set of values that governs society's cultural outlook are part of the long list of key institutions. In societies everywhere, cultural institutions and practices, economic processes, and political structures are interactive and relatively autonomous. In the Marxist framework, infrastructures and superstructures are made up of multiple levels, and there are various types of transformations from one level to another. There is also an interactive relationship between structure and agency, inasmuch as structural changes are linked to "consciousness"—whether this be class consciousness (of interest to Marxists) or gender consciousness (of interest to feminists).

One of the main markets for women workers is the textile industry. Photo:
International Labour Office

Social change and societal development come about principally through technological advancements, class conflict, and political action. Each social formation is located within and subject to the influences of a national class structure, a regional context, and a global system of states and markets. The world-system perspective regards states and national economies as situated within an international capitalist nexus with a division of labor corresponding to its constituent parts—core, periphery, and semiperiphery. As such, no major social change occurs outside of the world context.[1] Thus, to understand the roles and status of women or changes in the structure of the family, for example, it is necessary to examine economic development and political change—which in turn are affected by regional and global developments. As we shall see in the discussion of women's employment, the structural determinants of class location, state legal policy, development strategy, and world market fluctuations come together to shape the pace and rhythm of women's integration in the labor force and their access to economic resources. Figure 1.1 illustrates the institutions and structures that affect and are affected by social changes in a Marxist-informed world system perspective. The institutions are embedded within a class structure (the system of production, accumulation, and surplus distribution), a set of gender arrangements (ascribed roles to men and women through custom or law; cultural understandings of "feminine" and "masculine"), a regional context (the Middle East, Europe, Latin America), and a world system of states and markets characterized by asymmetries between core, periphery, and semiperiphery countries.

The study of social change is also often done comparatively. Although it cannot be said that social scientists have a single, universally recognized "comparative method," some of our deepest insights into society and culture are reached in and through comparison. In this book, comparisons among women within the region will be made, and some comparisons will be made between Middle Eastern women and women of other Third World regions. Indeed, as a major objective of this book is to show the changing and variable status of women in the Middle East, the most effective method is to study the subject comparatively, emphasizing the factors that best explain the differences in women's status across the region and over time.

Yet such an approach is rarely applied to the Middle East, and even less so to women in Muslim societies in general.[2]

▲ The Debate on the Status of Arab-Islamic Women

That women's legal status and social positions are worse in Muslim countries than anywhere else is a common view. The prescribed role of women in Islamic theology and law is often argued to be a major determinant of women's status. Women are perceived as wives and mothers, and gender

Figure 1.1 **Social Structures and Principal Institutions in Contemporary Societies;
Their Embeddedness Within Class, Gender, Regional, and
Global Relations**

SOCIAL
FORMATION

Cultural-Ideological Structure
  Religious institutions
  Educational system
  Media
  Family
  Political culture

Political-Legal Structure ("The State")
  Government
  Political parties
  Courts
  Military
  Police

Economic Base
  System(s) of production/exchange/distribution
  Infrastructure

CLASS SYSTEM/GENDER ARRANGEMENTS

REGIONAL CONTEXT

WORLD SYSTEM OF STATES AND MARKETS

segregation is customary, if not legally required. Whereas economic provision is the responsibility of men, women must marry and reproduce to earn status. Men, unlike women, have the unilateral right of divorce; a woman can work and travel only with the written permission of her male guardian; family honor and good reputation, or the negative consequence of shame, rest most heavily upon the conduct of women. Through the Shari'a, Islam dictates the legal and institutional safeguards of honor, thereby justifying and reinforcing the segregation of society according to sex. Muslim societies are characterized by higher-than-average fertility, higher-than-average mortality, and rapid rates of population growth. It is well known that age at marriage affects fertility. An average of 34 percent of all brides in Muslim countries in recent years have been under twenty years of age, and women in Muslim nations bear an average of six children.

The Muslim countries of the Middle East and South Asia also have a distinct gender disparity in literacy and education, as well as low rates of female labor force participation.[3] In 1980 the proportion of women to men in the paid labor force was lowest in the Middle East (29 percent, though not far behind Latin America) and highest in Eastern Europe and the Soviet Union, where the proportion was 90 percent.[4]

High fertility, low literacy, and low labor force participation are commonly linked to the low status of women, which in turn is often attributed to the prevalence of Islamic law and norms in Middle Eastern societies. It is said that because of the continuing importance of values such as family honor and modesty, women's participation in nonagricultural or paid labor carries with it a social stigma, and gainful employment is not perceived as part of their role.[5]

Muslim societies, like many others, harbor illusions about immutable gender differences. There is a very strong contention that women are different beings—*different* often meaning *inferior*—which strengthens social barriers to women's achievement. In the realm of education and employment, not only is it believed that women do not have the same interests as men and will therefore avoid men's activities, but also care is exercised to make sure they cannot prepare for roles considered inappropriate. Women's reproductive function is used to justify their segregation in public, their restriction to the home, and their lack of civil and legal rights. As both a reflection of this state of affairs and a contributing factor, very few governments of Muslim countries have signed or ratified the United Nations Convention on the Elimination of All Forms of Discrimination Against Women. Half of the forty-nine countries that have not signed have large Muslim populations. In many Muslim countries, where gender inequality exists in its most egregious forms, it claims a religious derivation and thus establishes its legitimacy.

Is the Middle East, then, so different from other regions? Can we understand women's roles and status only in terms of the ubiquity of deference to Islam in the region? In fact, such conceptions are too facile. It is my contention that the position of women in the Middle East cannot be attributed to the presumed intrinsic properties of Islam. It is also my position that Islam is neither more nor less patriarchal than other major religions, especially Hinduism and the other two Abrahamic religions, Judaism and Christianity, all of which share the view of woman as wife and mother. Within Christianity, religious women continue to struggle for a position equal with men, as the ongoing debate over women priests in Catholicism attests. In Hinduism a potent female symbol is that of the *sati,* the self-immolating widow. And the Orthodox Jewish law of personal status bears many similarities to the fundamentals of Islamic law, especially with respect to marriage and divorce. The gender configurations that draw heavily from religion and cultural norms to govern women's work, political praxis, and other aspects of their lives in the Middle East are not unique to Muslim or Middle Eastern countries.

Religious-based law exists in the Middle East, but not exclusively in Muslim countries; it is also present in the Jewish state of Israel. Rabbinical judges are reluctant to grant women divorces, and, as in Saudi Arabia, Israeli women cannot hold public prayer services. The sexual division of labor in the home and in the society is largely shaped by the Halacha, or Jewish law, and by traditions that continue to discriminate against women. Marital relations in Israel, governed by Jewish law, determine that the husband should pay for his wife's maintenance, while she should provide household services. According to one account, "The structure of the arrangement is such that the woman is sheltered from the outside world by her husband and in return she adequately runs the home. The obligations one has toward the other are not equal but rather based on clear gender differentiation."[6]

Neither are the marriage and fertility patterns mentioned above unique to Muslim countries; high fertility rates are found in sub-Saharan African countries today and were common in Western countries in the early stage of industrialization and the demographic transition. The low status accorded females is found in non-Muslim areas as well. In the most patriarchal regions of West and South Asia, especially India, there are marked gender disparities in the delivery of health care and access to food, resulting in an excessive mortality rate for women.[7] In northern India and rural China, the preference for boys leads to neglect of baby girls to such extent that infant and child mortality is greater among females; moreover, female feticide has been well documented. Thus, the low status of women and girls is a function not of the intrinsic properties of any one religion but of kin-ordered patriarchal and agrarian structures.

Finally, it should be recalled that in all Western societies women as a group were disadvantaged until relatively recently.[8] Indeed, Islam provided women with property rights for centuries while women in Europe were denied the same rights. In India, Muslim property codes were more progressive than English law until the mid-nineteenth century. It should be stressed, too, that even in the West there are marked variations in the legal status, economic conditions, and social positions of women. The United States, for example, compares poorly to Scandinavia and Canada in terms of social policies for women. Why Muslim women lag behind Western women in legal rights, mobility, autonomy, and so forth, has more to do with developmental issues—the extent of urbanization, industrialization, and proletarianization, as well as the political ploys of state managers— than with religious and cultural factors.

Gender asymmetry and the status of women in the Muslim world cannot be solely attributed to Islam because adherence to Islamic precepts and the applications of Islamic legal codes differ throughout the Muslim world. For example, Tunisia and Turkey are secular states, and only Iran has direct clerical rule. Consequently, women's legal and social positions are quite varied, as this book will detail. And within the same Muslim society there are degrees of sex-segregation, based principally on class. Today upper-class women have more mobility than lower-class women, although in the past it was the reverse: Veiling and seclusion were upper-class phenomena. By examining changes over time and variations within societies and by comparing Muslim and non-Muslim gender patterns, one recognizes that the status of women in Muslim societies is neither uniform nor unchanging nor unique.

▲ Assessing Women's Status

In recent years the subject of women in the Middle East has been tied to the larger issue of Islamic revival, or "fundamentalism," in the region. The rise of Islamist movements in the Middle East has once again reinforced stereotypes about the region, in particular the idea that Islam is ubiquitous in the culture and politics of the region, that tradition is tenacious, that the clergy have the highest authority, and that women's status is everywhere low. How do we begin to assess the status of women in Islam or in the Middle East? Critics and advocates of Islam hold sharply divergent views on the matter. One author has sardonically classified much of the literature on the status of women as representing either "misery research" or "dignity research." The former focuses on the utterly oppressive aspects of Muslim women's lives, while the latter seeks to show the strength of women's positions in their families and communities. In either case, it is the status of women *in Islam* that is being scrutinized. Leila Ahmed once concluded that Islam is incompatible with feminism—even with the more mainstream/ modernist notion of women's rights—because Islam regards women as the weak and inferior sex. Freda Hussein has raised counterarguments based on the concept of "complementarity of the sexes" in Islam. Mernissi and others, although critical of the existing inequalities, have stressed that the idea of an inferior sex is alien to Islam, that because of their "strengths" women had to be subdued and kept under control.[9]

As noted by the Turkish sociologist Yakin Ertürk, these arguments draw attention to interesting and controversial aspects of the problem, but they neither provide us with consistent theoretical tools with which to grasp the problem of women's status nor guide us in formulating effective policy for strategy and action. They are either highly ethnocentric in their critique of Islam or too relativistic in stressing cultural specificity. The former approach attributes a conservative role to Islam, assuming that it is an obstacle to progress—whether it be material progress or progress with respect to the status of women. Ertürk argues that overemphasizing the role of Islam not only prevents us from looking at the more fundamental social contradictions that often foster religious requirements but also implies little hope for change, because Islam is regarded by its followers as the literal word of God and therefore absolute. The cultural relativist approach produces a circular argument by uncritically relying on the concept of cultural variability/specificity in justifying Islamic principles. Ertürk notes that many Western observers who resort to relativism in their approach to Islam hold liberal worldviews and treat Islamic practices within the context of individual freedom to worship; any interference with that freedom is seen as a violation of human rights. But gender tends to become occluded by this preoccupation with the human rights of cultural groups. As for the Muslim thinkers, a relativist stand is essentially a defensive response and imprisons its advocates in a pseudonationalistic and religious pride.[10]

However, as stated earlier, one premise of this book is that Islam is neither more nor less patriarchal than the other major religions. Moreover, Islam is experienced, practiced, and interpreted quite differently over time and space. The Tunisian sociologist Abdelwahab Bouhdiba convincingly shows that although the Islamic community considers itself unified, Islam is fundamentally "plastic," inasmuch as there are various Islams— Tunisian, Iranian, Malay, Afghan, Nigerian, and so on.[11] Thus, in order to understand the social implications of Islam, it is necessary to look at the broader sociopolitical and economic order within which it is exercised. As Ertürk correctly observes, and as can be discerned from the two contrasting quotes at the beginning of this chapter, whether or not the content of the Quran is inherently conservative and hostile toward women is relevant, but it is less problematic than it is made out to be.

An alternative to the conceptual trap and political problem created by the devil of ethnocentrism and the deep blue sea of cultural relativism needs to be developed. In this regard it is useful to refer to various "universal declarations" and conventions formulated within the United Nations and agreed upon by the world community. For example, the Universal Declaration on Human Rights (of 1948) provides for both equality between women and men and freedom of religion. The practical meaning of gender equality and means to achieve it have been reflected in the United Nations Convention on the Elimination of All Forms of Discrimination Against Women, adopted on December 10, 1979. The Convention entered into force in 1981 and by July 1992 had 114 government signatories. Similarly, the type of actions necessary to achieve equality by the year 2000 are set out in the Nairobi Forward-looking Strategies adopted by the United Nations General Assembly by consensus in 1985, at the end of the World Decade on Women. While the Strategies are not legally binding, they reflect a moral consensus of the international community and provide an understanding of how equality should be interpreted in practice. The Strategies strongly emphasize the necessity of fully observing the equal rights of women and eliminating de jure and de facto discrimination. They address in particular social, economic, political, and cultural roots of de facto inequality. The Strategies provide a set of measures to improve the situation of women with regard to social participation, political participation and decisionmaking, role in the family, employment, education and training, equality before the law, health, and social security.

The Universal Declaration on Human Rights, the Convention, and the Strategies are all intended to set out universally agreed-upon norms. They were framed by people from diverse cultures, religions, and nationalities and intended to take into account such factors as religion and cultural traditions of countries. For that reason, the Convention makes no provision whatsoever for differential interpretation based on culture or religion. Instead, it states clearly in Article 2 that "States Parties . . . undertake . . . to take all appropriate measures, including legislation, to modify or abolish existing laws, regulations, customs and practices which constitute discrimination against women. . . ."[12] All three international standards are thus culturally neutral and universal in their applicability. They provide a solid and legitimate political point of departure for women's rights activists everywhere.

As for social-scientific research to assess and compare the positions of women in different societies, a sixfold framework of dimensions of women's status adopted from Janet Giele—a framework that is quite consistent with the spirit of the Convention and the Nairobi Forward-looking Strategies—can usefully guide concrete investigations of women's positions within and across societies.[13]

- *Political expression:* What rights do women possess, formally and otherwise? Can they own property in their own right? Can they express any dissatisfactions within their own political and social movements?
- *Work and mobility:* How do women fare in the formal labor force? How mobile are they, how well are they paid, how are their jobs ranked, and what leisure do they get?
- *Family:* Formation, duration, and size: What is the age of marriage? Do women choose their own partners? Can they divorce them? What is the status of single women and widows? Do women have freedom of movement?
- *Education:* What access do women have, how much can they attain, and is the curriculum the same for them as for men?
- *Health and sexual control:* What is women's mortality, to what particular illnesses and stresses (physical and mental) are they exposed, and what control do they have over their own fertility?
- *Cultural expression:* What images of women and their "place" are prevalent, and how far do these reflect or determine reality? What can women do in the cultural field?

This is a useful way of specifying and delineating changes and trends in women's social roles in the economy, the polity, and the cultural sphere.

It enables the researcher (and activist) to move from generalities to specificities and to assess the strengths and weaknesses of women's positions. It
focuses on women's betterment rather than on culture or religion, and it has
wide applicability. At the same time, it draws attention to women as actors.
Women are not only the passive targets of policies or the victims of distorted development; they are also shapers and makers of social change—especially Middle Eastern women in the late twentieth century.

▲ Diversity in the Middle East

To study the Middle East and Middle Eastern women is to recognize the
diversity within the region and within the female population. Contrary to
popular opinion, the Middle East is not a uniform and homogeneous region.
Women are themselves stratified by class, ethnicity, education, and age.
There is no archetypal Middle Eastern woman, but rather women inserted
in quite diverse socioeconomic and cultural arrangements. The fertility
behavior and needs of a poor peasant woman are quite different from those
of a professional woman or a wealthy urbanite. The educated Saudi woman
who has no need for employment and is chauffeured by a Sri Lankan
migrant worker has little in common with the educated Iranian woman who
needs to work to augment the family income and also acquires status with a
professional position. There is some overlap in cultural conceptions of gender in Iran and Saudi Arabia, but there are also profound dissimilarities
(and driving is only one of the more trivial ones). Saudi Arabia is far more
conservative than Iran in terms of what is considered appropriate for
women.
      Women are likewise divided ideologically and politically. Some
women activists align themselves with liberal, social democratic, or communist organizations; others support Islamist/fundamentalist groups. Some
women reject religion as patriarchal; others wish to reclaim religion for
themselves or to identify feminine aspects of it. Some women reject traditions and time-honored customs; others find identity, solace, and strength
in them. More research is needed to determine whether social background
shapes and can predict political and ideological affiliation, but in general
women's social position has implications for their consciousness and
activism.
      The countries of the Middle East and North Africa differ in their his-
torical evolution, social composition, economic structures, and state forms.
All the countries are Arab except Turkey, Iran, Afghanistan, and Israel. All
the countries are Muslim except Israel. All Muslim countries are predominantly Sunni except Iran, which is predominantly Shi'a. Some of the countries have sizable Christian populations (Egypt, Lebanon, Syria, Iraq, the
Palestinians); others are ethnically diverse (Iran, Lebanon, Afghanistan);

some have had strong working-class movements and trade unions (Egypt, Tunisia, Iran, Turkey) or large communist organizations (Egypt, Sudan, Iran, the Palestinians). Others have nomadic and semi-sedentary populations (Saudi Arabia, Libya, Oman). In almost all countries, a considerable part of the middle classes have received Western-style education.

Economically, the countries of the region comprise oil economies poor in other resources, including population (United Arab Emirates [UAE], Saudi Arabia, Oman, Qatar, Kuwait, Libya); mixed oil economies (Tunisia, Algeria, Syria, Iraq, Iran, Egypt); and non-oil economies (Israel, Turkey, Jordan, Morocco, Sudan, Yemen). The countries are further divided into the city-states (such as Qatar and the UAE); the "desert states" (for example, Libya and Saudi Arabia); and the "normal states" (Turkey, Egypt, Iran, Syria). The latter have a more diversified structure, and their resources include oil, agricultural land, and large populations. Some of these countries are rich in capital and import labor (Libya, Saudi Arabia, Kuwait), while others are poor in capital or are middle-income countries that export labor (Algeria, Egypt, Tunisia, Turkey, Yemen). Some countries have more-developed class structures than others; the size and significance of the industrial working class, for example, varies across the region. There is variance in the development of skills ("human capital formation"), in the depth and scope of industrialization, in the development of infrastructure, and in standards of living and welfare.

Politically, the state types range from theocratic monarchism (Saudi Arabia) to secular republicanism (Turkey). States without constitutions are all Gulf states except Kuwait. Many of the states in the Middle East have had consistent legitimacy problems, which became acute in the 1980s. Political scientists have used various terms to describe the states in the Middle East: "authoritarian-socialist" (for Algeria, Syria, Iraq), "radical Islamist" (for Iran and Libya), "patriarchal-conservative" (for Saudi Arabia, Morocco, Jordan), and "authoritarian-privatizing" (for Turkey, Tunisia, Egypt). Some of these states have strong capitalistic features, while others have strong feudalistic features. In this book I use "neopatriarchal state," adopted from Hisham Sharabi, as an umbrella term for the various state types in the Middle East.[14] In the neopatriarchal state, unlike liberal democratic societies, Middle Eastern countries bind religion to power and state authority, resulting in a situation whereby the family, rather than the individual, constitutes the universal building block of the community.

In the Middle East there is a variable mix of religion and politics. For example, Islam is not a state religion in Syria, whose constitution provides that "freedom of religion shall be preserved, and the state shall respect all religions and guarantee freedom of worship to all, provided that public order is not endangered." Syria's Muslim majority coexists with a Christian minority totaling about 12 percent of the population. Christian holidays are recognized in the same way as Muslim holidays. Syria observes Friday rest but also allows time off for Christian civil servants to attend Sunday religious services. The constitution also guarantees women "every opportunity to participate effectively and completely in political, social, economic, and cultural life." Although women, especially in Syrian cities, enjoy a degree of freedom comparable to their counterparts in the West, it is difficult to reconcile women's rights with Quranic law, which remains unfavorable to women with regard to marriage, divorce, and inheritance.

Table 1.1 illustrates some economic characteristics of Middle Eastern countries, as well as juridical features relevant to women. A key factor shared by all countries except Tunisia and Turkey is the absence of a comprehensive civil code. Most of the countries of the Middle East and North Africa are governed to some degree by Islamic canon law, the Shari'a. (Israeli law is based on the Halacha.) Only in Turkey is there a constitutional separation of church and state.

Given the wide range of socioeconomic and political conditions, it

Table 1.1 Some Characteristics of Middle Eastern and North African Countries, 1989

Country	Income level High	Medium	Low	Oil Exporter	Labor Exporter	Highly Indebted	Signatory of CEDAW[a]	Comprehensive Civil Code
Afghanistan			X					
Algeria		X		X	X	X		
Bahrain	X			X				
Egypt		X		X	X	X	X	
Iran		X		X				
Iraq		X		X			X	
Israel		X						
Jordan		X			X			
Kuwait	X			X				
Lebanon					X			
Libya	X			X			X	
Morocco		X			X	X		
Oman	X			X				
Qatar	X			X				
Saudi Arabia	X			X				
Sudan			X		X	X		
Syria		X		X	X			
Tunisia		X		X	X	X	X	X
Turkey		X			X	X	X	X
UAE	X			X				
Yemen (YAR)[b]		X			X			
Yemen (PDRY)[b]		X			X	X	X	

Sources: ILO, *World Labour Report 1984*; World Bank, *World Development Report 1985*; United Nations, *The World's Women: Trends and Statistics 1970–1990*, pp. 115–116.

Notes: a. Convention on the Elimination of All Forms of Discrimination Against Women, adopted by the UN General Assembly in 1979.

b. The two Yemens united in 1990.

Table 1.2 Women's Political Participation

Middle East	Year of Right to Vote	Parliamentary Seats Occupied by Women, 1987 (percent)	Women Decisionmakers[a] in All Government Ministries, 1987 (number)
Algeria	1962	2.4	1
Bahrain	—	—	4[b]
Egypt	1956	3.9	0
Iran	1963	1.5	0
Iraq	1980	13.2	0
Israel	1948	8.3	16
Jordan	1973	0.0	0
Kuwait	—	—	5[b]
Lebanon	1957	0.0	0
Libya	—	—	0
Morocco	1963	0.0	0
Oman	—	—	1[b]
Qatar	—	—	0
Saudi Arabia	—	—	1[b]
Sudan	1953	0.7	0
Syria	1949	9.2	0
Tunisia	1956	5.6	3
Turkey	1934	3.0	0
UAE	—	—	0
Yemen, AR	1970	0.0	0
Yemen, PDR	1967	9.9	n.a.
Selected Comparative Countries			
Brazil	1934	5.3	3
India	1950	8.3	4
Indonesia	1945	n.a.	2
Ireland	1918	8.4	2
Malaysia	1957	5.1	1
Mexico	1953	10.8	1
Pakistan	1947	8.9	3
South Korea	1948	2.5	n.a.
Sweden	1921	28.5	4
United States	1920	5.3	27

Sources: All data from *The World's Women: Trends and Statistics 1970–1990* (United Nations, 1990), Table 3, pp. 39–42, except the year of women's right to vote in Lebanon, which is from *Compendium of Statistics and Indicators on the Situation of Women, 1986* (United Nations, 1989).

Notes: a. Decisionmakers are ministers, deputy or assistant ministers, secretaries of state and deputy secretaries of state, or their equivalents.

b. The apparent discrepancy between the lack of voting rights and absence of parliamentary seats on the one hand, and the number of female decisionmakers in the Gulf sheikhdoms on the other is explained by elite recruitment patterns, whereby women from elite families have access to the limited opportunities for women.

n.a. = not available

follows that gender is not fixed and unchanging in the Middle East (and neither is culture). There exists internal regional differentiation in gender codes, as measured by differences in women's legal status, education levels, fertility trends, employment patterns, and political participation. For example, gender segregation in public is the norm and the law in Saudi Arabia but not in Syria, Iraq, or Morocco. In Iran, Egypt, Tunisia, and elsewhere, women vote and run for parliament. In Turkey, the female share of certain high-status occupations (law, medicine, judgeship) is considerable. Following the Iranian Revolution, the new authorities prohibited abortion and contraception, and lowered the age of consent to thirteen for girls. But in Tunisia contraceptive use is widespread, and the average age of marriage is twenty-four.[15] Afghanistan has the highest rate of female illiteracy among Muslim countries, but the state took important steps after the Saur Revolution of April 1978 to expand educational facilities and income-generating activities for women. And, as seen in Table 1.2, women's participation in government as key decisionmakers and as members of parliament varies across the region.

If all the countries we are studying are Muslim (save Israel), and if the legal status and social positions of women are variable, then logically Islam and culture are not the principal determinants of their status. Of course, Islam can be stronger in some cases than in others, but what I wish to show in this book is that women's roles and status are structurally determined by state ideology (regime orientation and juridical system), level and type of economic development (extent of industrialization, urbanization, proletarianization, and position in the world system), and class location. A sex/gender system informed by Islam may be identified, but to ascribe principal explanatory power to religion and culture is methodologically deficient, as it exaggerates their influence and renders them timeless and unchanging. Religions and cultural specificities do shape gender systems, but they are not the most significant determinants and are themselves subject to change. The content of gender systems is also subject to change.

▲ A Framework for Analysis:
Gender, Class, the State, Development

The theoretical framework that informs this study rests on the premise that stability and change in the status of women are shaped by the following structural determinants: the sex/gender system, class, the state, and development strategy that operate within the capitalist world system.

Sex/Gender System

A useful definition of gender is provided by de Lauretis:

The cultural conceptions of male and female as two complementary yet mutually exclusive categories into which all human beings are placed constitute within each culture a gender system, that correlates sex to cultural contents according to social values and hierarchies. Although the meanings vary with each concept, a sex-gender system is always intimately interconnected with political and economic factors in each society. In this light, the cultural construction of sex into gender and the asymmetry that characterizes all gender systems cross-culturally (though each in its particular ways) are understood as systematically linked to the organization of social inequality.[16]

The sex/gender system is primarily a cultural construct that is itself constituted by social structure. That is to say, gender systems are differently manifested in kinship-ordered, agrarian, developing, and advanced industrialized settings. Type of political regime and state ideology further influence the gender system. States that are Marxist (for example, the former German Democratic Republic), theocratic (Saudi Arabia), conservative democratic (the United States), and social democratic (the Nordic countries) have quite different laws about women and different policies on the family.[17]

The thesis that women's relative lack of economic power is the most important determinant of gender inequalities, including those of marriage, parenthood, and sexuality, is cogently demonstrated by Blumberg and Chafetz, among others. The division of labor by gender at the macro (societal) level reinforces that of the household. This dynamic is an important source of women's disadvantaged position and of the stability of the gender system. Another important source is juridical and ideological. In most contemporary societal arrangements, "masculine" and "feminine" are defined by law and custom; men and women have unequal access to political power and economic resources, and cultural images and representations of women are fundamentally distinct from those of men—even in societies formally committed to social (including gender) equality. Inequalities are learned and taught, and "the non-perception of disadvantages of a deprived group helps to perpetuate those disadvantages."[18] Many governments do not take an active interest in improving women's status and opportunities, and not all countries have active and autonomous women's organizations to protect and further women's interests and rights. High fertility rates limit women's roles and perpetuate gender inequality. Where the state's policies and rhetoric are actively pronatalist, as with neopatriarchal states, and where official and popular discourses stress sexual differences rather than legal equality, an apparatus exists to create stratification based on gender. The legal system, educational system, and labor market are all sites of the construction and reproduction of gender inequality and the continuing subordination of women.

According to Papanek, "Gender differences, based on the social construction of biological sex distinctions, are one of the great 'fault lines' of societies—those marks of difference among categories of persons that govern the allocation of power, authority, and resources." Contemporary gender systems are often designed by ideologues and inscribed in law, justified by custom and enforced by policy, sustained by processes of socialization and reinforced through distinct institutions. But gender differences are not the only "fault lines"; they operate within a larger matrix of other socially constructed distinctions, such as class, ethnicity, religion, and age, that give them their specific dynamics in a given time and place. Gender is thus not a homogeneous category. To paraphrase Michael Mann, gender is stratified and stratification is gendered.[19] Nor is the gender system static. In the Middle East, the sex/gender system, while still patriarchal in the classic sense, has undergone change.

Class

Class constitutes a basic unit of social life and thus of social research. Class is here understood in the Marxist sense as determined by ownership or control of the means of production; social classes also have differential access to political power and the state. Class location shapes cultural practices, patterns of consumption, lifestyle, reproduction, and even worldview. As Ralph Miliband puts it, class divisions "find expression in terms of power, income, wealth, responsibility, 'life chances,' style and quality of life, and everything else that makes up the texture of existence."[20] Class shapes women's roles in the sphere of production, and it shapes women's choices and behavior in reproduction.

In the highly stratified societies of the Middle East and North Africa, social class location, along with state action and economic development, acts upon gender relations and women's social positions. Although state-sponsored education has resulted in a certain amount of upward social mobility and has increased the number of women willing and able to fill administrative and welfare jobs, women's access to resources, including education, is largely determined by their class location. That a large percentage of urban employed women in the Middle East are found in the services sector or in professional positions can be understood by examining class. As in other Third World regions where social disparities are great, upper- and upper-middle-class urban women in the Middle East can exercise a greater number of choices and thus become much more "emancipated" than lower-middle-class, working-class, urban poor, or peasant women. In 1971 Safilios-Rothschild wrote that women could fulfill conflicting professional and marital roles with the help of cheap domestic labor and the extended family network.[21] In 1990 this observation was still true for women from wealthy families, although, except in Morocco, middle-class women in the large Middle Eastern countries are less likely to be able to afford domestic help these days and more likely to rely on a mother or mother-in-law. As noted by Badran, while at the level of ideology and policy some states are committed to women's participation in industrial production (such as in Egypt), the system extracts the labor of women in economic need without giving them the social services to coordinate their productive roles in the family and workplace.[22]

Economic development has led to the growth of the middle class, especially the salaried middle class. The middle class in Middle Eastern countries is internally differentiated; there is a traditional middle class of shopkeepers, small bazaaris, and the self-employed—what Marxists call the traditional petty bourgeoisie. There is also a more modern salaried middle class, persons employed in the government sector or in the private sector as teachers, lawyers, engineers, administrators, secretaries, nurses, doctors, and so on. But this modern salaried middle class is itself differentiated culturally, for many of its members are children of the traditional petty bourgeoisie. The political implications are profound, for Islamist movements seem to be recruiting from the more traditional sections of the contemporary middle class.

Economic Development and State Policies

Since the 1960s and 1970s, the Middle East has been participant in a global process variously called the internationalization of capital, the new (or changing) international division of labor, and global Fordism. Transnational corporations, national development plans, and domestic industrialization projects led to significant changes in the structure of the labor force, including an expansion of nonagricultural employment. Oil revenues assisted industrial development projects, which also led to new employment opportunities and changes in the occupational structure. The Middle East has historically been a region with thriving cities, but increased urbanization and rural-urban migration since the 1950s occurred in tandem with changes in the economy and in property relations. Property ownership patterns changed concomitantly from being based almost exclusively on land or merchant capital to being based on the ownership of large-scale industrial units and more complex and international forms of commercial and financial capital. The process of structural transformation and the nearly universal shift toward the nonagrarian urban sector in economic and social terms produced new class actors and undermined (though it did not destroy) the old. Industrial workers, a salaried middle class, and large-scale capitalists are products of and participants in economic development. Mass education and bureaucratic expansion led to prodigious growth in the new middle class; the creation and absorption into the public sector of important productive, commercial, and banking assets spawned a new managerial state bourgeoisie.[23] Other classes and strata affected by eco-

nomic development and state expansion are the peasantry, rural landown-
ing class, urban merchant class, and traditional petty bourgeoisie. High
population growth rates, coupled with heavy rural-urban migration, concentrated larger numbers of semiproletarians and unemployed people in
major urban areas.

Although female labor force participation rose in all Third World
regions, the largest increase was reported in the Middle East. In the heyday
of economic development, most of the large Middle East countries, such as
Iran, Egypt, Turkey, and Algeria, embarked on a development strategy of
import-substitution industrialization (ISI), where machinery was imported
to run local industries producing consumer goods. This strategy was associated with an economic system characterized by central planning and a large
public sector. State expansion, economic development, oil wealth, and the
region's increased integration within the world system combined to create
educational and employment opportunities for women in the Middle East.
For about ten years after the oil price increases of the early 1970s, a massive investment program by the oil-producing nations affected the structure
of the labor force not only within the relevant countries but throughout the
region as a result of labor migration. The urban areas saw an expansion of
the female labor force, with women occupying paid positions as workers,
administrators, and professionals.

In developing countries, the state plays a major role in the formulation
of social policies, development strategies, and legislation that shape opportunities for women. Family law; affirmative action; provisions for or
restrictions on working mothers; policies on education, health, and population; and other components of social policy designed by state managers
crucially affect women's status and gender arrangements. Strong states
with the capacity to enforce laws may undermine customary discrimination
and patriarchal structures—or they may reinforce them. The state can act as
a facilitator for or an obstacle to the integration of female citizens in public
life. As Jean Pyle has found for the Republic of Ireland, state policy can
have contradictory goals: development of the economy and expansion of
services on one hand, maintenance of the "traditional family" on the
other.[24] Such contradictory goals could create role conflicts for women,
who may find themselves torn between the economic need or desire to
work and the gender ideology that stresses family roles for women.
Conversely, economic development and state-sponsored education could
have unintended consequences: The ambivalence of neopatriarchal state
managers notwithstanding, there is now a generation and stratum of educated women who actively pursue employment and political participation in
defiance of cultural norms.

The positive relationship between female education and nonagricultural employment is marked throughout the Middle East. Census data reveal
that each increase in the level of education is reflected in a corresponding

increase in the level of women's nonagricultural employment and a decrease in fertility. Education seems to increase the aspirations of women in certain sectors of society for higher income and better standards of living.[25] Moreover, it has weakened the restrictive barriers of traditions and increased the propensity of women to join the labor force and public life. These social changes have had a positive effect in reducing traditional sex segregation and female seclusion and in producing a generation of middle-class women who have achieved economic independence and no longer depend on family or marriage for survival and status.

At the same time, it is necessary to recognize the limits to change—including those imposed by a country's or a region's location within the economic zones of the capitalist world system. Development strategies and state economic policies are not formulated in a vacuum; they are greatly influenced, for better or for worse, by world-systemic imperatives. Although most of the large countries in the Middle East are semiperiphery countries, the function of the region within the world system thus far has been to guarantee a steady supply of oil for foreign, especially core-country, markets, and to import industrial goods, especially armaments, mainly from core countries. One result has been limited industrialization and manufacturing for export. Another result has been limited employment opportunities for women in the formal industrial sector, as capital-intensive industries and technologies tend to favor male labor. And in the 1980s, socioeconomic problems bedeviled the region, with wide-ranging implications for women.

The section that follows examines in more detail the gender dynamics of social change in the region—and, by extension, the organization of this book.

▲ Social Changes and Women in the Middle East

One of the ways societies influence each other economically, politically, and culturally is through international labor migration, which also has distinct gender-specific effects. In the Middle East and North Africa, oil-fueled development encouraged labor migration from labor-surplus and capital-poor economies to capital-rich and labor-deficit oil economies. For example, there was substantial Tunisian migrant labor in Libya and Egyptian migrant labor in the Gulf emirates.[26] This migration affected, among other things, the structure of populations, the composition of the households, and the economies of both sending and receiving countries. Many of the oil-rich Gulf states came to have large populations of noncitizens, and female-headed households proliferated in the labor-sending countries. During the years of the oil boom, roughly until the mid-1980s, workers' remittances were an important factor in not only the welfare of families and households but also in the fortunes of economies such as

Jordan's and Egypt's. Labor migration to areas outside the Middle East has been undertaken principally by North Africans and Turks. Historically, North Africans have migrated to the cities of France, although large populations of Moroccans settled in Spain as well. And in the late 1980s Italy became another destination for North African migrant workers. Turkish "guest workers" have been an important source of labor to West German capital since the 1950s.

Labor migration may be functional for the economies of the host country (in that it receives cheap labor) and sending country (in that unemployment is reduced and capital inflows through workers' remittances are increased); emigration, especially of professionals (the so-called brain drain) also may be advantageous to receiving countries. Like exile, however, labor migration and emigration have other consequences, including social-psychological, cultural, and political effects. In the case of Iran—characterized by the brain drain of Iranian professionals following the 1953 Shah-CIA coup d'état, the massive exodus of students to the West in the 1960s and 1970s, a second wave of emigration and exile following Islamization, and the proliferation of draft-dodgers in the mid-1980s—the society became fractured and contentious. When, in 1978–1979, tens of thousands of Iranian students in the United States and Europe returned en masse to help construct the new Iran, they brought with them both organizational and leadership skills learned in the anti-Shah student movement *and* a secular, left-wing political-cultural orientation that put them at odds with the Islamists.[27]

Exile, emigration, and refugee status almost always result in changes in attitudes and behavior, but whether these changes improve or worsen women's lot depends on many intervening factors. In the refugee camps on the Algeria-Morocco border, where 160,000 Sahrawis have spent over a decade, the women who make up three-quarters of the adult population have played a central role in running the camps from the time of their arrival. They set up committees for health, education, local production, social affairs, and provisions distribution.[28] Janet Bauer informs us that among Algerian Muslim immigrants in France, women have a strong role in maintaining religious rituals and symbolic meanings that are important in preserving cultural identity and adaptation. The same is true for many Turkish residents in Germany. The situation for Iranian refugees, exiles, and immigrants seems to differ, however, as they may be ambivalent about the very traditions and religious rituals from which individuals are said to seek comfort in times of modernity and crises. Socioeconomic status and political ideology may also explain differences between Algerian, Turkish, and Iranian immigrants. In her study of Iranian immigrants in France, Vida Nassehy-Behnam states: "Since the initiation of 'theocracy,' Iranian emigration in general has been partly motivated by the pervasiveness of a religious ideology which impinges so dramatically upon individual lifestyles."

She then offers two categories of emigrants: (1) political emigrants—that is, those whose exodus began in February 1979, including monarchists, Nationalists, communists, and the Iranian Mojahedin; and (2) sociocultural emigrants, defined as those Iranians who were not politically active to any great extent but left the country out of fear over an uncertain future for their children and/or because of the morose atmosphere that prevailed in Iran, especially for women and youth. In their study of Iranian exiles and immigrants in Los Angeles, Bozorgmehr and Sabagh show that some 65 percent of immigrants and 49 percent of exiles have four or more years of college. These findings for Iranians stand in contrast to the figures for other migration streams. Another difference between Iranian exiles, refugees, and immigrants and those of North Africa and Turkey is the greater preponderance of religious minorities—Christians, Jews and Baha'is—among Iranians. Such minorities are especially prevalent within the Iranian exile group in Los Angeles. Bozorgmehr and Sabagh offer these religious patterns as an explanation for why the Iranian exiles they surveyed perceived less prejudice than other groups, which may contain a larger share of Muslims.[29]

These factors—socioeconomic status, education, and political ideology—shape the experience of women in exile, immigrants, and refugees. Bauer notes that although women in Middle Eastern Muslim societies are rarely described as migrating alone, many Iranian women do go into exile alone. The women she interviewed in Germany typically had been involved in secular left political and feminist activities in Iran; many had high school or college educations. She elaborates: "Some married young in traditional marriages; others were single or divorced. Some were working class; others middle or upper middle class . . . but most of those I interviewed did come into exile with some ideas about increasing personal autonomy and choice."[30]

Can there be emancipation through emigration? Bauer notes the growing feminist consciousness of Iranian exiles and writes that among those she interviewed, there was a general feeling that the traumatic events of 1979–1982 had initiated cross-class feminist cooperation among women and rising consciousness among all Iranians on the issue of gender relations. She adds that larger political goals may be lost, however, as people put aside notions of socialist revolution, social transformation, and political activity and wrap themselves in introspection and their individual lives. (These are both points with which I, from an inside vantage point, concur.)

The key elements of social change that are usually examined are economic structure and, tied to that, class and property relations. The major source of social change in the Middle East in the post–World War II period has been the dual process of economic development and state expansion. There can be no doubt that over the past thirty years, the economic systems of the region have undergone modernization and growth, with implications for social structure (including the stratification system), the nature and capacity of the state, and the position of women. Much of this economic modernization was based on income from oil, and some came from foreign investment and capital inflows. Economic development alters the status of women in different ways across nations and classes. How women have been involved in and affected by economic development is the subject of Chapter 2. As the state is the manager of economic development in almost all cases, and as state economic and legal policies shape women's access to employment and economic resources, this chapter underscores the government's role in directing development and its impact on women.

Another source of social change is revolution, whether it be a more limited political revolution or a large-scale social revolution. In some Middle Eastern countries, notably Saudi Arabia, change comes about slowly and is carefully orchestrated by the ruling elite. But where revolutions occur, change comes about rapidly and dramatically, with unintended consequences for the masses and the leadership alike. Revolutions frequently result in strong, centralized states whose programs may or may not be in accord with the spirit of the revolutionary coalition (as in the case of the Iranian Revolution). Still, modernizing revolutionary states have been crucial agents in the advancement of women by enacting changes in family law, providing education and employment, and encouraging women's participation in public life. For example, the Iraqi Ba'th regime in its radical phase (1960s and 1970s) undertook social transformation by introducing a land reform program that utterly changed the conditions of the peasantry and by establishing a welfare state for the urban working classes and the poor. In its drive against illiteracy and for free education, the Ba'thist revolution produced one of the best-educated intelligentsias in the Arab world. Even a hostile study of Iraq credits the regime with giving women the right to have careers and participate in civic activities.[31] Such radical measures effected by states and legitimized in political ideologies have been important factors in weakening the hold of traditional kinship systems on women—even though the latter remain resilient. On the other hand, weak states may be unable to implement their ambitious programs for change. The case of Afghanistan is especially illustrative of the formidable social-structural and international hurdles that may confront a revolutionary state and of the implications of these hurdles for gender and the status of women. The sociology of revolution has not considered changes in the status of women as a consequence of revolution and has so far been oblivious to the overriding importance of the "woman question" to revolutionaries and reformers. Chapter 3 examines the effect of radical reforms and revolutions in the Middle East on the legal status and social positions of women, including variations in family law. This chapter underscores the gender dynamics of reforms and revolutionary changes, with a view also to correcting an oversight in the sociology of revolution.

Political conflict or war can also bring about social change, including change in the economic and political status of women, a heightened sense of gender awareness, and political activism on the part of women. World War II has been extensively analyzed in terms of gender and social change.[32] Wartime conditions radically transformed the position of women in the work force. Ruth Milkman notes that virtually overnight, the economic mobilization in the United States produced changes that advocates of gender equality both before and since have spent decades struggling for. Postwar demobilization rapidly restored the prewar sexual division of labor, and American culture redefined woman's place in terms of the now famous "feminine mystique." But it is also true that in many Western countries involved in World War II, female labor force participation rose rapidly in the postwar decades. Some authors have begun exploring the complex relationship between gender, consciousness, and social change, suggesting a strong link between the wartime experience and the emergence, two decades later, of the second wave of feminism. The Middle East has encountered numerous kinds of wars and political conflicts since the 1950s, with varying implications for societies and for women. In some cases, an unexpected outcome of economic crisis caused by war could be higher education and employment of women. A study conducted by a professor of education at the Lebanese University suggests that Lebanese parents feel more strongly that educating their daughters is now a good investment, as higher education represents a financial asset. In addition to offering better work opportunities and qualifications for a "better" husband, a degree acts as a safety net should a woman's marriage fail or should she remain single. In a study I undertook of women's employment patterns in postrevolutionary Iran, I was surprised to discover that, notwithstanding the exhortations of Islamist ideologues, women had not been driven out of the work force and their participation in government employment had slightly increased relative to 1976. This I attributed to the imperatives of the wartime economy, the manpower needs of the expanding state apparatus, and women's resistance to subordination.[33] In Iraq the mobilization of female labor accelerated during the war with Iran, though this was apparently coupled with the contradictory exhortation to produce more children.[34]

The most obvious case of the impact of political conflict is that of the Palestinians, whose expulsion by Zionists or flight from their villages during periods of strife was a major cause of changes in rural Palestinian life and the structure of the family.[35] There is evidence that the prolonged uprising, which has organized and mobilized so many Palestinians, has had a positive impact on women's roles, inasmuch as women have been able to participate politically in what was probably the most secular and democratic movement in the Arab world. Internationally, the best known have been the guerrilla fighter Leila Khaled and the negotiator and English professor Hanan Ashrawi—two contrasting examples of roles available to Palestinian women in their movement. During the 1970s Palestinian women's political activity and participation in resistance groups expanded, whether in Lebanon, the West Bank, Gaza, in universities, or in refugee camps. And during the intifada, or uprising against occupation, which began in 1987, Palestinian women organized themselves into impressive independent political groups and economic cooperatives. A feminist consciousness is now more visible among Palestinian women. Some Palestinian women writers, such as Samira Azzam and Fadwa Tuqan, have combined a critique of patriarchal structures and a fervent nationalism to produce compelling work.[36] Likewise, the long civil war in Lebanon has produced not only suffering and destruction but a remarkable body of literature with strong themes of social and gender consciousness. Miriam Cooke's analysis of the war writings of the "Beirut Decentrists" in the late 1970s and early 1980s shows the emergence of a feminist school of women writers. Indeed, Cooke's argument is that what has been seen as the first Arab women's literary school is in fact feminist.[37]

At the same time, the Palestinian movement has exalted women as mothers and as mothers of martyrs. This emphasis on their reproductive role has created a tension on which a number of authors have commented.[38] During the latter part of the 1980s, another trend emerged among the Palestinians, especially in the impoverished Gaza Strip: Islamist vigilantes who insisted that women cover themselves when appearing in public. The frustrations of daily life, the indignities of occupation, and the inability of the secular and democratic project to materialize may explain this shift.

One important dimension of social change in the region has been the weakening of the patriarchal family and traditional kinship systems. Specifically, demographic changes, including patterns of marriage, have followed from state-sponsored economic development, state-directed reforms, and educational attainment. Industrialization, urbanization, and proletarianization have disrupted kinship-based structures, with their gender and age hierarchies. In some cases, revolutionary states have undermined patriarchal structures, or attempted to do so, through legislation aimed at weakening traditional rural landlord structures or the power of tribes. Often this type of change comes about coercively. Whether changes to the patriarchal family structures come about gradually and nonviolently or rapidly and coercively, the implications for the status of women within the family and in the society are profound. Yet most Middle East states have been ambivalent about transforming women and the family. They have sought the apparently contradictory goals of economic development and strengthening of the family. The latter objective is often a bargain struck with more conservative social elements, such as religious leaders or traditional local communities. Changes in the patriarchal social structure, the contradictory role of the neopatriarchal state, and the profound changes occurring to the structure of the family are examined in Chapter 4.

One of the most vexed issues of the region, with significant implications for the rise of Islamism and the question of women, is the nonresolution of the Palestinian-Israeli conflict. A deep sense of injustice directed at Zionist actions and American imperialism pervades the region. In Iran the 1953 CIA-sponsored coup d'état against the government of Prime Minister Mohammad Mossadegh and subsequent United States support for the second Pahlavi monarch linger in collective memory. That the Shah gave Israel near-diplomatic status in Iran in the 1960s was also used against him during the Iranian Revolution. Significantly, one of the first acts of the new revolutionary regime in Iran in 1979 was to invite Palestine Liberation Organization chairman Yasir Arafat to Tehran and hand over the former Israeli legation building to the PLO. Throughout the region—in Lebanon, Iraq, Syria, Algeria—large segments of the population find the displacement of fellow Arabs or Muslims (Palestinians) and the intrigues of Israel and the United States an enormous affront. Although this sense of moral outrage is common to liberals, leftists, and Islamists alike, it is typically strongest among Islamists, who make the elimination of Zionism, the liberation of Jerusalem, and other such aspirations major goals and slogans of their movements.

The implications for women are significant, inasmuch as anti-Zionist, anti-imperialist, and especially Islamist movements are preoccupied with questions of cultural identity and authenticity. As women play a crucial role in the socialization of the next generation, they become symbols of cultural values and traditions. Some Muslim women regard this role as an exalted one, and they gladly assume it, becoming active participants, in some cases ideologues, in Islamist movements. Other women find it an onerous burden; they resent restrictions on their autonomy, individuality, mobility, and range of choices. In some countries, these nonconformist women pursue education, employment, and foreign travel to the extent that they can, joining women's associations or political organizations in opposition to Islamist movements. In Algeria, the Islamist movement has spurred a militant feminist movement, something that did not exist before. In other, more authoritarian countries, nonconformist women face legal restrictions on dress, occupation, travel, and encounters with men outside their own families. Their response can take the form of resentful acquiescence, passive resistance, or self-exile. The latter response was especially strong among middle-class Iranian women during the 1980s. The emergence of Islamist movements and women's varied responses, including feminist responses, will be examined in Chapter 5.

To veil or not to veil is a recurring issue in Muslim countries. Polemics surrounding hijab (modest Islamic dress for women) abound in every country. During the era of early modernization and nation-building, national progress and the emancipation of women were considered synonymous. This viewpoint entailed discouragement of the veil and encouragement of schooling for girls. The veil was associated with national backwardness, as well as female illiteracy and subjugation. But a paradox of the 1970s and 1980s is that more and more educated women, even working women (especially in Egypt), have taken to the veil. It is true that the veil has been convenient to militants and political activists. For example, in the Algerian war for independence against the French and the Iranian Revolution against the Shah, women used the *chador,* or all-encompassing veil, to hide political leaflets and arms. But is veiling always a matter of individual choice, or does social pressure also play a part? In the case of compulsory veiling in the Islamic Republic of Iran, the answer is clear. But what of the expansion of veiling in Algeria, Iraq, and Egypt, and among the Palestinians? Chapter 5 takes up this question as well.

Certainly there are Islamist women activists. Much of feminist scholarship over the past fifteen years has sought to show that women are not simply passive recipients of the effects of social change. They are agents, too; women as well as men are makers of history and builders of movements and societies. This holds equally true for the Middle East. Women are actively involved in movements for social change—revolution, national liberation, human rights, and women's rights. Besides national groupings, there are regionwide organizations and networks within which women are active, such as the Arab Women's Solidarity Association, the Arab Human Rights Organization, and Women Living Under Muslim Laws, an international network. Women are also actively involved for and against Islamist/fundamentalist movements. Pro-Islamist women are discernible by their dress, the Islamic hijab. Anti-fundamentalist women are likewise discernible by their dress, which is Western, and by their liberal or left-wing political views. All in all, women in the Middle East, North Africa, and Afghanistan have participated in political organizations, social movements, and revolutions. Women have also been involved in productive processes and economic development. Whether as peasants, managers of households, factory workers, service workers, street vendors, teachers, nurses, or professionals, Middle Eastern women have contributed significantly to economic production and social reproduction—though their contributions are not always acknowledged, valued, or remunerated.

I have said that political conflicts and war are an important part of the process of social change in the Middle East, with implications for women and gender relations. Apart from the long-standing Arab-Israeli tensions, a conflict in the region that influenced women's positions was the Iran-Iraq war, which lasted eight long years (1980–1988). One result of the war in both countries was the ever-increasing allocation of central government expenditure to defense, at the expense of health, education, and services. Also, during the war women in Iran were constantly harassed by zealots if they did not adhere strictly to Islamic dress and manner. Those women who complained about hijab or resisted by showing a little hair or wearing bright-colored socks were admonished to "feel shame before the corpses of the martyrs of Karbala"—a reference to the dead soldiers in the battle with Iraq. However, as mentioned above, an unintended consequence of the war was to override early ideological objections to female employment in the civil service. As the state apparatus proliferated, and as a large proportion of the male population was concentrated at the war front, women found opportunities for employment in the government sector that Islamist ideologues had earlier denied them. Thus, data for 1983 showed that, far from being expelled from civil service employment, Iranian women had increased their participation by one percentage point relative to 1976 (the date of an earlier census). Eventually, the war had a deteriorating effect on employment for both men and women. Yet today the Iranian authorities actively encourage women to take up fields of study and employment they deem both socially necessary and appropriate for women, especially medicine and teaching.

Iran constitutes one of the two case studies in this book. The Iranian case deserved further amplification, I felt, because it has tended to be portrayed in an oversimplified way. (It is also the case of women and social change with which I am most personally involved.) Thus Chapter 6 examines the contradictions of Islamization and the changing status of women in Iran. The subject of Chapter 7 is the prolonged battle over women's rights in Afghanistan. The Afghan case needed its own chapter, too, if only to place the Marxist-inspired reforms of 1978 in proper historical and social context and to correct the tendentious view of the Afghan civil war as a national liberation struggle from Soviet imperialism and its domestic puppets. The elaboration of the Afghan case is necessary to demonstrate its gender dimension—occluded in almost all mainstream accounts—and to show its relevance to the study of social change.

This book, therefore, is an exploration of the causes, nature, and direction of change in the Middle East, particularly as these have affected women's status and social positions. The economic, political, and cultural dimensions of change will be underscored, and the unintended consequences of state policies as they affect women will be highlighted. The chapters will reveal the contradictions, paradoxes, and nonlinearity of social change. In particular, the chapters draw attention to the potentially revolutionary role of middle-class Middle Eastern women, Islamist and non-Islamist alike. These women are not simply acting out roles prescribed for them by religion, by culture, or by neopatriarchal states; they are questioning their roles and status, demanding social and political change, participating in movements, and taking sides in ideological battles.

▲ 2
Economic Development, State Policy, and Women's Employment

The position of women within the labor market is frequently studied as an empirical measure of women's status. Access to remunerative work in the formal sector of the economy—as distinct from outwork, housework, or other types of informal-sector activities—is regarded by many feminists and women-in-development (WID) researchers as an important indicator of women's social positions and legal status. For those who argue that women's economic dependence on men is the root cause of their disadvantaged status, change in the structure of labor force rewards is the key target. Many studies examining the global rise in female paid employment and the structure of work opportunities for women have concluded that women are better off in paid employment than in unpaid family labor. Employed women tend to have greater control over decisionmaking within the family. Households also benefit when women control income and spending, and the well-being of children is increasingly linked to female education and income. Societal benefits of increasing female employment include diminishing fertility rates and a more skilled and competitive human resource base.[1] Participation in the labor force is thus a key indicator of women's contribution to national development, and investment in women's education and employment is increasingly understood as integral to utilizing the national human resource base.

At the same time, much feminist and WID scholarship has documented the adverse conditions under which many women work, particularly in developing countries with authoritarian regimes and weak labor protection codes. Marxist and feminist researchers have been especially critical of transnational factory employment, and much ink has been spilled over the exploitation of women in export processing and free trade zones.[2] During the 1970s and 1980s, many studies argued that the changing international division of labor was predicated upon the globalization of production and the search for cheap labor, and that the feminization of labor, especially in textiles and electronics, was the latest strategy in that search. A major debate arose over whether this new utilization of female labor reduced women's economic status or improved it. Most of the case studies in the literature came from Latin America, especially Mexico, and from Southeast Asia, particularly South Korea and Malaysia.[3] Ester Boserup, whose landmark study *Women's Role in Economic Development* launched the field of women-in-development and argued that the process of industrialization marginalized female producers, has recently addressed the debate. She notes that economic development has opposing effects on different groups of women: "Whereas young women are drawn into industrial employment and increasing numbers of educated women obtain white-collar jobs in social and other services, the situation of older, uneducated women may deteriorate because the family enterprises in which they work may suffer from competition with the growing modern sector."[4]

The Middle East has not figured prominently in the WID literature, partly because of the difficulty of obtaining data and partly because of a common view that cultural and religious factors influence women's lives more than do economic factors. In the same recent essay cited above, Ester Boserup states that rapid development inevitably creates tension between sexes and generations and spawns pressure groups that seek to preserve or reintroduce the traditional hierarchical cultural pattern. She cites the "oil rich countries in the Arab world, which have attempted to preserve the family system of domesticated and secluded women by mass importation of foreign male labor, and in which mass movements of Muslim revival pursue the same aim."[5] Boserup does not specify which oil-rich countries she has in mind. The richest Arab countries have the smallest populations and must import labor; they are not beset by Muslim revivalism. Rather, it is the larger, labor-exporting Middle Eastern countries, where women have been participating in the work force in growing numbers, that have seen Muslim revivalism.

As was discussed in Chapter 1, myths and stereotypes abound regarding women's social positions in Muslim countries. A common view is that traditional gender relations are entrenched and women's economic roles are insignificant, especially in the modern sector. What are some of the patterns, or comparative indicators, that support such a view? In 1975 the percentage of economically active females among those of working age in Muslim countries (which would include those of Africa, South Asia, and Southeast Asia as well as the Middle East) was less than half of that in non-Muslim countries.[6] By 1980 the female share of the paid labor force was smaller in Middle Eastern countries than in the Southeast Asian newly industrialized countries and, of course, smaller than in the advanced industrialized countries, but not substantially different from that of Latin America or South Asia, with their huge informal sectors. In 1980 the ratio of women to men in the labor force was lowest in the Middle East (29 percent) and highest in Eastern Europe and the Soviet Union, where the ratio was 90 percent.[7] In 1990, as can be seen in Table 2.1, women's share of the labor force in the Middle East was lowest among the six regions surveyed. Such comparative data cannot be contested. But what explains the differences? According to a UN survey, "the level of women's work [is] consistently low in countries with a predominantly Muslim population, such as Bangladesh, Egypt, Jordan, Pakistan, and the Syrian Arab Republic, where cultural restrictions that discourage women from doing most types of work are common."[8] Note that only "culture" is provided as an explanation.

Table 2.1 Employment Profile: Cross-Regional Comparison, 1990

	Sub- Saharan Africa	Middle East and North Africa	Asia and Oceania	South Asia	East and South- east Asia	Latin America and the Caribbean
Labor Force	40.6	30.9	46.4	35.6	54.2	35.1
Women in Labor Force	37.8	18.7	33.2	22.0	41.2	26.3

Source: UNDP, *Human Development Report 1990* (New York: Oxford University Press, 1990), Table 23, pp. 173–175.

Following from the premise that an important indicator of women's status is the extent of their integration in the formal labor force, this chapter examines women's employment opportunities and describes the specific characteristics of the paid female labor force in the Middle East and North Africa. The chapter also identifies the structural determinants of women's access to remunerative work in the formal sector of the economy and explains the variations in the region. Attention to this region is important because (1) it is underresearched outside of Middle East studies; (2) it is frequently left out of book volumes on women workers in the world economy; and (3) it is a good test of assumptions and propositions about capital's global quest for cheap labor and about the relationship between female employment and female emancipation.

This chapter will show that although the region still lags behind other regions in terms of female labor force participation, such participation has been rising steadily since the 1960s in all Middle Eastern countries. I will try to show that women's employment patterns are largely shaped by the political economy of the region and that female employment has been constrained by overall limited industrialization. At the same time, there is considerable variation within the region in terms of women's status and employment opportunities. To explain these differences, we need to examine specific development strategies, state policies, the nature of political elites, and women's class location.

▲ The Internationalization of Capital and the Middle East

In the 1960s and 1970s, the Middle East was part of the global process of the internationalization of productive and financial capital. Relationships between countries and regions changed as the old colonial division of labor—whereby the periphery provided raw materials and the core countries provided manufactured goods (at very unequal pricing schemes)—underwent some modification. Increasingly, countries on the periphery (also known as Third World countries, developing countries, or less-developed countries) established an industrial base, sought to diversify their products, and aspired to export manufactures and industrial goods to the core. The term "newly industrialized country," or NIC, was coined to describe countries making a significant shift in the composition of their labor force, the source of the national product, and the direction of trade. Major changes occurred in the structure of national economies and the labor force.

During the 1970s the trends included the following: a regional and global decline in agriculture; an increase in the service sector; and a shift toward industrial employment, especially in the developing countries, many of which had embarked upon rapid industrialization as a key factor in their development. Significant factors influencing these trends were: the changing structure of world labor markets, involving massive rural and international migration; the relocation of labor-intensive industries; and the spread of new technologies, changing the nature of work.[9] Particularly important for women was the relocation of labor-intensive industries from industrially developed to developing countries in search of cheap labor; the laborers were mostly young, unmarried, and inexperienced women. Textiles and clothing were the first industries relocated, followed by food processing, electronics, and in some cases pharmaceuticals. In this process, various forms of subcontracting arrangements were made to relocate production or set up subsidiaries with foreign or partly foreign capital.[10]

During this period the large Middle Eastern countries, such as Iran, Egypt, Turkey, and Algeria, were pursuing import-substitution industrialization, where machinery was imported to run local industries producing consumer goods. This strategy was associated with an economic system characterized by central planning and a large public sector, and it opened up some employment opportunities for women, mainly in the expanded civil service but also in state-run factories or industrial plants in the private sector receiving state support and foreign investment. The rise of oil prices in the early 1970s led to a proliferation of development projects in the

OPEC countries, massive intraregional male labor flows from capital-poor to oil-rich countries, and considerable intraregional investment and development assistance. In the region as a whole, the augmentation in the activities of capital was followed by increased male employment and an increase in the portion of the labor force involved in industry and services. These changes also affected women, who were increasingly brought into the labor force.

Among those developing countries where female employment grew significantly during the 1970s, especially high increases were reported in Syria and Tunisia, where female labor gain topped that of men.[11] Massive interregional migration of men from the labor surplus countries of Jordan, Egypt, Lebanon, Syria, and North Yemen to better-paying jobs in the oil-rich states of the region (such as Libya, Saudi Arabia, Kuwait, and the UAE) also affected female employment patterns. In some countries the working-age population remaining in the rural areas came to be dominated by women.[12] The migratory trend created shortages in the labor markets of the sending countries, resulting in some cases in the agricultural sector's dependence on female workers.[13] In a 1982 special economic report on South Yemen (the People's Democratic Republic of Yemen [PDRY]), the World Bank estimated women's employment at more than 20 percent. Between 1976 and 1984 the number of women working in the public and mixed sectors doubled in South Yemen. Some of the labor-receiving countries also experienced a dramatic rise in female labor force participation; such was the case in Bahrain and Kuwait, although not in Libya and Saudi Arabia. In Kuwait the number of economically active women doubled between 1970 and 1980, by which time women represented 18.8 percent of total salaried employees. In Bahrain the female activity rate—the proportion of economically active persons to population of working age—reached 11 percent in 1981.

Concomitantly, new job vacancies were created in the service and industrial sectors, and they were filled by women. For relatively well-educated women, services (teaching, health, and welfare) offered the greatest possibilities, while in the more developed Middle Eastern countries (such as Turkey and Egypt) women's participation increased in commercial and industrial enterprises and public administration. During the period of rapid growth, some governments provided generous benefits to working women. Sudan in 1974, Kuwait in 1976, and Jordan in 1978 instituted comprehensive social security systems for workers, including women. Iran adopted the International Labour Organisation (ILO) Convention No. 3, which applies to all women employed in industrial and commercial undertakings and provides for twelve weeks' maternity leave, to be taken in two parts, one before and one after childbirth, the latter being compulsory. In Libya a woman on maternity leave received 100 percent of her previous salary. Legislation in nearly all Middle Eastern countries protected a woman employee from dismissal during pregnancy or maternity leave and in some cases (Jordan, Syria, Iraq) even provided for the establishment of workplace nurseries and breast-feeding breaks.[14]

The degree of occupational choice that women had within the structure of employment was linked to the type of industrialization the country was undergoing, the extent of state intervention, the size of the public sector, and the class background of women entering the labor force. In some places, development and state expansion afforded women a wider range of professional work opportunities than was available in the most industrialized societies of the West. This breadth of options is particularly striking in Turkey, where in the 1970s the female share of teaching, banking, and medical positions reached one-third, and where one in every five practicing lawyers was female.[15] A similar pattern has been found for other Third World countries, such as Mexico, Argentina, and India. Cross-national studies conducted in the 1970s indicated that in societies undergoing capitalist development, there is a curvilinear relationship between the level of development and the range of options open to women in professional careers. At intermediate levels there are higher proportions of women in professional schools and the professional labor market than at either extreme. In such countries, law, medicine, dentistry, and even engineering constitute a "cluster" of occupations open to women.[16] But class is another explanatory variable. A kind of affirmative action or quota system may be operating for the upper class, limiting the social mobility of the lower classes. Oncü suggests that under conditions of rapid expansion, the elite recruitment patterns into the most prestigious and highly remunerated professions are maintained by the admission of women from the upper reaches of the social hierarchy.[17]

In the Middle East, as elsewhere, the formal economy could not absorb all the entrants to the labor force, and the urban population in all developing countries grew rapidly because of natural population growth and high in-migration rates. Thus, the 1970s also saw unemployment, the expansion of the urban informal sector, and the rise of female-headed households resulting from male migration, separation, divorce, and widowhood. In 1980 women's share of unemployment was generally higher than their share of employment. For example, the female share of unemployment in Syria was 16 percent; in Tunisia, 18 percent.[18] Low wages tended to enlarge the informal sector and push women into it.

A Methodological Note

It is important to establish at the outset the problems entailed in studying women's economic activities in the Middle East. First, the region suffers from a paucity of data on women's productive activities and contributions to national development. Women are underrepresented in national accounts; census enumerators do not pose the correct questions and consequently receive wrong or inadequate answers regarding women's work, especially in the agricultural sector. As a result, census data in many countries frequently report an extremely small economically active female population. A major problem involves definitions of work and employment; much of what women perform in the informal sector or household is not recognized as a contribution to the national income or development but is rather perceived to be a private service to the family. This nonrecognition lies not only with statisticians and policymakers but also with ordinary men and women, who may be motivated by prevailing attitudes and modesty codes to refrain from providing an accurate description of women's productive activities. A second problem: inconsistency in data collection across government agencies. The census bureau may report a very small female agricultural work force, but a manpower or labor force survey, or an agricultural census, will account for women more properly and indicate a much larger female work force. There is also inconsistency in data collection across countries: Some countries count persons over the age of fifteen as part of the labor force, other countries count persons aged ten and above, still others include persons aged six and over. A third problem lies with the informal sector. Small workshops, such as textile enterprises, that rely on female labor may avoid taxation through nonregistration. Not only does this result in a further underestimation of women's industrial involvement in statistical studies, it entails more exploitative work conditions.

Because of such problems, extreme care must be exercised in reviewing and interpreting available data. However, this chapter is concerned principally with examining women's access to the formal sector of the economy and to salaried employment, where the data presented are more reliable. Women's employment data in public services and large-scale industry are virtually free from gaps in coverage.[19]

Let us now turn to the economic features of the region in order to better understand the constraints and possibilities regarding women's employment. In particular I will try to show the connection between patterns of industrialization and patterns of female employment.

▲ The Political Economy of the Middle East

Chapter 1 noted the social structural diversity of the Middle East, which has implications for gender relations generally and for women's roles and status more specifically. Let us examine the political economy of the region and its implications for women's employment.

It may be helpful to begin with two complementary typologies of the region. In his discussion of industrialization in the Middle East, Robert Mabro offers the following classification:

• Oil economies poor in other resources, including population (UAE, Saudi Arabia, Oman, Qatar, Kuwait, Libya)
  • Mixed oil economies (Algeria, Tunisia, Syria, Iraq, Iran, Egypt)
  • Non-oil economies (Israel, Turkey, Jordan, Morocco, Sudan, Yemen)

In their study of the political economy of the region, Alan Richards and John Waterbury offer the following taxonomy:

• The Coupon Clippers: Libya, Kuwait, Oman, UAE, Bahrain, Qatar. These states have much oil and little of anything else, including people. They have been and will continue to be almost entirely dependent upon oil and any money earned from overseas investments.
  • The Oil Industrializers: Iraq, Iran, Algeria, and Saudi Arabia. The first three states share the main features of large oil exports, a substantial population, other natural resources, and a chance to create industrial and agricultural sectors that will be sustainable over the long run. Saudi Arabia lacks the non-oil resources of the first three countries.
  • The Watchmakers: Israel, Jordan, Tunisia, and Syria. These four small countries have limited natural resources and must therefore concentrate on investing in human capital and exporting skill-intensive manufactures. Manufactured goods now account for 84 percent of Israeli, 52 percent of Jordanian, and 42 percent of Tunisian exports.
  • The NICs: Turkey, Egypt, and Morocco. These countries have relatively large populations, relatively good agricultural land or potential, and a long experience with industrial production.
  • The Agro-Poor: Sudan and Yemen. These are the poorest countries of the region and ones where the agricultural-development-led strategy of industrial growth seems to offer the best hope.[20]

The two classifications differ somewhat, but the essential point is that patterns of women's employment generally follow from the given political economy. Unlike Latin America and Southeast Asia, the Middle East has seen fairly limited industrialization, which has served, among other things, to limit female labor force participation. But, as we shall see below, there are interesting variations in women's labor force participation.

Concerted industrialization began in Latin America and Southeast Asia earlier than it did in the Middle East. In the case of South Korea, first the Japanese and then the Americans played a role in expanding agricultural and industrial production as well as education. In Brazil and Mexico, foreign investment played an important role in propelling industrialization. The success of the Southeast Asian countries in making a transition to export-oriented industrialization (EOI) in the early 1960s contributed to their rapid economic growth, which was facilitated by the rapid expansion of world trade in the 1960s.[21] By contrast, in the Middle East the rate of industrial expansion remained slow until the mid-1950s. The industrialization drive gained momentum when revolutionary regimes took over in Egypt, Iraq, and Syria and the Shah of Iran decided to divert oil revenues to finance industrialization. Between 1955 and 1975 the industrialization of the Middle East (with the notable exception of Israel) followed a classic pattern of import-substitution industrialization.[22]

Those countries rich in oil and poor in other resources (Mabro's first category) have chosen an industrial strategy based on petroleum products and petrochemicals. A strategy relying on oil, gas, and finance, which is heavily capital-intensive and minimizes the use of labor, is not conducive to female employment. The industrialization of other countries (Mabro's second and third groups) has followed a typical pattern of ISI, although Algeria, Iran, and Iraq remained dependent on oil revenues for foreign exchange. Mabro notes that in the Middle East, unlike Latin America, ISI did not evolve into manufacturing for export. Because of oil revenues, governments chose to extend the import-substitution process, moving into capital-intensive sectors involving sophisticated technology.[23] For the OPEC countries, foreign exchange from oil revenues constituted the accumulation of capital, although an industrial labor force in the manufacturing sector was also created. In both the oil and mixed oil economies, the contribution of petroleum to the national income is such as to make the apparent share of other sectors appear insignificant. It should be added that investment in iron and steel plants, petrochemicals, car assembly plants, and similar industries turned out to be not only costly and inefficient but also not especially conducive to increased female employment.

By 1980, a number of Middle Eastern countries turned to EOI. In particular, the non-oil economies have pursued development strategies of export-oriented manufacturing and agriculture. For example, although Tunisia exports oil, oil's share of its exports is lower than that of OPEC countries (42 percent in 1985 compared to Saudi Arabia's 97 percent or Iran's 85 percent). Non–oil-producing countries other than Tunisia have had to rely on exports of manufactured and agricultural goods. Notable among them is Turkey; in 1984 manufacturing constituted 54 percent of GDP.[24] (Egypt under Sadat tried to follow the Turkish model and liberalize its economic system to promote industrial exports, but it was less successful than Turkey.) It should be noted that in the non-oil industrializing economies (the Watchmakers and NICs), female labor force participation is higher than elsewhere and in some countries is encouraged by policymakers.

▲ Industrialization and Female Proletarianization

By 1980 global trends in female employment included the following: the proletarianization of women and their sectoral distribution in services and industry; the globalization of female labor via TNCs and female labor migration; and the feminization of poverty, with the interrelated phenomena of high unemployment rates, growth of the urban informal sector, and the proliferation of female-headed households. TNC relocation has mainly affected women in Latin America, the Caribbean, and Southeast Asia. The most important areas of activity for foreign investors in the export manufacturing sector in developing countries have been the textile, clothing, and electronics industries. Five countries dominate in terms of the size of their export processing zone (EPZ) operations: Hong Kong, South Korea, Puerto Rico, Singapore, and Taiwan. Rather less important but still substantial are EPZs in Brazil, Haiti, Malaysia, and Mexico. Over the years a majority of jobs created in the export manufacturing sector has gone to women. Indeed, Joekes and Moyaedi note "the disproportionate access that women have to export manufacturing employment and their overwhelming importance as suppliers for the export manufacturing sector."[25]

In the Middle East, free production zones were established in Bahrain, Jordan, Lebanon, Syria, PDRY, Egypt, and Tunisia. In Iran a world market factory, commencing operations in 1974 with US and West German capital investment, produced shoes, leather goods, textiles, and garments.[26] However, most of the workers were male. The high concentrations of female labor in TNCs characteristic of Southeast Asian and some Latin American countries are rarely found in the Middle East, partly because EOI has not been pursued by all the countries of the region and partly because of reliance on revenue and foreign exchange from oil exports. Mabro has written that Iran probably would have embarked upon an export-oriented strategy if the revolution and the war with Iraq had not arrested the process of industrial development.[27] This theory would also explain the decline in female industrial employment in the years immediately following the revolution and the subsequent fall of overall female employment in the Islamic Republic. (See Chapter 6 for details.)

Industry in Middle Eastern countries has failed to make progress comparable to that achieved in India, Brazil, or South Korea. Richards and Waterbury note that total manufacturing value-added (MVA) in the region is approximately equal to that of Brazil. It is instructive "to compare MVA for Turkey and Iran with that of Italy, which has roughly the same number of people: Italy's MVA is more than five times that of Turkey, and roughly ten times that of Iran."[28] This ratio has implications for patterns of female employment: Lower levels of industrialization or manufacturing for export means less female proletarianization and activity in the productive sectors.

Among Arab nations, Morocco is the country in which industry makes the largest relative contribution to GDP: 18.6 percent. Manufacturing accounts for 32 percent of Morocco's merchandise exports. At the same time, it has the highest recorded percentage of women in production. Nearly half of the economically active women in the urban areas of

Morocco are engaged in textile work, although many of them work at home.[29] Middle Eastern countries with the largest shares of manufacturing in their merchandise exports are Israel with 80 percent and Turkey with 57 percent.[30] Other countries in the region do not usually come near the top fifty in ranking of world manufacturing production.

The evidence from the Middle East would confirm the view in the WID literature that export-led industrialization and female employment are positively related. Israel, Morocco, Tunisia, and Turkey all have export-led industrial (and agricultural) strategies and higher levels of female labor force participation. During the 1980s in Tunisia, 40 percent of all employed women worked in the industrial sector; nearly 30 percent did so in Morocco. A study of the Moroccan clothing industry showed that the proportion of women workers was higher both within and between firms when the product was for foreign markets.[31] The Middle East also provides evidence that oil-centered industrialization inhibits female employment. Algeria and Iran have relied heavily on oil revenues, and both report a very small female labor force.

In the case of Turkey, more women are engaged in agricultural work than in the modern industrial sector. Although Turkey's proximity to Europe and its greater participation in the international division of labor have drawn more women into world market activities, most of these activities are in the informal sector—unwaged, family-based production of agricultural goods or carpets. Agriculture, light manufacturing industry (tobacco, textiles/apparel, food/beverages, packaging of chemicals), and certain subdivisions of service industries are typically "feminine" occupations, but they constitute a relatively small percentage of Turkey's female labor force. In 1985 fully 69 percent of the economically active female population of 5.5 million was in agriculture, and only 7.6 percent were production workers. Indeed, work in the manufacturing sector remains a predominantly male phenomenon in Turkey, at least according to official statistics, and certainly in the formal sector. In Israel, too, the most industrialized nation in the region, the role of women in industrial work is also negligible; the female share of production workers is about 14 percent. By contrast, the female share of production workers in South Korea is about 30 percent.

Table 2.2 provides data on the percentage of women among production workers and manufacturing employees. The table illustrates the diversity in the region. (Data on Mexico and South Korea are included for comparative purposes.)

As can be seen in Table 2.2, the female share of production work ranges from a low of 1 percent in Libya and Jordan (and next to nothing in the Gulf city-states) to highs of 23 percent in Morocco and 17 percent in Tunisia. Table 2.2 also provides data on salaried employment in the production sector and shows that most female production workers are not

Table 2.2 Female Shares of Production Workers and Manufacturing Employees

Country	Year	Production All Statuses[a]	Salaried[b]	Country	Year	Female Share
		Percentage of Females Among Production Workers			Percentage of Females Among Manufacturing Employees	
Algeria	1966	4.0	2.4	Algeria	1977	6.9
	1987	2.5	2.4		1987	7.8
Egypt	1975	2.4	2.8 (1976)	Bahrain	1971	1.0
	1984	5.8	—		1981	2.4
Iran	1966	25.0	18.2	Egypt	1976	6.5
	1976	19.8	7.9		1984	12.3
	1986	15.0	7.1	Iran	1976	38.4
Iraq	1977	5.5	3.7		1986	14.4
	1987	4.0	—	Iraq	1977	17.2
Israel	1972	12.1	—		1987	14.6
	1987	13.4	14.3	Israel	1972	24.0
Jordan	1979	1.0	—		1982	25.2
Kuwait	1975	0.3	0.2	Jordan	1980	9.6
	1985	0.2	0.2	Kuwait	1975	13.8
Lebanon	1970	10.0	8.1		1985	2.5
Libya	1973	1.0	0.4	Libya	1973	7.4
Morocco	1971	15.5	—	Morocco	1971	—
	1982	23.0	—		1982	36.1
Sudan	1973	5.4	—	PDRY	1973	13.5
Syria	1970	5.3	4.0	Qatar	1986	0.8
	1981	4.0	3.0	Sudan	1973	16.5
	1984	3.8	—	Syria	1970	10.5
Tunisia	1975	23.9	10.5		1981	10.5
	1980	22.1	—	Tunisia	1975	51.6
	1984	17.6	—		1984	55.5
Turkey	1975	7.8	—	Turkey	1975	17.6
	1985	7.6	6.9		1985	15.2
UAE	1975	0.1	0.1	UAE	1975	0.6
	1980	0.1	0.1		1980	1.2
Mexico	1960	10.4	—	Mexico	1980	21.2
	1970	12.8	10.9		1985	24.5
	1980	16.8	15.3		1986	25.7
South Korea	1966	25.2	19.3	South Korea	1980	45.2
	1975	28.0	27.7		1985	42.0
	1980	25.8	28.5		1986	42.3
	1988	31.1	29.3			
	1989	31.0	31.6			

Sources: ILO, *Yearbook of Labour Statistics 1989–1990,* Tables 2A and 2B, and *Retrospective Edition, 1945–1989,* Tables 2A and 2B; *National Census of Population and Housing,* November 1986 (Total Country), Table 14, p. 39 (Tehran: Central Statistical Office, 1987); Guy Standing, "Global Feminisation Through Flexible Labour" (Geneva: ILO, 1989), Tables 4 and 5.

Notes: a. Includes own-account, employer, unpaid family worker, and wage worker
b. This column refers to the female share of salaried production workers.

wage workers. Rather, they seem to be either unpaid family workers or own-account workers—in both cases informal-sector rather than formal-sector workers. In contrast, female production workers in Mexico and South Korea seem to be employed in registered factories.[32] The female share of total manufacturing employees is lower in the Middle East than in Latin America, East Asia, and Southeast Asia, although Tunisia and Morocco again depart from the pattern of low recorded female involvement in industry. In some cases there have been declines in the measured female work force in production—for example, in Iran, Iraq, Syria, and Tunisia. This may be due to economy difficulties—but it may also be related to the measurement problems discussed above.

Care must be taken in interpreting the high percentages of women in production and manufacturing recorded for Iran; much of what purports to be industrial activity for women is in fact rural and traditional work, such as carpet-weaving. In the 1970s Iran was sometimes listed as an NIC, and the development literature stressed a significant increase not only in male but also in female participation in industry. One study placed Iran's increase in female labor force participation in the same category as that of Hong Kong, Japan, and Singapore.[33] By 1976 industry's share of the total labor force was about one-third. According to ILO data, some 33 percent of the female economically active population in 1976 was engaged in industrial work. However, this statistic masked the dualistic nature of Iranian industry. The industrial labor force (both male and female) was actually divided between workers in small, traditional workshops and workers in large, modern factories, a polarization that intensified in the years after the Iranian Revolution.[34] Of the roughly 660,000 female production workers in 1976, 16 percent were own-account workers, 27 percent were salaried, and fully 55 percent were unpaid family workers. Two-thirds of the women in the category "female employees/own-account workers" were in manufacturing.[35] These figures suggest that most female industrial workers were actually rural women involved in traditional manufacturing (carpets, handicrafts, clothing for the domestic market, and so on) rather than wage workers employed in the larger urban factories. By 1986 women's involvement in manufacturing had declined dramatically in Iran (see Table 2.2), and only 30 percent of women in manufacturing were salaried workers.

In the cases of Morocco and Tunisia, both of which report high percentages of women in manufacturing, female contributions to national industrial development and exports are certainly considerable, but whether these women are properly remunerated is unclear. Although precise data are not available on the status of their industrial employment, one can assume that a high percentage are "self-employed."

Thus, Joekes's argument that industrialization in parts of the Third World "has been as much female-led as export led" must be qualified for the Middle East. And Standing's contention that "women are being

A growing number of married women are entering or remaining in the work force. Photo: International Labour Office, J. Maillard 89

This woman works in a small family shoe-making business. Photo: International Labour Office, J. Maillard 89

substituted for men in various occupational categories, including manufacturing and production work" also does not quite apply in the Middle East, where men predominate in the industrial sector.[36] To be sure, in nearly all the large countries women are engaged in light manufacturing—clothing, woven goods, shoes, food processing, confectioneries. But in the cities of the Middle East, most women are marginalized from production and especially from the formal-sector productive process, concentrated instead in community, social, and personal services. There does seem to be a widespread Middle Eastern attitude that factory work is not suitable for women, although this belief may itself be a function of the limited demand for women's labor, given the current stage of industrialization and the high rates of male unemployment in the Middle East. Economic development has led to the creation of a female labor force, but that labor force is small in part because industrialization, an important stage of economic development, has been fairly limited in the region. From a world-system perspective, because the region functions as a source of oil and petrodollars, international capital and Middle East states alike have not aggressively pursued foreign investment in the kinds of industry likely to enhance female employment. As Mabro observes: "The Arab countries, Iran, and, to a lesser extent, Turkey have still a long way to go on the road to industrialization."[37]

▲ Characteristics of the Female Labor Force

During the 1980s the highest rates of economic activity for women were in East Asia (59 percent) and the Soviet Union (60 percent).[38] Economic activity rates of Middle Eastern women ranged from a low of less than 7 percent in Jordan, Syria, Algeria, Iran, and Egypt to highs of 18 percent in Kuwait, 22 percent in Turkey, and 27 percent in Israel.[39] In relation to Latin America, East Asia, Southeast Asia, and the advanced industrialized countries, female activity rates in all age groups in the Middle East are quite low. Moreover, in general female labor force participation tends to be concentrated in the age group fifteen to twenty-nine years old. The exceptions are Turkey and Israel, where female activity rates are both the highest in the region (over 45 percent) and fairly consistent across the age groups. They are followed by Tunisia, which has a 30 percent activity rate for women aged fifteen to thirty-four. Kuwait and Qatar also report fairly high activity rates (37 percent) for women aged twenty-five to forty-nine; these are professional women who, in fact, make up the entire female labor force in those countries. Table 2.3 illustrates the evolution of labor force participation since the 1960s. These patterns generally follow but are not entirely consistent with the two political economy typologies mentioned earlier in this chapter, suggesting that other factors, such as gender bias and

Table 2.3 Evolution of Labor Force Participation in Selected Countries[a]
(in percent)

Country	Year	Male	Female	Total
Algeria	1966	42.2	1.8	21.7
	1975	43.4	1.9	22.3
	1982	38.9	2.9	21.1
	1987	42.4	4.4	23.6
Egypt	1966	51.2	4.2	27.9
	1975	50.4	4.1	27.9
	1982	48.2	5.8	27.3
	1986	48.1	6.2	27.7
Iran	1966	50.7	8.3	30.2
	1976	48.1	8.9	29.1
	1982[b]	46.3	7.0	27.6
	1986	45.5	5.4	25.9
Jordan	1961	42.4	2.6	22.9
	1971	43.1	2.6	23.1
	1975	44.4	3.0	24.2
	1979	38.0	3.3	21.3
Kuwait	1965	61.3	4.8	39.4
	1970	53.0	5.2	32.4
	1975	49.5	7.8	30.6
	1980	55.1	10.9	36.2
	1985	55.8	18.1	39.5
Libya	1964	46.6	2.7	25.6
	1975	47.4	2.7	25.9
Morocco	1960	50.1	5.9	28.0
	1971	44.5	8.0	26.3
	1975	44.4	7.9	26.1
	1982	47.9	11.6	29.6
Syria	1960	46.0	5.4	26.3
	1970	42.7	5.5	24.8
	1981	42.2	4.1	23.6
	1984	40.3	6.8	23.9
Tunisia	1966	44.4	3.0	24.1
	1975	48.9	12.6	31.0
	1984	47.4	13.3	30.6
Turkey	1985	50.1	21.9	36.2

Sources: ILO, *Yearbook of Labour Statistics, Retrospective Edition, 1945–1989*, Table 1, p. 60; ILO, *Yearbook of Labour Statistics 1981, 1985, 1991*, Table 1.

Notes: a. The labor force participation rate—or activity rate—is the proportion of the economically active labor force in relation to the population of working age.

b. The 1982 figures for Iran are for urban areas only.

specific state policies, are also necessary to explain the patterns of female labor force participation.

As seen earlier in this chapter, the female share of the region's economically active population (EAP) is reaching 20 percent. Table 2.4 shows that there are higher shares in Israel, Turkey, Tunisia, and Egypt. Other countries with large populations overlook many rural women and thereby report very small female economically active populations. For example, Iran's 1986 census counted only about a million women in the economically active population. Table 2.4 also provides data on employment status, including the female share of the salaried work force. As with the female share of the EAP, the proportion is generally under 20 percent, from a low of 5.2 percent in the UAE and 9 percent in Iran to 17 percent in Morocco in 1982. Kuwait reports a 20.8 percent female share, while Israel's female share is highest at 41.5 percent. In Turkey the female share of the salaried work force is a mere 17 percent, suggesting a high percentage of women in nonregular or unpaid family labor.

Table 2.5 presents more data on women's employment status. The percentage of the female EAP that receives a wage or salary is high in Kuwait (98 percent) and Israel (79 percent), average in Syria (51 percent in 1989) and Egypt (38 percent in 1984), and low in Turkey (19 percent in 1989). In Iran the proportion of the female EAP that receives a wage appears artificially high (nearly 52 percent in 1986) because the Iranian enumerators do not count most rural women as part of the EAP; if they did, the percentage would probably be closer to Turkey's. The distribution of the female EAP in branches of industry is shown in Table 2.6. The distribution in Algeria, Israel, Kuwait, and Iran is skewed in favor of Group 9 of the major industry branches—that is, community, social, and personal services. Turkey's female EAP is skewed in favor of Group 1, or agriculture. In some cases, women in agriculture are not counted as part of the labor force, but large percentages of female agricultural workers are recorded for Egypt, Syria, and Turkey. The female EAP of both Tunisia and Morocco is more evenly distributed across the three branches, and, in a departure from the Middle Eastern pattern, more women are found in industry than in services. Considering the fact that Turkey is the most developed country in the region, it is somewhat jarring to realize that nearly 70 percent of the female labor force was classified "unpaid family labor" in 1989 (Table 2.5) and that an equally high percentage of the female EAP is in agriculture (Table 2.6). Turkey's EOI strategy was adopted in 1980, so it will be interesting to see if this results in a shift in female employment from agriculture to industry and services.

Patterns of women's employment in the Middle East may be compared with those elsewhere in the world in Table 2.7. Only a handful of countries report large numbers of women in the agricultural work force—Malawi, Haiti, Indonesia, Pakistan, Sri Lanka, and Thailand. Among European

Table 2.4 **Characteristics of the Economically Active Population:**
Various Countries, 1980s

Country (Year)	Total Population	Total EAP	% Female	Total Salaried	% Female
Algeria					
(1983)	20,192,000	3,632,594	6.8	n.a.	n.a.
(1987)	22,600,956	5,341,102	9.2	3,293,200	10.5
Bahrain					
(1981)	278,481	142,384	11.3	122,256	11.4
Egypt					
(1984)	45,231,000	14,311,300	21.4	6,376,800	14.0
Iran					
(1986)	49,400,000	12,820,291	10.0	5,327,885	9.4
Iraq					
(1977)	12,000,477	3,133,939	17.3	1,864,701	7.9
(1987)	16,335,199	3,956,345	11.6	n.a.	n.a.
Israel					
(1987)	4,365,200	1,494,100	39.0	1,110,800	41.5
Kuwait					
(1985)	1,697,301	670,385	19.7	619,722	20.8
Morocco					
(1982)	20,449,551	5,999,260	19.6	2,429,919	17.6
Qatar					
(1986)	369,079	201,182	9.4	196,488	9.6
Sudan					
(1973)	14,113,590	3,473,278	19.9	905,942	7.4
(1983)	18,058,673	6,342,981	29.0	n.a.	n.a.
Syria					
(1984)	9,870,800	2,356,000	13.8	1,216,781	12.4
(1989)	11,719,000	3,068,832	15.4	1,661,000	14.5
Tunisia					
(1984)	6,975,450	2,137,210	21.2	1,173,630	14.3
(1989)	7,909,500	2,360,600	21.0	1,443,000	16.8
Turkey					
(1985)	50,958,614	18,422,980	27.7	6,978,181	15.3
(1989)	53,614,017	20,616,733	31.7	7,782,584	16.7
UAE					
(1980)	1,042,099	559,960	5.0	518,969	5.2

Sources: CERED, *Femmes et Condition Feminine au Maroc* (Rabat: Direction de la Statistique, 1989); *Recensement Général de la Population et de l'Habitat 1987* (Algiers, 1989); ILO, *Yearbook of Labour Statistics 1988, 1991,* Tables 1, 2A, and 2B; ILO, *Yearbook of Labour Statistics, Retrospective Edition 1945–1989,* Table 2A; World Bank, *World Development Report 1985* (1990).

Note: n.a. = not available

Table 2.5 Percent Distribution of Economically Active Women by Status of Employment in Selected Countries (various years)

Country (Year)	Employers and Own-account Workers	Salaried Employees		Unpaid Family Workers	Not Classified by Status
Algeria					
(1977)	1.7	42.1	(8.1)[a]	0.5	55.7
(1987)[b]	2.8	70.1	(10.5)	1.6	25.2
Bahrain					
(1981)	0.9	88.6	(11.7)	—	10.3
Egypt					
(1984)	14.2	38.0	(14.0)	36.3	11.5
Iran					
(1976)	6.9	28.6	(12.0)	24.9	39.6
(1986)	19.7	51.7	(9.5)	21.5	7.0
Iraq					
(1977)	10.6	27.3	(8.0)	58.0	3.6
Israel					
(1982)	11.1	79.7	(40.0)	3.2	6.0
(1986)	11.0	78.5	(41.1)	2.3	7.9
Kuwait					
(1985)	0.2	97.7	(20.8)	—	2.0
Morocco					
(1982)	14.5	36.3	(18.0)	27.5	21.6
Syria					
(1979)	9.9	41.7	(12.0)	44.5	3.9
(1981)	11.4	60.9	(8.7)	22.2	4.0
(1983)	9.8	48.0	(12.4)	36.9	4.7
(1989)	1.5	50.9	(14.5)	7.8	39.5
Tunisia					
(1984)	27.3	38.8	(14.3)	20.6	13.3
Turkey					
(1985)	4.7	14.0	(15.3)	79.2	2.0
(1989)	6.9	18.8	(16.7)	67.7	6.4
UAE					
(1980)	0.8	97.5	(5.2)	—	1.5

Sources: ILO, *Yearbook of Labour Statistics 1991*, Table 2A; ILO, *Yearbook of Labour Statistics, Retrospective Edition, 1945–1989*, Table 2A; *Recensement Général de la Population et de l'Habitat 1987* (Algiers, 1989).

Notes: a. This column refers to the female share of total salaried employees, in percent.

b. Algeria's 1987 census lists a female EAP of 492,442. Of that figure, 74 percent are employed ("occupées"), 13 percent are unemployed, and 13 percent are partly employed housewives ("femmes au foyer partiellement occupées").

Table 2.6 Percent Distribution of Female Economically Active Population in Branches of Industry: Selected Countries, 1980s

Country (Year)	Total Number	Industry Branches									
		Group 1	Group 2	Group 3	Group 4	Group 5	Group 6	Group 7	Group 8	Group 9	Other[a]
Algeria (1985)	326,000	3.7		12.0[c]		2.7	2.7	3.1	75.8[d]		—
Egypt (1984)[b]	2,354,600	41.2	0.03	8.6	0.3	0.6	6.8	1.1	1.3	23.8	16.0
Iran (1986)	975,305	26.5	.05	21.6	.22	.95	1.5	.87	1.06	42.4	4.6
Israel (1983)	556,495	2.7	14.0[e]		0.3	0.9	10.6	2.9	11.3	48.2	8.6
Kuwait (1983)	132,128	0.08	0.25	0.96	0.05	0.89	2.2	1.5	2.2	89.2	1.9
Morocco (1982)	1,181,280	30.6	.18	28.5	.11	.27	2.0	.34	23.7[f]		14.0
Syria (1984)	327,200	44.5	0.3	10.7	0.4	1.5	2.9	1.5	1.2	30.0	6.7
Tunisia (1984)	433,630	22.1	0.4	40.6	1.1[g]	0.7	2.3	—	4.6	13.0	14.5
Turkey (1985)	5,543,862	69.5	0.07	7.0	0.01	0.08	1.5	0.4	1.4	7.8	11.4

Source: ILO, *Yearbook of Labour Statistics 1988, 1991,* Table 2A, and *Retrospective Edition, 1945–1989,* Table 2A.

Notes: a. Not adequately defined, unemployed persons not previously employed, and/or unemployed persons previously employed.
b. The data for Egypt derive from a labor force survey sample; the census figures for 1986 are inexplicably different, showing a female labor force reduced by one million and a proportion of only 5 percent in agriculture. This is typical of inconsistencies in enumeration across government departments, a problem in Iran as well.

c. Includes Groups 2, 3, 4
d. Includes Groups 8, 9
e. Includes Groups 2, 3
f. Includes Groups 8, 9
g. Includes Groups 4, 7

Group 1 = agriculture, hunting, forestry, and fishing
Group 2 = mining and quarrying
Group 3 = manufacturing
Group 4 = electricity, gas, and water
Group 5 = construction
Group 6 = wholesale/retail trade, restaurants, and hotels
Group 7 = transport, storage, and communication
Group 8 = financing, insurance, real estate, and business services
Group 9 = community, social, and personal services

Table 2.7 Women's Employment by Sector: Various Countries, Various Regions,
1988–1989 (in percent)

	1	2	3	4	5	6
AFRICA						
Botswana	3.3	9.0	26.7	2.7	6.5	48.9
Kenya	22.3	6.4	5.8	2.6	4.6	55.5
Malawi	45.7	25.9	4.5	2.4	2.0	18.1
Mauritius	13.1	65.0	3.3	1.3	2.2	14.6
Niger	8.5	10.9	22.3	10.3	24.4	22.8
Swaziland	23.3	15.9	14.6	3.3	5.8	35.3
Tanzania	7.9	10.5	3.0	3.3	5.5	65.5
Zimbabwe	35.0	5.0	6.6	2.0	3.2	43.8
AMERICA AND CARIBBEAN						
Barbados	6.6	14.3	25.6	3.0	4.8	45.7
Bermuda	—	2.4	34.5	4.6	19.0	37.7
Bolivia	27.9	10.8	17.4	1.1	0.7	40.8
Brazil	15.4	12.1	11.1	0.9	2.5	54.2
Canada	2.6	11.0	25.3	4.0	13.6	40.9
Colombia	7.0	22.3	25.9	1.7	7.0	6.9
Costa Rica	5.9	25.7	19.2	0.9	3.2	43.4
Cuba	10.9	17.6	16.3	4.1	2.2	44.4
Chile	5.8	14.8	23.3	1.9	4.9	48.0
Haiti	49.6	7.4	29.4	0.3	0.2	7.9
Honduras	0.5	15.1	30.1	1.0	3.8	48.0
Jamaica	17.9	12.8	—	3.1	23.9	42.5
Panama	4.1	9.5	19.7	3.1	4.4	55.7
Peru	0.7	16.7	38.5	1.7	2.9	38.5
Puerto Rico	0.3	21.5	15.2	1.5	4.6	55.5
Trinidad and Tobago	7.6	8.4	25.0	3.8	9.3	41.4
United States	1.4	13.4	21.6	3.7	13.9	43.9
Uruguay	0.5	21.8	15.0	2.1	5.8	53.6
Venezuela	1.7	15.8	22.0	1.6	7.8	49.0
ASIA						
China	8.3	39.3	12.2	4.2	1.4	25.2
Cyprus	17.4	23.5	26.1	3.5	6.6	39.5
Hong Kong	8.4	35.3	26.8	3.5	8.4	23.7
India	13.4	18.3	0.7	3.5	4.0	54.7
Indonesia	55.6	5.4	19.6	—	4.6	10.7
Japan	8.8	23.8	27.3	2.1	8.6	24.8
Korea	21.6	28.8	27.7	1.0	4.5	14.4
Malaysia	30.8	20.2	19.7	1.2	4.1	22.9
Pakistan	72.2	13.3	2.2	0.3	0.3	10.5
Philippines	31.0	13.6	25.1	0.6	1.9	27.0
Singapore	—	33.7	22.6	5.1	11.4	25.3
Sri Lanka	60.7	26.6	5.1	1.4	3.6	1.7
Thailand	64.5	9.2	12.9	0.4	—	11.7

(continues)

Table 2.7 (*continued*)

	1	2	3	4	5	6
EUROPE						
Belgium	1.7	12.7	21.2	2.7	8.6	51.9
Czechoslovakia	9.9	32.7	18.3	4.6	3.8	25.9
Denmark	2.8	14.0	15.3	4.3	8.6	52.0
Spain	11.2	16.0	26.4	2.1	4.9	38.4
Finland	6.2	15.5	18.4	4.3	9.2	44.0
GDR	3.0	36.5	16.3	5.8	—	36.2
FRG	4.9	23.4	21.4	3.5	9.0	35.6
Greece	34.0	16.2	17.8	2.0	4.9	24.3
Hungary	15.5	25.9	13.9	4.7	—	27.8
Ireland	3.3	17.4	22.4	3.5	10.4	41.2
Italy	9.5	21.3	22.7	2.2	4.6	38.2
Luxembourg	2.6	9.1	30.9	3.4	15.9	35.5
Malta	1.3	35.9	10.6	3.1	5.0	43.3
Netherlands	3.3	9.6	20.3	3.0	9.9	51.9
Norway	4.0	8.9	21.4	5.2	8.0	49.7
Sweden	1.9	12.9	15.0	4.5	7.9	56.2
OCEANIA						
Australia	3.6	10.8	23.3	3.8	13.4	41.9
New Zealand	7.4	12.5	23.9	4.3	11.5	38.0

Source: ILO, *Yearbook of Labour Statistics 1991; Retrospective Edition, 1945–1989.*
Note: 1 = Agriculture
2 = Manufacturing
3 = Wholesale, retail trade, restaurants, and hotels
4 = Transport, storage, and communications
5 = Financing, insurance, real estate, and business services
6 = Community, social, and personal services

countries, only Greece has more women in that sector than any other. The manufacturing sector claims over 25 percent of the female labor force only in the NICs, the former socialist countries, and, in the Middle East, Tunisia and Morocco. In many countries 25 percent or more of the female work force is in wholesale, retail trade, restaurants, and hotels, a sector that absorbs very small percentages in countries as diverse as Sweden, the former GDR, and Malta. Throughout the world, the largest concentrations of women workers are in public service; in this regard, most Middle Eastern countries follow a global pattern.

Middle Eastern women are concentrated in professional occupations. The high incidence of women workers in the "professional, technical, and related workers" group in most countries may be the outcome of occupational stereotyping prevalent in the region, where women cluster around specific jobs such as teaching and nursing. It may also be a function of the

Table 2.8 Percent Distribution of Female Labor Force by Occupation:
Major Groups, 1980s

Country (Year)	Group 1	Group 2	Group 3	Group 4	Group 5	Group 6	Groups 7–9	Not Classified/ Unemployed
Algeria (1987)	33.5	0.7	15.0	1.0	13.2	1.7	7.3	27.2
Egypt (1984)	17.6	1.8	12.9	5.5	2.7	41.3	6.5	11.4
Israel (1983)	28.9	1.7	27.1	5.3	14.9	1.6	8.9	10.2
Kuwait (1985)	27.4	0.2	14.3	0.75	54.3	0.04	0.37	1.7
Morocco (1982)	6.6	5.4a		1.4	13.7	32.5	33.2	6.8
Syria (1984)	26.0	0.9	8.2	1.2	2.6	44.0	10.4	6.7
Tunisia (1984)	2.2	0.4	13.2	0.18	6.5	22.0	28.2	27.0
Turkey (1985)	5.5	0.1	4.5	0.9	1.6	69.0	6.9	10.8
(1989)	4.0	0.2	3.6	1.5	2.0	72.2	7.1	9.4

Source: ILO, *Yearbook of Labour Statistics 1988, 1991; Retrospective Edition, 1945–1989*, Table 2B.

Notes:

Group 1 = Professional, technical, and related workers
Group 2 = Administrative and managerial workers
Group 3 = Clerical and related workers
Group 4 = Sales workers
Group 5 = Service workers
Group 6 – Agricultural, animal husbandry, and forestry workers, fishermen and hunters
Group 7–9 = Production/related workers, transport equipment operators, and laborers
a. Includes groups 2 and 3

relationship between class, income, and work participation, whereby women from elite families are most likely to be those who are employed, especially in the Gulf countries.

In terms of occupational distribution, all countries have minimal female presence in administrative and managerial occupations. There also appears to be a marked disinclination for women to enter sales work or even clerical work, except in Israel. Ghazy Mujahid explains women's avoidance of such jobs in terms of cultural norms, as these are occupations

The High Institute of Public Health in Alexandria is a training center for doctors, engineers, and chemists. This photo shows an instructor during a lecture at the institute. Photo: International Labour Office

with the highest likelihood of indiscriminate contact with outsiders.[40] It should be noted that the merchant class has been typically male, and the traditional urban markets—bazaars and souks—have been the province of men. The absence of women in sales work is also a function of socialization. In their study of sex role socialization and Iranian textbooks, Higgins and Shoar-Ghaffari note that in both pre- and postrevolutionary textbooks nearly half the lessons that portray women working show them doing housework, and in both eras three-quarters of the lessons portraying women at work outside the home show them in professional positions (almost always teaching). The remainder portray women in agricultural work; no lessons in either set of texts portrayed women in blue-collar, clerical, sales, or service positions.[41] Indeed, throughout the Middle East, the largest percentages of employed women are in the teaching professions.

I have discussed the political economy of the region, the specificities of development strategies, the limited nature of industrialization, and the consequent patterns of female employment. In the 1980s all Middle Eastern countries were beset by economic and political difficulties, which also affected women's economic status and employment possibilities. The economic crisis in the Middle East occurred in the context of a worldwide crisis resulting in part from the drop in real prices of primary commodities, including oil. The global oil market became very unstable, leading to fluctuating and declining prices. The near-collapse of prices in 1986 (from $28 per barrel to $7 per barrel) had repercussions throughout the Middle East: austerity measures were introduced, availability of development aid decreased, and major development projects were reevaluated or suspended. The Iraqi invasion of Kuwait in August 1990 raised the price of oil again, but the damage had already been done. In the 1980s countries of the Middle East, and especially North Africa, experienced low or negative economic growth rates, declining state revenues, and high levels of indebtedness to foreign creditors. In some cases (Egypt, Morocco, Algeria), debts became truly enormous in relation to the country's economic capacities; Turkey was placed on the World Bank's list of "severely indebted middle-income countries." According to the UN, debt as a percentage of GNP for the Middle East and North Africa in 1989 rose to 70 percent; during the 1980s the region's debt increased from $4.4 billion to $118.8 billion.[42]

The most active Arab borrowers from the World Bank—Algeria, Egypt, Jordan, Morocco, Syria, Tunisia—had to impose austerity measures on their populations as a result of World Bank and International Monetary Fund (IMF) structural adjustment policy packages, and several experienced "IMF riots."[43] High population growth rates coupled with heavy rural-urban migration has concentrated larger numbers of the unemployed in major cities. The livelihood of lower-middle-class and working-class women (and men) has been adversely affected by the debt and the inflationary-recessionary cycles plaguing the region, especially in Morocco, Algeria, Iran, and Egypt. In Israel the serious economic plight has been alleviated by massive American aid. But elsewhere, tough economic reforms, along with poverty, unemployment, and debt servicing—as well as political repression—have served to delegitimize "Western-style" systems and revive questions of cultural identity, including renewed calls for greater control over female mobility. It is in this context of economic failures and political delegitimation that Islamist movements are presenting themselves as alternatives. (See Chapter 5 for a full discussion.)

▲ State Policies and Women's Status

If natural resource endowments, national development strategies, and international economic factors have largely shaped women's employment patterns, what distinct role has the national state played? What is the impact of state-directed legal measures, public campaigns, educational programs, and investment decisions? We find that (1) there are variations in state policies in the region, particularly with regard to the mobilization of female labor and women's integration into the formal economy and public life, and (2) in all cases the state is a major determinant of women's legal and economic status. In some cases a regime's search for political legitimacy, a larger labor force, or an expanded social base has led it to construct health, education, and welfare services conducive to greater work participation by women, and to encourage female activity in the public sphere. Examples are the Iraqi Baathists during the 1960s and 1970s, the Pahlavi state in Iran in the same period, Tunisia under the late President Habib Bourguiba, and Egypt under Nasser and afterward. In other cases state managers remain wedded to the ideology of domesticity and refrain from encouraging female participation in the paid labor force. Examples are Saudi Arabia, Algeria, and Jordan.

In most Middle Eastern countries, women remain an underutilized human resource because of limited industrialization, the gender ideology stressing women's family roles, and ambivalence on the part of state managers toward the full participation of women in economic development and policy formulation. As a result, Middle Eastern women have not yet established labor attachment, and they have a long way to go before they attain the labor force participation rates and access to salaried employment of women in other Third World regions, not to mention the advanced industrialized world. Nevertheless, economic development, the expansion of the state, legal reform, and educational attainment by women have had interesting consequences, some intended, others wholly unintended. Let us examine these on a country-by-country basis.

Turkey

Turkey provides a nearly unique example (the other being Tunisia) of a country that replaced the Islamic personal status laws with a civil law code regulating personal and family relations and equalizing the duties and responsibilities of the sexes. As we will see in Chapter 3, Kemalist reforms in the 1920s introduced secular legal codes based on Western models. Such legal codes provide an important basis for women to act as autonomous persons. In the late 1960s there were signs that women in one region of western Turkey were exercising their full legal right to sue for divorce to protect their personal reputations and their claims to property. Another result of the Kemalist reforms is that Turkey is unique among Middle Eastern or Muslim countries in having large numbers of women in the legal profession.[44] But during the 1980s there was a shift in state orientation. The social democratic years of the 1970s were halted by a military coup in 1980. Between 1983 and 1990 some 700 Quranic schools were established throughout the country, and their graduates have raised calls for Islamization. During this period Prime Minister Turgut Ozal, the architect of a tough stabilization and structural adjustment program, was also the most openly Islamic Turkish leader in modern times.

One area where the Turkish state has been deficient is in the provision of literacy and education, especially for girls. Between 1975 and 1985 the illiterate female population declined from 49 percent to 32 percent, but the reduction of male illiteracy was much steeper, from 24 percent to 13 percent. In 1985 women constituted fully 70 percent of the illiterate population, and most were rural.

For the majority of Turkish women, wage work is elusive, primarily because of the structure of Turkey's agrarian sector, in which so many women are involved. Unlike many developing countries, Turkey's countryside is characterized by what Keyder calls a system of "peasant proprietorships."[45] This system, along with Turkey's pursuit of agricultural production for export, leaves most Turkish women as unwaged family workers, poorly educated, and situated in rural patriarchal gender arrangements. A study on social security legislation conducted for the ILO stated that in Turkey all agricultural workers, whether wage-earning or self-employed, "have been protected by compulsory insurance since 1 January 1984."[46] But this protection would not apply to the vast majority of rural women, who are deemed family workers rather than self-employed or waged.

There is evidence from Turkey that, in contrast to farm work or traditional manufacturing (monetized rural carpet-weaving), wage work in the formal sector seems to improve women's standing in the household. Ecevit's study of Turkish factory workers showed that "married women factory workers in Bursa have gained a considerable degree of power over decision-making in their families as a result of their employment. Over half the married women who were interviewed reported that they and their husbands took decisions together and often consulted each other."[47]

Egypt

In the late 1950s and during the administration of the late Gamal Abdul Nasser, Egypt's public sector expanded significantly through a series of Egyptianization decrees (1956–1959) that gave the government control of foreign-owned assets such as the Suez Canal. These decrees were followed in the early 1960s by the adoption of a highly centralized development policy approach and a massive wave of nationalizations of Egyptian-owned enterprises in industry, banking, trade, and transport. At the same time, the government embarked on an employment drive that required state-owned enterprises to include among their annual targets the creation of significant numbers of new jobs; the administrative apparatus of the state was also expanded rapidly at both the central and local government levels. Equally important was the objective of spreading health and education services, bringing a corresponding growth of government employment in these services.[48] The state's guarantee of a job to all high school and university graduates encouraged women, including women from working-class and lower-middle-class families, to take advantage of the government's free education policy.

A distinctive feature of the Nasser government was its political support for the education of women and their integration into national development. Labor Law 91 of 1954 guaranteed equal rights and equal wages, and made special provisions for married women and mothers. As Hoodfar notes, these provisions were expanded under Sadat to facilitate women's labor market participation. "This law was applied primarily in the public sector, which made jobs in this area particularly attractive to women. As a result, the state became the single most important employer of women."[49]

By the mid-1980s the Egyptian government was faced with the difficult issue of how to reduce its commitment to job creation in the face of severe recessionary conditions. These conditions included a record level of 15.5 percent overall (open) unemployment, according to the 1986 population census (up from 7 percent in the 1976 census), and with poor prospects for either the domestic productive sectors or the oil-rich Arab markets to create significant job opportunities for Egyptian workers. Moreover, high inflation effectively eroded the financial advantage of the white-collar work force. The recession fueled social tensions and led to a growth in Islamism, with its attendant ideological and social pressures on women. Employed women now feel compelled to appear in hijab at work, even though they will claim that the turn to Islamic dress is their own choice.

Since Nasser's time many women have entered previously male strongholds—universities, the administration, professions, industry, the business world, diplomacy, politics. But the economic crisis in Egypt and rapid population growth limit formal employment opportunities for women. Thus, the vast majority of Egyptian women are engaged in the informal sector as street vendors and hawkers, working at home as seamstresses, or taking part in a myriad of small-scale income-generating activities.

Tunisia

Government policy since independence has prioritized women's emancipation and integration into the economy, and the constitution and civil code have reflected and reinforced that position. Staunchly secular, President Bourguiba made the participation of women in public life a major policy goal. The constitution ensured all citizens the same rights and obligations. Polygamy and male repudiation were outlawed, allowing women the right to petition for divorce and custody of their children. Such legal reform has made Tunisia the most liberal country in the Arab world.

In 1960 a law gave the minority of women who are members of the social insurance service (mainly those employed in industry, handicrafts, and services, with the exception of housework) the right to pregnancy leave—six weeks before delivery and six weeks afterward. During this period 50 percent of monthly wages were to be paid.[50] More recently the length of maternity leave has been set at thirty days, apparently as part of government policy to lower the birthrate. Public employees are also entitled to child-care leaves. Law No. 81–6 of February 12, 1981, introduced a social security scheme for wage-earning agricultural workers and those engaged in cooperative undertakings. The following year this scheme was extended to cover small farmers and the self-employed—a law that would benefit women as well.

In the 1980s the distribution of the female labor force was more balanced in Tunisia than in many other Middle Eastern countries: 26 percent in agriculture, 48 percent in manufacturing, 21 percent in services. The female share of government employment was 24.5 percent in 1987; of the country's magistrates, 13.5 percent were women; of medical personnel, 20.6 percent; of paramedical personnel, 48 percent; of the country's teachers, 31.5 percent. Women's participation in formal politics matched the trends in employment. In 1981 there were seven female deputies in Parliament; in 1983 there were 50,000 female members of the ruling social-democratic Neo-Destour Party and 57,000 members of the National Union of Tunisian Women; and in 1985 some 492 women were voted municipal councillors around the country.[51]

Economic problems have encouraged Islamist forces and threatened women's gains. In May 1989 Islamists competed openly in Tunisia's parliamentary elections, winning 14 percent of the total vote and 30 percent in Tunis and other cities to beat the main secular opposition party, the Movement of Democratic Socialists, into third place.[52] Although the Tunisian state remains opposed to Islamist political aspirations, more mosques have been built and Quranic universities restored since the removal of Habib Bourguiba.

Iraq

During the 1960s and 1970s, the Ba'th Party had an interest both in recruiting women into the labor force to alleviate a continuing labor shortage and in wresting women's allegiance away from kin, family, or ethnic group and shifting it to the party-state. The 1978 Personal Status Law, although limited in its objectives, aimed to reduce the control of extended families over women. In November 1977 the government conducted a census to determine the characteristics of the illiterate; of 2.2 million illiterates aged fifteen to forty-five, 70 percent were women. The government then passed laws requiring attendance at adult literacy classes, made extensive use of trade unions and other "popular organizations" and daily use of TV, and so forth. Different textbooks were prepared for peasants, workers, housewives, and so on.[53] Women were recruited into state-controlled agencies and put through public education as well as vocational training and political indoctrination.

In 1979, 51 percent of Baghdad University medical school's first-year class was female, as were 75 percent of students in the English translation department at Mustansiriyah University. The General Federation of Iraqi Women grew in importance, even organizing sports events for women athletes. The ruling Ba'th Party encouraged a wide range of employment for women, who by the late 1970s accounted for 29 percent of the country's medical doctors, 46 percent of all dentists, 70 percent of pharmacists, 46 percent of teachers and university lecturers, 33 percent of the staff of government departments, 26 percent of workers in industry, and 45 percent of farm employees.[54] Maternity leave was generous, and jobs of pregnant women were protected. Many young Iraqi women traveled abroad and studied on scholarships.

The onset of the war with Iran brought about a toughening of the state's position on women. In April 1982 the government issued a regulation stating that married women were not allowed to travel unless accompanied by their husbands; unmarried women were required to have the written consent of their fathers or guardians. Women were told that it was their patriotic duty to fill jobs vacated by men now at the front; they also were told that they should bear five children to narrow the gap between Iraq's population (then 15 million people) and Iran's (47 million). In 1986 birth control devices disappeared from pharmacy shelves. What impact these changes have had or will have is as yet unclear, but according to one account, women's participation in the formal labor force more than doubled in the 1980s.[55]

Iran

Iran provides an interesting example of unintended consequences of development and state policies on women's gender consciousness. In 1962 the Pahlavi state granted women the vote and in 1967 introduced the Family Protection Act, which limited polygamy, allowed women to initiate divorce, and increased their child custody rights after divorce or widowhood. However, the Shah himself was opposed to "women's lib" and frequently derided the demands of Western feminists. Moreover, his reforms were in place for only ten years and did not have widespread impact. In 1979 the new Islamic state abrogated many of these liberal codes. Among other things, the new authorities adopted a pronatalist stance that deemed women, especially young mothers, inappropriate for full-time work. Significantly, the very first display of opposition to the Islamists—and this at the height of the new regime's popularity and support—came from educated middle-class women in early March 1979. These were the women who had been the principal beneficiaries of several decades of modernization. Development—however limited and skewed in its Iranian variant—combined with state reforms had allowed a segment of the female population upward social mobility through education and employment. There was a stratum and generation of women who opposed veiling and rejected Islamist exhortations that working women in the civil service return to the joys of domesticity. These women were subsequently silenced—and some were imprisoned, killed, or exiled—but their political activism must be regarded as nothing less than remarkable.

By the mid-1980s a number of factors converged to modify and liberalize the Islamist state's position on women, education, and work. These factors included the expansion of the state apparatus, the dearth of male labor in a war situation, and women's own resistance to their second-class citizenship. What is especially interesting is that it is now educated and employed Islamist women in Iran—university professors, members of Parliament, the widow of a former prime minister—who are demanding a modification of the rigid gender rules implemented in the early 1980s and pushing for changes in family law and labor legislation to increase women's rights. This activism is illustrative of both the interplay of structure, consciousness, and agency, and of unexpected outcomes of state policies. (See Chapter 6 for details on Iran.)

For the small percentage of women in the formal sector, government employment provides many advantages. Nearly all women who are waged and salaried are in the public sector, where they enjoy insurance, pensions, and other benefits. Labor legislation enacted in 1990 provides women with ninety days of maternity leave, at least half of which must be taken after childbirth. There is also a job-back guarantee with no loss of seniority and a half-hour break every three hours for breast-feeding, with a crèche provided at the workplace.[56] But in the private sector, most women are likely to be "self-employed" or unpaid family workers in agriculture or rug-weaving workshops, where they have no benefits at all.

Algeria

Throughout the 1960s and 1970s, the Algerian government promoted industrialization in tandem with the preservation of the close-knit family union. The state's attitude toward family law and personal status oscillated for over twenty years. Both the industrial strategy and the pronatalist Boumedienne social policy worked against female employment. By the 1980s, as a result of a galloping birthrate, nearly three-quarters of Algeria's population was under the age of thirty, and many were unemployed. According to the 1987 census, the employed population numbered 3.7 million men and a mere 365,000 women—out of a total population of 13 million people over the age of fifteen. The female share of the employed population was 8.8 percent. Still, these figures represented a steady increase in female employment since 1966.

Reasons for the low levels of female employment are Algeria's chronically high unemployment, a conservative cultural stance on the part of the leadership, and the specific development strategy pursued by the state. Algeria's strategy emphasized heavy industrialization (partly on the assumption that this approach would eventually encourage mechanized agriculture). The new, large-scale factories, such as steel works and petrochemical plants, required skilled workers, and it was men who were trained for those jobs. The result was very low female labor participation in industry. Consequently, women are an underutilized source of labor, with implications for fertility, population growth rates, and overall societal development.

In the early 1980s the Algerian government began to make concessions to the growing Islamist faction in the National Assembly. A family code was drafted, which alarmed many women and provoked protest demonstrations. In the midst of a privatization effort and faced with high rates of unemployment (on the order of 22 percent), a heavy debt-servicing burden, and other assorted economic ills, Algerian policymakers were unwilling to risk legislation that could potentially aggravate the situation and thus conceded to the Islamists in the National Assembly. The final bill, passed in 1984, gives women the legal right to work but renders them economic dependents of men.[57] In the municipal elections of June 1990, the Islamist party won the most seats, a situation North African feminists and democrats felt was bound to adversely affect women's already fragile and limited rights. (See Chapter 5 for details.)

As a result of the Algerian state's cultural conservatism, women's participation in state and other social agencies is quite low compared to male participation. For example, women constitute only 11 percent of the employees of ministries, 34 percent of schoolteachers, 24 percent of higher education instructors, and 36 percent of public health workers. There are no women in the sectors *affaires religieuses* and *protection civile*. Still, Algerian women are more likely to work in the government sector than in the private sector. Indeed, 86 percent of employed Algerian women are employed in the public sector, as against 14 percent in the private sector. For Algerian men, the respective rates are 55 percent and 45 percent.[58] Thus, as in Iran's case, any contraction of the public sector would have devastating effects on women's employment situation.

Jordan

In Jordan one finds a low overall participation rate (19.6 percent in 1984 for both men and women), partly due to a very high rate of population growth (about 3.8 percent annually), a large under-fifteen population, high out-migration, and low female economic activity. During the 1970s the state encouraged education and indeed made school compulsory for nine years. There has consequently been an impressive increase in female education: by 1984–1985 girls accounted for some 48 percent of the total school enrollment.[59] The area of women's employment, however, has shown less impressive progress, despite the fact that social policy provides for generous benefits to employed women. In 1979 the percentage of economically active women in the total labor force was only about 4 percent, and the female share of employees was only 9 percent. As in Yemen, out-migration of Jordanian male labor did not cause an increasing number of women to enter the wage labor market; rather, their activities in the informal sector and as unpaid family workers increased. Labor shortages due to migration led to labor importation, mainly from Egypt, at all skill levels instead of the training of women in marketable skills.[60]

Jordan's five-year plan (1980–1985) ostensibly sought to further integrate women into the development process and predicted an increase in female labor force participation and a larger female share of the total labor force. But by 1984 the female participation rate was only 4.8 percent. Only 8.4 percent of females of working age (15–65) were reported as economically active, constituting a mere 10.5 percent of the total work force.[61] Nearly half of all women in the modern sector are in education, while textile workers represent about 30 percent of Jordan's female labor force. In an untoward economic situation characterized by a large external debt and high male unemployment, there has in fact been an implicit government policy to discourage female employment.[62] In the November 1989 parliamentary elections, the first held since 1967, thirty-four out of eighty seats were won by members of the Muslim Brotherhood and like-minded Islamists. This political development, too, is likely to stymie efforts to integrate women into public life.

Saudi Arabia

State personnel have designed policy not only to promote economic growth and development but also to reproduce traditional familial relations and sex-segregation in education and employment. In Saudi Arabia women's place is in the home, and their life is more circumscribed than in any other Middle Eastern country: The percentage of Saudi women who work outside the home, mainly in the teaching and health sectors, is about 5 percent. Elements of Saudi culture—devotion to Islam, extended-family values, the segregated status of females, and the al-Saud monarchic hegemony—have been formulated in an increasingly deliberate fashion into a new political culture that acts as a screen to ensure that technological and human progress remains within acceptable bounds.[63]

The first private school for girls was started in the late 1950s and was the initiative of a princess from the royal family. Fifteen private girls' schools subsequently opened in four Saudi Arabian cities. In 1960 the female education system was placed under the auspices of the government, with supervision by the religious order. Expatriate teachers were employed to start with, then replaced progressively by Saudi women teachers from a well-planned training program. Educational facilities for girls have become available nationwide and provide for general, technical, vocational, and university-level education. Nearly a million female students are now enrolled at various levels and constitute nearly 45 percent of the national student population. Professional education includes medicine, pharmacy, teaching, commerce, and the social sciences. Educational progress has prepared the ground for women's employment on a broad front. By 1987 over 80,000 Saudi women were employed in the government, education, and health sectors.[64] To minimize sensitivities concerning male physicians and female patients, a substantial number of Saudi female physicians are being trained, whose efforts will be directed toward female patients.

In the wake of the Gulf crisis following Iraq's invasion of Kuwait in August 1990, Saudi authorities called for wider participation of women in the labor force "in the area of human services and medical services within the context of fully preserving Islamic and social values."[65] In November 1990 a group of forty Saudi women, most of them university lecturers, took this opportunity to demonstrate their desire for change by driving their own cars through the streets of Riyadh, an extraordinary action that stunned the country.

A Wider Range of Options for Women

The Middle East provides a positive example of the benefits for women of large public sectors. Women's entry into public life has been facilitated by state-sponsored education and by job opportunities in the expanding government sector and public services. Formal/modern sector employment, and especially opportunities in the civil service, have been an important source of status and livelihood. Throughout the Middle East, the active role of the government in national development has meant that many women no longer rely on a male guardian as provider, but rather the state. As we have seen in the examples above, the government sector is a crucial source of women's livelihood and entry into public life. In this regard, the Middle East is not so different from other countries, for around the world the public sector and government employment have provided women with jobs and benefits that may elude them in the private sphere.[66] As Mernissi remarks, "The North African woman of today usually dreams of having a steady, wage-paying job with social security and health and retirement benefits, at a State institution; these women don't look to a man any longer for their survival, but to the State. While perhaps not ideal, this is nevertheless a breakthrough, an erosion of tradition. It also partly explains the Moroccan women's active participation in the urbanization process: they are leaving rural areas in numbers equaling men's migrations, for a 'better life' in the cities—and in European cities, as well."[67]

▲ Integration or Marginalization: Development and the Status of Women

"Integrating women in development" has come under attack by feminist researchers of Latin America, Asia, and Africa. They argue that women have indeed been integrated into development projects—much to their disadvantage, as they have become the latest group of exploited workers, a source of cheap and expendable labor. It has also been argued that capitalist development has everywhere reduced the economic status of women, resulting in marginalization and impoverishment.[68] It is true that the term "development" obscures the relations of exploitation, unequal distribution of wealth, and other disparities (not to mention environmental degradation) that ensue. But it also true that within a national economic framework there is room to improve working women's lot. Sex-segregated occupational distribution can be challenged and altered, as can gender-based wage differentials, inadequate support structures for working mothers, unfair labor legislation pertaining to women, unhealthy work environments, and so on. Moreover, although the proletarianization of women entails labor control (as it does for men), wage work also provides prospects for women's autonomy—not an insignificant consideration in patriarchal contexts.

Whether modernization and paid employment have resulted in an increase or a diminution of women's economic status continues to be a matter of debate for the Middle East as for other regions of the Third World. Some have argued that men's work and women's work are complementary in nomadic communities, and that modernization reduces, marginalizes, and devalues women's work. Women of rural backgrounds, it is argued, suffered a decline in status; they lost the productive role they traditionally played in the pre-industrial economy as the goods they produced were replaced by imported or locally produced factory ones.[69] Mernissi's research, however, suggests a link between the deterioration of women's position and their preexisting dependence on men. Her interviews with Moroccan women working in various craft industries (such as weaving textiles and rugs) indicate how dependent women are upon men as intermediaries, a situation that only increases their precarious economic position. She concludes that the increasing capitalist penetration of such industries has had the consequence of further degrading women's status.[70] Thus, patriarchal gender arrangements constitute an intervening factor in the impact of development on women's status.

The complex and contradictory nature of the relationship between development and women's status has been explored by a number of Turkish and Iranian researchers. Kandiyoti's research in the 1970s comparing the status of Turkish women in nomadic tribes, peasant villages, rural towns, and cities found that the influence of the patrilineal extended household—where the father dominates younger men and all women, and there is a hierarchy by age among the women—was pervasive in all sectors, but less so in the towns and cities because of neolocal residence and the diminished importance of elders. It is true that, compared to peasant and nomadic women, urban women play a sharply reduced role in the productive process, even though they are more likely to head their own households. But peasant and nomadic women do not receive recognition for their own labor, not even for their offspring, as these belong to the patrilineal extended family. In many parts of rural Turkey, women have been traditionally called the "enemy of the spoon," reflecting the perception that they share the food on the table without contributing economically to the household. Berik's study of carpet weavers in rural Central Anatolia reveals that the labor of female weavers, and the wages that accrue to them, are controlled by male kin. This pattern has also been found for Iran and Afghanistan. Abadan-Unat refers to the persistence of "archaic and patriarchal family structures," and Kandiyoti observes that "we cannot speak of a simple decline in women's status with the transition to an urban wage labor economy. Their diminished role in production may be offset by other factors, which are, however, increasingly specific to certain class sectors."[71]

In a patriarchal context, therefore, the effects of development on women's status vary by class and by region. Women are likely to have more options in an urban setting, whereas in rural areas patriarchal family arrangements limit their options. Moreover, the major beneficiaries of the development process will likely be middle-class and upper-middle-class women, even though national development, legal reforms, and especially public education will result in some mobility for women of other social classes. There can be no doubt that expanding education and employment opportunities have created a generation of Middle Eastern women who are accustomed to working in the formal sector and indeed expect it. It should not be surprising that middle-class educated and employed women should be the ones agitating for more progressive social change—for women as women and for women as workers.

Development must be seen, therefore, to have had a differential impact on women's lives. Its effects have been positive as well as negative, depending on region, culture, and class. Positive effects of development, and especially of wage employment, on working-class women include their greater participation in decisionmaking in the household. Ecevit's study of Turkish factory workers, cited earlier in this chapter, is instructive. There is growing evidence from around the world that employed women, including working-class women with factory jobs, value their work for the economic independence and family support it provides and for the opportunity to delay marriage and childbearing. In many countries, young women in particular are able to escape restrictive family circumstances and enjoy horizon-broadening experiences and the companionship of other women.[72] Even women in EPZs or world-market factories have been known to express satisfaction with their jobs, although their working conditions are usually poor. In one study of Mexican *maquila* workers, however, almost two-thirds of respondents declared that they would keep working even if they did not need the money.[73] Fatima Mernissi's interviews with working women in a world-market electronics plant show the value these women place on their jobs and the satisfaction employment brings to them.[74] During a visit I made to a large pharmaceutical plant (not an EPZ) outside Casablanca in early December 1990, women workers revealed that they enjoyed their jobs, were cognizant of the better conditions of work and higher wages at that plant, and would continue to work even if the household did not require their additional income. The work force was unionized (the result of a bitter labor dispute some ten years earlier), and several of the women with whom I spoke had been or were workers' representatives.[75]

Transnational firms are not known for providing long-term stable jobs, and women's continued employment in the large-scale private sector depends to a great extent upon the vagaries of international trade and the world market.[76] At the same time, the public sector wage bill everywhere is in a state of contraction as a result of privatization and the structural adjustment policies of the 1980s. If Middle Eastern women were to lose their position in the labor market, it would certainly not be for reasons of religion or culture. Economic and political forces shape their employment opportunities to a far greater extent.

▲ Conclusions

This chapter has surveyed patterns of female employment over the past three decades in the modernizing countries of the Middle East and North Africa. An essential point of the endeavor has been to underscore the diversity of women's positions within the region and to link women's status and work opportunities to their class location, as well as state policies, development strategies, and the region's political economy. Many studies on the

Middle East and commentaries by Islamists themselves tend to understate the heterogeneity of the region; they project a uniform culture and exaggerate its importance, elevating culture or religion to the status of single explanatory variable. My alternative position is that there is an interactive relationship of economic processes, political dynamics, and cultural practices. Only through such an approach can variations within the region and changes over time be understood.

Since the 1960s state expansion, economic development, oil wealth, and increased integration within the world system have combined to create educational and employment opportunities favorable to women in the Middle East. Although benefits have spread unevenly, female education and employment are undermining patriarchal attitudes and practices. But it appears that just as women have been making inroads into public life, including the work force, a cultural and political backlash in the form of conservative Islamist movements has taken shape and targeted them.

Female labor force participation is still low in relation to that of other regions of the world and, of course, in relation to male labor force participation. Several explanatory factors have been discussed in this chapter. One factor is the ambivalence of state managers to equality and empowerment for women. Another is the economic crisis facing the region. A third factor is the general low level of industrialization and transnational activity in the region, and the correspondingly small percentage of women in industrial jobs. The oil economies chose a strategy that relied on oil, gas, and finance, thereby minimizing the use of labor and offering few opportunities for women. Elsewhere, although ISI opened up some employment for women—for example, in state-run factories or industrial plants in the private sector receiving state support—the strategy tended to be capital-intensive and to favor male employment. In contrast, an export-led development approach accompanied by an influx of multinational corporations into a country seems to result in significant increases in female labor force participation, in particular increases in the female share of manufacturing.

Equity and empowerment remain elusive for women when access to economic resources is reserved mainly for men. In the Middle East there continues to exist an exceedingly large population of underutilized labor—that is, women. Attention to the ways and means of integrating women in development therefore remains a pressing item on the national agenda of each country of the region. Policymakers must be persuaded of the positive payoff of investing in the education and employment of women: a more skilled work force, stabilized population growth, healthier children, more prosperous households, an expanding tax base. It is likely that as countries turn toward economic liberalization, encouraging manufacturing for export and increased trade, women's employment will increase. On the other hand, women may be the most adversely affected by the contraction of the public sector wage bill, while the growth of small-scale manufacturing—as distinct from employment in large and modern firms or in the public sec-tor—may not be in their best interests. At the end of the twentieth century, Middle Eastern working women have come a long way, and in many coun-tries they have significantly contributed to national development and eco-nomic growth, but economic development should be able to serve them bet-ter than it has.

▲ 3
Modernizing Women: Reforms, Revolutions, and the Woman Question

The proletariat cannot achieve complete freedom unless it achieves complete freedom for women.—Lenin

Woman was transformed in this society so that a revolution could occur.
—Iranian magazine editorial

Around the world, changes in women's status have come about through a combination of long-term macrolevel change processes (industrialization, urbanization, proletarianization, education, and employment) and collective action (social movements and revolutions). In the context of both socioeconomic development and political change, legal reforms have been pursued to improve the status of women in the family and in the society. The Bolshevik Revolution in Russia provides the first historical example of sweeping legal reform in favor of women. Here the leadership adopted an official discourse of sexual equality and enacted policies of affirmative action, quotas, and political education that many countries subsequently emulated. In Scandinavia the welfare state plays an important role in relieving women of some of the responsibilities of child care and other forms of care-giving, releasing them for employment and participation in formal politics. In the former German Democratic Republic, a policy of combating sex discrimination, indeed of discrimination in favor of women, was in place from 1949 until the demise of the GDR in 1990. Elsewhere, revolutionary movements and developmentalist, welfarist states—both socialist and nonsocialist—have been crucial agents of the advancement of women, promoting reforms in family law, encouraging education and employment, and formulating social policies intended to facilitate women's participation in public life.[1]

In many Third World countries, including Middle Eastern ones, concepts of the emancipation of women emerged in the context of national liberation, state-building, and self-conscious attempts to achieve modernity in the early part of the century.[2] In many cases, male feminists were instrumental in highlighting the woman question. Among the earlier generation of male women's rights advocates are Qassem Amin (author of the 1901 study *The New Woman*) and Muhammad Abduh (1849–1905); Turkey's Ziya Gökalp and Mustafa Kemal; Afghanistan's Mahmud Tarzi (1866–1935); Iraq's Jamal Sudki Azza Khawy (who in 1911 advocated doing away with the veil); and Iran's Malkum Khan (who in an 1890 issue of his journal, *Qanun* [Law], wrote an article advocating women's education). Many other intellectuals, inspired by socialist or liberal political thought, advocated unveiling women and liberating them through education. In most cases, especially in the first half of the twentieth century, these ideas were used to call for revolt against corrupt, feudalistic governments. In the post–World War II period, integrating women into national development may have been an objective for many male reformers. In postindependence Tunisia, President Habib Bourguiba replaced Islamic family law (based on the Shari'a) with a civil law code regulating personal and family relations and equalizing the responsibilities of the sexes. Polygamy and unilateral male divorce were abolished, and the state assumed a strong stance in favor of female emancipation. In Syria and Iraq following the Baathist "revolutions" of the 1950s, women were granted political and social rights and encouraged, especially in Iraq, to utilize state-sponsored educational facilities. Nasserism as a reformist and developmentalist philosophy created unprecedented educational and employment opportunities for women in Egypt. In Iran women were granted the right to vote in 1962, and in 1967 the Pahlavi state introduced the Family Protection Act, which limited polygamy, allowed women to initiate divorce, and increased their child custody rights after divorce or widowhood.

Although male reformers have been instrumental in changing laws pertaining to women, women activists have been crucial agents themselves of legal and political change. In the early twentieth century, well-known women activists included Egypt's Huda Sharawi, who formed the Egyptian Feminist Union in 1923 and dramatically threw her veil into the sea; Turkey's Halide Edip (1883–1964), a nationalist who had served in Mustafa Kemal's forces; Iran's Qurratul Ayn, the famous Baha'i leader who fought in battles and caused a scandal in the 1840s by going unveiled; and Sediqheh Dowlatabadi, who, like Qurratul Ayn, was a fierce nationalist opposed to concessions to the British and publisher of the short-lived *Zaban-e Zanan* ("Women's Tongue"). Since then, women in the Middle East, like women in other countries, have been engaged in all manner of political manifestations: reform movements, anticolonial struggles, national liberation movements, anti-imperialist struggles, religious movements, bread riots, street demonstrations, and so on. Their formal political participation has not been as extensive as that of men because they have been unfairly handicapped by existing custom and law. But precisely because of this handicap, their participation in political movements must be considered remarkable. In some cases, as a direct result of their involvement in a movement, women's legal status improved. In other cases, women's political activities had little or no bearing on their subsequent legal status and social positions; if anything, their legal status in fact diminished. It is essential to recognize that women in the Middle East have been actors in political movements, that these movements have had a variable effect on their social positions, and that gender and the woman question have been central features of political movements, reforms, and revolutions.

In their book *Female Revolt,* Chafetz and Dworkin state that "independent women's movements are totally absent" in the Middle East.[3] This is rather an exaggeration, for independent women's movements have been especially persistent in Egypt (see Chapter 5). It is also surprising that Chafetz and Dworkin nowhere mention the strong opposition mounted by women against the Khomeini regime in 1979 and the many independent women's groups that emerged that year (see Chapter 6). There is also an independent Iranian feminist movement in exile, with a number of journals, the most lively being *Nimeh-ye Digar,* published in the United States. And in Algeria an independent women's movement first emerged in the early 1980s in opposition to the state's draft bill on a Muslim family code, subsequently after the political opening of 1988, and especially since the 1990 electoral victory of the Islamist organization Front Islamique du Salut.

This chapter will not describe the many political movements in which Middle Eastern women have participated. The purpose of this chapter is to examine a number of revolutionary movements in which the woman question figured prominently and as a result of which women's legal status and social positions underwent considerable change. Two sets of cases are examined. In one, national progress and societal transformation were viewed by the leadership as inextricably bound up with equality and the emancipation of women. I call this the Women's Emancipation model of revolution. Such movements occurred within the context of the struggle against feudalism and backwardness and were in some cases inspired by socialist ideals. Education, employment, and unveiling were encouraged as a way of integrating women into the development of the country and thereby accelerating the process of social change. The Middle Eastern cases considered here are the radical Kemalist reforms in Turkey during the 1920s; the 1967 revolution in South Yemen and reform of family law in what came to be called the People's Democratic Republic of Yemen; and the April 1978 Saur Revolution in Afghanistan, which sought to implement a controversial decree pertaining to marriage and the family. In the second set of cases, the leadership regarded cultural identity, integrity, and cohesion as strongly dependent upon the proper behavior and comportment of women, in part as a reaction to colonialist or neocolonialist impositions.

Veiling, modesty, and family attachment were encouraged for women. I call this the Woman-in-the-Family model of revolution. The two Middle Eastern cases considered here are the Algerian Revolution and the period following independence in 1962; and the Iranian Revolution of 1979 and the subsequent issue of veiling.

Quite apart from what this examination tells us about the varied positions of women and the role played by states in legislating gender in the Middle East, this chapter underscores the centrality of gender and the strategic role of the woman question in sociopolitical change processes. As such it offers theoretical lessons of a wider relevance regarding political battles and the reproduction of state power.

▲ Bringing Women into the Study of Revolution

Feminists and social scientists of gender from across the disciplines have examined some of the ways women affect and are affected by national, ethnic, and state processes.[4] Some scholars of the French Revolution have examined how gender was constructed in the political discourse and discovered the legal disempowerment and exclusion of women based on the "natural fact" of sexual difference.[5] Unlike standard studies on revolution, feminist scholarship has been especially attentive to the theme of women and revolution. Siân Reynolds makes the interesting point that the participation of women as mothers and food distributors has a profoundly legitimizing effect on revolution—at least in its early stages.[6] In social science studies of revolution, however, gender has yet to be treated systematically in the causes, course, or even outcomes of revolutions, despite the fact that the woman question has been so closely entangled with the entire course of revolutions.[7] In the sociology of revolution, gender, unlike class or the state or the world system, is not seen even as a constitutive category.[8]

Let us begin this discussion of women and revolutionary change by defining revolution. The *Oxford English Dictionary* defines it as "a complete overthrow of the established government in any country or state by those who were previously subject to it; a forcible substitution of a new ruler or form of government." As Kimmel notes, this definition implies that revolutions take place on the political level. Other definitions cite the use of violence, as in Samuel Huntington's description of revolution as "a rapid fundamental and violent domestic change in the dominant values and myths of a society, in its political institutions, social structure, leadership, government activity, and policies." More than anyone else, Theda Skocpol has insisted upon the structural features of revolutionary causes and outcomes. She defines social (as distinct from the more limited political) revolutions as "rapid, basic transformations of a society's state and class structure; they are accompanied and in part carried through by class based revolts from below." The definition by John Dunn includes the purposive dimension of revolutions: "a form of massive, violent, and rapid social change. They are also attempts to embody a set of values in a new or at least renovated social order."[9] Finally, Perez Zagorin's definition is perhaps most useful for our present study, as it combines political change, attempts at social transformation, and concepts of the ideal society:

> A revolution is any attempt by subordinate groups through the use of violence to bring about (1) a change of government or its policy, (2) a change of regime, or (3) a change of society, whether this attempt is justified by reference to past conditions or to an as yet unattained future ideal.[10]

Let us agree, then, that revolutions are attempts to rapidly and profoundly change political and social structures; they involve mass participation; they usually entail violence and the use of force; they include notions of the "ideal" society; and they have some cultural reference points. Let us also note that revolutions have thus far occurred in societies undergoing the transition to modernity. The major theories of revolution—Marxist class analysis, relative deprivation, and resource mobilization—link revolution to the dynamics and contradictions of modernization.[11] Certain conditions are necessary for the seizure of state power and the successful transformation of social structures, but these conditions vary, particularly over historical eras and types of societies (that is, causes of the Iranian Revolution are necessarily different from causes of the Bolshevik Revolution, and of course their outcomes completely diverge).

Revolutionary programs are not always fulfilled, and the intentions of the revolutionary leadership and state may be subject to various constraints, such as poor resource endowments, civil war, a hostile international environment, or external intervention. There is increasing consensus among students of revolution that in addition to the state, class conflict, resource bases, and the world system, cultural dynamics also should be investigated. That is, because of the complexity of causality, revolutions should be explained in terms of the interaction of economic, political, *and cultural* developments within national, regional, and global contexts.[12] However, what the study of revolution has not yet considered systematically is the prominent position assumed by gender—the position of women, family law, the prerogatives of men—in the discourse of revolutionaries and the laws of revolutionary states. Yet, as mentioned above, outside of the sociology of revolution, a separate body of prolific research on the position of women in revolutionary Russia, China, Vietnam, Cuba, Algeria, Nicaragua, Ethiopia, Iran, and elsewhere strongly suggests that gender relations constitute an important part of the culture, ideology, and politics of revolutionary societies.

This chapter is in part an initial attempt to use gender as a constitutive category of the analysis of revolution. That is, in addition to describing how revolutions in the Middle East have affected women's legal status and social positions, this chapter seeks to contribute to the ongoing refinement of the sociology of revolution. But in order to avoid inferences that gender is politicized and that women are political and cultural signifiers only in Muslim societies or that concepts of liberty, equality, and solidarity in Western countries have always been extended to women, I have included in this chapter two Western revolutions to add to the comparative perspective: the French Revolution and the Bolshevik Revolution. I will try to show that the first exemplifies the Woman-in-the-Family model of revolution, whereas the second is the quintessential Women's Emancipation model of revolution.

The French Revolution

That the French Revolution was an event of world historical significance is uncontestable. Even before the 1840s, Marx was well aware that the French Revolution had become a representative event destined to be played out not once, but again and again. Elements of its progressive discourse are found in many subsequent revolutions in Europe and in the Third World. Popular sovereignty, civil liberty, equality before the law—these are among the rich legacy of the French Revolution, itself a product of the Enlightenment. But feminist scholars have argued that women were the marginalized Other in the development of the liberal democratic state. Bonds between men *qua* men were constituted in opposition to women. In Western societies the division between the public sphere of state and civil society was conceptualized in opposition to the family, which was constructed as a natural and private institution headed by a man.[13] Even champions of the Enlightenment and of the French Revolution must concede that the woman question represents a serious drawback.[14]

What were the gender dynamics of the French Revolution? Reynolds cites Mary Wollstonecraft to the effect that in the minds of many of the French revolutionaries, women were associated with weakness, corruption, frailty, and specifically with the court and the ancien régime. Indeed, under the ancien régime, certain privileged women of all three estates took part in the preliminary voting for the Estates General of 1789, which may explain in part why the French republicans did not extend the new liberties to women.[15] On the other hand, with the collapse of the Church's authority, the revolutionaries sought a new moral basis for family life counterposed to that of the old regime. They made divorce possible, they accorded full legal status to illegitimate children, and they abolished primogeniture. They also abolished slavery and gave full civil rights to Protestants and Jews. But it is important to note that the emerging political culture of the French Revolution was rather biased in favor of men. Subsequently, Napoleon reversed the most democratic provisions of the laws on family life, restoring patriarchal authority.

Harriet Applewhite and Darlene Levy describe the crucial participation of women of the popular classes during the spring and summer of 1792, a period of acute military/political crisis in Paris and throughout France. Their participation in armed processions was tolerated, if not positively encouraged and protected, by Girondin authorities such as Jerôme Pétion, the mayor of Paris, for its potential to co-opt key elements of the armed force and to apply collective pressure on both the national legislature and the royal executive. The marches reached insurrectionary proportions on June 20, when the thousands of men and women hastened the erosion of the constitutional monarchy. Finally, on August 10, 1792, the monarchy was brought down and a republic established. Both supporters and opponents of these fully mobilized democratic forces were sensitive to the strategic significance of women's involvement in these armed marches. According to Applewhite and Levy: "Revolutionary leaders exploited women's presence to create a gendered image of a national alliance of comrades in arms, mothers, sisters, and children. Authorities on both sides argued that it was extraordinarily difficult if not impossible to exercise repressive force effectively; they strongly implied that these armed families of *sectionnaires* constituted an insuperable popular force."[16]

The women who participated in the armed processions of 1792— women who bore weapons, shouted slogans, displayed banners, forged ties with National Guard battalions, demonstrated their solidarity with the passive male citizenry of the sections, and identified themselves as the sovereign people in arms—contributed to mobilizing the forces that democratized principles of sovereignty and militant citizenship. Such acts were necessary to the struggle for democratization but not sufficient to break through gender-based limitations on the meaning of political democracy. Authorities such as Pétion, who honored, tolerated, or even orchestrated women's involvement in the ceremonial and insurrectionary movements of 1792, never intended to grant women the expanded political rights under the republic. In the autumn of the following year, Jacobin leaders who, during their struggle against the Girondins, had encouraged the organized militancy of the Society of Revolutionary Republican Women, did not hesitate to outlaw women's political clubs when women's activism began to threaten their power base.

Robert Darnton notes that at the height of the French Revolution, virtue was the central ingredient of the new political culture. But to the revolutionaries, virtue was virile. At the same time, the cult of virtue produced a revalorization of family life. Darnton explains that the revolutionaries took their text from Rousseau and sermonized on the sanctity of motherhood and the importance of breast-feeding. "They treated reproduction as a civic duty and excoriated bachelors as unpatriotic."[17] Banners and slogans proclaimed: "Citizenesses! Give the Fatherland Children!" and "Now is the time to make a baby." Mothers had a certain legitimacy that unmarried *citoyennes* did not. Robespierre's Reign of Virtue involved an ideal of women as passive nurturers: Women should bear children for the revolution and sacrifice them for France. He abhorred the active women from the revolutionary club, describing them as "unnatural" and "sterile as vice." In contrast, Sheila Rowbotham writes that the action of women in the crowd over prices or in pushing for a part in popular sovereignty hinted at an active creation of women's roles, while Claire Lacombe attempted to appropriate revolutionary virtue for an extension of the power of the left-wing women. The deputation of the Society of Revolutionary Republican Women that came to the National Convention to protest the ban on their organization described the Society as "composed in large part of mothers of families."[18]

Although Lynn Hunt's study does not focus on gender, she argues that in the French Revolution the radical break with the justification of authority by reference to historical origins implied the rejection of patriarchal models of authority. On the republic's official seal, in engravings and prints, and in the *tableaux vivants* of the festivals, feminine allegorizations of classical derivation replaced representations of the king. These female figures, whether living women or statues, always sat or stood alone, surrounded most often by abstract emblems of authority and power. The republic might have her children and even her masculine defenders, but there was never a father present. In the early years of the French Revolution, the symbol of the republic was Marianne.

Eventually Marianne was replaced by Hercules, a distinctly virile representation of sovereignty and an image with connotations of domination and supremacy. The introduction of Hercules served to distance the deputies from the growing mobilization of women. For both the Jacobin leaders and their *sans-culottes* followers, politics was a quarrel between men.[19] On the grounds that women's active participation would lead to "the kinds of disruption and disorder that hysteria can produce," the convention outlawed all women's clubs at the end of October 1793. The Jacobin Chaumette said, "The *sans-culotte* had a right to expect his wife to run the home while he attended public meetings: hers was the care of the family, this was the full extent of her civic duties."[20] If the revolution had been female, the republic was to be male. The founding of the republic legitimized male power and banned women from the political stage.

What was to be the place of women in the new society? According to the Jacobin deputy André Amar: "Morality and nature itself have assigned her functions to her: to begin the education of men, to prepare the minds and hearts of children for the exercise of public virtues, to direct them early in life towards the good, to elevate their souls, to educate them in the cult of liberty—such are their functions after household cares . . . When they have carried out these duties they will have deserved well of the father-land."[21] In other words, the French woman was not a citizen but the chief source of civic education, responsible for the socialization of children in republican virtues. As we shall see, the Iranian case is very similar.

"O my poor sex," wrote feminist playwright Olympe de Gouges. "O women who have gained nothing from the Revolution!" Her *cri de coeur* that the advancement of men in the French Revolution had been accomplished at the expense of women suggests interesting theoretical possibilities, including an analogy with André Gunder Frank's development/underdevelopment thesis (whereby the two processes are symbiotic) or, perhaps more aptly, with Hegel's master/slave template.

The exclusion of women from the construction of the republic, their relegation to the sphere of the family, and their education in Catholic schools (until the 1850s) made them especially vulnerable in the anticlerical politics of the Second and Third Republics. The association of women with cultural and political conservatism led to their exclusion from the "universal suffrage" of 1848. As Michelet put it, giving women the vote would mean "giving thousands of votes to the priests."[22] This argument peaked under the Third Republic (1870–1940) and was shared by all anticlerical parties. Not until after World War II did women in France obtain the right to vote.

The Bolshevik Revolution

In contrast to the Woman-in-the-Family model of revolution as represented by the French Revolution, the Women's Emancipation model constructs women as part of the productive forces, to be liberated from patriarchal controls expressly for economic and political purposes. Here the discourse more strongly stresses sexual equality than sexual difference. The first example historically of such a movement is the Bolshevik Revolution in Russia, which remains the avant-garde revolution par excellence, more audacious in its approach to gender than any revolution before or since.

With the onset of World War I, women had entered production in greater numbers, and by 1917 one-third of Petrograd's factory workers were women. The Bolsheviks published a paper for women workers, *Rabotnitsa,* and encouraged women to join factory committees and unions. Split over the question of organizing women, the party moved steadily in 1917 toward a policy of separate organizations for them. Support for the Bolsheviks, in turn, grew among laundresses, domestic servants, restaurant and textile workers, and soldiers' wives. Although the party was theoretically opposed to separate organizations for women, in practice *Rabonitsa*'s success resulted in the organization of the Petrograd Conference of Working Women in November 1917 and the formation of the Zhenotdel, or women's department, within the party in 1919.[23]

Under Alexandra Kollantai, people's commissar for social welfare, labor legislation was passed to give women an eight-hour day, social insurance, pregnancy leave for two months before and after childbirth, and time at work to breast-feed. It also prohibited child labor and night work for women. The early months of the revolution also saw legislation to establish equality between husband and wife, civil registration of marriage, easy divorce, abolition of illegitimacy, and the wife's right not to take her husband's name or share his domicile. Under Kollantai's directorship in particular, the Zhenotdel saw itself as a force for women's interests and the transformation of society. In Central Asia it organized mass unveilings of Muslim women and ran literacy classes. (As we shall see below, this was attempted fifty years later in South Yemen and in Afghanistan.) All these developments followed from the view that the emancipation of women was an essential part of the socialist revolution, something to be accomplished through "the participation of women in general productive labor" and the socialization of domestic duties. Lenin sometimes expressed his views on the subject of women, revolution, and equality in rather forceful terms:

> Woman continues to be a *domestic slave,* because *petty housework* crushes, strangles, stultifies and degrades her, chains her to the kitchen and to the nursery, and wastes her labor on barbarously unproductive, petty, nerve-racking, stultifying and crushing drudgery.
>
> Enlightenment, culture, civilization, liberty—in all capitalist, bourgeois republics of the world all these fine words are combined with extremely infamous, disgustingly filthy and brutally coarse laws in which woman is treated as an inferior being, laws dealing with marriage rights and divorce, with the inferior status of a child born out of wedlock as compared with that of a "legitimate" child, laws granting privileges to men, laws that are humiliating and insulting to women.

The Bolsheviks also stressed the need for political participation of women, as the following quote from Lenin reveals: "We want women workers to achieve equality with men workers not only in law, but in life as well. For this, it is essential that women workers take an ever increasing part in the administration of public enterprises and in the administration of the state."[24]

The Bolsheviks took the initiative in calling the First Communist Women's Conference in 1920, and prepared the position paper for the occasion, *Theses of the Communist Women's Movement.* Apart from its commitment to the political equality of women and the guarantee of their social rights, the *Theses* included an attack on housewifery and "the domestic hearth." The document reflected the Engelsian view that female emancipation would be a twofold process, incorporating both the entry of women into the national labor force and the socialization of domestic labor.[25] The document also reflected the views of the outstanding Communist women who contributed to its formulation, among them Alexandra Kollantai, Inessa Armand, and Clara Zetkin.

Like the French revolutionaries before them, the Bolsheviks strongly supported "free union" and therefore legalized divorce. But in other matters they parted company with the French revolutionaries. Debates on sexuality reflected the Bolsheviks' commitment to gender equality and their critique of the family. The liberation of peasant women could only come about through a massive change in the mode of production, as well as a revolutionary transformation of social values and practices. The implementation in the 1920s of the Land Code and the Family Code, with their emphasis on individual rights and freedoms—including women's rights to land and for maintenance—was an extremely audacious act that challenged centuries of patriarchal control. It also undermined the collective principle of the household, the very basis of peasant production, and was thus strongly resisted. In Soviet Central Asia in the 1920s, where there was virtually no industrial working class, Bolshevik strategists directed their campaigns at women because they were considered the most oppressed social category.[26]

Despite the Zhenotdel's best efforts, material scarcity crippled the Bolshevik vision of liberation, although jurists and party officials maintained their commitment to the "withering away" of the family, and convocations such as the Women's Congress in 1927 showed the potential of an active socialist women's organization. This potential was cut short in the 1930s with the consolidation of the power of Stalin and his associates, who ushered in a more culturally conservative era, disbanded the Zhenotdel, ended open discussions of women's liberation, and resurrected the family. The earlier critique of the family was replaced by a strong emphasis on the "socialist family" as the proper model of gender relations. Family responsibilities were extolled for men as well as for women. By this time, economic, political, and ideological factors had converged to undermine the early libertarian views. Yet it cannot be denied that gender relations were altered, and significantly, by conscious deed and were an integral part of the construction of the new social order, the new socialist economy, and the new political culture of the Soviet Union.

Let us now turn to reforms, revolutions, and the woman question in the modern Middle East. As will be evident, they follow the two models described above.

▲ The Tanzimat Reforms and the Kemalist Revolution in Turkey

At the end of the nineteenth century, the Ottoman Empire was in the process of disintegration. It faced external pressure from the European powers who wished to expand their influence into the Middle East.

Internally, the pressure came from two sources: growing feelings of nation-alism among the non-Turkish population of the empire (Greeks, Arabs, Armenians, and people of the Balkans) and a desire for modernization and democratic institutions on the part of the Turks themselves. Among the lat-ter, the strongest influence came from the ideals of the French Revolu-tion.[27] The process of modernization along European lines had already begun in the late eighteenth century. During the first half of the nineteenth century, military officers were sent to France for training, and in Turkey two schools were established to produce civil servants.

The wide-ranging reforms known as the *Tanzimat* (reorganization) began in 1839 under the rule of Abdul Majid and inaugurated Turkey's shift from theocratic sultanate to modern state. The security of the subject's life, honor, and property was guaranteed, and fair public trials and a new penal code were instituted. The principle of equality of all persons of all religions before the law was considered a very bold move for the times.[28] The tax structure was reformed, and a new provincial administration based on the centralized French system was set up. Primary and secondary state schools were established alongside the religious schools, and in 1847 the creation of a Ministry of Education effectively took away the *ulamas'* power of sole jurisdiction over education. The reforms continued during the sultanate of Abdul Aziz and included the introduction of a new civil code in 1876, which, however, was based on the Shari'a. In 1871 the American College for Girls was started, although for two decades it was restricted to Christians. (The first Muslim girl to complete her studies there was Halide Edip, a future women's leader.[29]) But the trend had started, and many women educated in this manner were to make their mark as novelists and writers on women's emancipation.

Toward the end of the nineteenth century, opposition to the sultan was manifested in the Young Turks movement, officially called the Committee of Union and Progress. One of the principal tenets of the Young Turks was the need for modernization; they were also unabashedly for Westernization. Closely linked to the need for modernization through Westernization was the emancipation of women. Jayawardena reminds us that the process of Europeanization was not only ideological; it also entailed the forging of economic links with the capitalist countries of Europe. Around this time, the writer and sociologist Ziya Gökalp, who was often referred to as the theoretician of Turkish nationalism and was strongly influenced by the Comtean and Durkheimian tradition in French sociology, advocated equali-ty in marriage and divorce and succession rights for women.[30]

World War I hastened the breakup of the Ottoman Empire and the emergence of a new group from among the Young Turks. This faction advocated the building of a modern Turkish national state that was "repub-lican, secular and non-imperialist." Mustafa Kemal, an army captain, set up a revolutionary government in Ankara in 1920, oversaw a peace treaty with the British, and established the Turkish Republic in 1923, with himself as president and leader of the Republican People's Party. The Kemalist reforms were the most far-reaching in both intent and effect. Ataturk, as he came to be known, furthered the process of Westernization through economic development, separation of religion from state affairs, an attack on tradition, Latinization of the alphabet, promotion of European dress, adoption of the Western calendar, and the replacement of Islamic family law by a secular civil code. The influence of the French Enlightenment and anticlericalism is clear in these reforms. By 1926 the Shari'a was abolished and the civil and penal codes thoroughly secularized. Ziya Gökalp urged the Turks, "Belong to the Turkish nation, the Muslim religion and European civilization." Ataturk distanced himself from Islam much farther than Gökalp did.[31]

Where the Turkish reformers diverged from their French predecessors was on the woman question. Turkish women obtained the legal right to vote in 1934, many years before French women did. Unlike the French, for whom the emancipation of women was not on the agenda, a central element of the conceptualization of Turkish nationalism, progress, and civilization was "Turkish feminism"—the exact words of Gökalp.[32] Not only Ataturk and Gökalp but also Kemalist feminists such as the nationalist fighter and writer Halide Edip and Ataturk's adopted daughter, Afet Inan (author of *The Emancipation of the Turkish Woman*), played major roles in creating images of the new Turkish woman. According to Kandiyoti, the new Turkish woman was a self-sacrificing "comrade-woman" who shared in the struggles of her male peers. She was depicted in the literature as an asexual sister-in-arms whose public activities never cast any doubt on her virtue and chastity. Turkish national identity was "deemed to have a practically built-in sexual egalitarianist component."[33] In this sense the image of the emancipated Turkish woman was in line with the "true" identity of the collectivity—the new Turkish nation.

Why was the question of women's rights so strategic to the self-definition of the Turkish reformers? It appears that Mustafa Kemal had been highly impressed by the courage and militancy of Turkish women during the Balkan wars and World War I. As Jayawardena notes, Turkish women had taken up new avenues of public employment as nurses on the war fronts and had worked in ammunition, food, and textile factories, as well as in banks, hospitals, and the administrative services. Political events caused their involvement in militant activities. The occupation of various parts of Turkey by European troops in 1919 aroused protests in which women joined, and women in Anatolia were part of Kemal's army, which had launched a war against the invaders. In his speeches in later years, Kemal constantly referred to the role played by Anatolian women in the nationalist struggle. In a speech at Izmir in 1923 he said, "A civilization where one sex is supreme can be condemned, there and then, as crippled. A people which has decided to go forward and progress must realize this as quickly as possible. The failures in our past are due to the fact that we remained passive to the fate of women."[34] On another occasion, also in 1923, he said, "Our enemies are claiming that Turkey cannot be considered as a civilized nation because this country consists of two separate parts: men and women. Can we close our eyes to one portion of a group, while advancing the other, and still bring progress to the whole group? The road of progress must be trodden by both sexes together, marching arm in arm."[35]

This sentiment has parallels with one shared by a number of Turkish writers who stressed the harmful individual and national effects of the subordination of women. Various stories and essays depicted individual women who suffered from subjugation, children who suffered because of their mother's ignorance, households that suffered because women could not manage money properly. The solution to these individual and household problems was education for women. Other writings depicted women who descended into abject poverty when their husbands or fathers died. The solution to that particular problem was work for women. Other stories sought to show that society and progress suffered when women were kept illiterate and subordinated to men.[36] Ziya Gökalp in particular linked education and employment of women with the development of the country. One of his poems reads:

> Women are also human beings, and as human beings
> They are equally entitled to the basic rights of human beings:
> education and enlightenment.
> So long as she does not work, she will remain unenlightened,
> Which means, the country will suffer.
> If she does not rise, the country will decline.
> No progress is complete without her contribution.[37]

In answer to Kandiyoti's question in the title of an essay, "Women and the Turkish State: Political Actors or Symbolic Pawns?" one may conclude that to the Turkish reformers, the women of Turkey were both participants in the political struggles *and* symbols of the new Turkey. As Suna Kili argues, the Kemalists' hatred for, suspicion of, and experiences with the traditional order became the source of the processes leading to the initiation of the Turkish Enlightenment. Women's rights and women's emancipation were integral parts of Turkey's Westernization plan. Kemal Ataturk viewed women's equality to men as part of Turkey's commitment to Westernization, secularization, and democracy.

▲ National Liberation, Revolution, and Gender in Algeria

The French took over Algeria in June 1830. In contrast to their colonial policy in Morocco after 1912 and Tunisia after 1882, the French made an attempt in Algeria to dismantle Islam, its economic infrastructure, and its cultural network of lodges and schools. By the turn of the century, there were upwards of half a million French-speaking settlers in Algeria.

European competition ruined most of the old artisan class by 1930. Small shopkeepers such as grocers and spice merchants survived, but others suffered severely from the competition of the *petits colons*. Industrialization in Algeria was given a low priority by Paris during the interwar period. Local development and employment generation were severely hampered, and there was considerable unemployment and male migration. Fierce economic competition, cultural disrespect, and residential segregation characterized the French administration. In this context, many Algerians regarded Islam and the Muslim family law as sanctuaries from French cultural imperialism.[38]

To many Algerian men, the unveiled woman represented a capitulation to the European and his culture; she was a person who had opened herself up to the prurient stares of the foreigners, a person more vulnerable to rape. The popular reaction to the *mission civilisatrice* was a return to the land and to religion, the foundations of the old community. Islam became transformed, the patriarchal family grew in importance, and the protection and seclusion of women were seen by Algerians as increasingly necessary.

When the Front de Liberation Nationale (FLN) was formed, there was no provision for women to enjoy any political or military responsibilities. Nonetheless, military exigencies soon forced the officers of the Armée de Liberation Nationale (ALN) to use some women combatants. Upwards of 10,000 women participated in the Algerian Revolution. The overwhelming majority of those who served in the war were nurses, cooks, and laundresses.[39] But many women played an indispensable role as couriers, and because the French rarely searched them, women were often used to carry bombs. This practice recalls the function of women in the street processions of Paris in 1792. Among the heroines of the Algerian Revolution were Djamila Bouhired (the first woman sentenced to death), Djamila Bouazza, Jacqueline Guerroudj, Zahia Khalfallah, Baya Hocine, and Djoher Akrour. Women who fought and did not survive the war of liberation included twenty-year-old Hassiba Ben Bouali, killed in the Casbah, and Djennet Hamidou, who was shot and killed as she tried to escape arrest. She was seventeen. Yamina Abed, who was wounded in battle, suffered amputation of both legs. She was twenty.[40] These Algerian women, like the women of Vietnam after them, are the stuff of legends.

One emancipatory development during the national liberation struggle was the admittance of unmarried women into the ranks of the FLN and ALN and the emergence by default of voluntary unions (marriage without family arrangement) presided over by an FLN officer. (This was poignantly depicted in a scene in Pontecorvo's brilliant film *Battle of Algiers*.) Alya Baffoun notes that during this "rather exceptional period of struggle for national liberation," the marriage of Djamila Bouhired to an "infidel" non-Muslim foreigner was easily accepted and assimilated by her community.[41]

After independence the September 1962 constitution guaranteed equality between the sexes and granted women the right to vote. It also made Islam the official state religion. Ten women were elected deputies of the new National Assembly and one of them, Fatima Khemisti, drafted the only significant legislation to affect the status of women passed after independence.[42] In this optimistic time, when heroines of the revolution were being hailed throughout the country, the Union Nationale des Femmes Algeriennes (UNFA) was formed. Indeed, one consequence of the Algerian Revolution and of women's role in it was the emergence of the *Moudjahidates* model of Algerian womanhood. The heroic woman fighter was an inspiration to the 1960s and 1970s generation of Algerians, particularly Algerian university women.[43]

But another, more patriarchal tendency was at work during and after the Algerian Revolution. One expression of this tendency was the pressure on women fighters during the liberation struggle to get married and thus prevent spurious talk about their behavior. Moreover, despite the incredible sacrifices of Algerian women, and although the female militants "acceded to the ranks of subjects of history," the Algerian Revolution has tended to be cast in terms of male exploits, and the heroic female feats have not received as much attention.[44]

Following independence, and in a display of authoritarianism, President Ben Bella proceeded to ban all political parties; the Federation of the FLN in France, which had advocated a secular state, had been dissolved; the new FLN general secretary, Mohammed Khider, had purged the radicals—who had insisted on the right of workers to strike—from the union's leadership. And of women, Khider said: "The way of life of European women is incompatible with our traditions and our culture . . . We can only live by the Islamic morality. European women have no other preoccupations than the twist and Hollywood stars, and don't even know the name of the president of their republic."[45] In a reversal of the political and cultural atmosphere of the national liberation struggle, "exacerbated patriarchal values" became hegemonic in independent Algeria. In this context, the marriage of another Algerian heroine, Dalila, to a foreigner was deemed unacceptable. Alya Baffoun reports that Dalila's brother abducted and confined her "with the approving and silent consent of the enlightened elite and the politically powerful."[46]

Thus, notwithstanding the participation of upwards of 10,000 women in the Algerian Revolution, their future status was already shaped by "the imperative needs of the male revolutionaries to restore Arabic as the primary language, Islam as the religion of the state, Algeria as a fully free and independent nation, and themselves as sovereigns of the family."[47] This is why, *pace* the optimistic vision of Frantz Fanon, the country's independence did not signify the emancipation of women. Indeed, the FLN organ, *El Moudjahid,* opposed the term emancipation (identified with the French colonizers) and preferred Muslim Woman—"which in this context had a political rather than a religious meaning."[48]

In the 1960s Algerian marriage rates soared. In 1967 some 10 percent of Algerian girls were married at fifteen years of age; at twenty years of age, 73 percent were married. The crude fertility rate was 6.5 children per woman. The Boumedienne government's policy on demographic growth was predicated on the assumption that a large population is necessary for national power. It was, therefore, opposed to all forms of birth control unless the mother had already produced at least four children.[49] By the end of the Boumedienne years in 1979, 97.5 percent of Algerian women were without paid work. (Some 45 percent of Algerian men were unemployed or underemployed.) The UNFA had become the women's auxiliary of the FLN, devoid of feminist objectives.

On the positive side, state-sponsored education has created a generation of Algerian women who could become a restive force for progressive social change in Algeria. These are the women who loudly and visibly challenged the Chedli government's conservative family code in 1982, who continued to protest it after it was passed in 1984, and who today are confronting the Islamist fundamentalist movement in Algeria. (See Chapter 5 for an elaboration.)

▲ The People's Democratic Republic of Yemen

In November 1967 the National Liberation Front came to power after five years of guerrilla fighting and terminated 128 years of British colonial rule in South Yemen. The People's Democratic Republic of Yemen (PDRY) was born. In June 1969 the revolutionary government took a more radical turn that aimed at "the destruction of the old state apparatus," the creation of a unified, state-administered legal system, and rapid social structural transformation. Tribal segmentation and the local autonomy of ruling sheikhs, sultans, and emirs had resulted in a country devoid of a unified national economy, political structure, and legal system. Such a social order was seen by the revolutionaries as an obstacle to economic development and social reform. At the same time, it was clear that development and change required the active participation of women. Kin control over women, and the practice of seclusion, consequently had to be transformed.

In this context the constitution of 1970 outlined the government's policies toward women, and a new family law was proposed in 1971 and passed in 1974.

Quite unlike the Algerian FLN, the National Liberation Front of Yemen described itself as "the vanguard of the Yemen working class," and its official doctrine was inspired by the writings of Marx, Engels, and Lenin. Article 7 of the constitution, which described the political basis of the revolution as an "alliance between the working class, the peasants, intelligentsia and petty-bourgeoisie," went on to add that "soldiers, women, and students are regarded as part of this alliance by virtue of their membership in the productive forces of the people."[50] The constitution recognized women as both "mothers" and "producers," consequently as forming part of the "working people." In addition to giving all citizens the right to work and regarding work as "an obligation in the case of all able-bodied citizens," the constitution called upon women not yet involved in "productive work" to do so.

According to the preamble of the family law, the "traditional" or "feudal" family is "incompatible with the principles and programme of the National Democratic Revolution . . . because its old relationships prevent it from playing a positive role in the building up of society." As Maxine Molyneux explains, the law began by denouncing "the vicious state of affairs which prevails in the family" and proclaimed that "marriage is a contract between a man and a woman who are equal in rights and duties, and is based on mutual understanding and respect." It established the principle of free-choice marriage; raised the minimum legal age of marriage to sixteen for girls and eighteen for boys; abolished polygamy except in exceptional circumstances such as barrenness or incurable disease; reduced the dower (*mahr*); stipulated that both spouses must bear the cost of supporting the family; ended unilateral divorce; and increased divorced women's rights to custody of their children.[51]

As in Soviet Russia, family reform was seen simultaneously as a precondition for mobilizing women into economic and political activity and as an indispensable adjunct of both economic change and social stability.[52] What was distinctive and especially problematic about the process in the PDRY was that improvements in women's social and legal status involved reforming codes that were derived from Islam and were considered to be of divine inspiration. The introduction of the new family law in the PDRY, as elsewhere (see the discussion of Afghanistan below), involved challenging both the power of the Muslim clergy and orthodox interpretations of Islam. After 1969 the government sought to curb the institutional and economic base of the traditional clergy and transferred its responsibilities to agencies of the state. Religious education in schools was made the responsibility of lay teachers. Kin, class, and tribal control over women were outlawed and to some degree delegitimized. As Maxine Molyneux has noted, women were interpolated in new ways—as workers, national subjects, political subjects—in order to help construct the new order. The rearticulation of gender was an integral part of the restructuring of state and society. Gender redefinition was both a reflection of the new regime's political agenda *and* the means by which it could establish its authority and carry out its revolution.

As with the Bolsheviks, the Yemeni revolutionaries encouraged women's entry into the political realm, and women were given the vote in 1970 when universal suffrage was implemented. According to Molyneux, a special effort was made to ensure that some women candidates ran for election in the first national poll of 1977. Women were also drawn into political activity through such organizations as the General Union of Yemeni Women, the party, neighborhood associations, and other mass organizations. In 1977 the women's union had a membership of 14,296, which included 915 women workers employed in factories and workshops; 528 agricultural workers and members of co-ops and state farms; 253 employees of various government agencies; secondary school and university students; and housewives. The women's union became especially active in the literacy campaign and in the campaign to gain support for the family law.[53]

As mentioned above, the Yemeni family law was passed in 1974 following extensive debate in what was a very conservative society. The law restricted polygamy but did not ban it. Men and women had equal rights when it came to divorce, and indeed there was a rise in the number of divorces immediately after the law was passed because it had become easier for women. The family law also required both spouses' consent to the marriage; set a limit to the dower; stipulated that the cost of running the household must be shared between husband and wife; and favored the mother for custody of the children even if she remarried, although the court had to decide in the child's best interests. A women's conference was held in April 1984, a decade after the family law had been passed, to see whether it needed any changes. The conference concluded that while there was nothing wrong with the law as it stood, there were still some problems in implementation.[54]

The government, party, and women's union retained a commitment to integrate Yemeni women into public life. Here is how one activist described it:

> We cannot speak of liberating women without making them participate in social life to convince them of their role in society. In our constitution we have included a commitment to the principle of women's liberation. It is women's right now to work in factories. By encouraging women to work in factories and to go to school we will achieve the right orientation. The state has also abolished the existence of women as a special stratum. No text in the laws or constitution discriminates against women. If a woman wants to work in any sphere no one will stop her.[55]

In fact, not all women were able to enter public life. Notwithstanding some socioeconomic development and expansion of state authority, the PDRY government could not achieve its vision of a literate and productive society and emancipated women citizens. South Yemen remained poor, and there was still a cultural stigma attached to women performing income-generating activities outside the home. Disagreements within the party and pressures from surrounding countries forced a change in the PDRY. In 1990 the PDRY merged with its northern half, the Republic of Yemen, which is conservative and tribal-dominated. A retreat on the woman question is inevitable.

▲ Revolution, Islamization, and Women in Iran

The Iranian Revolution against the Shah, which unfolded between spring 1977 and February 1979, was joined by countless women. Like other social groups, their reasons for opposing the Shah were varied: economic deprivation, political repression, identification with Islamism. The large street demonstrations included huge contingents of women wearing the veil as a symbol of opposition to Pahlavi bourgeois or Westernized decadence. As in Algeria and revolutionary France, the massive participation of women was vital to the success of the insurrection. Many women who wore the veil as a protest symbol did not expect hijab (veiling) to become mandatory. Thus when the first calls were made in February 1979 to enforce hijab and Ayatollah Khomeini was quoted as saying that he preferred to see women in modest Islamic dress, many women were alarmed. Spirited protests and sit-ins were led by middle-class leftist and liberal women, most of them members of political organizations or recently formed women's associations. Limited support for the women's protests came from the main political groups. As a result of the women's protests, the ruling on hijab was rescinded—but only temporarily. With the defeat of the left and the liberals in 1980 and their elimination from the political terrain in 1981, the Islamists were able to make veiling compulsory and to enforce it strictly.

The idea that women had "lost honor" during the Pahlavi era was a widespread one. Anti-Shah oppositionists decried the overly made-up "bourgeois dolls"—television announcers, singers, upper-class women in the professions—of the Pahlavi era. As in Algeria, the Islamists in Iran felt that "genuine Iranian cultural identity" had been distorted by Westernization, or what they called *gharbzadegi*. The unveiled, publicly visible woman was both a reflection of Western attacks on indigenous culture and the medium by which they were effected. The growing number of educated and employed women terrified men, who came to regard the modern woman as the manifestation of Westernization and imperialist culture and a threat to their own manhood.[56] Islamists projected the image of the noble, militant, and selfless Fatemeh—daughter of the Prophet Muhammad, earlier popularized by the late radical Islamic sociologist Ali Shariati—as the most appropriate model for the new Iranian womanhood.

It is necessary to point out that in the 1979–1980 period, the women's movement, then quite dynamic, was bifurcated; there were pro-Khomeini and anti-Khomeini women, and even among Islamist women there were different perspectives on women's rights issues, including the veil. Moreover, many women were comfortable with the veil because of the prevalence of male harassment of women in Western dress. During the 1960s and 1970s, when I was growing up in Tehran, just waiting for a taxi or shopping downtown entailed major battles with men, who variously leered, touched, made sexual remarks, or cursed. Women were fair game, and it is understandable that many would want to withdraw to the protective veil when in public. But the legal imposition of hijab was not about protecting women, and it was certainly not part of any struggle against male sexism: It was about negating female sexuality and therefore protecting men. More profoundly, compulsory veiling signaled the (re)definition of gender rules, and the veiled woman came to symbolize the moral and cultural transformation of society.

The full implications of the Islamic dress code are spelled out in a booklet entitled *On the Islamic Hijab* by a leading Iranian cleric, Murteza Mutahhari, who was assassinated in May 1979. In the preface by the International Relations Department of the Islamic Propagation Organization, it is argued that Western society "looks at women merely through the windows of sexual passion and regards woman as a little being who just satisfies sexual desires. . . . Therefore, such a way of thinking results in nothing other than the woman becoming a propaganda and commercial commodity in all aspects of Western life, ranging from those in the mass media to streets and shops." Mutahhari himself writes:

> If a boy and a girl study in a separate environment or in an environment where the girl covers her body and wears no make-up, do they not study better? . . . Will men work better in an environment where the streets, offices, factories, etc., are continuously filled with women who are wearing make-up and are not fully dressed, or in an environment where these scenes do not exist? . . .
> The truth is that the disgraceful lack of *hijab* in Iran before the Revolution . . . is a product of the corrupt western capitalist societies. It is one of the results of the worship of money and the pursuance of sexual fulfilment that is prevalent amongst western capitalists.[57]

The idea that women had lost their modesty and men had lost their honor during the Pahlavi era was a widespread one. Afrasiabi recounts a conversation he had in early February 1979 with a striking worker named Alimorad, who had just returned from Shahr-e Now (the red-light district in downtown Tehran), which had been destroyed by a fire set by Islamist militants.

> We burnt it all. Cleansed the city, he said.
> And women? I asked.
> Many were incinerated [*jozghaleh shodand*].
> Who are you? Where do you come from? I asked him.
> I am a worker from Rezaieh, married with children.
> What is your business in Tehran?
> To take part in the revolution!
> What is happening in Rezaieh?
> In Rezaieh there is just a movement [*jombesh*], but here there is a revolution.
> Why do you support the revolution?
> Islam, freedom, poverty, *zolm* [oppression], he answered without hesitation.
> What else? I insisted.
> Dignity [*heisiat*].
> Dignity?
> Yes brother. Shah took our dignity. He took man's right from him. My wife is now working. What is left of family when the wife works?
> And what is your expectation of Islam?
> Islam is our dignity. I want to bring bread on my own—to have a wife at home to cook and nurse the children, God and Islam willing.[58]

Such attitudes were behind the early legislation pertaining to women. The 1979 constitution spelled out the place of women in the ideal Islamic society the new leadership was trying to establish: within the family, through the "precious foundation of motherhood," rearing committed Muslims. Motherhood and domesticity were described as socially valuable, and the age of consent was lowered to fifteen (or thirteen, in some accounts). Legislation was enacted to alter gender relations and make them as different as possible from gender norms in the West. In particular, the Islamic Republic emphasized the distinctiveness of male and female roles, a preference for the privatization of female roles (although public activity by women was never barred, and they retained the vote), the desirability of sex-segregation in public places, and the necessity of modesty in dress and demeanor and in media images. Yet the Iranian Islamists were aware of modern sensibilities. The introduction to the constitution mentions women's "active and massive presence in all stages of this great struggle" and states that men and women are equal before the law. But this stated equality is belied by differential treatment before the law, particularly in the area of personal status or family law, based on the Shari'a.

The significance of the woman question to the Islamist revolutionaries and state-builders is captured in the following passage from an editorial in *Zan-e Rouz*, discussed by Afsaneh Najmabadi:

Colonialism was fully aware of the sensitive and vital role of woman in the formation of the individual and of human society. They considered her the best tool for subjugation of the nations. . . . In the underdeveloped countries . . . women serve as the unconscious accomplices of the powers-that-be in the destruction of indigenous culture. So long as indigenous culture persists in the personality and thought of people in a society, it is not easy to find a political, military, economic or social presence in society. . . . And woman is the best means of destroying the indigenous culture to the benefit of imperialists. . . .

In Islamic countries . . . Islamic belief and culture provide people of these societies with faith and ideals. . . . Woman in these societies is armed with a shield that protects her against the conspiracies aimed at her humanity, honor and chastity. This shield verily is her veil. For this reason, in societies like ours, the most immediate and urgent task was seen to be her unveiling, that is, disarming woman in the face of all calamities against her personality and chastity. . . . It is here that we realize the glory and depth of Iran's Islamic Revolution. This revolution transformed everyone, all personalities, all relations and all values. *Woman was transformed in this society so that a revolution could occur* (emphasis added).[59]

There can be no doubt that gender relations and the question of women were among the central components of the political culture and ideological discourse of the Islamic Republic of Iran.

▲ Afghanistan: The Saur Revolution and Women's Rights

The Afghan Revolution represents an extreme case illustrating the problems of implementing modernizing and socialist reforms in the face of poverty and underdevelopment, precapitalist structures, counterrevolution, and external intervention. This revolution had profound implications for the woman question.

In April 1978 the People's Democratic Party of Afghanistan (PDPA) seized power in what came to be called the Saur (April) Revolution and established the Democratic Republic of Afghanistan. Soon afterward the PDPA introduced rapid reforms to change the political and social structure of Afghan society, including patterns of land tenure and gender relations—and this in one of the poorest and least developed countries in the world. The government of President Noor Mohammad Taraki targeted the structures and relations of "tribal-feudalism" and enacted legislation to raise women's status through changes in family law (including marriage customs) and policies to encourage female education and employment. As in other modernizing and socialist experiments, the woman question constituted an essential part of the political project. The Afghan state was motivated by a modernizing outlook and socialist ideology that linked Afghan backwardness to feudalism, widespread female illiteracy, and the exchange of girls. The leadership resolved that women's rights to education, employment, mobility, and choice of spouse would be a major objective of the "national democratic revolution." The model of revolution and of women's emancipation was Soviet Russia, and the Saur Revolution was considered to belong to the family of revolutions that also included Vietnam, Cuba, Algeria, the PDRY, and Ethiopia.

In addition to redistributing land, cancelling peasants' debts and mortgages, and taking other measures to wrest power from traditional leaders, the government promulgated Decree No. 7, meant to fundamentally change the institution of marriage. A prime concern of the designers of the decree, which also mandated other reforms, was to reduce material indebtedness throughout the country; they further meant to ensure equal rights of women with men. In a speech on November 4, 1978, President Taraki declared: "Through the issuance of Decrees No. 6 and 7, the hard-working peasants were freed from bonds of oppressors and money-lenders, ending the sale of girls for good as hereafter nobody would be entitled to sell any girl or woman in this country."[60]

The first two articles in Decree No. 7 forbade the exchange of a woman in marriage for cash or kind and the payment of other prestations customarily due from a bridegroom on festive occasions; the third article set an upper limit of 300 afghanis (afs.), the equivalent of $10, on the *mahr*. President Taraki explained, "We are always taking into consideration and respect the basic principles of Islam. Therefore, we decided that an equivalent of the sum to be paid in advance by the husband to his wife upon the nuptial amounting to ten 'dirhams' [traditional ritual payment] according to shariat be converted into local currency which is afs. 300. We also decided that marriageable boys and girls should freely choose their future spouses in line with the rules of shariat."[61]

The legislation aimed to change marriage customs so as to give young women and men independence from their marriage guardians. Articles 4 to 6 of the decree set the ages of first engagement and marriage at sixteen for women and eighteen for men (in contrast to what happened in the Iranian case). The decree further stipulated that no one could be compelled to marry against his or her will, including widows. This last provision referred to the customary control of a married woman (and the honor she represents) by her husband and his agnates, who retained residual rights in her in the case of her widowhood. The decree also stipulated that no one who wanted to get married could be prevented from doing so.

Along with the promulgation of Decree No. 7, the PDPA government embarked upon an aggressive literacy campaign. This was led by the Democratic Organization of Afghan Women (DOAW), whose function was to educate women, bring them out of seclusion, and initiate social programs.[62] Throughout the countryside, PDPA cadres established literacy classes for men, women, and children in villages. By August 1979 the government had established 600 new schools. The PDPA's rationale for pursuing the rural literacy campaign with some zeal was that all previous reformers had made literacy a matter of choice; male guardians had chosen not to allow their females to be educated, and thus 99 percent of all Afghan women were illiterate. It was therefore decided not to allow literacy to remain a matter of (men's) choice, but rather a matter of principle and law.

This was an audacious program for social change, one aimed at the rapid transformation of a patriarchal society with a decentralized power structure based on tribal and landlord authority. Revolutionary change, state-building, and women's rights subsequently went hand in hand. The emphasis on women's rights on the part of the PDPA reflected (1) its socialist/Marxist ideology; (2) its modernizing and egalitarian outlook; (3) its social base and origins—the urban middle class, professionals, and those educated in the United States, USSR, India, and Europe; and (4) the number and position of women within the PDPA.

The PDPA was attempting to accomplish what reformers and revolutionaries had done in Turkey, Soviet Central Asia, and South Yemen and to carry out what earlier Afghan reformers and modernizers had tried to do. (See Chapter 7 for a full exposition.) But PDPA attempts to change marriage laws, expand literacy, and educate rural girls met with strong opposition. Decrees 6 and 7 deeply angered rural tribesmen and the traditional power structure. In the summer of 1978, refugees began pouring into Pakistan, giving as their major reason the forceful implementation of the literacy program among their women. There was also universal resistance to the new marriage regulations, which, coupled with compulsory education for girls, raised the threat of women refusing to obey and submit to family authority. The attempt to impose a minimum age for marriage, prohibit forced marriage, limit divorce payments, and send girls to school "inevitably aroused the opposition of Afghan men, whose male chauvinism is as massive as the mountains of the Hindu Kush," according to one account.[63] An Islamist opposition began organizing and conducted several armed actions against the government in the spring of 1979. By December 1979 the situation had deteriorated to such an extent that the Soviet army intervened. To a great extent, then, the failure of the revolution was linked to its audacious policy on women.

In 1980 the PDPA slowed down its reform program and announced its intention to eliminate illiteracy in cities in seven years and in provinces in ten. Unlike Soviet Russia, Turkey, or Iran, the Afghan state was not a strong one, able to impose its will through an extensive administrative and military apparatus. As a result, it was far less successful than other revolutionary regimes in carrying out its program—in Afghanistan's case, land redistribution and women's rights. Nor did twelve years of civil war and a hostile international climate provide conditions propitious for progressive social change. In 1987 the name Democratic Republic of Afghanistan was changed to the Republic of Afghanistan and the liberation of women took a backseat to national reconciliation. In 1990 the PDPA changed its name to the Homeland Party, or Hizb-e Watan. Similarly, the party made constitutional changes, dropping clauses that expressed the equality of men and women and reinstating Muslim family law. In 1992 the whole experiment collapsed, and the mujahidin set up an Islamic regime. Their very first act was to make veiling compulsory.

▲ Revolution, State-Building, and Women

Revolutions are a special case of social change that attempts to rapidly transform political and economic structures, social and gender relations, and societal institutions to conform to an ideology. The twentieth century has been called the century of revolutions, and many Third World countries, including countries in the Middle East, have experienced revolutionary change. Where revolutions result in the emergence of strong, centralized states, as in Turkey, Iran, and Algeria, revolutionaries or state-builders are more successful in implementing their vision of the ideal society. But where revolutions occur in underdeveloped areas, states are not strong enough to carry out their program for rapid and radical social change, as was the case in Afghanistan and South Yemen. In all cases, however, gender plays a role in the course of revolution and in the programs of state-builders. Changes in gender relations, practices, and laws should be part of the explanation of the causes, preconditions, and outcomes of revolutions. The nature of gender discourse (for example, the radical language of the Bolsheviks versus the moralist rhetoric of the Islamists in Iran—i.e., gender equality versus gender difference) reveals a great deal about the nature of the revolution and the regime. During periods of revolutionary transformation, changes in societal values and ideologies affect gender relations and vice versa. Laws about women are closely bound to the power of the state. That is why, to paraphrase Hanna Papanek, states and movements raise the woman question even when it creates so much trouble.[64]

Beginning at least as early as Marianne in the French Revolution, the idealized woman has historically played a major role as a national or cultural symbol. During transitional periods in a nation's history, women may be linked to either modernity or tradition. The woman question may be framed in the context of modernizing projects or in tandem with religious and moral movements; it may be raised to legitimize women or to mobilize them toward specific ends. At times of regime consolidation and state-building, questions of gender, family, and male-female relations come to the fore. The state becomes the manager of gender. Cultural representations of women, and of course legislation on family law and women's rights, reflect the importance of gender in politics and ideology and signal the political agenda of revolutionaries and regimes. Whether political discourses support women's emancipation and equality or whether they glorify tradition, morality, the family, and difference, the point remains that political ideologies and practices are gendered and that social transformation and state-building entail changes in gender relations as well as new class configurations and property rights.

The twentieth century has seen two models of womanhood emerge in the context of societal reform and revolutionary change. One model, which I have called the Woman's Emancipation model, draws its inspiration from the Enlightenment, the socialist tradition, and the Bolshevik Revolution. This model emerges when revolutionaries target feudalism, tribalism, or backwardness and recognize the need to integrate women into programs for development and progress. The other archetype I called the Woman-in-the-Family model, and it occurs in cases of opposition to colonialist or neo-colonialist modes of control, where revolutionaries draw from their own cultural repertoire. The historical precursor of this model of gender outcomes is, ironically, the French Revolution.

As Jayawardena observes in her study of feminism and nationalism in the Third World, for modernizing states and revolutionary regimes of the first half of the twentieth century the image of the modern woman, unveiled, educated, and working in the public sphere, provided a potent symbol. Nationalism, state-building projects, and the emancipation of women were of a piece. The modern woman who cut her hair, worked outside the home, and was accepted, at least on paper, as a full citizen was associated with progress and modernity, as in Russia and Turkey (and later in China). As I have shown in this chapter, more recent extensions of the earlier model of societal transformation and women's emancipation were the revolutionary aims of the People's Democratic Republic of Yemen and the Democratic Republic of Afghanistan.

A second pattern of revolution and gender emerged in the second half of the twentieth century. With the rise of anti-colonialist and anti-imperialist movements, the modern woman came to be viewed with ambivalence, especially if she was associated with the culture of the colonialists and imperialists. We have seen in this chapter that in the Algerian and Iranian revolutions, the modern, unveiled woman was associated with social danger, moral decay, and imperialist culture. For "freedom fighters" who are staunchly opposed to modernizing projects, such as the Afghan mujahidin, the image of the modern woman is anathema. Elsewhere, at a time of economic difficulties, social uncertainties, and confrontations with the West, the image of the traditional woman seems to promise a return to a comforting, stable, and idyllic past; she is seen as the repository of old values and ways of life and is linked to a more "genuine" cultural identity. The modern woman is taken to be representative of everything that appears threatening in the new and quickly changing world, of alien cultures and external subterfuge. This perception explains why not all revolutions in the latter half of the twentieth century have had favorable outcomes for the status of women.[65]

Maxine Molyneux has argued that when revolutionary governments set about reforming the position of women in the first period of social and economic transformation, they tend to focus on three goals: (1) extending the base of the government's political support; (2) increasing the size or quality of the active labor force; and (3) helping harness the family more securely to the process of social reproduction. In all the cases examined here, Molyneux's third factor was present. But the first and second factors are present only in the cases of modernizing, developmentalist states—those following what I have called the Women's Emancipation model of revolution—whether guided by socialist ideology (as in the cases of South Yemen and Afghanistan) or bourgeois ideology (as in the case of Turkey). For the revolutionary leaders in Algeria or Iran, integrating women into the labor force to increase its size (which was not a goal in these labor surplus countries) or its quality (which should have been a goal but was not) was clearly not an objective. Rather, their keen desire to restore cultural authenticity, religious integrity, and national traditions, which they felt colonialism or imperialism had distorted, led to the policy of family attachment rather than labor attachment for women.

In all the cases reviewed—Turkey, Algeria, South Yemen, Iran, and Afghanistan, and, of course, the French and Russian revolutions—the woman question figured prominently in political discourses, state ideologies, and legal policies. Gender relations and the position of women have figured prominently in other revolutionary movements as well, as Table 3.1 shows. The outcome of the woman question is determined by both structure and agency, as well as by economic, political, and ideological factors: the prevailing material conditions of social life, the international environment, the nature of the revolutionary leadership and its social program, the extent of women's participation in the revolution, the degree to which women are organized and capable of articulating their interests, and the ability of the revolutionary state to realize its vision of liberation and social transformation. Concepts of the ideal society invariably entail concepts of the ideal woman. The formation of national identity is both a political and a cultural exercise; as such, constructions of gender are an integral part of the process of identity and state formation. Political-cultural projects, and the position of women, are inextricably linked. Transforming society and transforming women are consequently two sides of the same coin.

Table 3.1 Gender Dynamics of Revolutions: A Typology

Type of Revolution	Bourgeois Revolutions	Socialist Revolutions and Populist Revolutions
Women's emancipation a major goal or outcome	Kemalism in Turkey	France (1848) Russia (1917) China Cuba Vietnam Democratic Yemen Ethiopia Afghanistan Nicaragua El Salvador
Family attachment of women a major goal or outcome	French Revolution Perestroika in the Soviet Union "1989 Revolutions" of Eastern Europe	Mexico Algeria Iran

Notes: "Revolutions" are defined as attempts at rapid economic, political, and ideological transformation. There is very little information on the gender dynamics of African revolutions.

▲ 4
Women, Patriarchy, and the Changing Family

The social institutions under which men [and women] of a definite historical epoch and of a definite country live are conditioned by . . . the stage of development of labor, on the one hand, and of the family, on the other. . . . The less the development of labor, and the more limited its volume of production, . . . the more preponderatingly does the social order appear to be dominated by ties of sex.—Frederick Engels

This chapter examines the structure of the Middle Eastern Muslim family, the position of women within it, and the impact of social change, especially education, on the family and on patterns of marriage and reproduction. I define the Muslim family as a patriarchal unit and describe the contradictions and challenges it is encountering during the contemporary period of economic development and demographic transition. The persistence of patriarchy is a matter of debate, and some feminist theorists argue that industrialized societies are also patriarchal. In this chapter the term patriarchy is used in its strict rather than liberal sense—that is, in terms of Caldwell's "patriarchal belt" and Kandiyoti's "classic patriarchy," based on kinship systems in agrarian settings. I have also adopted Sharabi's concept of "neopatriarchal society," the result of the collision of tradition and modernity in the context of oil-based dependent capitalism and, I would add, limited industrialization.[1]

The family is perhaps the only societal institution that is conceptualized as "essential" and "natural." The biological basis of kin ties and women's reproductive capacities have historically conferred such a status on the family. This emphasis on biology has led to reductionist and functionalist accounts of the family, accounts that transcend cultural barriers and unite Muslim and Western conservatives. Consider Talcott Parsons's functionalist perspective. He argued that the modern family has two main functions: to socialize children into society's normative system of values and inculcate appropriate status expectations, and to provide a stable emotional environment that will cushion the (male) worker from the psychological damage of the alienating occupational world. These functions are carried out by the wife and mother. It is she who plays the affective, "expressive" role of nurturance and support, and it is the husband who plays the "instrumental" role of earning the family's keep and maintaining discipline. The Parsonian view is very similar to a contemporary Muslim view, which sees the family as the fundamental unit of society and stresses the mother's role in the socialization of children—particularly in raising "committed Muslims" and transmitting cultural values. These two similar accounts of the family and women are not only descriptive but also prescriptive.

Proponents of the family as a natural unit or a haven in a heartless world frequently warn of its impending death. Throughout the world, the alarm tends to be sounded by persons and groups of the right: Christian fundamentalists and Orthodox Jews in the United States, anticommunists in Eastern Europe and the former Soviet Union, Islamists in the Middle East. What are some of the indicators of the weakening of the family? According to Kingsley Davis, the state of marriage has become severely weakened in Western nations over the past forty years. He cites easy divorce, the postponement of marriage, a rise in the proportion of the never-married, an increase in nonmarital cohabitation, and the ready availability of contraception as forces that have eroded the family and compromised its ultimate function—the licensing of reproduction.[2] In the former Soviet Union and Eastern Europe, high divorce rates and low birthrates led demographers to warn that these societies may not be able to reproduce themselves.[3]

Laments about the current condition of the family imply that at an earlier time in history the family was more stable and harmonious than it is today. Yet, despite massive research, historians have not located a "golden age of the family." One historian lists as causes for the small family size in fourteenth-century England, "birth control, infanticide, high infant mortality, late marriages, infertility due to poor diet, high female mortality, and economic limitations on nuptiality."[4] The marriages of seventeenth-century Europe were based on family and property needs, not on choice or affection. In one of the most famous historical observations, Thomas Hobbes described mid-seventeenth-century life as "solitary, poore, nasty, brutish, and short." In other words, people lived a lot less than we do now. Two in ten children died in infancy; another two died before reaching puberty; and more either died before reaching marrying age or simply never married. Those who did survive and marry spent most of their adult lives reproducing and raising the next generation.[5] Loveless marriages, tyrannical husbands, high death rates, and the beating, abuse, and abandonment of children add up to a grim image.[6] Caldwell notes that many writers have tended to romanticize the peasant family, even though Chayanov calculated that

Russian peasant women and girls worked 1.21 times as many hours as men and boys. Teodor Shanin writes that despite their heavy burden of labor (both housework and fieldwork) and their functional importance in the Russian peasant household, women were considered second-class members of it and were nearly always placed under the authority of males. Quarrels and tensions seem to be endemic to the extended household and family everywhere.[7] Amartya Sen's model of "cooperative conflicts" within households and Hanna Papanek's concepts of "unequal entitlements to resource shares" and "socialization for inequality" contradict idealized notions of harmony.[8]

But myths about golden ages are easy to construct, especially during times of rapid social change, socioeconomic difficulty, or political crisis. At times like this, the family question and its correlate, the woman question, come to the fore. These questions are tackled and answered quite differently by different social groups and political forces. For example, many conservatives feel that a major source of family dissolution is female employment. In the former Soviet Union during perestroika, social problems were blamed on the "overemployment" of women and their "forced detachment" from the family under communism. The solution, according to this view, is to reduce female labor-force attachment and increase women's family attachment. In Eastern Europe, too, a romanticization of the family, of domesticity, and of the private sphere, combined with an emphasis on women's maternal roles, has followed the end of communist rule. Somewhat inconsistently, many writings and speeches regard the family as having been the site of resistance to the monolithic state *and* as having been destroyed by the communist policy of imposing public activity on women and substituting institutionalized child care for mother's care. Barbara Einhorn explains that postcommunist ideology includes the frequently voiced opinion that politics is men's prerogative in a return to a "natural order" in which women have privacy in the home and men in the public sphere.[9] There are parallels with the ideology of the new conservative movement in America, as described by Rebecca Klatch:

> The ideal society, then, is one in which individuals are integrated into a moral community, bound together by faith, by common moral values, and by obeying the dictates of the family and religion. . . .
> While male and female roles are each respected and essential and complementary components of God's plan, men are the spiritual leaders and decision-makers in the family. It is women's role to support men in their position of higher authority through altruism and self-sacrifice.[10]

The parallels with modern Middle Eastern ideals of the role of women and the family are quite interesting. According to the late Murteza Mutahhari, one of the major Iranian Islamist thinkers, "For Muslims, the institution of marriage based on mutuality of natural interest and cordiality between spouses represents a sublime manifestation of the Divine Will and Purpose." He continues:

> Marriage and family living are very significant aspects of a society. They are responsible institutional aspects for the benefit of posterity. Family upbringing of children determines the quality of successive generations. . . .
>
> A wife's entitlement to alimony and to practically sharing her husband's wealth represent the most significant economic and financial provisions instituted for marriage and family living. These are in consideration of the exclusiveness of the spouses' conjugal relationship. The genuine interaction between a couple, which is anticipated in marriage and family living, is envisaged in terms of their individual and collective endeavours, as well as in the broader context of appropriately maintaining their social environment.
>
> Mutual affection and sincerity, as well as humane compassion and tenderness, are highly desirable attributes in married couples, in the context of their mutual and social interactions. These are often in evidence in societies governed by Islamic moral and legal checks and balances. In the others, such as those in the West, these qualities are seldom noticeable.[11]

In similar fashion, the late Egyptian Islamist Seyid Qutb placed far more significance on the role of marriage and the family than did historical Islam, which considered both as down-to-earth civil contracts, according to one account of Qutb's work. In accordance with conservative theories of motherhood and education, Qutb spoke in glowing terms of the family as "the nursery of the future," breeding "precious human products" under the guardianship of women. Qutb further celebrated the holy bond of pure love between a man and a woman, who both voluntarily enter into a relationship of marriage as two equal partners, each discharging functions assigned by nature and biology. A woman fulfills her functions by being a wife and mother, while a man is to be the undisputed authority, the breadwinner, and the active member in public life.[12]

To the Islamist intellectual, the Muslim family is by no means the site of oppression or subjugation. Consider the views of the Iranian woman writer Fereshteh Hashemi, who in 1981 wrote that in the context of marriage and the family,

> women have the heavy responsibility of procreation and rearing a generation: this is a divine art, because it creates, it gives birth; and it is a prophetic art, because it guides, it educates. God, therefore, absolves the woman from all economic responsibilities so that she can engage herself in this prophetic and divine act with peace in mind. Therefore, He makes it the duty of the man to provide all economic means for this woman, so as there shall not be an economic vacuum in her life. . . .
>
> And in the exchange for this heavy responsibility, that is, the financial burden of the woman and the family, what is he entitled to expect of the woman? Except for expecting her companionship and courtship, he

cannot demand anything else from the woman. According to theological sources, he cannot even demand that she bring him a glass of water, much less expect her to clean and cook.[13]

In the Islamic Republic of Iran, a study by the Research Group for Muslim Women's Studies explains low female employment by suggesting that Iranian women are by choice more attached to maternal and family roles:

> After the victory of the Islamic Revolution, in order to guarantee the implementation of the legal right of *nafaghe* (a continual allowance being paid by husband to his wife and children), many women who are not specialized in a particular field have chosen to limit their activities to their homes by taking care of their families. They have also realized that the real place for them is their homes, where they are able to raise and train Muslim children and disseminate revolutionary culture, a woman's effective role in the success of Islamic Revolution.[14]

The notion of the family as a woman-tended haven against a heartless world seems to be universal—or at least universal among middle classes in modern industrial societies—rather than specific to any culture or religion. Some have argued that in the West, this concept of the family emerged in the course of real struggles against the market and the state.[15] But the haven ideology is deficient on a number of counts. It obfuscates the extent to which this ideal is socially limited; for example, it most obviously is not experienced in households maintained by women alone, a phenomenon that is becoming statistically significant throughout the world, especially in regions with considerable male out-migration. In the United States nearly 25 percent of children are being raised in female-headed households, and three-fifths of all chronically poor households with children are supported by single women. In Iran tens of thousands of women became widows during the Iran-Iraq war. Of what use to them is the ideology that their "real place" is at home rearing children while their husbands are earning the family's daily bread? Moreover, one wonders whether the millions of Iranian women who were not counted in the labor force really *chose* to limit their activities to the domestic sphere. One may conjecture that, in fact, millions of Iranian women are engaged in a myriad of informal sector activities and other survival strategies, although such activities escape the attention of enumerators and ideologues alike. The haven ideology obscures the very different opportunity structures available to men and women in the society and the economy; it occludes power differentials and inequality within the family; and it suggests a public/private dichotomy and separation of family and state that do not exist.

The relationship between the family and the state illustrates the fine line between the public and private spheres. Nowhere is the family free of state regulation. This intervention takes various forms: Apart from marriage registration (and defining what is acceptable and unacceptable), there is family law, the content of which differs across societies. There are also laws pertaining to reproductive rights, contraception, and abortion. There may or may not be legal codes regarding the provision of care within families and the responsibilities of family members to each other. In many cases female family members are understood, if not legally required, to be care providers (to children, to in-laws, and to parents). In other cases, a father is legally required to provide for his family. In yet other cases there are social policies creating extra-family supports: day care, homes for the aged or infirm, nursing help, and so on. There may or may not be legal codes pertaining to domestic violence, child abuse, wife battering, or spousal rape. There are invariably laws pertaining to family disintegration (which may come about through divorce, death, abandonment, or migration). Far from being an enclave, the family is vulnerable to the state, and the laws and social policies that impinge upon it undermine the notion of separate spheres. Yet the haven ideology persists and is often strategically deployed by state authorities and dissidents alike.

There are some similarities and some differences between the trajectory of the Arab-Islamic family and that of the family in Western countries. They share a patriarchal structure that undergoes change as a result of economic and political developments. The timing, pace, and extent of the changes differ. In the contemporary Middle East, the family is a powerful signifier, and there is a strong conservative trend to strengthen it and reinforce women's family and maternal roles. This trend seems to have arisen in the context of two parallel developments: (1) the erosion of classic patriarchy and the extended household unit, and (2) the rise of middle-class movements, Islamist and non-Islamist alike, that evince values and attitudes reminiscent of the moral discourse of the European bourgeoisie. Let us examine patriarchal social structures in order to place in proper context changes in the family, fertility, and the status of women in Middle Eastern countries.

▲ The Patriarchal Society and the Extended Household

Patriarchal society is a precapitalist social formation that has historically existed in varying forms in Europe and Asia in which property, residence, and descent proceed through the male line. In classic patriarchy, the senior man has authority over everyone else in the family, including younger men, and women are subject to distinct forms of control and subordination. As noted by Kandiyoti, the key to the reproduction of classic patriarchy lies in the operations of the patrilocally extended household, which is also commonly associated with the reproduction of the peasantry in agrarian societies. The subordination of women in kinship-ordered or agrarian societies is linked to the reproduction of the kin group or the peasantry, as well as to the sexual division of labor. Childbearing is the central female labor activity. But just as in capitalism what a worker produces is not considered the property of the worker, so in a patriarchal context a woman's products—be they children or rugs—are not considered her property but those of the patriarchal family. There is a predisposition to male dominance inherent in the relation between the precapitalist peasant household and the world of landlords and the state and in the reproduction of kinship-ordered groups, wherein women are exchanged and men are the transactors in what Gayle Rubin has called "the traffic in women." In a patriarchal context, women are considered a form of property. Their honor—and, by extension, the honor of their family—depends in great measure on their virginity and good conduct.[16]

Michael Mann's elaboration of the trajectory of patriarchy historically and cross-culturally provides a useful perspective and framework.[17] Mann has identified and traced the interrelations of five principal stratification nuclei—five collective actors that have affected gender-stratification relations over recent history. They are: the atomized person (more pertinent to liberal, bourgeois society); the networks of household/family/lineage; genders; social classes; and nations and nation-states. According to Mann, the patriarchal society is one in which power is held by male heads of households. There is also clear separation between the public and private spheres of life. In the private sphere of the household, the patriarch enjoys arbitrary power over all junior males, all females, and all children. In the public sphere, power is shared between male patriarchs according to whatever other principles of stratification operate. Whereas many, perhaps most, men expect to be patriarchs at some point in their life cycle, no female holds any formal public position of economic, ideological, military, or political power. Indeed, females are not allowed into this public realm of power. (It goes without saying that men have the monopoly on the means of violence.) Within the household they may influence their male patriarch informally, but this is their only access to power. Contained within patriarchy are two fundamental nuclei of stratification: the household/family/lineage nexus and the dominance of the male gender.

Although Mann regards this framework as an ideal-type, his narrative is remarkably consistent with Gerda Lerner's theory of the creation of patriarchy.[18] It also accords well with what we know about the legacy of *patria potestas,* the Roman paternal authority. In his study of abandonment of children in Western Europe, Boswell explains that the paterfamilias—the family patriarch—had total authority over all members of his household and could sell his children into slavery or prostitution. Roman law and custom also allowed parents to kill deformed children.[19] The Christians of the first five centuries were not unaffected by these aspects of Roman culture.

In addition, according to Boswell, abandonment of children was spurred by the Christian injunction against nonprocreative forms of sexuality. Sheer increase in the size of families may have led fathers to "offer" one or two of their children to the Church. Prostitution also produced unwanted and abandoned children. Apparently, abandonment was so widespread that it necessitated a Church decree warning men that in having sex with a prostitute they may be committing incest![20]

Patriarchal societies distinguished the public arena from the private. In the public sphere, power relations overwhelmingly involved male household-heads (patriarchs), and the private sphere was usually ruled formally by a patriarch. This arrangement left no basis for collective action by women. If women sought public influence, they had to go through patriarchs. Social stratification was thus two-dimensional. One dimension comprised the two nuclei of household/family/lineage and male dominance. The second dimension comprised whatever combination of public stratification nuclei (classes, military elites, etc.) existed in a particular society. The latter dimension was connected to the former in that public power-groupings were predominantly aggregates of household/family/lineage heads. But apart from this connection, the two dimensions were segregated from each other.

As the particularism of agrarian societies gave way before the stratification of modern society, stratification became gendered internally with the entry of women into the public sphere. Mann notes that in Western Europe, from about the sixteenth to the eighteenth centuries, the stratification system changed under the pressure of emerging capitalism, first in agriculture and then in industry, as more of economic life became part of the public realm. Louise Tilly and Joan Scott have explored the effects of this change on women in terms of work and family relations.[21] Mann goes on to note that the particularist distinction between the public and the private was eroded first by employment trends and the emergence of more universal classes, second by universal citizenship, and third by the nation-state's welfare interventions in the private household/family. Thus Mann presents a model of the trajectory from patriarchy to neopatriarchy to a stratification system based on gendered classes, personhood, and the nation. Women's rights movements have emerged in the course of this trajectory and have contributed to the elimination of some of the more egregious aspects of the patriarchal legacy.[22]

As Judith Stacey found for contemporary China, patriarchy is fostered in a social system in which male power over women and children derives from the role of fatherhood, and is supported by a political economy in which the family unit retains a significant productive role.[23] Young brides marry into large families, gain respect mainly via their sons, and late in life acquire power as mothers-in-law. Over their life-cycle, their dependence shifts from father to husband and finally to son.

Like Judaism and Christianity before it, Islam came into being in a patriarchal society. Indeed, Tillion argues that the origin of women's oppression in Muslim societies has nothing to do with Islam but can be traced to ancient times and the beginnings of patrilineal society, itself the product of the agricultural revolution. It was endogamy, the practice of marrying within the lineage, that set the shape for the oppression of women in patrilineal society, long before the rise of Islam. Endogamy kept property (land and animals) within the lineage and protected the economic and political interests of the men. Quranic reforms provided women with certain legal rights absent in Judaism and Christianity and also corrected many injustices in pre-Islamic Arabian society. For example, Islam entitled women to the right to contract their marriage, receive dower, retain control of wealth, and receive maintenance and shares in inheritance. At the same time, family laws were formulated to meet a woman's needs in a society where her largely domestic, childbearing roles rendered her sheltered and dependent upon her father, her husband, and her close male relations.[24] A woman's right to inherit property was often circumvented by more powerful male relatives, including her brothers, uncles, or husband's agnates. In the Shari'a, the custody of children is first accorded to mothers, but ultimately the children of Muslim marriage are taken into the formal custody of the father's patrilineal kin group, generally at the age of seven for boys and nine for girls, or puberty for the boy and the time of marriage for the girl, depending upon interpretation.[25] As Alya Baffoun has noted, although men and women are in theory equal before religious law, "an imbalance is introduced through sexual and economic inequality—polygamy, unequal inheritance rights and male monopoly of the production of commodities."[26] Islamic law gives male members of the kin group extensive control over key decisions affecting women's lives, as Mounira Charrad states. Islamic law, especially in its Maleki version (which has historically predominated in North Africa), "encourages kin control of marriage ties and thus facilitates both marriages within the lineage and collectively useful outside alliances." Charrad continues, "By favoring males and kin on the male side, inheritance laws solidify ties within the extended patrilineal kin group. The message of the Maleki family law is that the conjugal unit may be short-lived, whereas the ties with the male kin may be enduring. Maleki law defines the kin group rather than the nuclear family as the significant locus of solidarity. It facilitates—and reflects—the maintenance of tribal communities."[27]

The "belt of classic patriarchy" includes North Africa, the Muslim Middle East (including Turkey and Iran), and South and East Asia (Pakistan, Afghanistan, northern India, and rural China). In the contemporary world, the tribal structure is the pristine type of patriarchal organization and can still be found in the Arab world and in Afghanistan. The social organization of the tribe (*qabila*) or the communal group (*qawm*, especially in Afghanistan) is based on blood ties and is patriarchal in the classic sense.

Tribal identity, such as that of the Arab Bedouin or the Iranian Qashqa'i, is generally based on notions of common patrilineal descent. Quite unlike the "primitive" groups studied by Lévi-Strauss, which were exogamous, the Arab-Islamic tribes are endogamous and favor cousin marriage, as noted also by Goody. Tillion, Keddie, and Baffoun have pointed out that endogamy increases the tendency to maintain property within families through the control of women in tightly interrelated lineages. Keddie writes that nomadic tribal groups "have special reasons to want to control women and to favor cousin marriage." Pastoral nomadic tribes, the most common type in the Middle East, trade animal products for agricultural and urban ones. Tribal cohesion is necessary to their economy, which requires frequent group decisions about migration. Groups closely tied by kin are desirable because they make decisions amicably. The practical benefits of close kinship, Keddie argues, are surely one reason cousin marriage has long been preferred among Middle Eastern people: It encourages family integration and cooperation. Keddie feels that continuing "controls on women are connected to the pervasiveness of tribal structures in the Middle East," or what Tillion calls "the republic of cousins," and notes that "even though most nomadic women are not veiled and secluded, they are controlled."[28] Patriarchy is thus strongest in rural areas, within peasant as well as tribal communities.

The patriarchal belt is characterized by extremely restrictive codes of behavior for women, rigid gender segregation, and a powerful ideology linking family honor to female virtue, as Kabeer notes. "Men are entrusted with safeguarding family honor through their control over female members; they are backed by complex social arrangements that ensure the protection—and dependence—of women." In contemporary Muslim patriarchal societies, such control over women is considered necessary in part because women are regarded as the potential source of *fitna*—that is, moral or social disorder. Men traditionally have the unilateral right of divorce and the authority to decide whether their wives work outside the home or travel. A family's honor and reputation rest most heavily on the conduct of women. The Shari'a itself does not enjoin women to veil, but certain *hadith,* or sayings of the prophet, do. Sex-segregation, also legitimated on the basis of *hadith,* is part of the Islamic gender system. In South Asian Muslim societies in particular, *purdah* (literally "curtain," also meaning covering, seclusion, and segregation) remains common and is also strongly linked to men's honor. As Mandelbaum put it, "Honor is the key good for these men, and their honor is balanced on the heads of the women."[29] Women's life-options are severely circumscribed in the patriarchal belt. One typically finds an adverse sex ratio, low female literacy and educational attainment, high fertility rates, high maternal mortality rates, and low female labor force participation in the formal sector. Some analysts, noting these demographic facts, have characterized societies such as those in Afghanistan,

Pakistan, Bangladesh, and northern India as "a culture against women," in which women are socialized to sacrifice their health, survival chances, and life options.[30]

Patriarchy, therefore, should not be conflated with Islam but rather should be understood in social-structural and developmental terms. The emergence of a modern middle class tied to the capitalist economy or the state bureaucracy would seem to represent a weakening of the patriarchal order. Certainly, patriarchal structures are stronger in rural areas, and many Middle Eastern countries—among them Jordan, Libya, Morocco, Saudi Arabia, Sudan, Yemen, and Afghanistan—are predominantly rural. In many of these countries, precapitalist forms of social organization, including various forms of nomadic groups, may be found. Turkey provides an apposite example of the split between a highly patriarchal countryside and an urban context where gender and family relations are more egalitarian.[31]

Patriarchy can be intensified as a result of political and economic changes. An example is provided by the experience of the Palestinians. Zionism left them landless and proletarianized, disrupting the traditional structure of the extended peasant family. Endogamous marriage was gradually replaced with exogamous marriage. But the proletarianization of Palestinian men, which was very unstable and insecure, was not accompanied by a similar process for women. As a result, family size did not decrease, fertility rates did not decline, and women's status did not improve. According to Nahla Abdo-Zubi, "The family in this period was transformed from a productive and reproductive unit—producing agricultural goods as well as a new generation of workers—into an almost exclusively reproductive unit. Whereas production took place outside the family, and was done by males, reproduction became centered in the family, as the women's main task."[32] In this modern context, a new form of the patriarchal family was strengthened.

State policy, including the legal system, exerts a further influence on the persistence, modernization, or weakening of patriarchy and, by extension, women and the family. Let us examine the contribution of Middle Eastern states to the position of women, gender relations, and the fate of the patriarchal family.

▲ The Neopatriarchal State and Personal Status Laws

The centrality of the family in Islam is reflected in Muslim family law, which is derived from the Shari'a and from pre-Islamic customary practice in Arabia. In the tenth century the elaboration of Islamic law was considered complete, and for the next nine centuries family law remained intact and unchanging. Islam privileges patrilineal bonds and enjoins men to take responsibility for the support of their wives and children. In the Arab-

Islamic family, the wife's main obligations are to maintain a home, care for her children, and obey her husband. He is entitled to exercise his marital authority by restraining his wife's movements and preventing her from showing herself in public. This restriction of the wife mirrors the prevailing medieval social customs of veiling and seclusion of women, practices intended to protect their honor.[33]

Toward the end of the nineteenth century, Muslim family law became subject to challenges from reformers and modernizers who sought changes in rules governing marriage, divorce, polygamy, child custody, and inheritance in order to improve women's position. The first reform movement took place in Egypt in the early twentieth century; reforms were also made in the Nasser period. The Ataturk reforms of the 1920s were the most comprehensive; these were followed by the Bourguiba reforms in Tunisia in the 1950s, which abolished polygamy and unilateral male divorce, and reforms in Syria and Iraq. In Iran, the Pahlavi state instituted the Family Protection Act in 1967, meant to offer women more rights in family matters and to raise the legal age of marriage. Other reforms to bolster women's position in the family were undertaken in the People's Democratic Republic of Yemen in the late 1960s and early 1970s. In all Muslim countries, family law is derived from Shari'a, though in varying degrees. Jamal Nasir reports that in general the legal age of marriage for girls is fifteen, but in some countries it is higher: In Syria and Tunisia a girl must be seventeen and in Iraq eighteen, although parents may petition the court for permission to marry their fifteen-year-old daughter. An innovation in the Syrian, Jordanian, and Moroccan laws regulates the age gap between the two spouses-to-be. According to Nasir: "Under the Syrian law if they are disproportionate in age, and no good is seen to be forthcoming, the judge may withhold permission for them to marry. The Jordanian law is more categorical and precise, ruling that no marriage contract shall be solemnized for a woman under 18 years of age if the husband-to-be is over 20 years older than her, unless the judge makes sure of her consent and free choice, and that the marriage is in her interests."[34] Change in family law is a significant index of social change in the Middle East, a barometer of the internal debate within Islam, and an illustration of the capacity for Islamic reform. It is also highly indicative of the role of the state and of state legal policy in matters of gender and the family.

During the twentieth century the Arab-Islamic family and its concomitants—rigid sex roles, women's legal status as minors, the prerogatives of fathers and husbands, high fertility—have been challenged by socioeconomic developments (industrialization, the expansion of the urban labor market, and education) and political action (state legal reform and popular social movements). Today the application of Muslim family law varies throughout the Middle East, depending principally on the type of political regime and the strength of modern social classes. In some cases, state legal policies have worked to undermine the patriarchal Arab-Islamic family; in other cases, policies foster and perpetuate family structure and the authority of male members in a more modernized form of patriarchy, or what Sharabi calls neopatriarchy. Thus, two parallel, apparently contradictory developments may be discerned: (1) the expansion of industrialization, urbanization, proletarianization, and state-sponsored education, which undermine patriarchal family authority; and (2) the retention of Muslim family law, which legitimates the prerogatives of male family members over female family members. Polemics surrounding women and the family are responses to the contradictions of social change and emerge in the context of patriarchal societies undergoing modernization and demographic transition.

Outside of the household, the source of patriarchal control is political-juridical: the state and legislation. The nature of the political system, objectives of state managers, and orientation of ruling elites constitute crucial factors in the equation that determines the legal status and social positions of women. As Charrad argues, legislation is a key element in the strategies available to the state in its efforts to produce social changes or to maintain the status quo. Through the law, and especially through family law, the state can maintain existing gender arrangements; it can alter social policies and laws in the direction of greater restrictions on women; or it can introduce new legislation to foster more equality within the family and raise women's social and economic status. "Family law regulates marriage, divorce, individual rights and responsibilities, and the transmission of property through inheritance; it is thus a prime example of state policy affecting women."[35]

According to Charrad, variations in the balance of power between the national state and local communities in Tunisia, Morocco, and Algeria during accession to independence account for the significant differences in family legislation. "The Moroccan personal status code essentially reiterates Islamic family law in a more concise and codified manner. Consent to marriage is expressed not by the bride but by her father or male guardian. The bride need not be present at the marriage ceremony for the marriage to be valid." Polygamy remains legal, and the husband has the prerogative in divorce. In contrast, "the Tunisian code gives greater rights to women and decreases the legal control of male kin over them. With respect to the kinship structure, the code weakens the extended patrilineal kin group while strengthening the conjugal unit." The Tunisian code establishes minimum ages for marriage at twenty for men and seventeen for women (unlike Morocco's eighteen and fifteen, respectively) and stipulates that the bride must attend her own marriage ceremony and express her consent to marriage. Unilateral repudiation was abolished in 1956, allowing spouses equal rights to file for divorce. Polygamy was outlawed, and women now receive larger shares in inheritance.[36]

Charrad continues: "Algeria's attitude toward family law and personal status oscillated for over twenty years. Legislation consisted of a perplexing mismatch of Maleki law and secular codes." In July 1984 the government adopted a conservative family code that strengthened the legal prerogatives of husbands, retained unequal inheritance between women and men, legalized polygamy, and reconfirmed the principle of matrimonial guardianship. An innovation is that if the father dies, the mother (and not agnatic kin) now automatically becomes the child's guardian.[37] Algeria's post-Boumedienne turn toward conservatism in family law was met with fierce opposition by women who quickly organized themselves into feminist and democratic groupings. But this resistance has not stemmed the tide toward neopatriarchy.[38]

Neopatriarchal state is useful as an umbrella term for the various types of political regime in the Middle East. Whether the regimes be monarchies or republics, radical or conservative, socialist or populist, they share the essential features of neopatriarchy. Hisham Sharabi applies the term even more broadly to describe discourses, relations, and institutions in the Arab world. For Sharabi, the concept refers equally to macrostructures (society, the state, the economy) and microstructures (the family or the individual). Neopatriarchy is the product of the encounter between modernity and tradition in the context of dependent capitalism; it is modernized patriarchy. Whatever the outward (modern) forms of the contemporary neopatriarchal family, society, or state, their internal structures remain rooted in the patriarchal values and social relations of kinship, clan, and religious and ethnic groups. A central feature of this system is the dominance of the father within the household and at the level of the state. Thus, for Sharabi, "the most advanced and functional aspect of the neopatriarchal state . . . is its internal security apparatus, the *mukhabarat*. . . . In social practice ordinary citizens not only are arbitrarily deprived of some of their basic rights but are the virtual prisoners of the state, the objects of its capricious and ever-present violence. . . . It is in many ways no more than a modernized version of the traditional patriarchal sultanate."[39]

Neopatriarchal state practices build upon and reinforce particular normative views of women and the family, often but not exclusively through the law. States that legitimize their own power on patriarchal structures such as the extended family foster its perpetuation through legislation that subordinates women to the control of men. Examples are laws about women's dress and behavior passed in the 1980s by the Islamist state in Iran and the sexual conduct laws of the Zia ul-Haq regime in Pakistan. Muslim family laws that render women legal minors and dependents of men reflect and perpetuate a modernized form of patriarchy.

Constructions of gender and discourses about women are sometimes a convenient weapon between contending political groups. Political elites or neopatriarchal states may raise the woman question to divert attention from economic problems or political corruption. As Susan Marshall has put it: "The elite defense of the family, religion, and culture, demonstrated by the reactivation of patriarchal traditions, may serve as evidence of unswerving national loyalty."[40]

Another reason states may find it useful to foster patriarchal structures is that the extended family performs vital welfare functions. The joint household system and intergenerational wealth flows that are characteristics of patriarchal structures provide welfare and security for individuals. This, of course, is incumbent upon an adequate supply of household members, especially sons. The material consequences of reproductive failure is disastrous, as Mead Cain observes for Bangladesh.[41] It is especially dire for women, who attain status and old-age security through their sons. In all cases, the persistence of patriarchy relieves the state of the responsibility to provide welfare to citizens.[42]

Some of the stronger critics of Muslim family law complain that there is heavy resistance in the Arab world to changing anything having to do with the family.[43] Yet some states have challenged local and communal patriarchal interests, with important consequences for family legislation and more general policies affecting women. Modernizing, developmentalist elites—particularly but not exclusively those with a socialist orientation—have tended to see the emancipation of women as part of their program for change. These states would be more inclined to curb the power of traditional and rural elites, which would entail an attack on forms of patriarchal control over women and young men, as in Soviet Central Asia.[44] As discussed in Chapter 3, states in the patriarchal belt that have undertaken such actions are Turkey under Kemal Ataturk, the People's Democratic Republic of Yemen in the late 1960s and the 1970s, and the Democratic Republic of Afghanistan (DRA) in the late 1970s and early 1980s. In Iraq the Ba'th Party had an interest both in recruiting women into the labor force in the context of a continuing labor shortage and in wresting women's allegiance away from kin, family, or ethnic group and shifting it to the party-state. Women were recruited into state-controlled agencies and put through public education, vocational training, and political indoctrination. The 1978 personal status law, although limited in its objectives, aimed at reducing the control of extended families over women.[45]

Nevertheless, the patriarchal family and patriarchal ideology persist in these countries and throughout the Middle East. As a British jurisprudence expert once noted, the law is always out of step with society; there is always a gap between the legal rules and the existing social reality. Caldwell, too, taking a cue from Marx, has noted that culture, or the superstructure, lags behind changes in the economic structure.[46] An equally important reason for the persistence of patriarchy is that most neopatriarchal states in the Middle East have an instrumentalist approach toward women, gender, and the family: Policies and laws that strengthen the position of the state itself are the ones that will be enacted.

▲ The Middle Eastern Muslim Family

The families of the Middle East have been described as extended, patrilineal, patrilocal, patriarchal, endogamous, and occasionally polygynous, a description that, with the exception of endogamy, fits well enough from Morocco to Bangladesh and even, until recently, across China.[47] In Islam plural marriages are allowed but are rare.[48] The concept of sanctity and privacy of family life in the Middle East remains more developed than in the West. The honor of the family is more closely bound to the good sexual conduct of its female members. In the past, such conduct was guaranteed via segregation of women in the "forbidden" sectors of the house—the *hareem,* or harem. Today, the confinement of women is more a result of their closer association with the domestic chores and living arrangements of the household. Outside the home, this is managed by segregating men and women in workplaces and in educational institutions. Although the preferred marriage among Arabs and Muslims of the Near East has been cousin marriage, particularly between children of two brothers (parallel patrilateral cousins), it is of course not the exclusive form of marriage. Among Arabs and Iranians, ties to the natal family are hardly ever broken, even in out-marrying situations, and so the daughter has recourse to her own family in the event of repudiation, widowhood, or domestic problems. There is some evidence that the situation in South Asia, prerevolutionary China, and rural Turkey is different: A girl's ties to her natal family tend to be weakened after marriage, making her more vulnerable before her husband's agnates. One reason for these differences may be the different kinds of "bridewealth," or "endowments of the bride."[49] Although dower amounts have come to vary greatly by class, they represent a major potential source of financial security for the woman and an important disincentive to divorce.

Among Arabs and Muslims there are different, and direct and indirect forms of bridewealth: (1) endowing of the bride by her father (*jahaz*) or her in-laws (*mahr*); (2) in Iran and Afghanistan, indirect dower consisting partly of the *shirbaha* (literally, milk price), which is cash provided by the groom and given to the bride's father to buy a *jahaz,* to which he is expected to add at least the equivalent cash amount; and (3) direct *mahr,* which may be immediate or deferred but is intended as a sort of social insurance and financial protection for the wife in the event of repudiation or widowhood.[50] Again, these marriage transactions are elaborated by class. A woman from a wealthy family may control relatively large amounts of wealth, which enhances her standing within her new family.

Some scholars argue that in a rural setting, the payment of brideprice to a woman's kinsmen symbolizes men's control over a woman and over the transfer of her productive and reproductive capacities to her husband's kin group. But marriage does not necessarily terminate a woman's ties with her relatives. In fact, these ties are maintained throughout her life, and she may utilize the support of her kin in production and to bring pressure against her husband and his family. The support of kinsmen, however, is subject to variation. A woman may count on the aid of her brother. But a woman may also be beaten by her brother or father and sent back to her husband's household when she turns to kinsmen of limited resources with complaints of illness or maltreatment. In fact, the woman's own relatives may condone the husband's action and blame his fury on her bad attitude or her "long tongue."[51]

The early years of marriage in patriarchal settings are usually stressful for young brides. They are subjected to orders from older sisters-in-law and are clearly subservient to the authority of their husband's mother. In this extended family setting, the products of new brides' domestic and agricultural labor, like those of other members of the household, are under the control of the senior male and senior female (mother- and father-in-law in extended family households, older brother and wife in fraternal joint family households). Senior males and females are the center of authority. Soheir Morsy notes that quarrels between women in domestic groups reflect the conflicts and tensions between the men upon whom they are dependent.[52]

The pattern of cousin marriage is one strategy for keeping property within the lineage; it also seems to mitigate the view of women as property, argues Goody, rejecting the Lévi-Straussian view of women as pawns who embody transaction and exchange. But the exchange of women does seem to take place and has been discussed with respect to Afghanistan. There brideprice is more customary, especially in out-marrying situations. As Tapper explains, mobility and migration patterns revolve around brideprice. Men from one region will travel to another to find inexpensive wives, while fathers will travel elsewhere in search of a higher price for their daughters. Goody notes that pastoralists (such as the Bedouins) are closer to the exclusively patrilineal and patriarchal model. Nasir explains that "in rural and bedouin areas," girls are married at ages below the required minimum age and frequently at thirteen.[53]

Whereas the patrilineal extended household is characteristic of rural areas in many Middle Eastern countries, it is less typical in cities, especially in large metropolitan areas. There, neolocal residence is assumed upon marriage, and the nuclear family form prevails. Some of the most extensive studies on changes in household or family types and the impact of economic changes on women's status have been undertaken in Turkey. In the 1970s Kandiyoti delineated six socioeconomic categories of women: nomadic, traditional rural, changing rural, small town, newly urbanized squatter (*gecekondu*), and urban, middle-class professionals and housewives. Family form and household composition varied across these groups, as did the gender division of labor. An interesting discovery was that although patriarchal attitudes and practices remained strongest in the countryside, the patrilocal extended household was being undermined by market incorporation, migration, and poverty. The wealthier landed households were in a better position to sustain extended families. As Kandiyoti put it, "The role of the father as the sole holder of economic resources has been clearly undermined for the poorer strata: the displaced sharecropper turned wage-worker, or the marginal smallholder who is increasingly dependent on wage income, are hardly in a position to command the labor of their married children beyond any obligations arising from their contribution to the cost of their weddings."[54] In general, postmarital residence is linked to class, mode of production, resources, and bridewealth.[55]

Whereas most of Asia has experienced considerable fertility decline in recent decades—a function of increased female education and employment—a handful of countries stand out for their lack of significant fertility change. According to the World Fertility Survey (WFS), conducted in forty-one countries between 1977 and 1982, high fertility persists in the Middle East and sub-Saharan Africa compared to other regions, as well as in South Asia, where the crude fertility rate is six children per woman in Bangladesh, Nepal, and Pakistan. Among Middle Eastern countries fertility rates have generally declined since the 1950s and 1960s, although not in Yemen. And in Iran, fertility increased between the 1976 census and the 1986 census due mainly to the pronatalism of the Islamic government in the early 1980s.[56]

▲ The Demographic Transition and the Family

The demographic transition is a process as far-reaching and important for the history and structure of populations as is industrialization. It involves a change from the high mortality and high fertility characteristic of preindustrial societies to patterns of low mortality and low fertility. The demographer John Caldwell argues that in Western Europe the economic and demographic transitions co-evolved: The transition from the traditional peasant (family-based) economy to the capitalist economy entailed changes in decisions about and need for reproduction. Large families became less rational as the cost of each additional child increased. But the process of change took place in two steps. First, mortality declined while fertility remained high or even increased, thus accelerating population growth. Harris explains that in the transition from peasant to commodity production, the stage of proto-industrialization entailed whole families working as a labor collective. Wages were so low that an adult male could not support himself, let alone a wife and family. As a result, the number of children increased. Levine cites Michel Foucault to explain why: "The accumulation of men and the accumulation of capital . . . cannot be separated."[57] Then, as mortality continued to drop and as child and then infant mortality fell sharply, fertility began to decline as well, slowing rates of population growth.

In England and France, the rate of population growth increased by 1780, then slowed down after 1820 for France and 1879 for England.[58] Although lower fertility came about in Western societies in the course of industrialization and urbanization, another important source of instability in the family-based system of production and reproduction, according to Caldwell, was "the egalitarian strain in the modern European ideology, powerfully augmented by the spread of education."[59] The following trends, therefore, were significant in lowering the rates of fertility further: the enforcement of universal, compulsory education; an intensification of the movement for women's suffrage and more equal rights for women; and an increase in the availability of the wares of the consumption society and their advertisement.[60] These trends are consistent with Mann's trajectory of patriarchy to neopatriarchy to gendered societies.

Marriage patterns changed, too, in the course of the demographic transition in Western Europe. The age at which couples married fell (from twenty-six to under twenty-four for women in France) and the number of people who married increased. Marriage and employment became compatible, and proletarian women continued to work after marriage. During the nineteenth century people still delayed marriage in both rural and urban areas in England and France, and fertility was higher in urban industrial than in rural areas. In the twentieth century, birthrates continued their downward trend because of the practice of birth control, though there were periodic increases.[61] Tilly and Scott stress that mortality, marriage, and fertility patterns differed by class and region.

Carla Makhlouf Obermeyer points to the "diversity of demographic transitions, both historical and contemporary," and adds that although correlation analyses between demographic and socioeconomic indicators show a moderate negative correlation between GNP, urbanization, and primary school enrollment on the one hand and infant mortality on the other, she finds a limited relationship between socioeconomic development and total fertility rates.[62] However, in Chapter 2 I argued that women's employment patterns may be understood and explained in terms of the political economy of the region and development strategies of specific countries. Let us explore this connection further with respect to fertility rates.

In the Middle East, as in other developing regions in the twentieth century, the demographic transition is occurring more rapidly than it occurred in Europe. The result has been accelerated population growth. Nevertheless, contemporary Middle Eastern countries are in significantly different stages along the continuum of transition and development, as noted by Basheer Nijim.[63] Table 4.1 illustrates the demographic transition in the Arab world: Iran would be in Stage 3, and Afghanistan in Stage 1 or 2. As can be seen from Allman's table, in 1980 high fertility was found in the oil-rich Gulf states (Saudi Arabia, UAE, Libya) and in countries with substantial poverty (Morocco, Sudan, Yemen). Fertility was declining in Tunisia, Egypt, and Lebanon, three non-oil economies. Within these countries, fertility rates were (and are) variable by region, class, education, and employment.

Table 4.1 The Demographic Transition in the Arab World (after Allman, 1980)

Stage	Mortality	Fertility	Growth Rate	Fertility Differentials[a]	Modern Contraception	Countries in This Stage
1	High	High	Low	None	None	None
2	Declining	High and possibly increasing	High	None or slight	None or little	Saudi Arabia, UAE, Qatar, Oman, Libya, Iraq, Sudan, YAR
3	Declining	High, probably at a maximum	High	Some	Beginning, but generally very little	Morocco, Algeria, Jordan, Bahrain, Kuwait, PDRY, Syria
4	Declining	Declining	Decreasing	Marked	Increasing use	Tunisia, Egypt, Lebanon
5	Low	Low	Low	Slight	Widespread use	None

Source: Basheer Nijim, "Spatial Aspects of Demographic Change in the Arab World," in S. G. Hajjar, ed., *The Middle East: From Transition to Development* (Leiden: E. J. Brill, 1985), p. 37. Reprinted with permission.
Notes: a. "Fertility Differentials" refers to differences within the country, such as between rural and urban areas, among socioeconomic groups, or according to educational status.
UAE: United Arab Emirates
YAR: Yemen Arab Republic (North Yemen)
PDRY: People's Democratic Republic of Yemen (South Yemen)

The view that macrolevel social and economic changes affect members of different classes in different ways seems to be gaining credence and represents a move away from classic demographic transition theory. Comparative studies on the causes of high fertility have tended to concentrate on two variables: the cost of children and the status of women. Lower status means restricted access to education and employment and hence higher fertility. As women from elite families are generally those with the most access to education and employment, fertility is also variable by class. There are exceptions, however; in some countries (for example, Saudi Arabia) elite women will receive private, Western-style education but will not seek employment or will abandon it after marriage. Large families may be found in these cases; however, they may be statistically insignificant. What is more certain is that poor women who are economically dependent and who are not the beneficiaries of a social security system need adult sons in order to survive. Thus, the cost of children and the status of women are themselves shaped by social class; reproductive behavior and fertility patterns, therefore, are class-differentiated. And as reproduction is so closely linked to production, the economic system within which families live and work will also explain and predict fertility patterns.[64] Simply put, there are rational reasons why the fertility behavior and needs of peasants, proletarians, professionals, and the poor differ. It should come as no surprise that salaried middle-class women are probably the ones having the fewest children.

High fertility persists in those areas with the traditional rural extended family: North Africa and Southwest and South Asia.[65] Many of the countries in the patriarchal belt are predominantly rural, with large populations dependent upon agriculture. High fertility is advantageous to the peasant family and its most powerful members; it is also justified on cultural-religious grounds. However, though the familial mode of production is typically found in circumstances of subsistence production, it can adapt for at least a time to urban life and the market economy without fully succumbing to the rules of the market. Poor rural-urban migrants need their children to secure a purchase on town life and enable them to stay. The traditional elite, the merchants, organize their families much as do farmers and feel few, if any, ill effects from high fertility.[66] By contrast, the fully developed labor market mode of production offers no rewards for high fertility.

For these reasons, there is variability within the Middle East and rapid demographic change over the last two decades. As can be seen in Table 4.2, infant mortality and under-five child mortality have declined, in some countries quite dramatically. Life expectancy varies; it is highest in the oil-rich Gulf states and Israel, lowest in Yemen and Afghanistan. But it has definitely increased since 1960. Maternal mortality is highest in Sudan and Afghanistan, both very poor countries. At 280 deaths per 100,000 live births, the maternal mortality rate for the region is lower than the average for developing countries.

The World Fertility Survey found that fertility is highest in the Middle East and sub-Saharan Africa. But it also found that "substantial fertility declines have been observed over recent years in all regions except sub-Saharan Africa."[67] Where fertility rates are still high, there might be a "cultural lag" or a "knowledge lag": People in the midst of a changing mortality matrix have imperfect knowledge of their increasing survival chances. But ongoing high fertility may also be explained by the persistence of the patriarchal household, incomplete proletarianization and industrialization, and pronatalist state policies. The process of proletarianization is not yet complete, as large segments of the urban population are informal workers rather than formal-sector wage workers. When households are engaged in cottage industries, it is rational for them to increase the number of "workers," as was the case in Europe during the protoindustrial stage. For capital, large supplies of cheap labor are functional and profitable. And for many newly independent Third World states, at least until recently, a large population was associated with national strength. This idea was stated quite explicitly by leaders of Algeria, Kenya, India, and China, to name a few. A pronatalist policy was adopted in 1979 by the authorities in the Islamic Republic, which also banned abortion and prohibited the importation of contraceptives. Among the Arab countries, Saudi Arabia explicitly supports population growth.[68] In the wake of the Gulf War in early 1991, it is highly likely that Kuwait, hoping to reduce its long-standing dependence on foreign workers, will adopt an explicit pro–population-growth policy.

Female illiteracy is high in these areas, and female employment in the formal sector of the economy remains low. Overall unemployment is high, and informal-sector economic activities are often small family enterprises not incompatible with high fertility. In many countries, although illiteracy among women has been declining, it remains high, certainly when compared with male illiteracy. These characteristics are illustrated in Table 4.3. The lowest fertility rates are found in Israel, Kuwait, Tunisia, and Turkey, where female literacy, educational attainment levels, and employment shares are relatively high, and where there is access to contraception.

Table 4.4 provides data on the Middle East and North African participants in the World Fertility Survey, measured for nuptiality, fertility, child mortality, breast-feeding, fertility preferences, family planning, and contraceptive use. Note the variations in fertility preferences.

As we have noted earlier, state policy, including population or family-planning policies, affect women's productive and reproductive choices. Nijim explains that the Arab countries exhibit a variety of population policies and concerns. "Population policy" is understood to be an intention to improve the overall well-being of the nation's citizens. Definitions of well-being vary and are certainly debatable, as are prescriptions of how to reach objectives. Those countries that are concerned about the rate of population growth, such as Tunisia and Turkey, face the dual goal of seeking to improve health facilities on the one hand, thus reducing natal and infant mortality, and of seeking to decrease the birthrate. Other countries seek to reduce mortality rates and improve the population's health but do not seek to reduce birthrates. At the level of state policymaking, the approach to population growth ranges from pronatalist to laissez-faire to pro–family planning.

Table 4.2 Trends in Maternal Mortality, Life Expectancy, and Infant Mortality

Country	Maternal Mortality (per 100,000 live births) 1980–1987	Life Expectancy (men and women) 1960	1987	Infant Mortality (under age 1, per 1,000 live births) 1960	1987–1988	Child Mortality (under age 5, per 1,000 live births) 1960	1987–1988
Afghanistan	690	33	42	215	171	380	300
Algeria	130	47	63	168	73	270	107
Bahrain	—	—	—	130	27	208	32
Egypt	320a	46	62	179	83	300	125
Iran	120	50	66	169	61	254	90
Iraq	50	48	65	139	68	222	94
Israel	5	69	76	33	11	40	14
Jordan	—	47	67	135	43	218	57
Kuwait	18	60	73	89	19	128	22
Lebanon	—	—	—	68	39	92	51
Libya	80	47	62	160	80	268	119
Morocco	330	47	62	163	80	265	119
Oman	—	40	57	214	40	378	64
Qatar	—	—	—	145	32	239	43
Saudi Arabia	52	44	64	170	70	292	98
Sudan	660	39	51	—	—	—	—
Syria	280	50	66	135	47	218	64
Tunisia	310	48	66	159	58	255	83
Turkey	210	50	65	190	74	258	93
UAE	—	53	71	145	25	239	32
Yemen (North)	—	37	52	214	115	378	190
Yemen (South	100	37	52	214	118	378	197

Sources: UNICEF, *The State of the World's Children 1989* (New York: Oxford University Press, 1989), Tables 1 and 3; UNDP, *Human Development Report 1990* (New York: Oxford University Press, 1990), Tables, 4, 10, 11; World Bank, *World Development Report 1990* (New York: Oxford University Press, 1990), Table 32; World Bank, *Social Indicators of Development 1988* (Baltimore: Johns Hopkins University Press, 1988).

Notes: The average rate of maternal mortality for industrial countries in 1980–1987 was 24; the average for all developing countries was 290; the maternal mortality rate for the Middle East and North Africa was 280, according to the *Human Development Report 1990* (p. 149). In industrial countries, the average infant mortality rate in 1988 was 15 and the average under-five mortality rate was 18 (*Human Development Report 1990*, Table 10, p. 147).

a. *The State of the World's Children* lists a figure of 80, and the World Bank as high as 500.

Table 4.3 Literacy, Education, Labor Force, and Fertility Rates, 1980s

Country	Male Literacy 1985	Female Literacy 1985	Tertiary Enrollment (females as a % of males) 1987–1988	Female Share of Salaried L.F.	Fertility Rate 1988
Afghanistan	39	8	18	—	6.9
Algeria	63	37	45	8.8	5.4
Bahrain	79	64	142	—	—
Egypt	59	30	52	14.0 (1984)	4.5
Iran	62	39	43	9.4 (1986)	5.6
Iraq	90	87	64	—	6.3
Israel	97	93	94	41.5 (1987)	3.0
Jordan	87	63	—	—	6.4
Kuwait	76	63	171	20.8 (1985)	3.7
Lebanon	86	69	—	—	—
Libya	81	50	—	—	6.8
Morocco	45	22	49	17.6 (1982)	4.7
Oman	47	12 (1982)	71	—	7.1
Qatar	51	51 (1981)	—	9.6 (1986)	—
Saudi Arabia	71	31 (1982)	76	—	7.1
Sudan	33	15	62	—	6.4
Syria	76	43	59	12.4 (1983)	6.7
Tunisia	68	41	64	14.3 (1985)	4.1
Turkey	86	62 (1984)	55	15.3 (1985)	3.7
UAE	58	38 (1975)	—	5.2 (1980)	4.7
Yemen (North)	27	3	—	—	8.0
Yemen (South)	59	25	—	—	6.6

Sources: UNICEF, *The State of the World's Children 1989* (New York: Oxford University Press, 1989), Tables 4, 5; UNESCO, *Statistical Yearbook 1989.* (Paris: UNESCO, 1989), Table 1.3; UNDP, *Human Development Report 1990* (New York: Oxford University Press, 1990), Table 20; UNDP, *Human Development Report 1991,* Tables 10, 31.

Note: — indicates data not available.

▲ Social Change and the Family: The Significance of Education

The persistence or modernization of patriarchy notwithstanding, the processes of urbanization, industrialization, proletarianization, and mass schooling—so important to the demographic transition and the decline of classic patriarchy in the West—are present in the Middle East. There has been a concomitant change in the social structure, with the rise of the urban proletariat and salaried middle class. Developmentalist, welfarist states also have instituted legal reforms to bolster women's position in the family and

Table 4.4 Summary Measures of Demographic Characteristics from WFS Surveys: Middle Eastern and North African Participants, 1978–1982

	Egypt	Morocco	Sudan (North)	Tunisia	Jordan	Syria	Turkey	Yemen A.R.
Nuptiality								
1 Mean age at first marriage	21.3	21.3	21.3	23.9	21.6	22.1	20.4	16.9
2 % ever married ages 15–19	22.5	22.1	21.8	5.2	19.0	22.7	22.4	61.7
3 Time spent in marriage	94.3	92.5	94.3	97.1	97.4	97.7	98.2	93.8
Fertility								
4 Crude birth rate	43	44	39	35	45	45	31	48
5 Total fertility rate	5.3	5.9	6.0	5.9	7.5	7.5	4.5	8.5
6 Children ever born to women 45–49	6.8	7.1	6.2	7.0	8.6	7.7	6.3	7.2
Child mortality								
7 Under age 1	132	91	79	80	66	65	133	162
8 Under age 5	191	142	151	107	80	86	166	237
Breast-feeding								
9 Full breast-feeding (months)	7.4	5.5	5.6	6.2	—	5.5	—	4.5
10 Breast-feeding (months)	17.4	14.5	15.9	14.1	11.1	11.6	14.3	11.0
Fertility preferences								
11 % want no more children	53.7	41.8	16.9	48.9	41.8	36.5	59.3	19.3
12 Mean desired family size	4.1	5.0	6.4	4.2	6.3	6.1	3.0	5.4
13 Wanted total fertility rate	3.1	3.7	4.8	3.6	5.1	5.6	2.4	7.4
Family planning								
14 % aware of any contracept. method	90	84	51	95	97	78	88	25
15 % ever used any method	40	29	12	45	46	33	55	3
Currently using a method								
16 Efficient methods only	23	16	4	25	17	15	13	1
17 Any method	24	19	5	32	25	20	38	1
18 % willing to use contraception	43.1	23.7	8.7	27.0	36.6	20.4	39.0	4.9
19 Unmet need for contraception	17.9	10.8	7.6	12.5	10.6	10.5	12.8	10.7

Source: World Fertility Survey: Major Findings and Implications (Voorburg, The Netherlands: International Statistical Institute, 1984), Appendix Table, pp. 52–54.

(*continues*)

Table 4.4 (*continued*)

Note: Explanations of the indices are as follows: LINE 1 Singulate mean age at marriage, at the time of the survey; LINE 2 Percent ever married among women aged 15–19 at the time of the survey; LINE 3 Percent of time since the first marriage spent in married state; LINE 4 Crude birth rate from WFS: annual births per 1,000 population; LINE 5 Total fertility rate: no. of children a woman would bear if she experiences throughout her lifetime the rates that prevailed during the 5-year period to the survey; LINE 6 Average no. of children ever born by women aged 45–49 at the time of the survey; LINE 7 The no. of children who died before the age of 1 year, per 1,000 births, for the 5-year period before the survey; LINE 8 The no. of children who died before the age of 5 years, per 1,000 births, for the 5-year period before the survey; LINE 9 Mean duration of full breast-feeding (i.e., before introduction of supplementary food); LINE 10 Mean duration of total breastfeeding based on last live birth and penultimate live birth; LINE 11 Percent of currently married, fecund women who want no more children; LINE 12 Mean no. of desired children among currently married women; LINE 13 The no. of wanted births the average women would bear over her lifetime, if the preferences reported at the survey were to remain unchanged; LINE 14 Percent of ever-married women aware of any contraceptive method; LINE 15 Percent of ever-married women who have ever used any contraceptive method; LINE 16 Percent of currently married women who were currently using efficient methods of contraception; LINE 17 Percent of currently married women who were currently using any method of contraception; LINE 18 Percent of ever-married women willing to use contraception among those who are at risk and have never used contraception before; LINE 19 Percent of currently married, fecund, non-pregnant women who want no more children and who report that they are not using any method of contraception.

in the society. In Turkey in the 1920s, secular legal codes based on Western models were introduced; a study conducted in the late 1960s in a region of western Turkey showed that at least some women outside the large cities were exercising their full legal rights to sue for divorce and to protect their personal reputations and their claims to property.[69] Legal codes are an important basis for women to act as autonomous persons. Most important is the expansion of schooling for girls.

The combined and cumulative effect of these social changes has been differentiation among the female population and an expansion of the range of options available to women. Trends include later marriages, more education, formal-sector employment, smaller families, and greater decisionmaking among women. As Caldwell explains, a greater female role in reproductive decisionmaking would imply an important transition—a move toward a greater belief in female participation in work or social activities—and perhaps reflect and accelerate a decline (itself a function of increasing secularization) in strong moral views on the separate roles of the sexes and the sanctity of maternity.[70] These trends are relevant to a small percentage of the urban female population, but they have been visible enough to result in opposition by conservative forces. The relative rise in the position of females is seen by conservative forces as having the greatest potential of any factor to destroy the patriarchal family and its political, economic, and demographic structure.

Caldwell argues that mass schooling has probably had a greater impact on the family in developing countries than it had even in the West. First, mass schooling has come in many countries at an earlier stage of economic and occupational structure development than it did in the West. Second, schooling frequently means Westernization, including Western concepts of family and gender. According to Caldwell, "Schools destroy the corporate identity of the family, especially for those members previously most submissive and most wholly contained by the family: children and women."[71]

Fatima Mernissi has also emphasized the role of state-sponsored education in creating a generation of unveiled and independent women. Her thesis is worth quoting at length:

> As corrupt and inefficient as it proved to be, the national state did nevertheless carry out a mass educational programme (limited to males only in the rural area) after independence, and fostered the emergence of a new class: *educated youth of both sexes.* This class is the result of the interplay of three factors: (1) the demographic factor, the "youthification" of the population; (2) a political factor, the emergence of the welfare state; (3) a cultural factor, the change in women's self-perception as actors in society. . . .
>
> Centuries of women's exclusion from knowledge have resulted in femininity being confused with illiteracy until a few decades ago. But things have progressed so rapidly in our Muslim countries that we women take literacy and access to schools and universities for granted.[72]

Educational attainment by parents seems to have some effect on their children's aspirations. A study of female education in Egypt in the early 1980s found that all the students whose father had a university education saw nothing less for themselves than a comparable education. Similar aspirations were also noticed among students whose mother completed a university education. Girls whose mothers were illiterate were more likely to see secondary education as their ultimate goal. The great majority of daughters whose mothers could read and write or had completed primary, preparatory, or secondary education intended to seek a university degree. Further analysis of students' aspirations in relation to fathers' occupations showed a high correlation between a student's level of aspiration for university or postgraduate studies and her father's employment in a professional field. Fully 100 percent of the daughters of fathers who worked in professional jobs aimed for a university or postgraduate education. Similarly, 96 percent of the daughters of fathers working in semiprofessional jobs expressed the same desire. The percentage of students aiming at only a secondary education was higher among girls whose fathers worked as small business entrepreneurs (10 percent); religious functionaries, guards, and policemen (12 percent); skilled laborers (20 percent); and unskilled laborers (23 percent). The mother's employment status also showed a relationship to her daughter's hopes for higher education. The great majority (98 percent) of the daughters of working mothers expressed a desire to pursue a university education; the other 2 percent were satisfied with a secondary education as their goal. A higher percentage (12 percent) of the daughters of nonworking mothers did not intend to go beyond secondary school. When education was related to employment, the girls' responses were more positive regarding the employment of educated women. The overwhelming majority (93 percent) believed that once a young woman completes her education, she must work. They further asserted that the ultimate goal of education for women was future employment.[73]

Egypt and Iran, two large Middle Eastern countries, are representative of the profound changes under way in the region. Whereas a few decades ago the majority of women married before the age of twenty, today only 22 percent of that age group in Egypt and 18 percent in Iran are married.[74] As Mernissi puts it, "To get an idea of how perturbing it is for Iranian society to deal with an army of unmarried adolescents one has only to remember that the legal age for marriage for females in Iran is thirteen and for males fifteen." The legal age was lowered following the assumption of power by Islamists, but it is interesting that this has not been translated into a higher rate of marriage for girls under twenty. In Turkey 21 percent, in Morocco 17 percent, and in Tunisia only 7 percent of females aged fifteen to nineteen were ever married in the early 1980s. Mernissi argues that the idea of a young unmarried woman is completely novel in the Muslim world, for the whole concept of patriarchal honor is built around the idea of virginity, which reduces a woman's role to its sexual dimension: reproduction within an early marriage.[75] The concept of a menstruating and unmarried woman is so alien to the entire Muslim family system, Mernissi adds, that it is either unimaginable or necessarily linked with *fitna*. The unimaginable is now a reality.

As noted by Fatima Mernissi, young men, faced with job insecurity or lacking a diploma to guarantee access to desired jobs, postpone marriage. Women, faced with the pragmatic necessity to count on themselves instead of relying on a rich husband, see themselves forced to get an education. The average age of marriage for women and men in most Arab countries has registered a noticeable increase. In Egypt and Tunisia, the average age at marriage for women is twenty-two and twenty-four, respectively, and for men in both countries, twenty-seven. In Algeria the average age is twenty-one for women and twenty-four for men; in Iran the figures are twenty for women and twenty-four for men. In Morocco and Jordan the average age of marriage for women is twenty-two; men marry at around age twenty-five. The oil countries, known for their conservatism, have also witnessed an increase of unmarried youth: age at marriage for women is twenty, and for men, twenty-seven. The lowest age of marriage for girls, seventeen, is found in Yemen, where the fertility rate is also the highest in the region. Of course, the patterns of nuptiality are influenced by urbanization: The more urbanized youth marry later in all countries. And it should be noted that in

Table 4.5 A Demographic Profile of the Middle East

| | Population (in millions) | | Annual Population Growth Rate % | | Dependency Ratio | | Contraceptive Prevalence Rate % | Fertility Rate | Crude Birth Rate[a] | Crude Death Rate | Mean Age at 1st Marriage (F) |
	1960	1988	1960–1988	1988–2000	1960	1985	1985	1988	1988	1988	1980s
Afghanistan	11.0	16.0	1.4	4.5	80.2	80.1	2	6.9	50	22	17.8
Algeria	11.0	24.0	2.9	2.8	90.9	97.3	7	6.0	39	9	21.0
Egypt	26.0	51.0	2.5	2.2	84.3	79.8	32	4.8	35	10	21.4
Iran	20.0	53.0	3.5	2.9	96.7	86.7	23	5.6	41	8	19.7
Iraq	6.8	18.0	3.5	3.4	94.5	98.4	14	6.3	42	8	20.8
Israel	2.1	4.4	2.7	1.5	69.3	70.5	—	2.9	22	7	23.5
Jordan	1.7	4.0	3.1	4.0	94.2	103.3	26	7.2	45	7	22.6
Kuwait	.3	1.9	7.2	3.1	58.9	70.4	—	4.8	32	3	22.9
Libya	1.3	4.2	4.2	3.5	89.7	95.0	—	6.8	44	9	18.7
Morocco	12.0	24.0	2.6	2.3	90.1	85.4	36	4.8	35	10	22.3
Oman	.5	1.4	3.6	3.4	85.3	87.9	—	7.2	46	13	—
Saudi Arabia	4.1	13.0	4.3	3.9	87.4	90.5	—	7.2	42	7	—
Sudan	11.0	24.0	2.7	2.9	89.6	92.2	5	6.4	44	16	18.7
Syria	4.6	12.0	3.4	3.5	93.0	103.5	20	6.7	44	7	20.7
Tunisia	4.2	7.8	2.2	1.9	90.6	76.8	41	4.0	30	7	24.3
Turkey	28.0	54.0	2.4	1.8	81.1	68.4	51	3.5	28	8	20.6
UAE	.1	1.5	10.5	2.3	88.8	48.1	1	4.8	23	4	18.0
Yemen Arab R.	4.0	7.6	2.3	3.3	83.8	105.2	1	7.0	48	16	17.8
Yemen, PDR	1.2	2.3	2.4	3.2	91.0	91.8	—	6.7	47	16	17.8

Sources: UNDP, Human Development Report 1990 (New York: Oxford University Press, 1990), Table 20; World Bank, World Development Report 1990 (New York: Oxford University Press, 1990), Table 27; United Nations Statistical Office, Compendium of Statistics and Indicators 1988 (New York: United Nations, 1991), Table 10.

Notes: a. Annual number of births per 1,000 population.
— indicates information not available

all cases the average age of marriage is higher than the legal minimum. The mean age at first marriage for women is shown in Table 4.5, which also provides other sociodemographic data on Middle Eastern countries.

The single most important determinant in the age of marriage has been education. The World Fertility Survey report on Egypt, like many others, shows a definite positive relationship between education and age at first

Table 4.6 Primary, Secondary, and Tertiary School Enrollments

	% Primary School Enrollment (Gross)				% Secondary School Enrollment (Gross)				Tertiary Enrollment (Females as a % of Males)
	1965		1986–1988		1965		1986–1988		1987–1988
	Male	Female	Male	Female	Male	Female	Male	Female	
Afghanistan	26	5	27	14	4	1	10	5	18
Algeria	81	53	105	87	10	5	61	46	45
Bahrain	—	—	111[a]	110[a]	—	—	89[b]	83[b]	142
Egypt	90	60	100	79	37	15	79	58	52
Iran	85	40	122	105	24	11	57	39	43
Iraq	102	45	105	91	42	14	60	38	64
Israel	95	95	94	97	46	51	79	87	94
Jordan	105	83	98	99	52	23	80	78	—
Kuwait	129	103	95	92	59	43	86	79	171
Lebanon	118	93	105	95	33	20	57	56	—
Libya	111	44	—	—	24	4	—	—	—
Morocco	78	35	85	56	16	5	43	30	49
Oman	—	—	103	92	—	—	46	29	71
Qatar	—	—	124[b]	123[b]	—	—	64[b]	69[b]	—
Saudi Arabia	36	11	78	65	7	1	52	35	76
Sudan	37	21	59	41	6	2	23	17	62
Syria	103	52	115	104	43	13	69	48	59
Tunisia	116	65	126	107	23	9	46	34	64
Turkey	118	83	121	113	22	9	57	34	55
UAE	—	—	98	100	—	—	55	66	—
Yemen (N.)	16	1	141	40	—	—	46	6	—
Yemen (S.)	35	10	96	35	17	5	26	11	—

Sources: World Bank, *Social Indicators of Development 1988* (Baltimore: Johns Hopkins University Press, 1988); UNDP, *Human Development Report 1990,* Table 13; *Human Development Report 1991,* Tables 10, 31 (New York: Oxford University Press); UNICEF, *The State of the World's Children 1989* (New York: Oxford University Press, 1989), Table 4.
  Notes: a. 1984–1986
  b. 1980–1986
  — indicates information not available

marriage. Increasing education opportunities for young Egyptian women are largely responsible for the recent decline in early marriage and the upward trend in age at marriage, particularly in urban areas.[76] Table 4.6 provides data on primary and secondary school and tertiary enrollments for both men and women. Although with a few exceptions female educational attainment is low in comparison with that of men, female enrollments have been increasing since the 1960s, and quite dramatically at the secondary school level.

Education for women in the patriarchal belt has had a rapid and revolutionary impact. As Mernissi states: "Access to education seems to have an immediate, tremendous impact on women's perception of themselves, their reproductive and sex roles, and their social mobility expectations."[77] Higher levels of education tend to result in more knowledge and use of contraceptives. According to a summary report on the WFS, contraceptive use ranges from 1 percent of women surveyed in North Yemen and Mauritania to 64 percent in Costa Rica. In Middle Eastern countries there are moderate proportions of between 24 and 38 percent. Whereas on average women desire four children in Egypt, the mean jumps to 4.4 among illiterate mothers and drops to 2.1 for women with secondary school education. The mean number of children born to university-educated women is 1.8. Contraceptive use among the more educated is clearly a factor here. But although fertility and education are negatively correlated, small increases in education—for example, a few years of primary education— are insufficient for fertility decline. There is also some evidence that the work status of the wife, especially if she works in the modern sector of the economy (nonagricultural cash economy), is an important determinant of marital fertility, although education of both wife and husband seems to be the stronger socioeconomic determinant in the Middle East.[78] Fertility rates are still high, especially in Saudi Arabia, Oman, Yemen, and Libya, but all Middle Eastern countries have seen fertility declines since the 1960s; especially dramatic have been the fertility declines in Tunisia, Turkey, and Kuwait.

The WFS was important in making a connection between a mother's education and a child's well-being. The Sudan Fertility Survey of 1979 stated:

> There are significant differences in the levels and patterns of nuptiality, fertility, knowledge and use of contraception, fertility preferences, and mortality as between the groups of women who are better educated, living in urban areas, and married to men engaged in professional, technical, and clerical occupations, and the groups of women with no schooling, living in rural areas, and married to men engaged in agricultural occupations.

The Syrian Fertility Survey of 1978 found that "while those with no schooling have a rate of 8.6 children, those with incomplete primary and those with complete primary schooling or above have rates of 4.3 and 3.2, respectively." And this despite the fact that "Syria has no organized family planning programme." The report concluded, "The very large differences in recent fertility between women of varying educational background and between rural and urban sectors suggest the likelihood of further decline in the national level of fertility as the Syrian population becomes more educated and urbanized." Similarly, the Turkish Fertility Survey of 1978 found that "women with high socio-economic status tend to have higher age at marriage and may have lower fertility." The survey found pronounced sociocultural and demographic differences between urban and rural, eastern and western, and educated and uneducated people in Turkey.[79] All fertility surveys showed a positive relationship between age at marriage, education, and child health. As a result, state managers in many Middle Eastern countries now recognize that education of women is the most important long-term factor in reducing infant and childhood mortality. An analysis carried out in ten countries using WFS data confirms this theory and further confirms that the influence of maternal education on child survival is usually greater than that of paternal education.[80]

In an analysis of recent data from Arab countries, one demographer finds three major changes in fertility determinants: an increase in the age at marriage, steadily reducing the traditionally large age difference between spouses; an increase in women's education; and larger numbers of younger women entering the labor market. Where detailed data are available, analyses indicate that these three factors are associated with reduced fertility.[81]

There is some consensus that the dramatic increase in education among US women in the postwar era was a major cause of the women's movement. The baby boomers, even more than those born a few years earlier, went to college in massive and unprecedented numbers. College education in turn increased women's labor force participation; at the same time there was an expansion of married women's labor force participation.[82] A similar pattern may be discerned in Middle Eastern countries—activist women, married and unmarried, emerge from the ranks of the educated and employed. This rapid social change—the impact of industrialization, urbanization, and education on marriage, the family, and sex roles—has caused a conservative backlash in the form of the Islamist movement. According to Mernissi, fundamentalism is a "defense mechanism against profound changes in both sex roles and the touchy subject of sexual identity."[83] Fundamentalists are concerned that education for women has dissolved traditional arrangements of space segregation, family ethics, and sex roles.

Although Mernissi underscores the revolutionary impact of the education of women in Muslim societies, she fails to consider the phenomenon of the educated Islamist woman. Islamist movements have been recruiting in the universities, and throughout the Middle East one sees veiled university women who are also active participants in Islamist movements. This, too, can be explained in terms of both the contradictions of social change and class factors: Islamists, whether they be male or female, are typically lower-middle-class and of recent rural or small-town background, "experiencing for the first time life in huge metropolitan areas where foreign influence is most apparent and where impersonal forces are at maximum strength."[84] In Turkey, Egypt, Iran, and Algeria, Islamist movements have many women supporters drawn from the traditional middle class. Such women continue to see the family unit as essential and natural, even while deploying such concepts as "equality" and "women's rights." For example, the passage from the analysis of the Research Group for Muslim Women's Studies of the Ministry of Culture and Higher Education in Iran, cited earlier in this chapter, continues thus: "By participating in meetings and gatherings (demonstrations, women's societies, educational and training classes, etc.), [nonemployed Iranian women] have acquainted themselves with Islamic standards, and through their proposals they have played an important role in promoting women's rights." Similarly, Islamist women activists stress both women's rights and family roles for women (see Chapter 5).

Education seems to have been a more important variable than employment in changing the position and self-perception of women. Education, while still limited, has been extended to many more women than has formal employment. Moreover, women have always worked and engaged in productive activity in the Middle East, especially in the large agrarian countries. Their participation in rural production, while considerable, has been historically devalued by the pervasive patriarchal ideology that sees women as "lacking in mind and religion."[85] This ideology is so strong in the rural areas that even the rise of female-headed households caused by male out-migration to the oil-rich countries has not significantly changed women's position in the family or vis-à-vis men.[86] Cynthia Myntti observed that in Yemen, one of the Arab labor-exporting countries, "male relatives remaining behind make the decisions as surrogates for the absent emigrant."[87]

Mervat Hatem's proposition that "while changes in women's work roles could be observed . . . they did not constitute sufficient basis for challenging the character of the existing patriarchies" may be true.[88] But it may be so because (1) more time is needed for changes in gender ideology and cultural understandings to take root, and (2) patriarchal concepts and practices are strongest in the rural areas of Middle Eastern countries. Family production and the peasant household, still prevalent in the Middle East, are not known for egalitarian gender relations. Consequently, it is likely that urban formal-sector employment, accompanied by compulsory mass female education, will be the major sources of positive change for women in the family and vis-à-vis men. We also need to consider a longer time span in deciding whether the results of change have improved women's lives, even as we study the processes along the way.

▲ Conclusions

According to Esposito, "While tradition plays an important role in most cultures, in Islam it has been elevated to an almost sacrosanct status."[89] Esposito feels that the sacralization of tradition resulted from the way Islamic law was formulated in the early years and from the victory of conservative jurists over those who wished to retain interpretation and contingency in Islamic jurisprudence. This hypothesis may be true, but to explain the persistence of patriarchy and the preoccupation with women and the family, one must look at the social structure: forms of economic organization, property relations, the state, social classes, and forms of stratification and segmentation. It has been in the twentieth century, and most rapidly since World War II, that social structure in the Middle East has undergone sudden and rapid change through industrialization and modernizing state systems. The material bases of classic patriarchy crumble under the impact of capital penetration, infrastructural development, legal reform, mass education, and employment. In this context, women and the family have experienced change, and Muslim family law has been revised and modified accordingly. Particularly in urban areas, there has been a shift from the extended household unit characteristic of classic patriarchy to a more modernized version, or neopatriarchy. Some family forms in the contemporary Middle East are remarkably similar to those of the classic bourgeois nuclear family.

But it is also in this context of social change that legal conservatives and Islamist ideologues have sought to stem the tide by resisting progressive changes in family law and insisting that it be more strictly applied. In various countries, the conservatives have made gains. Whether or not this victory is temporary depends crucially upon the pace and extent of industrialization and the education and employment of women. It will also depend on women's own responses to laws about them and their ability to organize on their own behalf. It is clear that women do not represent a homogeneous social category in the Middle East. They are differentiated by region, class, and education; educated women are further divided politically and ideologically. Yet it is hard to avoid the conclusion that further socioeconomic development and increasing rates of female education and employment will affect not only the structure and size of the family but also women's gender consciousness.

Michael Mann has suggested an evolution, in the West, from classic patriarchy to neopatriarchy and a gendered class structure. The capitalist market and liberal bourgeois ideology worked in concert to break down the private/public and male/female dichotomies, while the growth of education "provided women with one of their furthest points of entry into the public sphere and into economic stratification."[90] Parallel to these socioeconomic changes were ideological, cultural, and discursive developments around women's equality, autonomy, and liberation. In the Western world, socio-economic changes—including mass education and mass employment—have resulted in a dramatically different female relationship to the family, as well as in the proliferation of family or household forms. Rather than being limited by the family, "women's prospects are that around two-thirds of their adult lives will be spent without children in the household, and possibly half to two-thirds without a husband."[91] In the last one hundred years, it has become increasingly possible for the individual to live without the insurance afforded by an extended set of ties. This is not yet the generalized case in the Middle East. The family remains important not only economically but emotionally, even for highly educated Middle Eastern women. But their range of choices regarding family formation, duration, and size has quite definitely expanded.

▲ 5
Islamist Movements
and Women's Responses

If fundamentalists are calling for the return to the veil, it must be because women have been taking off the veil.—Fatima Mernissi

Social changes in the Middle East and North Africa have given rise to an ideological movement of a specific type, sometimes called fundamentalism or political Islam but which I prefer to call the Islamist movement, advocating reconstruction of the moral order that has been disrupted or changed. Islamist movements have arisen in the context of socioeconomic crisis, a crisis of legitimacy of the state and political order, and the weakening of the patriarchal family structure. In this context, gender has become increasingly problematized and politicized. Community morality, the status of women, and the sexual differentiation of social and familial roles are central concerns of Islamist movements. Gender identity is linked to group identity—the group here being the radicalized Muslim community, which has a twofold raison d'être. First, it has been under attack by internal and external enemies and must reassert itself. Second, it sees itself as the solution to the country's cultural, political, and economic malaise and to the crisis of national identity. Islamization measures include the banning of alcohol; the imposition of *zakat,* an Islamic method of taxation; and the restoration or strengthening of Shari'a. But Islamists are especially critical of Western influences on gender relations. Nonetheless, as this chapter will show, Islamist women are far from passive and subservient. In many of these movements one finds women activists and ideologues. A women's movement certainly exists in the Muslim world, with roots in the late nineteenth century,[1] but it is clearly bifurcated along class and ideological lines. This chapter will examine the causes of Islamist movements, their complex gender implications, and women's varied responses to them.

▲ Causes and Social Bases of Islamist Movements

As we have seen in Chapter 3, recent feminist scholarship has shown that during periods of rapid social change, gender assumes a paramount position in discourses and political programs. Historical studies, too, have found that at times of abrupt change, many people have adhered to religious interpretations that can be regarded as fundamentalist in the sense of emphasizing what are held to be basic religious values, with their accompanying cultural practices often anchored in the past.[2] This type of fundamentalism often focuses on what is perceived to be a better or more moral past as an alternative to new values and ideas that are perceived to be threatening. This perception has often implied a return to traditional social roles. As women are seen as the main transmitters of societal values, the changing role of women is associated with changes in values and behaviors that are felt to be at odds with religious or moral beliefs. As a result, efforts are made to try to reimpose traditional behaviors for women as a remedy for crisis and destabilization.[3]

In summary form, anomie, cultural introspection, identity creation, and Islamist movements in the Middle East have emerged in the wake of three processes: (1) social and economic crisis, including the uneven distribution of socioeconomic advantage within societies and the economic downturn of the late 1970s and the late 1980s; (2) a crisis of political legitimacy, with a decline in popular support for existing state systems, widely viewed as authoritarian, corrupt, or ineffectual; and (3) changes in the patriarchal system, with the growing visibility and public participation of women. Below I present a set of propositions regarding the causes and characteristics of Islamist movements.

• Islamist movements have emerged in the context of a profound economic crisis in the Middle East and North Africa, which has affected oil economies and non-oil economies alike. What modernization has been achieved to date has been very lopsided because it has been the result of a single, highly prized commodity.[4] Since the late 1970s rising indebtedness, unemployment, and problems arising from austerity measures in the 1980s have added to tensions in the region. These are linked to restructuring and the worldwide socioeconomic downturn of the 1980s; the falling price of oil on the world market has had an adverse effect on development and on living standards in the region.

• Islamist movements have also arisen in the context of the demographic transition, even though Muslim countries are at different stages on the continuum of the demographic transition and economic development, as we have seen in Chapter 4. In the Middle East, as in many other developing regions, the demographic transition is occurring more rapidly than it occurred in Europe. The result has been accelerated population growth.

Also in contrast to Western European countries, in the developing countries the onset of rapid population increase occurred before the start of modern economic development, compounding the burden of a larger and more youthful—and thus more dependent—population.[5] In Algeria, for example, 47 percent of the population is under the age of fifteen. In a context of chronic unemployment and economic crisis, this large youthful population finds itself without secure prospects.

• Politically, the region is characterized by neopatriarchal state systems that have silenced left-wing and liberal forces while fostering religious institutions in their search for legitimacy. In the wake of the growth of left-wing movements in the late 1960s and 1970s, many Middle Eastern regimes encouraged the Islamic tide in hopes of neutralizing the left. This was the basic strategy of President Anwar Sadat, who released the Muslim Brothers from prison in an attempt to counter the Egyptian left in his campaign of de-Nasserization. Iran's Shah Mohammad Reza Pahlavi followed the same strategy in the early 1970s, as did Turkish authorities following the 1980 military coup. Indeed, in the latter case, as the generals' overriding objective was to rid Turkish society of Marxist ideology and parties, they encouraged Islamic ideas and education as an antidote. Thus, in 1982 the military regime made the teaching of Islam compulsory in schools; since 1967 it had been optional.[6]

• In the Middle East and North Africa, as in many developing areas, capitalist and precapitalist modes of production coexist. These have corresponding social and ideological forms as well as types of consciousness. There is an uneasy coexistence of modern and traditional social classes, such as the Westernized upper middle class on the one hand and the traditional petty bourgeoisie organized around the bazaar and the mosque on the other. The urban centers all have large numbers of people outside the formal wage market and among the ranks of the urban poor and uneducated.

• Female education and employment, while still limited, have been increasing, thanks to economic development and the expanding state apparatus. This trend has challenged and slowly weakened the system of patriarchal gender relations, creating status inconsistency and anxiety on the part of the men of the petty bourgeoisie. Changes in gender relations, the structure of the family, and the position of women have resulted in contestation between modern and traditional social groups over the nature and direction of cultural institutions. As such, Islamist movements represent the formation and politicization of identity informed by class.

• The experience with European colonialism seems to have left deep and abiding tensions and grievances. The nonresolution of the Israeli-Palestinian problem and a pervasive sense of injustice caused by Israeli and American actions engender Islamist movements. The failure of the secular-democratic project of the PLO has encouraged the Islamist alternative among Palestinians and throughout the region.

• In the absence of fully developed and articulated movements, institutions, and discourses of liberalism or socialism, Islam is the discursive universe. However, Islam is quite variable across the various movements and also competes with nationalism, much to the chagrin of Pan-Islamists. For some Muslims, the new Islamic ideology reduces anxiety because it is able to offer a new form of assurance, and the movement provides new forms of collective solidarity and support.

• In the context of economic, political, and ideological crisis, and in the absence of fully developed, socially rooted, and credible secular alternatives, the vacuum can be more easily filled by Islamist-populist leaders and discourses. Most of the Islamist movements may be called populist by virtue of their social base (multiclass but mainly petty bourgeois) and their discourses (articulation of "the people," exhortations against foreigners, and vague notions of social justice). Islamist movements are political projects and are concerned with power.

• In the new ideological formation, tradition is exalted—and frequently invented. Although there are traditional forms of veiling, the typical Islamist hijab (modest dress for women) is a novel contemporary ensemble, deployed as a uniform. A recurrent theme is that Islamic identity is in danger; Muslims must return to a fixed tradition; identity lies in the female private sphere (women's behavior, dress, appearance); and Muslim personal laws are necessary at the level of the state (in the case of majority Muslim societies) or in the community (in the case of minority Muslim groups, as in India).

• Historically, the Middle East has not experienced a complete bourgeois revolution or an Enlightenment; neither has Islam completed a process similar to the Christian Reformation. Modernizing and reformist movements have been part of Islamic/Middle Eastern history, but they have not succeeded in the way such movements did in Christian/European history.[7] Islamist movements are a product of the contradictions of transition and modernization; they also result from the North-South contention. What is unclear is whether they impede or accelerate the transition to modernity.

• Thus, culture, religion, and identity act both as defense mechanisms and as means by which the new order is to be shaped. These movements must therefore be seen as both reactive and proactive.

The Indian scholar Asghar Ali Engineer has provided a description and analysis of Indian communalism, in particular the emergence of a politicized Muslim identity, that accords well with the analysis presented here. But mention should be made of another factor in the growth of these movements. Saudi Arabia, and to a lesser extent Kuwait, have been major funders of Islamist movements. Some Islamist groups in India have been encouraged and funded by Saudi Arabian petrodollars. Saudi Arabia has likewise been a factor in the persistence of Eritrean separatist groups and of the Afghan mujahidin. Marie-Aimée Hélie-Lucas also mentions the external funding for Islamist movements in the Muslim world. This is not to say that the Islamist movements would not otherwise emerge, only to stress the complexity of the causes of these movements and the interconnectedness of internal and external factors. Engineer concludes that a fundamentalist or communalist movement is neither a purely religious and ethnic phenomenon nor a purely economic and political phenomenon.[8]

The Islamist movement has two types: (1) movements that seek to *acquire* political power (oppositional movements), and (2) movements that seek to *maintain* or legitimate political power by manipulating religious and cultural sentiments (state-sponsored fundamentalism). A well-known example of type (1) is the Iranian Islamist movement; more recent examples are the Afghan mujahidin and the Algerian Front Islamique du Salut (FIS). An example of type (2) is state-sponsored Islamism under the late President Zia ul-Haq of Pakistan. In Bangladesh, too, the move toward Islamism was undertaken by the former regime of President Ershad. During the war with Iran, Iraq's President Saddam Hussein sought to put himself in the role of defender of Islam.

As is to be expected of movements fueled by socioeconomic disadvantages and grievances, support for Islamist movements is found among the urban poor. The involvement of recently urbanized people in Islamist movements is clear in the cases of Lebanon, Iran, Egypt, Algeria, and Tunisia. In Lebanon, the impoverishment of rural areas and the gradual abandonment of agriculture following the outbreak of civil war sparked a rural exodus to Beirut. There, Imam Musa Sadr became the spokesman of Shi'a discontent, and the poor Shi'a community, *mahrumin,* embraced Khomeini-style fundamentalism. In Iran, Khomeini had considerable support among the urban poor, whom he referred to as the *mostazafin*—the oppressed or the wretched.[9] The impoverished Gaza Strip, under Israeli military occupation, produced the first Palestinian Islamist movement—and a challenge to the PLO. In Algeria the locus of rebellion and violence in 1991–1992 has been the *bidonvilles* of Bab-el-Oued—the shantytowns of Algiers.[10] Support for Islamist movements is also found among the traditional petty bourgeoisie, artisans, shopkeepers, and bazaaris. In Iran, for example, bazaaris and clerics have had long-standing cultural and political ties. Indeed, the bazaar-mosque alliance was crucial to the success of the revolution against the Shah.

One of the striking features of Islamist movements is the extent to which young and educated people are attracted to them. Indeed, the intellectual leaders of most Islamist movements are trained in the sciences, engineering, and medicine. In Iran, Turkey, Egypt, Algeria, and Tunisia, university and high school students are among those who challenge their parents to follow a more genuinely Islamic order. Islamists are also found among young professionals, such as engineers, doctors, and teachers. There is some evidence that this educated middle class—whose support for Islamist movements was the big surprise of the 1980s—is a first-generation urban and educated stratum. Saad Eddin Ibrahim's in-depth study of the family background and social mobility of thirty-four Egyptian Islamic militants showed that nearly all came out of the middle class or lower middle class, were from rural areas or provincial towns, and were products of the country's university or secondary school system. In Sudan the newly educated urban middle class calls for cultural nationalism and forms the recruiting base for the National Islamic Front and the Muslim Brotherhood.[11] Educated people from the upper middle class, bourgeoisie, and landed gentry generally do not join Islamist movements, tending to be found instead in liberal or left-wing parties or associations. In his study of Morocco's political culture, John Entelis shows that the relatively small progressive political subculture of both liberals and leftists is comprised almost exclusively of members of the elite.[12]

Islamist movements may appear to be archaic, but in fact they combine modern and premodern discourses, means of communication, and even political institutions. Robert Wuthnow notes that the institutionalization of ideological movements involves securing a stable and consistent flow of resources, especially organizational (leadership, communication, administration, and structural autonomy), financial, and symbolic ones (including legitimation).[13] The classic example was the Iranian Revolution, where cassette tapes of Khomeini's speeches were smuggled throughout Iran and the bazaar-mosque network was a crucial focal point for organizing and mobilizing against the Shah. In Algeria the FIS used electoral means to attain power. In all cases, Islamists use modern means, including elections and the media, for their purposes. The phenomenon of Islamic revival is thus both proactive and reactive. It is reactive in the sense that it seeks to maintain the authenticity of Islamic institutions and traditions and rejects what is borrowed and external. Islamic fundamentalists, like their counterparts in the West, insist on a conservative, literal interpretation of the scriptures and do not admit the wider spectrum of theological interpretation that has characterized the development of Islam. But Islamic revival is also proactive in the sense that many Islamic reformers seek to be modernists, to borrow from the West selectively and thus enter the advanced technological age with its benefits but with Islam intact. Such contradictory impulses may be found in the movements' approaches to gender and women's status.[14]

An example of an Islamist movement with a modern approach is that of Turkey. The Turkish movement represents a response of the marginalized sectors of society to rapid industrial growth and the concomitant structural and cultural transformation. This marginality, in the Turkish context, is social as well as economic. High-status groups of Turkish republican society have consistently excluded Islamic traditionalists from their ranks. Since the mid-1970s, but especially in the 1980s, Islamic traditionalists have been bidding for social status, intellectual respectability, and political power. They have largely succeeded in entrenching themselves within the state and party bureaucracies, in commercial and industrial firms, and in intellectual circles. In short, they have become a counter-elite. The women within the ranks of the Islamist movement are part of the marginals' larger search for respectability and a redefinition of status. The so-called turban and the long coat—the novel Turkish hijab—are uniforms that serve the same function blue jeans served in Western leftist and countercultural movements. Both forms of dress are oblivious to status and class distinctions. This search ultimately includes the possibilities for upward social mobility, a prospect some within the movement have achieved. Binnaz Toprak concludes that Islamist identity politics are at the same time network politics. They build a web of intragroup relations that become instrumental in terms of acquiring political power, economic wealth, intellectual prominence, and social respectability in Turkey.[15]

It should be clear that the causes of Islamist movements are complex— political, economic, demographic, and cultural, with social and class conflict an essential feature—and that their goals are not only cultural but also frequently political. That is to say, juridical changes, upward social mobility, the acquisition of political power, and even the assumption to state power are among the objectives of many Islamist groups. It is thus important that religious reassertion and cultural revival be placed in its socioeconomic and political context.

▲ Gharbzadegi: Problematics of Class and Gender

Islamist movements claim that Westernization has deculturated Muslims and that the return to Islam—to the Shari'a, to Muslim family law, to the hijab—will defeat the crisis and strengthen cultural identity and integrity. It is useful to examine this discourse, and to deconstruct it for its gender and class elements. The Iranian concept of *gharbzadegi* provides rich material for such an investigation. Variously translated as "Westoxication," "Westitis," "Euromania," and "Occidentosis," *gharbzadegi* denotes an illness, a virus, a "plague from the West," a phenomenon of excessive Westernization that renders members of the community (usually those with a Western education) alienated from their own culture. Through those members who are struck by the West, imperialism can penetrate the society and wreak havoc on the culture. It is believed that those members of the community most vulnerable to *gharbzadegi* are women. The claim is made that by depriving women of chastity, modesty, and honor through notions of autonomy, sex appeal, and so on, colonialists and imperialists have been able to weaken cultures. This is said to have happened in Algeria under French colonialism and in Iran during the rule of the pro-American Shah. It follows that the main antidote to the virus of *gharbzadegi* is hijab. Furthermore, veiling must be compulsory in order to protect the cultural identity and integrity of the group and of its female members.[16]

It should be noted that in Iran, this antidote was not delivered to working-class women, peasant women, or the women of the urban poor. For the Islamists, the main targets were upper-middle-class educated women, principally those who had had a Western-style education, whether in high schools or in university. One type of *gharbzadeh* woman is the child of educated parents who attended one of the better private girls' schools in Tehran or one of the international schools (which were coed). Neither she nor her mother was veiled. She dressed well in the Western style, following European fashions. After high school, she either took a job in the civil service or private sector (her knowledge of Western languages and her family's connections would land her a good job) or went to college in Iran or abroad. There, too, she mixed freely with members of the opposite sex, went on dates, saw foreign movies. These women of the upper middle class were among the major beneficiaries of the Pahlavi political and economic system. Indeed, the upper middle class acquired significant economic advantages during the Pahlavi era, leading to its total expropriation after the revolution. Another type of *gharbzadeh* woman was one who may have come from a more traditional family but who became Westernized in the course of getting a university education. Many such women became politically active, invariably against dictatorship and dependent capitalism, and could be seen in the ranks of the Iranian student movement in Europe and North America. But as far as Islamists were concerned, these women had cast off their authentic cultural identity and assumed that of a Westerner, complete with ideas about liberalism, socialism, Marxism, feminism, and sexual equality.

These ideas were anathema to the Islamist paradigm, and women were the persons who quite literally embodied them. Such women were derided as *gharbzadeh*—decadent, bourgeois traitors. Thus, when Ayatollah Khomeini and his associates assumed control of the state following violent battles with liberals, the left-Islamic group the Mojahedin, and socialists, the victorious traditional petty bourgeoisie enacted repressive legislation that was both an attack on women (gender conflict) and an attack on the upper middle class (class conflict). Compulsory veiling was a kind of punishment, a form of discipline. The losers were the women of the upper middle class. By contrast, the women of the lower middle class, those from traditional and religious families, found validation in the new system, as well as new educational and employment opportunities.

The new veil, in its various permutations, is now the distinguishing mark of the Islamist woman throughout the world. It is the line of demarcation between the Islamist community and other communities. It is a shield against the slings and arrows of imperialists. But compulsory veiling in

Iran is also a mechanism of social control: the regulation of women. Moreover, it symbolizes the lack of choice in the selection of identity: Identity, in the form of hijab, is imposed.

A similar construct of the Westernized Algerian woman has been described by Cherifa Bouatta and Doria Cherifati-Merabtine, two Algerian feminist activists and professors of social psychology. They have analyzed the discourse on women in *El Mounquid,* journal of the FIS, which had electoral successes in June 1990 and was officially banned in 1992. Bouatta and Cherifati-Merabtine systematically analyzed forty-two letters and articles to discern images of womanhood and of Islamist women's self-representation. A critical theme running through these texts is that there is no need to address the woman question in terms of new rights because Islam established these rights fourteen centuries ago. Moreover, to raise the issue of women's rights is to imitate the West; another line of argument is that feminism is a Marxist plot. In the fundamentalist discourse, it is claimed that women have rights equal to those of men—the right to education and to religious instruction; the right to respect; the right to vote; the right to employment; the right to struggle. There are also prohibitions, however. A woman cannot be a political ruler, nor can she be a judge. Women should refuse mixed gatherings, should always appear in hijab, should not use cosmetics or perfume or clothes that reveal the female form. The maternal function is exalted, and salaried work is deemed inappropriate. In the Islamist discourse of *El Mounquid,* these rights, obligations, and proscriptions are based on divine precepts and biological and psychological differences between the sexes.[17]

Bouatta and Cherifati-Merabtine also found two antimodels of the non-Islamist woman. First, the Western woman: She is depicted in the Islamist literature as a mere sexual object, a commodity, an exhibitionist, subjugated to male desires, sexually and socially exploited. The second representation is that of the Westernized Algerian woman. She is both a traitor and deformed: Neither a Muslim woman nor a Western woman, she is a caricature, an alien by way of dress, language, outlook. And what do these women want? They want to subvert women's natural and sacred tasks; to dominate men; to marry when they want and divorce when they want; to go out and return as they wish; to travel without a chaperon or guardian; to reject male authority; to demand the abrogation of the family law, the sole juridical text based on the Shari'a; to create *fitna* (conflict) between men and women. The rights these women want are described by the writers in *El Mounquid* as unacceptable, inconceivable, and imaginary.

Bouatta and Cherifati-Merabtine argue that the feminine model projected by the Algerian *intégristes* diverged from that of the state because the official state discourse combines notions of tradition and modernity, whereas the discourse of the FIS, in its construction of a new tradition, eliminated and refused modernity and any form of pluralism. The authors argue that the FIS adopted a homogeneous discourse and presented ideal-types of women to the detriment of real, actually existing women.[18]

▲ Personal Status Laws and the Control of Women

During the past two decades and especially during the 1980s, new revisions of Muslim family law, or personal status (*ahwal shakhsiya*) laws, have been at the center of Muslim identities. These laws are derived from the Shari'a and govern marriage, divorce, maintenance, child custody, inheritance, and *iddat* (a period of abstinence during which the wife remains unmarried after the dissolution of marriage by divorce or death, usually to determine pregnancy and paternity). Personal status laws vary from country to country, and most do not, for example, allow divorce of a wife by simple repudiation.[19] Still, the restoration or strengthening of personal laws in places such as Iran and Algeria in the 1980s is interpreted by feminists as an expression of the fundamentalists' power and the collusion of neopatriarchal states with Islamist movements. And, as pointed out by the noted Egyptian feminist Nawal El-Saadawi, these Shari'a-derived personal status laws contravene the spirit and letter of the United Nations Convention on the Elimination of All Forms of Discrimination Against Women.[20]

Though regimes may resist the Islamist agenda on other points, family affairs and women's subordination are generally recognized as the reflection of Islamist movements' definition of identity, and laws are passed or modified in order to meet their demands. In Egypt a 1979 presidential decree liberalizing the personal status laws came to be known as "Jehan's law" for its prime proponent, the wife of President Anwar Sadat. So overwhelming was conservative male reaction that in 1985 the state rescinded the law, only to restore it in diminished form. Algeria's first family code, passed in 1984, twenty-two years after independence, restores certain patriarchal codes. It stipulates that Algerian women be given in marriage by a *wali* (a matrimonial tutor) and deprives a woman of the right to divorce except in specific cases, restoring divorce as a male prerogative. In terms of child custody, the children of divorced parents may stay with the mother until the age of six for boys and ten for girls, provided the ex-husband is satisfied with her method of child-rearing; otherwise he can claim them, as the father is the official guardian. Mothers cannot remarry without losing their children; they also have to live close enough to their ex-husbands to enable them to exercise their right to control the children's education. Women are entitled to 50 percent of a man's share of inheritance. Men are permitted polygamy and the right to repudiate their wives. In the same year, Egyptian women lost the right to remain in the marital home after a divorce, a right they had previously won following a decade-long battle.

These developments alarmed many Muslim women. One result was the formation of an international solidarity network called Women Living Under Muslim Laws. In July 1984 the members of the first action committee of Women Living Under Muslim Laws defined themselves as "women whose lives are shaped, conditioned and governed by laws, both written and unwritten, drawn from interpretations of the Koran tied up with local traditions." The action committee's position was that "men and the State use these laws against women, and have done so under various political regimes." This network monitors laws affecting the status of women in Muslim communities around the world and publicizes gender-related acts of violence or oppression.

Areas outside the Middle East have also seen the politicization of gender and the restoration of patriarchal family codes, often in the context of growing fundamentalist and communalist agitation. In 1985 the government of India acquiesced to fundamentalist demands in the famous Shah Bano case and exempted Muslims from maintenance following divorce. In 1986 Sri Lanka appointed a commission to reform Muslim personal law in a way that is unfavorable to women. In 1987 and 1989 the socialist and secular government of Mauritius accepted the project pushed forward by the Muslim main opposition party to reintroduce Shari'a law for the Muslim community. Similar attempts have been made in several other countries in Africa, notably Nigeria. Shari'a law has also been passed in several countries (such as Sudan and Pakistan) where it could supersede personal status laws and restrict women's freedom even more, considering the present interpretations of Shari'a. In countries of emigration, such as Britain, France, and the Caribbean, Muslims have demanded that personal laws be introduced. Migrants from Muslim communities to France have demanded a major constitutional change from secularism to a multireligious state. Veiling in schools and the right to polygamy are two of the demands.[21]

These developments led Marie-Aimée Hélie-Lucas, who directs Women Living Under Muslim Laws, to stress the international dimension of Islamism. She has noted that after the Shah Bano case in India, the Sri Lankan government invited an Indian scholar to serve as adviser to its Commission to Reform Muslim Law. In Mauritius the main opposition party, the Muslim Party, proposed the Indian Muslim personal law as a model for the Mauritius Muslim personal law and brought in an Indian adviser. Elsewhere, Saudi, Pakistani, or Iranian advisers have been invited. The implementation and expansion of Muslim personal laws is an integral part of the Islamist agenda. The "Islamist International" includes the circulation of funds linked to Muslim private capital, the involvement of states in fostering fundamentalist movements, and fundamentalist groups operating locally, nationally, and regionally.[22]

Although Islamist movements share an interest in the restoration or enforcement of Muslim personal law, they differ in other aspects of their political agendas and strategies. In the Middle East, some Islamist movements seek state power (as in Iran and Algeria); elsewhere (Egypt, Jordan) they limit themselves to exerting pressure on the state to reassert traditional patriarchal controls, such as stricter application of the Shari'a, veiling, segregation, or Muslim personal laws. In some societies, the state itself is the manager of patriarchy (Pakistan under Zia ul-Haq, Saudi Arabia, Sudan). In other cases, Islamist movements arise in the wake of socioeconomic crisis and win support for regimes by identifying a concern—morality, values, cultural identity—and reassuring people that something is being done. In the case of Turkey, the Islamist movement and its journals seek to create or increase Islamic consciousness—particularly among women—through the development of an alternative culture of Islam and in explicit opposition to norms of the secular culture. In all cases Islamist movements are engaged in cultural contestation.

In the new ideological construction of Islamist movements, women are presented as symbols and repositories of religious, national, and cultural identity. In the context of fear and loss of economic and social status, the link between the honor of the family and the honor of the community leads men to attempt to control "their" women. Threats to or the loss of their women is seen as a direct threat to manhood, community, and family. It therefore becomes essential to ensure patriarchal controls over the labor, fertility, and sexuality of women. Benedict Anderson has pointed out that nationalism describes its object in the language of kinship or the home, both of which denote something natural and given. Similarly, cultural authenticity in Islamist movements is linked to an image of women unsullied by Western education and the modern world. Islamist movements frequently exhibit a reductionist ideology of gender that places a high premium on motherhood and domesticity, as earlier right-wing movements did in Europe. Alya Baffoun finds that in these two distinct historical settings, movement leaders argued that housework is more suited to female biology and psychology than is professional work; morbidity and mortality rates are higher among employed women than among women who stay at home; employed women are less moral; juvenile delinquency reflects the breakdown of the family; and female employment causes male unemployment.[23]

But as we shall see, not all Islamist movements call for domestication of women. In many movements, the official Islamist pronouncements concerning women's social positions are ambiguous and contradictory. Apart from a clear stand on Shari'a, they express varying views on women's educational attainment and labor force participation, ranging from misogynistic (as with the Afghan Islamist leadership) to fairly tolerant (for example, Islamists in Iran and Turkey).

The emphasis on male-female differences, on the desirability and necessity of distinctive sex roles, and on separate male and female natures is hardly unique to Islam or to the Middle East. Cynthia Epstein shows us how pervasive were explanations of biological determinism in US academic disciplines and social science research, explanations that attributed psychological and social characteristics of men and women to physiological causes. In the nineteenth century, US suffragist political rhetoric resounded with claims that women—at least white, native-born women—possessed a large proportion of patriotism, temperance, morality, and religion, and that, once enfranchised, they would transform and purify politics itself. Women were deemed to be "more exalted than the men" because "their moral feelings and political instincts" are "not so much affected by selfishness, or business, or party consideration."[24] Similar qualities are attributed to Islamist women today, as we shall see below.

What is quite interesting is the range of women's responses to these movements. There are, of course, secular feminists who are unalterably opposed to Islamist movements, to Shari'a law, and to veiling as a form of social control; they may be found in countries such as Algeria, Tunisia, Egypt, Iran, and Turkey, actively involved in feminist and democratic movements. Then there are the Islamist women themselves and the surprising activism they display. They staunchly defend the veil as liberation from a preoccupation with beauty, call for the education of women in order that they be more competent in raising "committed Muslims," and argue that Shari'a and women's emancipation are compatible. At the same time, they accept that men and women are physiologically and psychologically different and thus require different roles.

For some women, being designated as the carrier of culture and tradition is an onerous burden, one they would just as soon not assume, especially as it is predicated upon control and conformity. But for Islamist women, it is an honor and a privilege to be elevated to such a lofty and responsible position. Therefore, all fundamentalist movements have women supporters as well as women opponents, and feminism has female detractors. As we know, this situation is not limited to fundamentalist movements or the Islamic world. In the United States, feminism has its female opponents, not limited to the formidable Phyllis Schlafly. The participation of women in the US anti-abortion movement, as with female support for Islamist movements in the Middle East and North Africa, may also reflect deep-seated fears among women, especially economically dependent women. Perhaps these women are responding to the perceived normlessness of contemporary society and wish to avoid the increased pressures and demands on women. (In this sense, the American anti-abortion movement is a classic example of a reactive movement.) In the case of the Islamist movement, women seem to find value and purpose in the movement's endorsement and exaltation of their domestic activities and nature. Writing about the Islamist movement in Turkey, Feride Acar states that "women have been exposed to contradictory, dissonant messages and practices, filled with false expectations and aspirations. This has rendered them vulnerable and receptive to an ideology that simplifies reality and promises escape from role conflict and ambiguity."[25]

Islamist movements promise women security and meaning in what, from a conservative point of view, is a world gone mad. There are some similarities with the Orthodox Jewish women in the United States studied by Debra Kaufman. The latter claim to be psychologically alienated from sexual liberation, individualism, and the secular worldview. They have decided that their personal needs are better met in the religious community. As with Islamist women, these Jewish women fear the loss of boundaries; they celebrate gender differences and extol separatism. Islamist women also bear some similarities to the social conservative American women of the new right studied by Rebecca Klatch. They tend to see everything in religious terms and place the family firmly at the center. They fear the breakdown of the moral universe and blame feminists for it; narcissism and the degradation of housework are said to be the result of the women's movement. Such religious women of the new right also fear the masculinization of the world through the blurring of gender roles. At the same time, they evince a distrust of men for being noncommittal and support measures, such as a ban on pornography, that would "hold back man's animal nature."[26]

As mentioned above, one of the surprises of Islamist movements in the 1980s has been its appeal among university and educated women. One reason for this appeal—apart from that provided by Acar—is that many Islamist movements exhibit a degree of flexibility in their position on women. They encourage education for women, mainly so that women can be more informed mothers but also so they can provide teaching and medical services for other women, thus avoiding the problem of excessive male-female interaction. In an interesting twist to the preoccupation with culture and identity, pragmatism can work its way through ideology to encourage female labor force participation during wartime or periods of labor scarcity, as occurred in Iran.[27] Thus, the Islamist discourse on gender combines traditional and conservative ideas about "women's place," vague longings for a mythical, bygone golden age, and acceptance of the needs of a modern economy.

Women from traditional families in the lower middle class also support these movements because the movements and the veil provide space for them. Women from this class can legitimately study, work, and act politically and publicly, with their honor and modesty protected within the confines of the Islamist movement. Veiling becomes not only a cultural symbol and an assertion of identity but a matter of convenience—it allows women physical mobility in public spaces, free from the gaze and harassment of men and the disapproval of family members.

All of these trends reflect the weakening of classic patriarchy and the resultant "sexual anomie" analyzed by Mernissi. This situation is felt by both men and women. Men are frustrated and humiliated at being unable to fulfill their traditional role—because of, inter alia, chronic unemployment—and at the threat posed by women's increasing spatial mobility and access to paid employment. Kandiyoti adds that this breakdown of classic patriarchy is equally threatening to women, "who often resist the process of change because they see the old normative order slipping away from them without any empowering alternatives." The response of some women who have to work for wages in this context may be an intensification of traditional modesty markers, such as veiling. Often, through no choice of their own, they are working outside the home and thus "exposed"; they must now use every symbolic means at their disposal to signify that they continue to be worthy of protection. El-Guindy, Macleod, and Hoodfar all suggest that the new veiling of working women in Egypt represents concern with retaining respectability, although this seems to be a class-specific response, as Macleod shows for lower-middle-class women in Cairo.[28]

There is also some evidence that voluntary veiling is not necessarily an expression of affiliation with or support for an Islamist political movement, but rather that it paradoxically represents rejection of parental and even patriarchal authority among rebellious young women. This especially may be the case for young women from nontraditional families—for example, Palestinians, Algerians, and Tunisians—who by donning hijab aspire to personal autonomy and a more serious mien, especially at coeducational colleges. For example, an American Fulbright scholar in Algiers has described a scene at a lecture on thermodynamics at the University of Science and Technology. According to his account, the hijab-wearing Muslim sisters arrived early, occupied the entire two front rows of the lecture hall, and for nearly two hours sat in rapt attention, scribbling down notes furiously. Several rows back, most of the young men chatted and smoked away their boredom. "I don't know what to think about this hijab business," confided the professor after class, "but I sure like their attitude. I wish all my students were as disciplined and hardworking." Hafidha, an aspiring civil engineer, was eager to explain how she reconciled her fundamentalist lifestyle with her dream of designing high-tech factories. "I don't have to behave like a European or American to be a scientist," she says. "I can very well be an eminent scientist or engineer and wear my hijab!"

These young women told their American observer that nothing irritated them more than the efforts of many Algerian men to veil their women by force and abuse them into submission. "I think it's scandalous how men dominate women in Algeria!" seethed Aîcha as she mechanically pushed an errant lock of hair back under her hijab. "Listen, if I'm able to take on the hijab against the wishes of my father, another woman is also able to decide *not* to wear it, despite the wishes of her father. No woman should let herself be intimidated by a slap, a whack of the belt, or blackmail. A woman must

stand up for her rights." When asked if they envied the freedoms enjoyed
by their European and American counterparts, the response was uniform:
Aside from scientific and technical know-how, the West has nothing to
offer, they felt. Western societies are hopelessly materialistic, exploitative,
racist, and rotting from within. Women in them are even more exploited
economically, politically, and especially sexually—yet they have no source
of spiritual comfort. Coffman explains that this image of Western women
"has apparently been reinforced by a small but steady diet of old US sit-
coms and TV movies."[29]

▲ **Women and Islamist Movements: Some Cases**

The following sections are case studies of Islamist movements and
women's responses. Table 5.1 is a summary illustration. These cases illustrate the contradictory features of Islamist movements, including their gender discourses. At the same time, they raise questions about Islamist
women: Are they patriarchal women or Islamic feminists?

Tunisia and Algeria

Alya Baffoun argues that in both Tunisia and Algeria, the causes and roots
of fundamentalism are (1) a state system based on single-party rule and
external dependence, (2) the cultural duality of the (petty bourgeois) elite,
which draws from both modern and traditional culture to legitimate its
authority, and (3) failures of political development and economic modernization, and the economic crisis encompassing the region. Morocco and
Tunisia suffered serious economic losses, especially in export revenue,
when Spain and Portugal joined the EC in 1986. In Tunisia in November
1987, after a summer of mounting tension during which hundreds of supporters of the Mouvement de la Tendance Islamique were arrested and two
executed on terrorism charges, President Zine El Abiddine Ben Ali
replaced President Habib Bourguiba as head of state. In Algeria in 1990, 70
percent of the country's export earnings went to service the country's
crushing debt, compared with 30 percent in 1986. Official statistics
acknowledged a 22 percent unemployment rate. And although Algeria's
galloping birthrate has slowed somewhat, nearly three-quarters of its population is under thirty.[30] In this context, Islamist movements have risen that
focus on women as *the* vehicle to cultural identity.

However, there are significant differences between the two cases. In
Tunisia the state has strongly opposed *intégrisme* and denied it any legitimacy or legality. And within civil society there are many groups and
associations—particularly the women's organizations—that have taken
strong positions against the Islamists. Moreover, the Tunisian state has

Table 5.1 Islamist Movements and Women's Movements in Middle Eastern Countries, 1980s

	Islamist Organization/Party	Political Status in 1992	Women's Organizations
Afghanistan	Seven-party tribal-Islamist opposition, the mujahidin, based in Peshawar, Pakistan	UN negotiations to form a transitional coalition government including the mujahidin parties led to collapse of non-Islamist Najibullah government. The mujahidin parties call for a strict Islamic republic and hold extremely conservative views on women and law.	All-Afghan Women's Council, government-supported, dissolved following mujahidin takeover in 1992.
Algeria	Front Islamique du Salut (FIS), led by Abbasi Madani (pro-Saudi) and Ali Belhadj (pro-Iranian)	After electoral gains in 1990, an emboldened FIS presented political demands and engaged in street battles with authorities. A military government found FIS seditious and dissolved it in March 1992.	L'organisation de l'égalité devant la loi entre les femmes et les hommes; L'association indépendante pour le triomphe des droits des femmes; Women's organizations affiliated with the Front des Forces Socialistes and le Parti Avantgarde Socialiste.
Egypt	Muslim Brotherhood; other, smaller and more violent groups	Police vigilance and state distrust keep the Brotherhood a minority party. But it controls al-Azhar mosque and university complex in Cairo and is very influential in education and the media.	Nawal El-Saadawi's Arab Women's Solidarity Association (AWSA), banned by the government in fall 1991; other smaller women's groups.
Jordan	Muslim Brotherhood	In 1990 it won thirty out of eighty-two seats in parliamentary elections and was given five seats in the Cabinet by King Hussein. Following the lifting of a 1957 ban on political parties in 1991, the Brotherhood lost its privileged status.	
Iran (Islamic Republic of)	Islamic Republican Party (IRP) 1979–1985	The state and constitution are defined as Islamic.	Islamic Women's Council; Association of Muslim Women (both state-sponsored)
Palestine	Hamas	Continues to operate.	General Union of Palestinian Women
Morocco	Justice and Welfare Party, led by Abdesalam Yassine	Ordered to disband in 1990. Secular opposition groups are stronger.	Network of antifundamentalist women and men activists and intellectuals associated with Fatima Mernissi.

(continues)

Table 5.1 (continued)

	Islamist Organization/Party	Political Status in 1992	Women's Organizations
Saudi Arabia	Several underground radical groups	Underground. They oppose the fundamentalist Wahhabi regime and favor a constitutional republic.	None
Sudan	National Islamic Front, ruling Islamist group, led by Hassan Turabi	Controls government. Shari'a law introduced in 1990. Radical groups collect money from Saudi Arabia for jihad against the south.	Information not available
Syria	Muslim Brotherhood	Banned; suppressed by military in mid-1980s.	General Federation of Syrian Women
Tunisia	En-Nahda, also known as Islamic Tendency Movement	Not officially recognized. Its members, standing as independents, won 13 percent of the vote but no seats in parliamentary elections in June 1990. Al-Nahda was subsequently split by the Gulf conflict. Its leader, Rachid Ghannouchi, who is in exile, supported Saddam Hussein. Its deputy leader, Abdelfatteh Mourou, reluctant to offend the party's Gulf funders, did not. Following a series of terrorist attacks, Mourou suspended party operations. President Ben Ali jailed 100 of its leading members.	Union of Tunisian Women, government-supported. In addition, many independent women activists and professional groups, many of them with links to similar groups in Morocco and Algeria.
Turkey	Welfare Party (successor to the National Salvation Party, banned in 1980)	Although a law bans agitation for Shari'a, 700 Quranic schools have been set up since 1983. Kemalists remain staunchly secular, but the Motherland Party (Turgut Ozal) and True Path Party (Suleiman Demirel) are more indulgent, having allowed Islamic banks and financial institutions. Some companies now allow Islamic attire.	Various feminist groups

Sources: The Economist Newspaper Ltd., Foreign Report (April 11, 1991); "Militant Islam's Saudi Paymasters," *The Guardian*, February 29, 1992, p. 5; "Islam Resumes Its March," *The Economist*, April 4, 1992, pp. 55–56; Women Living Under Muslim Laws, various documents.

Note: Many of these movements have been funded by Saudi Arabia's fundamentalist Wahhabi regime. The exception is Iran. The Pakistani government under Zia ul-Haq also sponsored the Afghan mujahidin, especially the most ruthless group, led by Gulbeddin Hekmatyar. Hekmatyar's group also received the lion's share of US military aid.

been secular since its inception; under Bourguiba, a staunch advocate of women's rights, a family law was introduced in 1956 that remains the most progressive in the Arab world. Today *intégrisme* remains banned in Tunisia. In Algeria, on the other hand, the rise of Islamism has its origins in a state system whose ideology includes Islamic precepts, whose legal system adopted Islamic family law, and whose economy has suffered from chronically high rates of unemployment. It should also be noted that the Algerian state, ruling party, and media were enthusiasts of the Iranian Revolution and of Ayatollah Khomeini, in contrast to Tunisia, where support was at best tepid.

Leaflets distributed by the FIS during its campaign in 1991–1992 bring to mind early Iranian Islamist documents on law, women, and the economy. On solutions to Algeria's massive economic problems they were vague and populist, promising to "make the poor rich without making the rich poor." Notwithstanding radical rhetoric against free market economics, the Algerian debt, and the IMF, the FIS had no economic strategy and focused more on political and cultural (mainly gender) issues and most stridently on public morality. The FIS was committed to introducing Shari'a, which it claimed was superior to Western-style civil codes. Hijab would also be introduced, ostensibly to free women from the prying eyes of men. According to one leaflet, "The hijab is a divine obligation for the Muslim woman: It is a simple and modest way to dress, which she has freely chosen." Other leaflets repeated the theme identified by Bouatta and Cherifati-Merabtine that women are under attack from "pernicious Westernization" and that "a woman is above all a mother, a sister, a wife or a daughter." Even the participation of women in sports events is seen as immoral and corrupting. When Hassiba Boulmerka won the 1,500 meters at the World Athletics Championships in Tokyo in August 1991, becoming only the second Arab woman ever to receive a major sporting title, she was hailed by the Algerian sports minister, Leila Aslouani, by President Chadli Benjedid and Prime Minister Sid Ahmed Ghozali, and by many of her compatriots. However, fundamentalist imams affiliated to the FIS united to pronounce *kofr,* a public disapproval of her from the nation's mosques. The object of their disapproval was the fact that Boulmerka had run before the world's eyes "half-naked"—that is, in regulation running shorts and vest.[31] Nevertheless, Boulmerka went on to participate in the 1992 Summer Olympic Games, where her remarkable performance was a source of pride to her compatriots and to Arab women everywhere.

The fundamentalist discourse and agenda of the FIS were strongly supported by a segment of the female population, and in April 1989 a demonstration of 100,000 women in favor of Islamism and sex-segregation shocked antifundamentalist Algerian women. But this phenomenon also spawned a network of anti-*intégriste* feminist groups, with names such as l'Association Indépendante pour le Triomphe des Droits des Femmes and l'Organisation de l'Egalité devant la Loi entre les Femmes et les Hommes. The Front des Forces Socialistes has a feminist women's organization, as does the Parti Avantgarde Socialiste. The Rassemblement pour la Culture et la Démocratie (RCD) is staunchly secular. On January 1, 1992, a mass demonstration of some 300,000 women and men, under the sponsorship of the Front des Forces Socialistes, voiced opposition to *intégrisme,* as well as criticism of FLN policies and failures. One Algerian feminist, who blamed the rise of the FIS on the failures of the "parti unique," also insisted that an FIS government would spell "the death of freedom, of creativity, of women's rights."[32] When an Algerian court decided to ban the FIS in March 1992, the court ruling was read by Judge Ziani, a woman judge who could not have held her position under an FIS government or, for that matter, in a majority of Middle Eastern countries still inspired by Shari'a.[33]

Gender and Islam in Sudan

Sudan provides an intriguing case study of women's responses to social change and the rise of Islamist movements. In Sudan, Sondra Hale finds similarities and differences between Islamist and secularist strategies. The former manipulates religious ideology toward a more "native" culture, reiterates the centrality of women, and attempts to create new trends and stem recent changes in the gender division of labor. The latter relegates Islam to the "private sphere" or coexists with it, also stresses the centrality of women in the political process, and views women as playing a potentially significant role in the work force. Women's movements show a similar religious/secularist division, exemplified by women in the National Islamic Front (NIF) and the Sudanese Women's Union. Both practice a politics of "authenticity," a search for a uniquely Sudanese identity, including an attempt to define women's roles.[34]

Sudanese women won the right to vote in 1965, and later secured equal pay for equal work. The 1973 constitution guaranteed women a number of civil rights and gender-related protections. But in 1983 Islamization began, along with the attempt to enforce Shari'a. Islamic law gained precedence over civil and customary law, leaving women in a contradictory position. On the one hand, some rights are guaranteed; on the other hand, recent changes in criminal and civil law discriminate against them, with some rights simply being ignored. There is an ongoing national debate over women in medicine, with the NIF attempting to bar them from such "inappropriate" areas as surgery and obstetrics and channel them into child and mother health, public health, and general medicine. A debate is also taking place on the appropriateness of work performed by (lower-class) women in the informal sector—that is, as vendors of local brew, prostitutes, and some types of entertainers.

Hale's interviews with NIF women and university students illustrate the degree to which the Islamic ideal of women and the family has permeated the urban middle class, the contradictions and inconsistencies in the Islamist discourse on gender, and the enthusiasm and activism of Islamist women. Women of the NIF agree wholeheartedly with the goal of strengthening Islam and enforcing Shari'a in Sudan. To an NIF woman activist, there is no distinction between politics and religion, between public and private life. Women are among the most active and visible organizers of the NIF, which has considerable support at the university. Hale finds that women are not only participating in the formation of the NIF's "modern Islamic woman" but are in fact central to the effort. NIF women say they are activists because of equal rights in Shari'a. At the same time, Islamist women have internalized the biological paradigm, which holds that men and women are fundamentally different by nature, thereby necessitating different roles and responsibilities. Some even see women as essentially weak, emotional, and sentimental, with a primary duty in the domestic sphere. NIF women are aware of the importance of their roles in the movement. Devotion and commitment to the NIF follows from the NIF's receptivity to an enhanced role for women in the movement. But why should the NIF be thus? Hale argues that states and political movements alike must maintain gender ideology while balancing labor needs. Within the NIF, the imperatives of organizational strategies require utilization of available human resources. Despite some ideological prohibitions, women are needed in large numbers by the NIF for many political tasks.

Among those interviewed by Hale in 1988 were three well-educated, professional, upper-middle-class to upper-class NIF women who provided their view of the ideal Muslim woman. One of these women was Sudan's first woman Shari'a judge, though no longer politically active; another was a lawyer, wife, and sister of prominent NIF activists; the third was a former NIF representative in the government and a teacher of Arabic. Much to Hale's surprise, these activist women all agreed that men oppress women, that Arabs have a low opinion of women, and that Arab men try to give a false idea to women about their rights under Shari'a. One commented, "Sudan is still a man's society . . . the man is the boss." Another, referring to a very conservative group, Ansar al-Sunna, which opposes any public activity by women, said, "They are against women. . . . They think a woman's voice is like women's breasts showing." They went on to claim:

> They [Arab men] are against women, and that is why *we are much against them*. We know our rights; we have learned the Koran and Shari'a; we know what Shari'a gives us . . . we think that *women are better human beings* than they think. . . . And *we are standing up for our sex*. We are working in the NIF *to praise women* and to make women have a better status and to tell the world that we are as equal as men and as efficient as men and we are as educated as men and we are as good as men and as great as men [emphases by S. Hale].

Yet the Shari'a judge also justified polygamy by saying that it was more dignified than "running around" outside of marriage. She stressed that women were equal with men under Shari'a and that the Shari'a permitted women to work. All felt that a woman's primary duty was as wife and mother, but household economic need could justify entering the work force. Still, it was a woman's responsibility to be "respectable" at all times.

A dictate in Shari'a providing that two women are needed to offset the testimony of one man during criminal proceedings has been historically justified in terms of the nature of women and the inherent differences between men and women. The Arabic teacher explained the need for two woman witnesses in the following way:

> We know that women are different from men . . . women, by their *nature*, sometimes forget. Sometimes they sympathize with somebody. Perhaps he may be a criminal . . . when one of them [woman witness] forgets, the other will remind her, and if one of them sympathized with the criminal, the other could correct her. . . . I don't think it is a problem for women to find themselves treated differently in the court . . . because it is *natural* . . . the entire principle [in Shari'a] is in accord with the way women are *created,* since women are *naturally empathetic* [emphases by S. Hale].

On the same point, the lawyer asserted:

> In a situation of somebody taking a . . . knife and stabbing another, a woman would be so much *excited* that she would not recognize exactly what happened, because after all, a *woman is weaker than a man* and all her *nervous system* is made different [from a man's] . . . so she may say something that she believes . . . happened, not what she saw happen . . . women are more *sentimental,* because they are the mothers who breed children. . . . That is why, in Shari'a law we guard against the sentimentality ['*aatifiyya*,' 'empathy,' 'compassion,' 'sympathy'] of womankind [emphases by S. Hale].

She continued:

> This does not mean that a woman is less than a man, or that her mental *capacity* is less than a man. It means that her *disposition* is different than [a man's]. We are equal in all rights in Islam [emphases by S. Hale].

The existence of these strong NIF women notwithstanding, in November 1991 the Sudanese government ordered all working women and students to adhere to Islamic dress—not the traditional Sudanese *tobe,* a sari-like wraparound, but a novel ensemble modeled after the Islamist uniforms of Tehran, Cairo, and Algiers. Committees were set up to enforce hijab and public morality in Khartoum's streets, offices, and schools. Following the Iranian example of the early 1980s, the Sudanese authorities also spoke out against the use of cosmetics and perfume outside the home. According to Carolyn Fleuhr-Lobban, the Islamization of law has been pursued farther in Sudan than in many other Islamist settings.[35]

Feminists and Islamists in Egypt

In Egypt similarly contradictory voices can be heard, and these are representative of thoroughly modern tendencies and developments. The secular feminist movement has produced some renowned authors and activists, notably Nawal El-Saadawi, who in recent years has received a great deal of attention in the West for her radical views regarding the need for a socialist transformation of society to ensure women's rights. In the 1930s the Islamic right responded to the growth of a feminist and mainly secular consciousness in Egypt with the creation of the Society of Muslim Sisters (later called the Muslim Sisters when it became attached to the Muslim Brotherhood). Certain women in the contemporary Islamist movement, such as Ni'mat Sidqi, articulate the position that women's rights are fully ordained in Islam. Scholarly and intellectual voices have been added to the Islamic right (countering the contention that fundamentalists are "blind followers" who are uneducated or anti-intellectual), such as Aisha Abd al-Rahman, a noted Quranic scholar and university professor who affirms the principle of male authority over women and criticizes the degrading and dehumanizing aspects of modernity.

In the late 1980s the new Islamist movement in Egypt began to show elements of more traditional feminism tied to the secular nationalist movement, with core values extracted from Islam. Aisha Abd al-Rahman argues against the "men from our nation who want to eliminate our humanity in the name of Islam" as she decries "the other men from our nation who, in the name of civilization, want to tear off every covering, material and spiritual."[36] The "truly Islamic" and the "truly feminist" option, she says, is neither immodest dress and identical roles for the sexes in the name of modernity nor sexual segregation and the seclusion of women in the name of Islam. The right path is the one that combines modesty, responsibility, and integration into public life with the Quranic and naturally enjoined distinctions between the sexes.

The most visible expression of this sentiment is the widespread use of some form of Islamic dress by women, a marked difference from the Egypt of Nasser's days. Hijab encompasses a range of dress from wrist and ankle-length clothing with head covering to the more extreme use of the face veil and gloves so as not to reveal any portion of the female body. The latter extreme form of veiling is quite rare. The contemporary debate over the proper role for women in Egypt has focused on clothing, the most obvious symbol of identifying oneself as either Islamic and modest or secular-Western and, presumably, immodest. Some observers note that the revival of Islamic forms of dress has provided a way for the educated, professional woman to participate in public life and be both modern and Islamic. Islamic dress has been adopted most enthusiastically by urban female students and working women.

The Egyptian constitution of 1971, in wording similar to that used in the Iranian constitution, states that women are equal to men in every respect that does not contradict Islamic Shari'a. But the nature of that equality is subject to current interpretations of women's proper role in society. For the middle-class woman who does not have to work outside of the home for wages, the conservative Islamic ideal of confinement provides the perfect rationale for her remaining out of the work force. The state has done its part as well by providing extended parental leave for women (increased to two years without pay) and supporting the use of women in part-time work at reduced hourly wages. Despite these incentives, frequently couched in Islamic terms of "family," to keep women from joining the labor force, the percentage of women in the work force doubled between 1971 and 1981, increasing from 7 percent to 14 percent. These official statistics do not reflect the large number of women working in the informal sector or in domestic production.

In the state-encouraged shift away from Arab socialism following Sadat's arrival to power, Islam was used as a counterideology, which fed the rise of social conservatism. At the same time, because of the feminist movements in the first half of the century and Nasser's program of Arab socialism, women had made important inroads socially, economically, and politically. Margot Badran argues that as the second Islamist wave accelerated in the 1970s and reached a peak in the 1980s, previous gender trends in society, most notably the growing presence of women in the public sphere, were reversed. The Islamist wave idealized women's family and domestic role, reassigning women to the home and urging them out of the workplace, where they had become entrenched. A discourse of modesty, articulated mainly by men, further endangered women's public roles. Segregation of the sexes and a return to the home were part of this rising discourse of modesty articulated in the name of Islam. At the same time, the call to (re)veil reflected and reinforced heightened awareness of women as (vulnerable) sexual beings. Some women argued that hijab facilitated their presence in public. The movement to reveil set some Muslim women apart in a political as well as religious statement. As with the Sudanese NIF women, some Egyptian Islamist women insisted on playing active roles in society, thereby promoting a vision somewhat different from that of the conservative male agenda. However, and again like the NIF women, they continued to extol women's family roles.[37]

Badran writes that coincident with the ascendancy of second-wave conservative Islam was the rise of second-wave feminism associated with Nawal El-Saadawi, whose writings took feminism in a new direction. Her feminism, which called for social, economic, and cultural revolution, was not articulated, like the previous feminist movement, within an Islamic framework. A medical doctor, El-Saadawi published *Al-Mar'a wa al-Jins* (Woman and Sex) in 1972, focusing on physical and psychological disease resulting from sexual oppression of women and attacking the sexual double standard. She enlightened many women and helped raise the consciousness of a whole generation of women students in the democratic movement of the time. However, because she entered an area of taboo, she evoked intense popular criticism. Often misunderstood, her feminism was associated with encouraging immorality of women and violating religion. Feminism per se came to be widely seen in this light.

Organized feminism resurfaced in Egypt in the early 1980s with the creation of the Arab Women's Solidarity Association (AWSA), headed by El-Sadaawi. A less formal but equally committed attempt at collective feminist activism surfaced at the same time, when young women who had belonged to the students' democratic movement of the 1970s came together in a study group in 1984. They investigated the history of feminist movements in Egypt led by Huda Sharawi and others.[38] In the face of the growing Islamist movement, they wanted to recover some of the gains of the Nasser period. In 1986 this group issued the journal *Al-Mar'a al-Jadida* as a means of reaching out to other women. Meanwhile, in 1982 in Mansura, a town in the delta, a group of women who had organized with others in public protest over the Israeli invasion of Lebanon came together to form *Jam'iyyat Bint Al-'Ard,* the Society of the Daughters of the Land. They sought to continue activism along feminist lines, encouraging girls in the town and surrounding rural areas to develop their minds and take part in the life of their societies. Like the previously mentioned group, they also wished to connect with other women, and they, too, started a magazine, called *Bint al-'Ard,* in 1984. The first issue discussed the problem of calls for female domesticity.

In 1985, the rescission of the 1979 personal status law provoked the formation of the Committee for the Defense of the Rights of the Woman and the Family. It succeeded in obtaining the reinstatement of the law, albeit in truncated form, after disagreements among feminists split the united front. The membership in the AWSA grew around the time of the crisis, though it later declined. But the organization developed as a forum for feminist debate and outreach through its publications (including a quarterly magazine, *Nun*), international conferences (in 1986, 1988, and 1990), and periodic seminars. These events have attracted women of different ages, especially younger women, as well as men interested in gender issues. Audiences have also included Islamist women and men. Uneasy about AWSA feminism, the government prevented publication of the fourth issue of *Nun,* which thereafter appeared as an internal organ. AWSA feminism is ideological and confrontational, and despite more recent efforts to marshal religious justifications, it is essentially a secular feminism. El-Saadawi took a strong position against the Gulf War—despite Egypt's support for the Anglo-American war effort. No doubt for all these reasons, the government banned the organization in the summer of 1991.[39]

Feminists continue to respond to conservative Islamist calls for women to retreat to the home. A group of professional women, including lawyers, journalists, professors, and Egypt's first woman ambassador, felt it was critical to detail for women the legal rights they already enjoy in theory so that they may utilize them in practice. Their booklet, *The Legal Rights of the Egyptian Woman* (compiled in the late 1980s), has one chapter dealing with laws concerning work; another chapter, on personal status laws, reminds women that they can include the right to work outside the home as a stipulation in the marriage contract. Relevant international conventions and treaties to which Egypt is signatory are also described in the booklet.

In August 1990 the magazine *Al-Mar'a al-Jadida* issued a letter exhorting women to share their professional experience and skills in sectors such as education, health, and legal affairs through their own networks for the benefit of the broad mass of underprivileged women. Some feminists are engaged in various forms of practical outreach, such as training women in forms of income-generating work. In one village, Shahinda Maqlad, a heroine in the peasant uprising at Kamshish in the 1960s during Nasser's agrarian reform, is involved in similar forms of activism. Badran explains that as a leftist, Maqlad places women's struggle in this wider context of class struggle, and she cannot separate women's struggle from the wider struggle. The members of the New Woman group see their feminism lying between the AWSA brand, which they feel "is focused mainly on women," and the feminism of the left, mainly of the socialist Taggamu Party, which incorporates feminism within the socialist project.

Egyptian feminists and Islamist women remain ideological adversaries. For feminists religion is primarily an individual and personal matter. They do not advocate an Islamic government and they have a pluralist attitude toward society. For Islamists the goal of an Islamic state and society is basic. As in Sudan, it is believed that when this goal is achieved, women, and all other members of the *umma,* will enjoy true liberation. But Badran finds that both secular feminists and Islamist women in certain ways share a commitment to one cause, similar to what Hale found for Sudan. Badran calls this cause "gender activism." Well-known Islamist women activists in Egypt such as Zainab al-Ghazali and Safinaz Kazim are hostile to secular and Westernized feminism and extol women's roles as wives and mothers. But they also stress the importance for women to work in society, including *da'wa* (proselytizing) in the society and within one's profession. They believe in and preach the message of liberation of women within Islam.

The Turban Movement in Turkey

Although it defends the conservative view that women's primary capacities should be as mothers and housewives, the Islamist movement in Turkey has nevertheless come to accept a more active public role for Muslim women. In the past, Islamic groups were ambivalent and indecisive about mobilizing women for their political cause. The neo-Islamic National Salvation Party of the 1970s, for example, had a strong youth organization but was hesitant to establish affiliated women's associations. Once the Iranian Revolution showed the power militant Muslim women could wield, Islamic groups in Turkey began to profess active participation of women within the movement.[40] But in 1980 the military government led by General Kenan Evren, which had already cracked down on the Marxist left, also banned the wearing of Islamic dress at universities.

The most visible example of this new role assigned to Muslim women was their confrontation with state authorities over the question of covering their heads while attending the university. This "Turban Movement" started as a protest against the legal prohibition of the Islamic headscarf for women students; gradually it became an issue of militant Muslim politics. The students wearing the turban claimed to do so because their faith demanded it and argued that their freedom of conscience was under constitutional guarantee. But what originally started as sporadic and unorganized demands for freedom of entry into universities soon turned into organized sit-ins and demonstrations. Interestingly, the Turban Movement and the participation of women in it became instrumental in radicalizing the Islamist cause.

The education of Muslim women is a second example of the new understanding concerning women's role within the movement. The Islamists view the education of women as important primarily in terms of women's crucial duty of raising and socializing children. It is argued that educated women are better equipped to raise healthy children and ensure a good education for them. Indeed, a major Islamic magazine for women regularly publishes articles on modern methods of child care, suggestions for healthy living, advice on medical problems, and the like, obviously addressing women with some degree of education. But more important, the Islamic movement has come to realize that it needs its own educated women in certain professions, such as gynecology. Thus, there are contradictory implications for women within the Turkish Islamic movement, as there are for women in Sudan and Egypt.

In a study of a major Islamic journal for women, Yesim Arat argued that for the women who make up the overwhelming majority of editors and correspondents contributing to its pages, the work experience provides the opportunity to choose alternative lifestyles. Instead of being confined by the conservative backgrounds from which they come, work with the journal opens up new avenues for a search for more authentic, less community-defined, and perhaps eventually liberationist life patterns. Similarly, in a study of women wearing the turban based on extensive interviews, Nilufer Göle argued that the sociological significance of the movement rests not on an understanding of the ideological orientation and religious beliefs of these women but on an analysis of their social practices. She points out that on the one hand, women with the turban refer to the basic foundation of Muslim society through the symbol of the veil, a reminder of the role assigned to women in the private sphere and of the segregation of the sexes. On the other hand, through their claim to university education, they are already leaving this private sphere and developing individual strategies. Göle notes the paradox of these ambiguous traditional and modern identities.[41] Indeed, this ambiguity is becoming evident to some within the movement. For example, a leading weekly journal published a cover story under the title "Feminists with Turbans" in which a number of interviews with women within the Islamist movement showed that they were as rebellious against the roles assigned to them by patriarchal society as are their secular feminist counterparts. According to the journal, the discussion of patriarchy, feminism, and women's status in Islam was one of the most heatedly debated issues among Islamist groups.

Another study found that Islamist magazines target specific groups. One magazine contained many articles on medicine and health, sections on literature and history, and items on dress patterns, food recipes, and consumer tips. These assume an affinity with the bourgeois lifestyle, as well as a certain educational background. Acar describes the magazine's target group of readers as middle-class women of cities and towns. As relatively educated women, they have been subjected to the contradictory messages of gender equality and freedom on the one hand and the centrality of marriage and motherhood on the other. As such they are likely to experience role conflict, have problems of identity definition, and suffer from unfulfilled expectations. The magazine's Islamist message identifies Westernization as the source of all problems and offers reassurance and an alternative. Another magazine contains radical and uncompromising articles on veiling and sex-segregation that can be seen as an attempt to enhance women's security by minimizing competition with men. This same magazine also expresses an approval of an equitable division of labor between spouses at home.[42]

Parallel to the Islamist women's movement, an autonomous feminist movement emerged in Turkey during the 1980s. Unlike the Marxist left, which suffered seriously following the 1980 military coup, Turkish feminism flourished, in part because it was seen as an outgrowth of Kemalism and an extension of Turkish state feminism since the 1920s. According to Yesim Arat, the feminist movement has helped promote Kemalist goals, namely liberalism, democratization, and secularism.[43]

The Intifada and Hijab

The emergence of Islamism among the Palestinians closely follows the pattern of causes and consequences delineated above. The failure of the PLO to win its goal of a secular-democratic state, whether as a substitute for Jewish Israel or as part of the two-state solution (that is, a separate Palestinian state on the West Bank), is one cause of the rise of Islamism among Palestinians. As one newspaper account reports, "Gazans grew frustrated by 20 years of political failure by the PLO." Ziad Abu Amer, a political science professor at Bir Zeit University, states, "People resort to cultural references, like the veil, especially when they perceive their whole national existence is threatened."[44] The indignity of the Israeli occupation of the West Bank and the awful living conditions in the refugee camps of Gaza provide fertile ground for the rise of militant Islamism. The daily migration into Israel of more than half the work force had profound effects on Gazan society. Drug abuse and alcoholism were perceived as major problems related to the experiences of Gazan workers in Israel. Elements of the left had initially tried to stop workers from going into Israel, where they were in all events a superexploited labor force, but this only created resentment, because the left could provide no practical alternatives.

An Islamist group called Mujama emerged in Gaza during the 1980s and proposed a practical solution: a return to the moral social code as embodied in their interpretation of Islam. Mujama activists also turned their attention to women's appearance, at first encouraging, then pressuring women to cover their heads. Graffiti on walls would exhort women to wear hijab; in May 1988 religious youths broke into classrooms and demanded that schoolgirls wear hijab. Gaza is where hijab has proliferated and where non-Islamist women have been harassed, threatened, even assaulted. Hammami reports that Palestinian women of peasant background have always worn a version of hijab, partly as a sign of their rural origins and partly because their socioeconomic status did not permit the wearing of "modern dress." But in recent years hijab has been politicized to the point where by December 1988, one year after the intifada erupted, "it was almost impossible for women to walk around Gaza without wearing some form of headcover." Islamist vigilantes have also taken to denouncing coeducational institutes, such as the French Cultural Center and the British Council in Gaza, and have attacked what they perceived to be "gambling houses and dance halls."[45]

The politicization of gender and the preoccupation with women's bodies has therefore occurred in the context of economic dependency and malaise and the crisis of the existing political ideologies of secular nationalism. In Gaza as elsewhere, Islamists have put liberals and nationalists on the defensive by raising the sensitive issue of women's bodies and women's liberation. Thus, when the Unified National Leadership of the

Uprising (UNLU) finally issued a statement denouncing the harassment of women, the first point it made was: "We are against excessive vanity in personal dress and use of cosmetics during these times. This is applied to the same degree for men and women." The statement also refers in a deferential way to traditional social norms, claiming that the acts "are foreign to our traditions and Islamic religion." Thus, the PLO nationalists have taken a defensive and apologetic stance vis-à-vis the religious trend and more specifically toward Hamas (as the Islamist movement is now called).[46]

Nahla Abdo interviewed women activists in Gaza and found that they are not docile in the face of Islamist male aggression. They resent the imposition of the veil, blame the Palestinian leadership for not taking a strong enough stand in defense of women, and stress the irrelevance of the issue of hijab to the intifada. They are also cognizant of the salience of class in the matter of hijab, for it is the women in the streets, in the fields, and doing public work, as Abdo notes, that are being harassed. Upper-class women in Gaza do not appear to be bothered. As one woman put it: "They hide in their big cars and no one attacks them or throws stones at them."[47]

In the wake of growing Islamism and the fundamentalists' intimidation of women, many Palestinian women activists are beginning to call on the Palestinian nationalist movement to link the struggle for an independent state to a broad program of democratization and sociocultural modernization, especially on issues of women's rights. According to two West Bank feminists, however, the efforts of the women's movement to link democratization within the nationalist movement to the progress of women is shaped by fierce constraints and conditions: 35 percent of Palestinians in the West Bank and Gaza alone are unemployed and close to 80 percent live beneath the poverty line. They add: "A new apartheid-like pass system bans West Bank residents from entering Israel (including Arab East Jerusalem) and cuts the West Bank in two. Residents need permits to exit from Gaza and yet another permit to be in the West Bank. Under such conditions, the effort to initiate a democratic debate is a very difficult ordeal indeed."[48]

Nevertheless, at least one audacious feminist group, El Fanar ("The Lighthouse"), was formed in early 1991 with the explicit aim of establishing an independent women's movement outside the confines of political parties in order to more effectively push for women's rights. According to Mana Hassan, a founder, "It is our conviction that women must organize themselves in an autonomous feminist context. . . . [T]he existing political parties refuse to confront the patriarchal traditions which oppress women."[49]

Veiling and Activism in Iran

The revolution in Iran was especially important for demonstrating that massive mobilization of women could occur within an Islamist framework, but the political agenda for which women were demonstrating was, for the most part, unacceptable to the West and widely viewed as antifeminist. As noted by Nayereh Tohidi, the anti-American and anti-Western aspect of the Iranian Revolution reduced the potential impact that such large-scale participation of women in a revolutionary process might have had on Western public opinion. It has been difficult, at the level of ideology as well as objective fact, to make a fair assessment of what progress or retrogression has occurred with respect to the status of women in Iran since the revolution. Consider the following comment on the situation in prerevolutionary Iran: "Iran adopted the worst of the West, including the exploitation of women's bodies to sell modern merchandise. Because we didn't tackle the real feminist issues, we just went from being sex objects Oriental style to being sex objects Occidental style. Worse yet, we often got squeezed in between. Under such circumstances the *chador* [veil] could be a tool for reasserting a woman's human dignity by forcing people to respond to her talents and personality rather than to her body alone."[50]

Sanasarian's study documents the women's rights movement in Iran from the turn of the century up until Khomeini's victory, discussing the corruption of the movement under the Shah. Women in the anti-Shah movement did not make feminism an issue and therefore did not achieve much by the overthrow of the Shah. The official repression of women's rights under Khomeini is understood by Sanasarian as a hopeless step backward for Iranian women. Many other studies, particularly those written in the early 1980s, express similar views.[51]

Yet the state and the Islamist agenda have strong female supporters and representatives. Among them were the Baseej Women, who numbered about 4,000 and were organized in 1984 as an arm of the Islamic state. They were a volunteer force who underwent military training and were assigned to guard government ministries and banks. Entrusting women with such public responsibility was inconsistent with the earlier decisions of the Islamic Republic to remove women from the ranks of public officialdom, as in 1979–1980 when women holding judgeships and top government posts were forced to resign. More recently, the government has reversed some of its earlier discriminatory policies regarding women and repudiated the pronatalist policy of the early years.[52]

A question that has recently been raised in the Iranian case, and which is pertinent to the other cases examined, is whether one can speak of "Islamic feminism." Those women who adhered to the model of Islamic womanhood and participated in the revolution as Khomeini supporters became symbols of the transformation of society, thus gaining status as bearers and maintainers of cultural heritage and religious values. Khomeini himself frequently praised those women by calling them "the real teachers of men in the noble movement of Islam" and "the symbol of the actualization of Islamic ideals." Using a term coined by Pierre Bourdieu, we may say that these women have acquired the requisite "cultural capital."

Participation in politics and the social sphere both during and after the revolution has been a turning point in the lives of those women, most of whom have a traditional middle-class background. Of course, the official mobilization of women was not intended to liberate women but to strengthen the Islamic state. Nevertheless, the very politicization of women and their continuous exposure to ideological and political challenges undermine efforts to redomesticate and privatize them. These women, who now have gained status, legitimacy, and respect, feel rather empowered and self-confident. Tohidi points out that they have even appropriated the political purpose of the veil to their own advantage by arguing that in an Islamic society regulated and sanctified by clerics and immunized against Westoxication by hijab, women's public role can no longer be a source of *fitna*. I would add that because these women are "ideologically correct" and possess the right symbolic capital, they cannot be accused of *gharbzadegi;* rather, they are taken seriously in Iran.

Tohidi finds that two developments have influenced Islamist women's perception of gender roles, leading them to a reformist approach more in line with Islamic ideologues such as the late Ali Shariati than with fundamentalists. One is the impact of the international ideological and political campaign against social roles for women, a campaign embodied in the orthodox doctrine of Islam and the government's sexist policies; the other is Islamic women's own social praxis and daily confrontation with patriarchal barriers. These women demand to see Islam practiced in its "true spirit," under which they assume oppressed women can find salvation. They have started their own study groups, their own associations, their own publications, their exegesis and interpretation of the Quran, gradually generating a new woman-oriented reformist discourse in Islam. For instance, Maryam Gorji, a former representative in the Islamic Parliament who was known as a token Islamic female indifferent to and ignorant of women's issues, is writing a woman-centered reinterpretation of women's images in the Quran. Khomeini's own daughter, Zahra Mostafavi, founded the Association of Muslim Women in 1989; copying Western women, she has organized international women's conferences in Tehran. A state-affiliated Women's Council and several women's commissions have been established to study and assist women with their specific concerns.[53] Although during the 1980s women's representation in the Islamist Parliament (Majlis) never exceeded 4 women out of 270 members, some of them were quite vocal in raising women's issues and criticizing the government's policies. In particular they were successful in intervening in areas such as the family and education. In the parliamentary elections of 1992, nine women were elected. The leading figures among these Islamic activist women are usually associated with men in power—for example, Zahra Rahnavard, the wife of former Prime Minister Musavi; Azam Taleghani, the daughter of a late prominent ayatollah; and Mrs. Rajai, widow of the assassinated prime minister. These women have been influential in the recent reforms in family law and in social and educational policies. Like the women observed by Margot Badran in Egypt, these Iranian Islamist women are "gender activists," if not feminists. For these reasons, Tohidi concludes that it is difficult to state decisively whether the status of women is better or worse under the Islamists than under the previous system in Iran.

And how do non-Islamist middle-class Iranian women view their roles and status in postrevolutionary Iran? A unique survey conducted by sociologist Shahin Gerami in the summer of 1989 found that although middle-class Iranian women accept the idea of "complementarity of roles" and endorse "feminine" occupations, they reject notions of men's intellectual superiority, support advanced education for women as well as men, and insist upon gender equality within the household. In particular, they reject sex-segregation.[54]

▲ Conclusions: Women's Responses to Islamist Movements

Islamist movements arise in the context of economic failure, political authoritarianism, and changes in the patriarchal system, with the growing visibility of educated and employed women. As Bassam Tibi has put it, the function of Islamist movements, on the positive side, is to bridge change and absorb disappointment. Its negative side is that "Islam does not offer any concrete future structural perspectives and therefore cannot contribute to the solution of urgent social and economic problems of the Middle East."[55] Tibi wrote these words in 1983, and years later the record has shown that Islamist states have evinced a marked incapacity to tackle economic issues. Neither the Zia ul-Haq regime in Pakistan, nor the Islamic governments in Iran, nor the Islamists of Sudan have been able to adequately address poverty, unemployment, economic growth, and income redistribution. Rather, they have focused their attention on the spheres of law and culture, most significantly on gender and the position of women.

Islamization draws on distinct gender and class patterns prevailing in society. Women's responses to Islamist movements generally have followed from class and social positions. These responses show the impact Islamist ideologies have had not only on governments and subsequent legal decisions affecting women but also on the women's movement itself. Women's responses range from participation in the fundamentalist movement to advocacy of reform within the frame of Islam to pursuit of a secular state and secular laws. In spite of this wide range of tendencies and strategies, most of them have internalized some of the concepts developed and used by Islamists. Hélie-Lucas argues that women have accepted the notion of an external monolithic enemy and the fear of betraying their identity. The latter is defined as group identity rather than identity as women in the group. To a large extent, "they also accept tradition not as a living history that informs the present and future but as a dead body, inextricably linked to the group identity, to be revived."[56] And as we have seen, women acknowledge their central role in Islamist movements.

Women's internalization of Islamist philosophy, concepts, and biased hypotheses has many consequences at the level of strategy. Hélie-Lucas argues that internalizing the notion that Islam or the community is in danger results in an ordering of priorities established by the male leadership and an indefinite postponement of issues of equality and empowerment. As we have seen, Palestinian women are trying to build an autonomous movement, but priority is still given to the liberation struggle.

In many Middle Eastern countries, especially where Islamist movements are strong, women who try to defend their rights are frequently accused of being Westernized. As was the left before them, they are accused of importing a foreign ideology. But whereas the left's response was to point to universal values of social justice, women seem to find it difficult to argue for women's rights as human rights or as universal values of social justice. To be sure, women's equality and autonomy, gender roles, and the family are more sensitive issues than is the position of labor, for example. Consequently, many women try to demonstrate that they are genuinely rooted in their own culture rather than in "foreign" ideologies, that they do not side with external enemies, and that they are not alienated. Hélie-Lucas writes that they spend considerable energy in trying to distinguish themselves from Western feminists. Many groups in Muslim countries and communities devote time to research their feminist ancestors, not only to recover their own history but also to seek legitimacy and stop accusations of Westernization by Islamists and rightists. For example, Fatima Mernissi, the noted Moroccan feminist, has traversed the road from sociology of sex roles to historic excavations of Muslim women rulers and theologians; Aziza al-Hibri attempts a feminist exegesis of Islamic theology. In so doing, they seek to reclaim, as do their Christian and Jewish sisters in the West, their religion and religious history for themselves.

In this general context, Hélie-Lucas identifies three main strategies in the women's movement. In one strategy, "entryism," women join fundamentalist groups. This strategy avoids challenging identity and frees women from the fear of betrayal; moreover, fundamentalist groups have both the will and the funds to offer their members various gratifications and advantages, such as grants to study, free medical care, and loans without interest. Women followers also benefit from social and parental recognition and the ability to choose a husband within the group instead of going through an arranged marriage. In this context, hijab makes possible women's entry into and activity within the public spaces dominated by men. Another strategy is that of women working for change from within the frame of Islam, both at the level of religion and at the level of culture. Some women theologians try to promote a liberation theology by reviving the tradition of reinterpreting the Quran. Similarly, women historians attempt to track and recapture Islamic women's history. Even if these approaches are seen as threatening by fundamentalists, they do not cut women off from the masses. Such women contest the accusation of betrayal by closing themselves within an Islamic frame of thought. The third strategy is for women to fight for secularism and laws reflecting the present understanding of human rights in the world today. To these women, hijab is a form of social control and a patriarchal legacy, and they reject it, as they do Muslim personal laws.

One must conclude, therefore, that in Middle Eastern and Muslim countries there are two women's movements—one secular and liberal/left in orientation, the other decidedly Islamist. Both are concerned about the status of women.

To the extent that they remain with the Islamist framework, reform-minded women will face ideological contradictions and conflicts with Quranic injunctions. Is there a common ground between what may tentatively be called "Islamist feminists" and secular feminists? Are there issues around which both groups could unite in a common struggle for the advancement of women? In the case of Iran, some have suggested the examination of the possibilities for dialogue and strategies for issue-oriented coalitions between Islamic and secular feminists.[57] Literacy, education, employment, family planning, and maternal health are issues that could unite both groups. But the dividing line is constituted by two formidable issues: hijab and Shari'a.

Within an Islamist movement tensions may arise between men and women. For example, Zahra Rahnavard of Iran, a fierce defender of hijab and of Islamization, has bitterly criticized official and vigilante attacks on *bad-hijabi mal*-veiling, which may entail wearing bright colors or showing some hair. Elsewhere, women Islamists may find that in a situation of high unemployment they may encounter discrimination in hiring and recruitment practices, despite their technical skills or attainment of advanced degrees. The inevitable gender contradictions may lead them to question hijab and Shari'a as expressions of patriarchal authority after all.

Middle Eastern feminists walk the difficult tightrope between reclaiming a national identity and reaffirming progressive elements of the indigenous culture on the one hand and rejecting regressive traditions by subscribing to women's liberation and gender equity on the other. In so doing, women are contributing enormously to the process of modernity and democratization in the Middle East. It may be that there are different cultural and political paths to gender equality and female empowerment. One possible outcome—certainly a surprising one—of Islamist movements, of the politicization of gender, and of women's activism for and against these movements could very well be the subversion of the patriarchal order and its rapid demise. In tandem with mass female education and the entry of women into the formal work force, the expanded activities of women's organizations will be the strongest challenge to patriarchy and the neopatriarchal state. As Sharabi has put it, "The women's movement . . . is the detonator which will explode the neopatriarchal society from within. If allowed to grow and come into its own, it will become the permanent shield against patriarchal regression, the cornerstone of future modernity."[58]

▲ 6

Women in the Islamic Republic of Iran: Inequality, Accommodation, Resistance

How have women fared in the Islamic Republic of Iran since the Iranian Revolution of 1979? How have their legal status and social positions changed? And to what can this be attributed? This chapter examines the changing and contradictory status of Iranian women over the past decade by examining fertility, literacy and education, and employment. These are fruitful indicators of women's status, of women's capacity for mobilization and collective action, and of their contribution (actual or potential) to social change. We begin by considering the political-ideological context shaping women's status and conclude by showing that this milieu itself has been modified by economic imperatives and women's resistance.

▲ Ideological Images of Women and the Sex/Gender System

We can identify three elements of the dominant ideology in the Islamic Republic that have distinct implications for women's status: domesticity, difference, and danger. Together they represent for women, and particularly for modernized middle-class women, the extraordinary ideological pressures of postrevolutionary Iran. The fate of Iranian women since the consolidation of the Islamic Republic has been extensively examined. Guity Nashat expressed a common view when she wrote that one of the principal objectives of the leaders of the Islamist regime was "to restore women to what they consider women's primary role in society: domestic responsibility."[1] In the view of the new authorities, such a role is in keeping with the teachings of Islam:

> [As] the new leaders see it, while it was the religious duty of both men and women to rise up against oppression under the Shah, now that the "right type" of government is in power, women's religious duty requires

that they concentrate on fulfilling their real task of taking care of their husbands and children, and that they allow the men to run the affairs of government. Therefore, while extolling the role women played in overthrowing the Shah, the government is urging women to resume their traditional duties as wives and mothers.

Nashat added: "Judging by the results over the past three years, their efforts to push women out of public life and back into the home have been successful."[2]

The ideology of domesticity is closely tied to the ideology of gender difference, whereby the physical, physiological, and biological differences between men and women are translated into universal and immutable differences in their social and intellectual capacities. Because of physiological and psychological differences, husbands and wives are supposed to have different roles and expectations. However, they are not "different but equal"; there is a hierarchy operating here, as in all spheres of life, and a relationship of domination and subordination in which the man is master and sets the rules. In this hierarchy, women are regarded as the weaker sex, commonly referred to by the term *zaeefeh* ("weakling"). In her survey of magazine articles on the ethics of marriage, Haleh Afshar noted their view that "the greatest mistake of the ungodly and materialistic societies is the assumption that marriage is a partnership and a collaboration between the spouses. Such assumptions deny all the feminine attributes and ignore the female characteristics of modesty, chastity and shame." She goes on to state that this total subordination is prescribed because men are declared to be shouldering the heavy burden of paid employment and are required to respond to the call for participating in the holy war (*jihad*). According to Afshar, the Prophet Muhammad is quoted by the women's journal *Zan-e Rouz* as saying that "domesticity is the woman's holy war."[3]

Afshar has studied the writings of the late Ayatollahs Khomeini and Mutahhari and concluded that these Islamic theologians were deeply convinced of the natural inferiority of women, which they presumed on the basis of their construction of the reason/emotion dichotomy.[4] Even Hojatoleslam Hashemi Rafsanjani, considered by many a moderate on social as well as economic issues, once said: "A man's brain is larger. Women mature too fast. The breathing power of men's lungs is greater and women's heartbeats are faster. . . . Men heed reasoning and logic, whereas most women tend to be emotional. . . . Courage and daring are stronger in men."[5] But in reading further, one finds that these and other Islamic figures also show an awareness of women's modern susceptibilities and their desire for equal treatment. For example, Ayatollah Yahya Nuri has asserted that despite their emotionality, women are not inferior in Islam; they are not *equal*. but they are not inferior.[6] Ayatollah Khomeini himself was quoted as saying that Shi'a Islam not only does not exclude women from social life but actually "elevates them to a platform where they belong, a higher platform."[7] Moreover, he maintained that "to wear the hijab does not imply suppression or seclusion."[8] According to Ferdows, Khomeini "refers with pride" to women's right under Islam to own property as an indication of their economic independence.[9]

It can be argued that exploring the late Ayatollah Khomeini's words on the subject of women would be of little value because his views were, as Ferdows and Afshar have stressed, foursquare in the conservative traditionalist school. But it is interesting to note that even Ayatollah Khomeini could make conciliatory comments regarding women's status and had to concede certain things to women. For example, in an address to a group of women in Qum on March 6, 1979, Khomeini praised Iranian women, saying, "I take pride in all the courageous deeds accomplished by the women of Iran . . . for you have been in the vanguard of our triumph and have encouraged the men." Elsewhere, he states, "Islam made women equal with men; in fact, it shows a concern for women that it does not show for men." Finally, he asserts, "In our revolutionary movement, women have likewise earned more credit than men, for it was the women who not only displayed courage themselves, but also had reared men of courage. Like the Noble Quran itself, women have the function of rearing and training true men. If nations were deprived of courageous women to rear true men, they would decline and collapse."[10]

The themes of gender difference (in fact, gender inequality) and the need for female domesticity are linked to another theme: the danger inherent in the female nature. Fatna Sabbah's study examined those Islamic writings that harp on the spurious theme of female sexuality (or omnisexuality) and enticement. It is the considered opinion of many Islamic ideologues that men are eminently susceptible to female lures; the mere presence of women is said to undermine men's better judgment, their sanity and rationality.[11] For example, the late Ayatollah Mutahhari has written: "Where would a man be more productive, where he is studying in all-male institutions or where he is sitting next to a girl whose skirt reveals her thighs? Which man can do more work, he who is constantly exposed to arousing and exciting faces of made-up women in the street, bazaar, office, or factory, or he who does not have to face such sights?" Mutahhari goes on to say:

> The truth is that the disgraceful lack of the modest dress in Iran (before the Revolution) whereby we were even moving ahead of America, is a product of the corrupt Western capitalist societies. It is one of the results of the worship of money and the pursuance of sexual fulfillment that is prevalent in Western capitalism. It is one of the means they use to manipulate human society and stimulate them by this force to become consumers of their products. If an Iranian woman only wants to put on makeup for her legal husband or only wants to get dressed up for gatherings

with women, she will not be a consumer of Western products. She will not be obliged to unconsciously corrupt the morals of young boys and girls, to weaken them so that they are no longer active members of society which is to the benefit of the exploiters.[12]

These ideas were advanced to justify hijab, or the modest attire required of women. They were also put forward as a critique of women's participation in the public sphere and, in some instances, as reason to reduce women's presence or to ban them altogether from certain arenas. In the early years of the Islamic Republic, the three dimensions of the ideology on women found their material expression in legislation and policy. The 1979 Islamic constitution has several clauses that pertain to the status and social positions of women. The preamble emphasizes the significance of the family: "The family is the fundamental unit of society and the main center of growth and transcendence for humanity." It also stresses women's primary role as mother: "A woman . . . will no longer be regarded as a 'thing' or a tool serving consumerism and exploitation. In regaining her important duty and most respectful role of mother in the nourishing of human beings who belong to the school of thought, as a pioneer along with men, as a warrior in the active living battlefields, the result will be her accepting a more serious responsibility. In the views of Islam, she will assume higher values and beneficence."[13]

The pronatalist sentiment that follows from the ideology of domesticity led to the discouragement of contraception and the banning of abortion; contraceptive devices were removed from pharmacies. In addition to institutionalizing domesticity, the constitution established Shari'a as the law of the land. Article 4 read: "All the laws and regulations concerning civil, criminal, financial, economic, administrative, cultural [and] military affairs must be based on the Islamic standards. This principle will be applied to all the articles of the Constitution and all other laws and regulations."[14]

The constitution of the Islamic Republic was put to a referendum in early December 1979 and was approved by the populace. But between February and December official statements had been made and steps taken that alarmed educated, non-Islamist women of the upper middle class. These women mounted the first serious challenge to the authority and legitimacy of the new leadership. In early March 1979, several thousand Iranian women demonstrated against the new sexual politics, especially Khomeini's statements that women should appear in public in hijab. Women also staged a sit-in at the Ministry of Justice and carried placards that read: "In the dawn of freedom there is no freedom." There was a week of meetings, rallies, and demonstrations, during which non-Islamist women expressed their outrage and anxiety over the issue of hijab. Prime Minister Bazargan announced that Khomeini's statement had been misunderstood by some genuine women militants and consciously manipulated by left-wing troublemakers. As Azar Tabari relates it, Bazargan said there would be no compulsory veiling in government offices and that it was the view of the Imam that women should be guided, not forced, to accept the veil. In fact, hijab was legislated the following year, when the Islamists' position strengthened. In the meantime, other steps were taken to redefine and regulate gender. The Ministry of Education banned coeducation, and the Ministry of Justice declared it would not recognize women judges. Childcare centers began to be closed down. Several Caspian Sea resort towns instituted sex-segregated beaches. The Family Protection Act of 1967 (amended in 1973) was abrogated and replaced by Shari'a laws, effectively denying women the right to initiate divorce.[15]

Another important factor in the formulation of the new gender codes was the notion of the excessively Westernized woman and the cultural danger she represented. Women were regarded as having been most vulnerable to *gharbzadegi*, to deculturation and imperialist culture. The stereotypical Westoxicated woman was a middle-class individual with no productive contributions or reproductive responsibilities. If she worked at all, she was a secretary, and her work was largely decorative and dispensable. Her access to money was considered a waste, because it was used to cover the cost of her own clothing, cosmetics, and imported consumer goods. She was preoccupied with her physical appearance and wore miniskirts and excessive makeup. She would mingle freely with men, smoke, drink, and laugh in public. If she read at all, she read a romantic novel; she picked her role models from among Hollywood stars, American soap operas, and pop singers. Her light-headedness and lack of interest in politics and national issues made her easy prey for commercialization and contamination by the West.[16] The solution to this vulnerability to the slings and arrows of the imperialists was compulsory veiling.

In the summer of 1980 veiling was made compulsory and throughout the decade was strictly enforced. Women were not permitted to wear cosmetics or perfume in public. Women's voices were banned from radio and female singers barred from television. Only those foreign films were imported in which actresses had hair coverings (an unintended consequence of which was to spur a lively and serious national film industry). An ideological campaign was waged to tie women to home and family. Women were restricted from certain professions, such as law, and women university students not allowed into programs such as agricultural engineering and veterinary sciences. The regime assumed a pronatalist stance, banning abortions and distribution of contraceptives, extolling the Muslim family, and lowering the age of consent. Women's responses to the new gender codes varied by class and political/ideological orientation, ranging from enthusiastic support to acquiescence to outright hostility. Some Islamist women criticized some of the changes, in particular compulsory veiling, which they felt would alienate many supporters of the Islamic revolution.

Fereshteh Hashemi pointed out that veiling is meant to be undertaken voluntarily by believers, saying, "Not only have we made the religious dress a job requirement for believing women and even for non-believers (of the religious minorities, the Christians and Jews), we are even specifying form and color of dresses—something that is not obligatory in Islam. . . . And if the Islamic system wants to establish Islamic norms in society in order to combat Westoxication, why is this done only to women?"[17]

Another critical view of compulsory veiling from Islamist women was expressed at a July 1980 seminar by Azam Taleghani, Zahra Rahnavard, Shahin Etezad Tabatabai, and Ansieh Mofidi. They suggested that "instead of imposition of hijab on women, public decency—meaning modest dressing and not using makeup—should be considered all over the country and lack of its observance punished," though only by those in charge, rather than by vigilantes. As an example of punishment, they offered the case of Algeria, where "this was done by painting the legs of women in short skirts."[18]

A rather apposite view of compulsory veiling was expressed by the communist Fada'i Khalq (Majority) organization: "The Islamic Republic of Iran claims that the imposition on women of the Islamic veil is a step towards the 'moral cleansing' of society and eradication of the degenerate culture of the monarchical order. Without smashing the social and economic foundations of contemporary capitalism upon which the monarchical order was based, however, cultural degeneration cannot be uprooted. Furthermore, the veil is totally irrelevant to the uplifting or degeneration of culture."[19]

In fact, the veil was far from irrelevant to the regime. The model of womanhood the Islamists sought to impose on the population was an integral part of the political-cultural project of Islamization. The transformation of Iran was seen as incumbent upon the transformation of women. (Re)definitions of gender are frequently central to political and cultural change, as we have seen in earlier chapters.

▲ Contradictions of the Islamist Discourse

The passages in the constitution and the statements by Islamic leaders discussed above are fairly straightforward in their approach to women, gender relations, and religious duty: the rights and responsibilities of men and women are not equal, women's role is as wife and mother, and the breadwinners and fighters are the men. However, this is not the whole story, for other passages in the constitution, as well as speeches by members of the political elite and practices in Iran, contradicted the notion of the inferiority of women and their relegation to the private sphere. For example, Article 20 of the constitution states: "Every individual citizen, whether male or female, will have equal protection of the law and all human, political, economic, social and cultural rights will be based upon Islamic precepts." Article 21 guarantees women's rights "according to Islamic criteria," but again emphasizes wives, mothers, widows, the family, and children. Article 28 states: "Every person has the right to pursue the occupation of his or her choice, insofar as this is not contrary to Islam, the public interest or the rights of others." These articles exemplify the contradictory and ambiguous ideological/political prescriptions vis-à-vis women in the Islamic Republic. On the one hand the constitution affirms gender equality; on the other it presents the "great qualifier"—the "laws of Islam"—which, as no one would deny (not even the clerics themselves), impose on women's behavior regulations of a very different order from those imposed on men's. For example, as Nashat has pointed out, the constitution may assert that men and women are equal, but Islamic law does not treat men and women equally, certainly not in such areas as divorce, child custody, polygamy, inheritance, and court testimony.[20]

In the first two years of the Islamic Republic, policies were enacted that adversely affected women and curtailed their participation in the public sphere. These policies resulted, in the first instance, in the loss of employment by elite women, who were the main target of the regime's policies. Women's participation in the legal profession was the first and most seriously affected area. A new law barred women from acting as judges; women judges who had been appointed during the Pahlavi era were dismissed. This action was followed by the removal of many women from top-level government posts; they were forced either to accept lower-level jobs or to retire completely. Many women in high posts resigned or retired rather than endure the hijab. The regime also passed a number of laws to encourage women to return to the home and ensure that they remained there. Various retirement programs allowed women who had worked as little as fifteen years to retire without loss of entitlements.[21] Later, another law was passed allowing working couples to enjoy the full benefit of the wife's salary if she decided to stay at home. Women with working husbands were told to forgo employment to open up positions for males. Many day-care centers that had been opened in various factories and government agencies under the previous regime were closed. As urban labor-force participation and, more specifically, access to prestigious professions are important indicators of women's status, these policies were considered by many writers to have resulted in a sharp decline in the position of women.

The fate of Iranian women immediately following the establishment of the Islamic Republic is not historically unprecedented, nor is it unique to Islam (or the Iranian Shi'a variant), as we have seen in Chapter 3. Some studies have noted the connection between authoritarian regimes and the control of women. As feminist historian Joan Scott has written:

> Whether at a crucial moment for Jacobin hegemony in the French
> Revolution, at the point of Stalin's bid for controlling authority, during
> the implementation of Nazi policy in Germany, or with the triumph in
> Iran of the Ayatollah Khomeini, domination, strength, central authority,
> and ruling power have been legitimized as masculine . . . and that coding
> has been literalized in laws (forbidding women's political participation,
> outlawing abortion, prohibiting wage-earning by mothers, imposing
> female dress codes) that put women in their place.[22]

The regime's attitude toward women was, in one sense, part of a broad
political/cultural/class project directed against the Westernized modern
middle class. For all men, ties and short-sleeved shirts in public were
banned. The outward signs of an Islamist man were a beard and a tieless
shirt buttoned at the neck. The foreign minister, Dr. Ali Akbar Velayati,
popularized a custom-made shirt that came to be known as *pirhan-e velayati,* or the Velayati shirt. But beyond this, the new public policies reflected
a reinforcement of patriarchy and its Islamic variant, whose defining feature is gender segregation.

Writing in 1985, Afshar and others noted the purging of women from
civil service and government agencies and suggested that domestic work or
the drudgery of badly paid activities in the informal sector were the only
real options for women in the Islamic Republic. "With the sole exception of
the right to vote, Iranian women are in all other respects formally recognized as second-class citizens who have no place in the public arena."[23]

The early literature focused on the content of clerics' statements and
speeches and emphasized the discriminatory laws against women. There
was also a tendency to engage in textual analysis of the Quran's references
to women as a way of understanding or explaining the new gender ideology
and the policies pertaining to women. These accounts could not explain
either contradictions in state policy or resistance on the part of some female
citizens. Analyses also glossed over the differentiation among Iranian
women and what this implied for the efficacy of the new ideology and policies. Pat Higgins offered an approach that differed from that of the majority
of writers in a 1985 essay on women and social change in the Islamic
Republic. She explained the relative paucity of opposition by Iranian
women to the official ideology of sex roles by suggesting that neither legal
changes nor social pressures had had a major impact on the lives of the
majority of the female population, who were rural and poor.[24]

One inconsistency in the Islamist ideology and discourse was that,
notwithstanding hijab and Shari'a, and despite sentiments on the part of certain Islamic ideologues against female participation in politics, women
retained the franchise. Nor were they barred from higher education,
although a quota system was established. There were fields of study that
were closed to women, open to women on a quota basis, restricted to
women only, or open to men only. Moreover, due to the chronic shortage of

medical personnel and in the interest of maintaining gender-segregated medical care, women were encouraged to study medicine. Women were allowed to run for Parliament (the first, second, and third Majlis had between two and four female parliamentarians) and hold administrative and supervisory posts in the public sector. A 1987 issue of the new literary magazine *Mofid* contained photos of women and men performing an Arthur Miller play as well as an interview with the woman writer Simin Daneshvar, who is perhaps the most widely read contemporary Iranian writer. Contrary to earlier speeches and policies designed to reduce their presence in government offices and the like, there *were* working mothers. Indeed, in December 1983 a legislative measure was introduced ostensibly to ease the burdens of working mothers by encouraging part-time rather than full-time work—but not, it should be noted, banning them from work altogether. Women also received military training; the "Zeinab Sisters"— female paramilitary enforcers—patrolled the streets for violations of Islamic dress codes and other offenses. Despite the regime's pronatalist policies banning abortion and discouraging contraception, World Bank data indicated that in 1983, some 23 percent of married women of childbearing age used contraceptives.[25] This can be regarded as a form of resistance to official impositions.

Of course, throughout the decade the authorities criticized women who resisted hijab by dressing "inappropriately" in public. The Persian word is *bad-hijabi,* which usually meant wearing bright colors; stockings that were not dark or thick enough; fashionable trousers, shoes, or bags; and/or revealing some hair beneath the headscarf. But the authorities also issued warnings against *hezbollahi,* the self-styled "partisans of God" who occasionally took it upon themselves to enforce the code on hijab. Fights were recorded in South Tehran between gangs of young *hezbollahi* and security patrols who admonished the youths for harassing women.[26] Hojatoleslam Ali Khamenei, Mir Hossein Musavi, and Hojatoleslam Hashemi Rafsanjani (who during most of the 1980s were president, prime minister, and Majlis speaker, respectively) were on record as having denounced these vigilantes. These and other officials of the Islamic Republic claimed that women's status was elevated after the revolution and that it would be further enhanced following the cessation of the war with Iraq as economic conditions stabilized. Indeed, in referring to the relative decline of female economic participation, Rafsanjani said: "When the war is over and the economy improves and expands, you will see that we will have a shortage of manpower, and then the need for women will be greater. . . . In the universities we have a shortage of women professors. In medicine we need women specialists."[27] Rafsanjani also urged men to "forget about virginity" and marry war widows; in addition, he encouraged women to propose to men, citing Khadijeh's proposal to the Prophet Muhammad as justification.[28] He even criticized such "extremism" as partitioning classrooms in grade school and enforcing the *chador* in all-girls' schools. He has been quoted as saying: "Who can quote a Quranic verse stating that there should only be four women members in the Majlis?"[29] And although Rafsanjani approves of a segregated labor market with women working in "appropriate" occupations, he once noted, "Our wives are basically the kind of people who in the past did not enter the social arena. . . . But our daughters are not like this. They go to university and get jobs and work. Right now the Imam's daughter works in the cultural and educational sector. My daughters do too, as does the wife of the Prime Minister [referring to Zahra Rahnavard]."[30]

Islamists have been divided over the issue of compulsory veiling. Some, women and men alike, are fierce advocates of strict enforcement of correct hijab. Others, such as Zahra Rahnavard and Hojatoleslam Rafsanjani, oppose excessive attention to the details of dress, even though they continue to defend the need for an Islamic dress code. At the Second International Women's Congress, held in Tehran in early 1989, Rafsanjani tried to assuage Islamist women militants who complained of increasing public laxity in hijab. His response was that while he was not satisfied with the situation in the streets, it was not as bad as the militants painted it. He then suggested that the group "try to raise more fundamental issues like the gap between rich and poor and the lack of availability of jobs for women."[31]

Ever since the revolution, women's participation in the revolt against the Shah has been acknowledged and praised, not only by the officials mentioned above but also, most importantly, by Ayatollah Khomeini himself. This has lent legitimacy to Islamist women's complaints of discrimination. Female Majlis deputies have charged in newspaper and magazine interviews that the suppression of women's rights is "un-Islamic" and "prejudicial." Veteran member of Parliament Maryam Behrouzi once complained to a leading women's magazine, "Women are never selected to chair committees; the Majlis merely reflects the male chauvinism that is rampant in our society."[32] During the 1980s the wife of then–prime minister Mir Hossein Musavi, Zahra Rahnavard—a well-known writer, university lecturer, and author of a book that presents a radical-populist Islamic perspective on social classes and inequality—was regarded by some as an "Islamic feminist." Always outspoken, she told a reporter, "Women have been active and present, at times in larger numbers than men, in all our public demonstrations. But when it comes to political appointments, they are pushed aside."[33] Nonetheless, Ms. Rahnavard has been among the staunchest supporters of the veil as a liberating force, although she is astute enough to recognize that discriminatory policies against women, especially in the spheres of education, employment, and politics, have undermined women's support for hijab. She has said:

> In our country there is a complex understanding about women . . .
> which produces a culture of inequality. . . . This culture is a far cry from

the true Muhammadan Islam. Thus, although women have shown their political support fully and at all social levels, in the past ten years they have not been allowed to play their part properly in the economic and social construction of our country.

Some of the activities that result in belittling women and lowering their status are conducted in the name of Islam. But these only have a religious cover and not a religious content. If we follow the true Muhammadan religion of Islam, then women would have no problems.[34]

It is clear that within the parameters of the Islamist system as it evolved in Iran, there was room for dissent, made possible by the fact that the Islamist discourse itself was never an integrated and coherent ideology; it has been a contradictory discourse, even on the question of women. Dissent is also made possible by the fact that women participated in massive numbers in the revolution against the Shah and supported the formation of an Islamic Republic. This involvement has allowed Islamist women room to maneuver in terms of access to education and employment, and in terms of the right to dissent.

It also should be noted that the gender system in the Islamic Republic was only partly "new," for many of its features were legacies of the past and/or inherited from the previous regime. Female physical mobility was not extensive in prerevolutionary Iran, and there were many legal and customary restrictions on women. They could not travel, obtain jobs, or rent apartments without the permission of their father or husband. Moreover, male sexist attitudes and behavior were notorious, making it difficult for women even to stand for taxis or go shopping. The beneficiaries of Pahlavi-style modernization were primarily middle-class and upper-class women, while the majority of women from working class and peasant households remained illiterate and poor. The 3.2 percent annual population growth rate resulted from this class division. Western-style dress abounded, but the *chador* was characteristically worn by working-class, traditional/lower-middle-class, and urban poor women. Most secondary schools (the exceptions being the international schools where the language of instruction was a European one) were gender-segregated; universities and workplaces, however, were not. Men could be taught by female instructors (for example, I taught English at the Air Force Language School in the early 1970s), but the matter of appropriate dress was always raised. Thus, after the revolution there were some continuities, and some breaks, in the gender system.

In the following sections, and in light of the foregoing discussion of the political-ideological context, let us survey women's social positions in postrevolutionary Iran, using data from the 1986 National Census of Population and Housing. The indicators to be examined are fertility rates, literacy and educational attainment, and employment patterns. As we shall see, gender inequality and female disadvantage are reinforced in the spheres of education and employment and expressed in the sex ratio and fertility rates. Even so, women continue to be present in public life in a way that would suggest conscious resistance to gender subordination. In turn, women's presence in the educational and employment spheres invariably subverts the patriarchal order.

▲ Population, Sex Ratio, Fertility

According to the census, the population of Iran was 49.9 million in November 1986. (This was adjusted upward to 50.6 million in 1989.) As shown in Table 6.1, the male population comprised a little over half of this figure (25.5 million), while women constituted 24.3 million, a ratio of 105 men to 100 women. In the 1970s and 1980s, Iran was among several countries in which males still had a higher life expectancy than females, the others being Bangladesh, Bhutan, India, the Maldives, Nepal, and Pakistan.[35] This was apparently also true for Afghanistan until recent years, when the escalation of the civil war resulted in more male deaths than female.[36] An adverse sex ratio indicates the low status of women, which within the overall cultural matrix and resource constraints would mean more nutritional deficiencies by females than males, and therefore higher rates of mortality among girls and women. Female mortality is also linked to high fertility and poor access to health care services during pregnancy and in childbirth.[37]

Table 6.1 Iran's Population, Various Years

Year	Total	Male	Female	Ratio
1956	18,954,704	9,644,944	9,309,760	104
1966	25,788,722	13,355,801	12,432,921	108
1976	33,708,744	17,356,347	16,352,397	106
1986	49,857,384	25,491,645	24,365,739	105

Sources: National Census of Population and Housing 1365 [1986], Table A, p. 1, and Table B, p. 2; *Statistical Yearbook 1366* [1987], Table 1, p. 55, and *1367* [1988], Table 2, p. 26.

In 1976 the population numbered 33.7 million. The increase of 15 million people over a ten-year period represents a rate of population increase of 3.9 percent, and a total fertility statistic of 5.6 children per woman, placing Iran among the countries with the highest growth rates.[38] As mentioned above, in the years following the revolution, the Islamic Republic had no official population-control or family-planning policy. Contraceptive devices and abortions were banned after the 1979 revolution. The high rate of marriage and the promotion of childbearing, the lack of any policy of birth control or family-planning services for older women, and the large number of women in their reproductive years kept the birthrate high in postrevolutionary Iran. Accordingly, in 1986 45.5 percent of the population was under the age of fifteen.[39]

The social and economic consequences of such population dynamics are clearly not compatible with the goal of improving the well-being of the population. Nor was the government's desire for economic growth consistent with such a high rate of population growth. In the latter half of the 1980s, a study by Hooshang Amirahmadi documented absolute poverty, inequality, and declining standards of living and quality of life, suggesting the government's inability to create jobs, meet basic needs, and invest in industry and agriculture.[40] The literature on demography and development shows that besides the strain placed on a country's resources and on economic development, high fertility is also linked to maternal mortality and infant and under-five mortality. During the years 1980–1987, the maternal mortality rate in Iran was 120 per 100,000. This may be compared to the low rates of Cuba (31) and Kuwait (18) and the high rates of Zaire (800) and Peru (310).[41]

Rising fertility rates adversely affect women's mobility, especially in educational attainment and labor force participation. Many studies have shown that fertility and labor force participation are negatively related. Economically inactive women tend to have more children than economically active women, and waged and salaried women tend to have fewer children. Women who work outside the home, particularly those who earn cash incomes, are presumed to have enhanced control over household decisions, increased awareness of the world outside the home, and subsequently more control over reproductive decisions. A recent study of rural women in the Dominican Republic has confirmed these presumptions.[42] The high fertility rate in Iran was clearly linked to the small percentage of women in the labor force and the even smaller percentage of women workers who are wage and salary earners (as we shall see in the discussion of employment below). Rising fertility is also linked to rising unemployment and diminishing job opportunities for women. That the marriage age was lowered from sixteen to thirteen for girls by the new Islamic state in 1979 further influenced the fertility rate. By the end of the 1980s, in an untoward macroeconomic context, the authorities in the Islamic Republic realized that they could ill afford rising birthrates and began to reconsider the earlier pronatalist policies.

▲ Literacy and Education

The 1986 census showed that over 7 million Iranian men and women, mostly in the provinces, did not speak or understand Persian, the official language of Iran.[43] Of that figure, 57 percent, or over 4 million, were women (17 percent of the female population). These women resided mostly in East and West Azerbaijan, Zanjan, Khuzestan, and Kurdestan. How did this compare with the male population? The number of men who did not know Persian was 2.9 million, or 11 percent of the male population. The male-female disparity in knowledge of Persian may be explained by educational and employment disparities (to be discussed below).

A steady improvement in literacy rates since the 1950s is evident from the censuses: In the decade 1956–1966 the literacy rate improved from 8 percent to 17.9 percent for women and 22.4 percent to 40.1 percent for men. In 1971 some 25.5 percent of women and 47.7 percent of men were literate; the corresponding figure for urban areas was 48.1 percent female and 68.7 percent male. According to the 1976 census, 55 percent of urban women were literate.[44] In 1986 the census showed that 65 percent of urban women (and 80 percent of urban men) were literate. The rural rates were, as expected, lower: 60 percent of the men, 36 percent of the women. While total literacy rates have improved over the decade, women's literacy rates do not compare favorably to those of men, as seen in Table 6.2. In all age groups, more males than females are literate.

Table 6.2 **Literacy Rates for Population 6 Years and Over, by Sex and Region, Iran, 1986**

	Total Literate	Percent	Urban Areas		Rural Areas	
			Numbers	Percent	Numbers	Percent
Men & Women	23,878,000	61.7	15,507,000	73.1	8,371,000	48.4
Men	14,052,000	70.9	8,765,000	80.4	5,287,000	60.0
Women	9,826,000	52.0	6,742,000	65.4	3,084,000	36.3

Sources: National Census of Population and Housing 1365 [1986], Table 7, p. 87; *Statistical Yearbook 1367* [1988], p. 97.
Note: Figures rounded.

Following the launching of the Islamic cultural revolution in 1980, which entailed the closing of universities and some high schools for two years, a number of steps were taken by the authorities to revise the educational system. Among the most widely noted changes were the conversion of all coeducational schools into single-sex institutions; the establishment of Islamic dress codes in schools; the encouragement of Arabic (rather than English) as a second language; the elimination of private schools, including those of the religious minorities; and the revision of textbooks. A recent study of sex-role socialization in Iranian textbooks (grade school through high school) concludes that the most dramatic change in textbooks lies in illustrations. Compared to prerevolutionary Iran, postrevolutionary society gives women much lower visibility in textbook illustrations, and there is a precipitous drop in their inclusion in lessons with a public as opposed to private setting. Moreover, all women in the textbook illustrations are veiled.[45] These findings are consistent with the Islamic Republic government's emphasis on the distinctiveness of male and female roles and the importance of family life and domestic responsibilities for women. Notions of gender difference/inequality are thus created and reproduced through school textbooks.

The 1986 census revealed that universal primary schooling had yet to be achieved, especially for girls. Both absolutely and proportionally, more males than females were receiving education at both the grade school and postsecondary school levels. The gap was narrowest at the primary school level (where boys constituted 55 percent of the student population and girls 44 percent) and began to widen at the intermediate ("guidance") school level, where the male and female shares were 60 percent and 40 percent, respectively. But the postsecondary student population had the most striking gender disparity. Out of nearly 182,000 students receiving higher education in 1986, 56,000 (or 31 percent) were female. (See Table 6.3.) The *Statistical Yearbook 1367* (March 1988–March 1989) lists forty universities, including one all-male seminary and one all-female seminary. The only institutions in which women's enrollment equaled or exceeded that of men's were the country's public health and medical schools, a reflection of the prevalent view that medicine is an appropriate field of study and profession for women—mainly so that they can provide medical services to women and thus avoid excessive male-female contact.

As in prerevolutionary Iran, admission to a university remains extremely difficult for both men and women. There are always more applicants than places in the universities, even though several new institutes of higher education were established in the Islamic Republic. In the entrance examination for academic year 1986–1987, 586,086 persons (383,245 males and 202,841 females) participated. Of the nearly 62,000 persons admitted, 19,000 were women (as against 42,000 men).[46] These figures represent 9.5 percent of the women who took the entrance exams and 11 percent of the men. But it means, again, that the female share of the university population is 31 to 33 percent.

Table 6.3 College Population and Fields of Study for Men and Women in Iran, 1986

	Total	Post-diploma	Bachelors	Masters	Doctorate
	181,889	60,490	96,353	10,394	14,652
Male	125,327	42,357	65,263	7,869	9,838
Percentage of Total	69	70	67.7	75.7	67
Teacher Training & Education	16,659	15,194	1,392	60	13
Health and Medicine	17,922	3,955	4,345	1,696	7,926
Engineering	34,569	8,870	22,866	2,433	400
Natural Sciences	10,271	1,958	7,522	661	230
Female	56,562	18,133	31,090	2,525	4,814
Percentage of Total	31	30	32.2	24	33
Teacher Training & Education	7,490	5,858	1,575	50	7
Health and Medicine	15,808	5,477	5,060	1,033	4,238
Humanities	6,934	1,318	5,298	183	35
Natural Sciences	6,257	931	5,011	251	64

Source: National Census of Population and Housing 1365 [1986], Table 10.2, p. 100.
Note: The academic fields were selected on the basis of the greatest concentration of male and female college populations.

And what were women studying? Nineteen academic disciplines were listed in the census. Women were represented in all of them, including engineering (2,259), but, as can be seen from Table 6.3, the largest numbers of women university students were in health and medicine, teacher training, humanities, and the natural sciences. Engineering was the most popular field for male students. Of 4,178 law students in academic year 1367–1368 (1988–1989), there were only 485 women.[47]

With the reopening of the institutions closed down in 1980, a nationwide *konkour* (entrance examination) was held. Mojab explains that considerable changes were introduced in the tests and test groups, fields of study, number of institutions, and criteria of admission. The government eliminated some programs of study it considered unnecessary, such as music and counseling. Another reform involved the centralization of diverse institutions by combining them into "complexes." By 1985 there were 114 institutions: 20 universities, 4 university complexes, 21 educational complexes, 7 colleges, 15 higher institutions, 31 two-year institutions, 12 technological institutes, and 4 instructional units. The general criteria for all applicants were (1) believing in Islam or one of the religions recognized by the constitution (Christianity, Judaism, Zoroastrianism), and (2) having no organizational connection with or advocacy of political parties, antigovernment groups, or atheistic groups. Male applicants also had to meet very strict requirements of military service based on the war with Iraq.[48]

Although there had been restrictions on women's admissions prior to the revolution (for example, the study of mining was off-limits to women; some nursing schools admitted only single women or widows without children), the restrictions following the cultural revolution were more extensive. Mojab explains that the program of mathematical and technical sciences offered eighty-four majors, of which fifty-five (64 percent) did not admit women. In the field of experimental sciences, forty majors were offered, of which seven (17 percent) did not admit women: veterinary technician, animal science, agrarian affairs, geology, disease control, veterinary science, and natural resources. Fourteen of the remaining thirty-three majors set maximum limits for female applicants: medicine, dentistry, optometry, radiology technics, speech therapy, audiometry, lab sciences, anesthesia, operation technician, and oral and dental hygiene technician, 50 percent; physiotherapy, 40 percent; pharmacology, environmental hygiene, and artificial limbs, 20 percent. Two majors, midwifery and family hygiene, accepted women only. A significant change occurred in nursing, which now allows 50 percent of students to be male, an apparent attempt at training male nurses to serve male patients.

Thirty-five majors were offered in the humanities, of which seven set a maximum for females: theology and Islamic learning, 50 percent; law, 25 percent (female graduates could not become lawyers or judges); archaeology and art history, 40 percent; physical education and sports, 40 percent. Art offered ten majors, of which design, sewing, and technical instructor for sewing and commercial sewing accepted women only. For women to be eligible for government scholarships to study abroad, they had to be married and accompanied by their husbands.

It should be noted that in the summer of 1989, the quotas for women at the universities were removed from many disciplines. Zahra Rahnavard, the wife of former prime minister Mir Hossein Musavi, was responsible for negotiating removal of these barriers. This reversal of policy indicates that women are hardly passive in the face of official discrimination and that Islamic feminists such as Zahra Rahnavard can maneuver on behalf of women's rights within the confines of the existing Islamist system.

In spite of an official policy of restricting women's access to higher education, available statistical data do not reflect any significant decline in women's participation. The failure to restrict women's access stems from

social changes: the growth of the urban middle class, urbanization, diversi-
fication of the urban economy, limited but steady industrialization, expansion of the state apparatus, and economic imperatives and labor needs.

▲ Employment

Before turning to the characteristics of the labor force, a note of caution is
in order. As is well known, figures for urban areas are more reliable than
they are for rural areas; but in either case, dealing with large informal sectors, seasonal employment, migrant workers, unstable work arrangements,
and part-time employment makes enumeration very difficult. Refugee populations (in Iran's case, large numbers of Afghan economic refugees work
as domestics or construction workers) could also complicate enumeration.
And then there is the notorious undercounting of women, a problem in all
developing countries, as was discussed in Chapter 2. Rural women in particular are frequently left out of the tabulations or are assumed to be
"homemakers." All of the Iranian censuses have overlooked large numbers
of women, most of them rural. The 1986 census categorized fully 11 million Iranian women as "homemakers." Consequently, there was a huge disparity in the activity rates of men and women, and only a tiny percentage of
Iranian women were calculated as part of the labor force.[49] Thus, what follows should not be regarded as exact; the description does, however, provide a picture of labor force participation patterns in Iran that accords with
earlier surveys and with informed expectations.

　　According to the census data, the economically active population in
1986 numbered 13,041,000 persons, constituting 19.3 percent of the total
population over ten years of age. Of the total employed population, 65 percent was engaged in the private sector and 31 percent in the public sector.[50]
About 1 million women were classified as employed, representing only
about 9 percent of the total employed population. (See Table 6.4.) Female
civil servants numbered about 420,000 (as against over a million men), or
28 percent of the total number of civil servants and 41 percent of the total
employed female population. The largest numbers of female government
employees were, predictably, in the Ministries of Education and Health.
(The same is true of male government employees.) This concentration
obtained in prerevolutionary Iran as well. Table 6.5 compares male and
female government employees for three periods before and after the revolution.

　　In the years following the revolution, female employment in modern
industry decreased relative to the prerevolutionary situation and to employment in government agencies and ministries. Women continued to work in
the large industrial establishments, but their participation in modern-sector
industrial activity was almost insignificant. In 1983 the yearly national

Table 6.4 Comparison of Male and Female Economic Activities in Iran, 1986

Activity	Male	Female
Total population	25,280,961	24,164,049
Population aged 10 and over	16,841,000	16,030,900
Employed	10,048,858	987,103
Unemployed seeking employment	1,486,138	332,602
Student	3,871,000	2,659,000
Homemaker	194,689	11,250,865
Activity rate (in percent)	45	8
Percentage of labor force	91	9

Sources: National Census of Population and Housing 1365 [1986], Table 16, p. 114, and Table 27, p. 237; *Statistical Yearbook 1367* [1988], Tables 3.1 and 3.2, pp, 57–59; *Iran Yearbook 89/90* (Bonn: M&B Publishing, 1989).

average (there are seasonal fluctuations) of female employees in the large industrial sector was nearly 40,000. (The number for men was 534,000.) This number was divided between *kargar* (blue-collar workers) and *karmand* (white-collar workers). The greatest number were *kargar* (32,000). Women production workers made up 6 percent of the labor force of the large industrial establishments in Iran in 1983.[51] About one-third of the blue-collar female work force in the large industrial establishments was in textiles/clothing/shoes/leather. (It should be noted that about one-fourth of male workers were also in textiles.) Next, women were found in food and beverages, followed by nonmetallic minerals, machinery, and chemical industries.[52] As shown in Table 6.6, white-collar female employees were found first in food and beverages, followed by machinery, tobacco, and chemicals.

Data in the 1976 census indicate that women earning wages and salaries in public and private sector manufacturing and mining/quarrying made up between 20 and 27 percent of the total.[53] As mentioned above, the 40,000 female wage and salary earners in urban factory employment in 1983 represented 6 percent of total employment here. Clearly there had been a sharp decline in female factory employment. One explanation may lie in different measurement techniques. Another explanation may be that many female industrial workers were employed by transnational corporations. When the latter closed down or changed owners, preferential treatment in hiring practices was accorded to men. As foreign contracts with

Table 6.5 Distribution of Male and Female Government Employees in Selected Ministries: Pre- and Postrevolutionary Iran

Ministry[a]	1974–1975		1983–1984		1986	
	Male	Female	Male	Female	Male	Female
Total	210,389	87,474	875,735	341,155	1,104,422	419,544
Education	93,976	66,539	316,735	218,703	381,710	286,103
Health	17,747	6,152	95,490	52,707	123,967	87,102
Economics and Finance	12,556	1,660	77,982	11,277	84,562	10,130
Roads and Transportation	18,814	627	54,908	2,310	58,801	2,863
Agriculture and Rural Development	12,562	1,660	41,672	2,733	47,778	2,940
Interior	5,848	638	37,333	4,844	14,132	1,126
Culture and Higher Education	6,326	4,105	31,832	14,154	26,622	6,152
Other[b]	42,560	6,093	219,785	38,878	366,850	23,128

Sources: Statistical Yearbook 2533 ["Imperial Year" corresponding to 1974–1975]; *Statistical Yearbook 1363* [1984–1985], p. 68; *Statistical Yearbook 1367* [1988–1989], p. 69.

Notes: a. The ministries were selected on the basis of the greatest concentration of male employees so as to better compare female concentration and distribution.

b. For 1983–1984: Prime Minister's Office, Islamic Guidance, Foreign Ministry, Commerce, Post/Telegraph/Telephone, Justice, Light Industries, Labor and Social Affairs, Housing and Urban Development, Industries and Mines, Power, Oil, Islamic Republic Media, Defense, Heavy Industries. This makes for a total of 1,216,890 employees. For 1974–1975: the same, excluding Islamic agencies and including the Ministry of War. This makes for a total of 304,404 employees. In the span of a decade, there was an increase in government employment roughly corresponding to the annual growth of the population. In 1986, male participation in the Rural Reconstruction Crusade numbered 54,388, but a mere 579 women were employed there.

TNCs were cancelled, the rate of unemployment for female industrial workers rose, furthering the marginalization of working-class women in the productive process. Similar patterns have been observed elsewhere in the Third World, usually following nationalization or the imposition of IMF austerity measures.[54]

By the mid-1980s there was a further decline in industrial work by women, although the *Statistical Yearbook 1364* [1985–1986] showed a decrease in industrial employment for both men and women, indicating the weakness of this sector of the economy. Compared with 1976, when the female share of manufacturing was reported to be 38 percent, in 1986 it had

Table 6.6 Distribution of Work Force in Large Industrial Establishments:
Iran, 1982–1983

Industry Total Number (Percentage)	Blue Collar		White Collar	
	Male 474,722 (94)	Female 32,022 (6)	Male 62,301 (90)	Female 6,787 (10)
Food and beverages	69,190	5,768	11,203	2,211
Textiles, clothing, leather, shoes	122,415	10,946	9,048	624
Woodworking	12,129	104	1,711	112
Furniture	2,718	31	308	30
Paper, cardboard, printing	12,336	327	2,726	231
Chemicals, pharmaceuticals, plastics	36,058	3,486	8,112	1,184
Nonmetallic minerals	86,759	5,633	6,424	415
Basic metals	29,018	123	3,402	147
Machinery	103,170	5,492	19,264	1,822
Miscellaneous	929	112	103	11

Source: Statistics for Large Industrial Establishments 1363 [1984–1985], pp. 263–266.
Note: The figures given are the yearly averages, as there are seasonal fluctuations.

declined to 14.5 percent. In 1986, most of the measured female labor force
was in services. The largest number of enumerated women were in private
and public services; agriculture ranked second, with about 263,000 workers, and industry third, with a mere 216,000 employees. Clearly, vast numbers of women were not being counted in the agricultural sector; the figure
for men in agriculture was nearly 3 million. The changes in the female economically active population since the 1960s are illustrated in Table 6.7,
which provides data from the 1966, 1976, and 1986 censuses.

In line with the economic sectors, most women in 1986 were found in
the following occupational groups: (1) professional, technical, and related
workers; (2) agricultural, animal husbandry, forestry, fishing, and hunting
workers; and (3) production and transport workers. Women were extremely
underrepresented in managerial, administrative, clerical, and sales work.[55]
Table 6.8 illustrates the distribution of the male and female work force
across the major occupational groups.

Among the most significant characteristics of the employed female
population during the 1980s that may be discerned from the 1986 census

Table 6.7 Economically Active Population by Industry, Status, and Sex: Iran, 1966, 1976, 1986

Year	Industry (Major divisions)	Total	Percentage Females	Employers and Own-account Workers		Employees		Unpaid Family Workers		Not Classified by Status	
				Total	Percentage Females	Total	Percentage Females	Total	Percentage Females	Total	Percentage Females
1966	Group 1	3,168,515	6.4	1,841,422	2.3	800,210	8.3	518,297	18.1	8,586	4.5
	Group 2	26,312	1.5	1,128	0.6	25,039	1.6	94	1.1	51	0.0
	Group 3	1,267,600	40.1	345,996	42.8	805,784	32.6	112,931	86.0	2,889	36.6
	Group 4	52,858	1.3	1,022	1.0	51,766	1.3	28	0.0	42	2.4
	Group 5	509,778	0.4	47,035	0.4	457,722	0.4	4,099	4.3	922	0.5
	Group 6	552,023	1.6	383,079	0.9	154,313	3.2	13,604	3.6	1,027	3.1
	Group 7	224,086	1.1	57,071	0.3	164,146	1.4	2,372	3.6	497	1.4
	Groups 8–9	929,685	18.3	120,924	6.7	788,106	19.9	18,869	25.2	1,786	30.5
	Other	853,228	12.1	13,797	8.9	75,275	4.5	6,777	21.0	757,379	12.8
	Total	7,584,085	13.2	2,811,474	7.2	3,322,361	15.0	677,071	29.2	773,179	12.8
1976	Group 1	3,615,314	22.8	1,741,540	1.1	662,072	11.3	587,430	22.8	624,272	95.5
	Group 2	90,230	3.8	1,380	2.1	88,385	3.7	70	27.1	395	33.2
	Group 3	1,682,188	38.4	357,607	28.6	900,856	19.6	411,249	87.3	12,476	70.0
	Group 4	61,761	3.2	606	1.2	60,981	3.1	8	0.0	166	24.7
	Group 5	1,202,061	1.5	117,897	0.4	1,065,730	0.7	4,388	2.5	14,046	71.0
	Group 6	671,735	2.0	479,654	0.9	176,561	3.8	12,021	8.2	3,499	24.9
	Group 7	433,364	2.2	156,539	0.3	272,352	3.1	2,123	1.9	2,350	26.0
	Group 8	100,653	9.4	16,061	0.8	84,202	11.0	102	5.9	288	11.5
	Group 9	1,523,689	18.9	115,217	8.1	1,399,951	19.7	3,052	29.2	5,469	0.5
	Other	415,061	8.4	5,939	6.9	33,929	12.0	869	45.8	374,324	44.7
	Total	9,796,056	20.2	2,992,440	4.5	4,745,019	12.0	1,021,312	48.5	1,037,285	75.8

(continues)

Table 6.7 (continued)

Industry (Major divisions) Year	Total	Percentage Females	Employers and Own-account Workers Total	Percentage Females	Employees Total	Percentage Females	Unpaid Family Workers Total	Percentage Females	Not Classified by Status Total	Percentage Females
1986										
Group 1	3,190,761	8.1	2,420,511	3.0	329,374	9.0	380,416	40.2	60,360	7.1
Group 2	32,370	1.7	1,491	1.0	30,034	1.6	21	4.8	824	3.8
Group 3	1,451,330	14.5	503,193	17.8	814,710	6.7	71,233	74.9	62,194	21.6
Group 4	91,044	2.5	5,090	0.9	83,095	2.5	85	1.2	2,774	5.2
Group 5	1,206,264	0.8	431,025	0.6	723,726	0.8	4,792	2.4	46,721	1.8
Group 6	875,458	1.7	655,280	1.1	183,304	3.2	10,788	3.9	26,086	3.9
Group 7	630,546	1.4	348,808	0.4	259,564	2.5	2,638	1.8	19,536	2.9
Group 8	114,288	9.2	12,946	2.0	97,325	9.7	124	12.1	3,893	18.6
Group 9	3,049,753	13.6	237,787	5.7	2,621,501	14.2	7,429	10.3	183,036	14.6
Other	359,721	12.7	115,519	5.2	185,252	9.0	6,467	32.2	52,483	39.4
Total	11,001,535	8.9	4,731,750	4.1	5,327,885	9.5	483,993	43.4	457,907	14.9

Source: ILO Yearbook of Labour Statistics, Retrospective Edition on Population Censuses (Geneva: ILO, 1990), Table 2A, pp. 268–269, and Table 2B, pp. 572–573.

Note:
Group 1 = Agriculture, hunting, forestry, and fishing
Group 2 = Mining and quarrying
Group 3 = Manufacturing
Group 4 = Electricity, gas, and water
Group 5 = Construction
Group 6 = Wholesale/retail trade, restaurants, and hotels
Group 7 = Transport, storage, and communication
Group 8 = Financing, insurance, real estate, and business services
Group 9 = Community, social, and personal services
Other = Not adequately defined, unemployed

Table 6.8 Employees Aged 6 and Above, by Occupational Groups, Sex, and Region, Iran, 1986

Major Occupational Groups	Total Country Male and Female Number^a	Percent	Percent Female^b	Urban Areas Male	Female	Rural Areas Male	Female
Total	11,036,000	100	8.9	5,433,000	527,000	4,558,000	455,000
Professional, technical, and related workers	1,054,000	9.6	32.5	593,000	316,000	118,000	28,000
Managers and supervisors	44,000	0.4	4.5	39,000	1,000	4,000	n.a.
Clerical and administrative workers	367,000	3.3	12.8	281,000	45,000	40,000	2,000
Sales, commerce, retail workers	762,000	6.9	1.4	648,000	10,000	103,000	2,000
Service workers	455,000	4.1	7.0	323,000	28,000	100,000	4,000
Agricultural, animal husbandry, forestry, fishing, and hunting	3,262,000	29.6	8.1	325,000	12,000	2,623,000	247,000
Production and transportation workers	3,648,000	33.1	6.3	2,334,000	71,000	1,080,000	159,000
Not adequately defined	1,443,000	13.1	4.0	890,000	44,000	492,000	15,000

Source: Statistical Yearbook 1367 [March 1988–March 1989], Table 3.12, p. 66.
Notes: a. rounded
b. female share of each occupational group
n.a. = information not available

are: (1) the female share of the total labor force was very small, at about 10 percent; (2) apart from carpet-weaving and traditional craftwork, women's role in modern industrial production was limited; (3) the majority of women employees were teachers and health workers; and (4) large numbers of employed women in the private sector were not receiving a wage for their work. Classified as "unpaid family workers" and "independent workers/self-employed," these women were found mostly in agriculture and industry. (Here industry really refers to carpet-weaving, largely rural and carried out in small workshops.) As in other countries, such as Turkey and Afghanistan, the products of their labor very often accrue not to themselves but to their husbands or male kin.[56] It is noteworthy that in the 1986 census the category "unpaid family worker" was very large for women and rather small for men. It represented 4 percent of the total male work force in the private sector but fully 42 percent of the female private sector work force. The proportion of women in the private sector receiving a wage or salary was only 19 percent. In contrast to the women in the private sector, all the women in the public sector were wage or salary earners, part of the country's social security program.[57]

These figures, and the classification system, suggest both a methodological bias and a social problem. The social problem is that women workers are subject to "double exploitation" (as workers and as women, or, to put it more analytically, by class and by gender), as fewer of them are wage earners and many more are unpaid family workers. Moreover, occupational sex-typing is carried to the extreme in the Iranian case. This social problem of the labor market (low employment, unwaged employment, sex-typing) spills into other areas of the social structure and is manifested in rising fertility rates, as discussed earlier. The methodological bias and inadequacy lie in the fact that most women are simply not being counted as part of the labor force and will therefore not be considered in any employment or social policies designed by the authorities.

Besides educational level and salary, the difference between work in the public sector (whether as production workers or as professionals) and in the private sector manifested itself in age structure as well. For such occupations as scientific/technical workers and teachers, the largest numbers of women were in the age groups 20–29 and 30–39. However, in agricultural occupations, the largest numbers of women were in the age group 10–19, followed by the age group 20–29. By the time we get to "industrial" occupations, such as rug-weaving, the largest numbers of women workers were in the 10–19 age group.[58]

The data thus reveal differentiation of the female population, with marked differences between rural and urban women. Women in the public sector tend to be largely professional, highly educated, salaried; they are found mainly in education and medicine; they are also less likely to be

Students like these learn to weave carpets at training centers that have been in operation since the early 1960s. Photo: International Labour Office

married. By contrast, a rural woman is typically married and illiterate or has attained only primary education.

▲ Fertility, Education, and Employment: The Connections

The census data pertaining to women in contemporary Iran discussed in this chapter suggest that beyond the limitations and restrictions there are opportunities for women's advancement. Certainly much could be improved, even within the confines of the Islamist system as it has developed in Iran. First of all, the female share of the total labor force declined by two percentage points between 1976 and 1986. Even accounting for differences in measurement in the two censuses, such a drop is significant. Male employment declined as well, reflecting overall unpromising economic conditions. But the female share of the total labor force in Iran is exceedingly low when compared to other countries. (See Table 6.9.)

Table 6.9 Female Share of Employed Population (in percent):
Iran Compared with Other Countries

Industrialized Country	Year	Female Share	Industrializing Country	Year	Female Share
Austria	1987	40.1	Egypt	1984	18.7
Bulgaria	1985	47.7	India	1981	25.9
Canada	1986	42.9	Indonesia	1985	35.9
France	1987	43.3	Israel	1983	38.5
West Germany	1987	39.5	South Korea	1987	39.9
Greece	1986	35.5	Mexico	1980	27.8
Italy	1987	36.4	Pakistan	1980	3.7
Japan	1985	38.6	Philippines	1987	36.2
Portugal	1987	42.0	Tunisia	1984	21.3
Sweden	1987	48.7	Turkey	1980	30.0
United States	1987	45.5	Venezuela	1987	27.7
Yugoslavia	1981	38.6	Iran[a]	1986	9.0

Source: ILO, *Yearbook of Labour Statistics 1988* (Geneva: ILO), Table 2A.
Note: a. Data from *National Census of Population and Housing 1365* [1986].

The data also reveal that men are concentrated in the high-status, high-paying occupations; the labor market is extremely gender-segregated. And it will continue to be so if the present educational patterns—wherein male students are overwhelmingly concentrated in engineering and related fields while women are tracked into health and medicine, the humanities, and teaching—persist. "Men's work" and "women's work" are not "natural" categories; they are social and cultural constructs. The market and other economic processes are not gender-neutral, nor are they divorced from political and ideological influences and noneconomic determinants (such as, in Iran's case, official interpretations of Islamic canon law). Thus, the education and employment patterns pertaining to women are neither accidental nor natural but derive from women's disadvantaged position in the stratification system and in the ideological/symbolic system.

Second, attention must be drawn to the large numbers of women in the private sector who are not receiving a wage for their work ("unpaid family workers"). Studies are needed to determine who these women are, how long they work per day or per week, what tasks they perform, how the income generated is allocated, who disposes of it, and so on. Their subordinate status as workers—determined solely by their gender—needs to be faced squarely, and steps must be taken to improve their situation. The first step is to transform work conditions in the private sector so that women are properly compensated for their labor.

As we have seen in Chapter 4, the connection between employment patterns and fertility rates has been widely made in the development literature. When women are marginalized from the productive process, they pursue strategies of childbearing, either because they are unable consciously to choose fertility reduction or because they may find such a reduction economically disadvantageous. Stripped of their economic/productive role, women depend on motherhood performance for status and prestige and on children's labor as a strategy for survival. The combination of low education, low employment, and the absence of a concerted family-planning strategy explains why fertility rates and population growth rates increased rather than decreased in Iran during the 1980s.

Spiraling population growth at a time of depleting fiscal resources and increasing pockets of poverty throughout the country eventually led authorities within the Islamic Republic toward a fundamental policy reversal—advocacy of family planning. In June 1989 the government formally lifted the ban on contraceptives at state hospitals and clinics. Still prohibited by law, however, is abortion. In January 1990 a seminar on population control convened in Tehran, with the result that the government is now openly favoring and encouraging family planning and the use of birth control devices—a marked departure from the early pronatalist position. The government is determined to reduce the population growth rate to 2.3 percent per annum. In July 1991 the Iranian cabinet approved a proposal by the Ministry of Health whereby any children born to families already having three will be deprived of the government's financial and economic privileges. Tehran University signed an agreement with the United Nations Fund for Population Activities to conduct population research and design a population policy. Iranian newspapers, especially *Kayhan* and the English-language *Tehran Times,* have devoted many editorials to calls for reduction of birthrates. The minister of health announced that, according to scientific theory, a 1 percent decrease in the growth of population would reduce the infant mortality rate by five per thousand.[59] The director of the family planning center of the Ministry of Health, Dr. Hamid Assadpour, expressed his concern over Iran's high population growth rate and stated the government's goal to reduce the growth rate to 2.9 percent per year in 1993–1994. In a statement to the press, Dr. Assadpour noted the levels of unemployment, illiteracy, and school enrollment.[60] Yet he did not take the next logical step and assert clearly that the target group for expanded literacy, education, and employment would be Iranian women. The authorities in Iran have not yet made the connection between birthrates and the status of women.

▲ Development Imperatives and Ideological Contradictions

There is no question but that the "second-sex" attribute of women—always present in Iran (as, indeed, in all patriarchal societies)—was intensified after the revolution. Nevertheless, the mere fact that women were present in such numbers in the formal sector of the economy, and especially in government employment, was a surprising and unexpected discovery. To what could this be attributed?

The women-in-development literature identifies three interrelated forces that condition and structure the position of women in the labor market: (1) supply factors that influence whether women are available for wage labor outside the household; (2) the specific structure of the economy, which conditions the demand for workers in the labor market; and (3) the implicit and explicit policies regarding the inclusion/exclusion of women in the labor market as reflected in hiring practices, segregation of jobs by sex, earnings/wage structure, and so on.[61] These three forces imply cultural, class, technical, and institutional determinants, all of which operate in a dynamic way. For example, cultural norms regarding women's role in society or the family influence the supply of female labor; the unidimensional view of women as wives/mothers and assumptions about women workers (for example, that they are less committed than men) affect policy formulation. We have seen that in many countries in the Middle East and South Asia, women represent a mere fraction of the labor force. However, at a certain point in the process of economic transformation and societal change, the emerging structure of production undermines the existing social and sexual divisions of labor. This transition is particularly apparent during or following periods of modernization, where updated industries and expanding public and private sectors create new labor markets. Moreover, dire material necessity increasingly propels women outside of the home and into the labor market. Finally, the preference for cheap, part-time, or temporary labor may prompt policymakers to include women in their formulations or employers to hire women. Certain industries and types of manufacturing work are also regarded as especially suited to female labor: Carpet-weaving, textiles, electronics wiring, and food processing tend to attract women workers.

In Iran other factors are salient as well. From 1980 to 1988, large segments of the male population over the age of fifteen were mobilized in the war effort. Employers and government agencies turned to women to compensate for the loss of vast numbers of males on the labor market. The war with Iraq—specifically, the mobilization, death, and disablement of so many men—was no doubt a major factor in widening female employment opportunities. It will be recalled that in other countries during wartime—such as the United States and England during World War II—women crowded the expanded payrolls of factories, offices, and retailers that had traditionally employed females as well as those of heavy industries and war-related agencies. Wartime labor shortages, therefore, may have increased employment opportunities for women throughout the expanding state apparatus. Thus, an unintended consequence of the Iran-Iraq war was to thwart the most conservative Islamist intentions by retaining women in the work force.

Another factor in women's employment is the phenomenon of women-headed households. In Iran in 1980, it was estimated that some 15 percent of households were headed by women.[62] This figure must have increased during the 1980s, given the death and displacement of so many men in the war with Iraq. War widows in Iran had several options: They could remarry, they could rely on assistance from the immediate or extended family, or they could survive on government monetary compensation for the "martyr-dom" of their husbands. Work remained an option forced by necessity; notwithstanding Rafsanjani's appeals to men to wed the war widows, many remained husbandless. Those that did not remarry would either join the formal sector as workers or, as is more likely, engage in various informal-sector activities. In summary form, the following factors explain why women have remained in the modern sector of the economy: (1) the ambiguities in the discourse and policies of the Islamic political elite and the conflicting cultural images of women, allowing women some room to maneuver within the confines of the Islamic system; (2) the imperatives of economic development and the expansion of the state apparatus, which created a demand, albeit limited, for female labor; (3) the exigencies of the war with Iraq, which also created a limited demand for female labor; and (4) economic need on the part of some women and the resistance to total subjection on the part of others, including educated women with prior work experience—"supply-side" factors.

Gender systems are designed by ideologues and inscribed in law, justified by custom and enforced by the police, sustained by processes of socialization and reinforced through distinct institutions. But they are not impervious to modification, change, and resistance. Modern societies are too heterogeneous for a single system to remain intact without challenges. Challenges to a strictly defined gender system (such as that envisioned by the early Islamist ideologues in Iran) may derive from economic imperatives and/or from the growth of the ranks of educated women who reject domestication. There is also a profound internal inconsistency in Iran's gender ideology, inasmuch as it seeks to associate womanhood with family life—marriage and childbearing—but does not deny women education and employment opportunities or the right to vote and run for Parliament. In

Iran today, women may be veiled, but they can be found in schools, universities, government offices, and even factories. Ideologies and practices of gender inequality may exist, but these are subject to the challenges of economic development and demographic changes, such as the growth of an educated female population. As universal schooling expands in Iran, the gender system will be further challenged.

There is every reason to believe that education among women will increase, mainly because of the pro-education stance of the current Iranian leadership. President Hashemi Rafsanjani officially inaugurated the 1991–1992 academic year with a visit to a boys' school and to a girls' school. In the latter, he expressed his satisfaction with the rising number of girl students. According to a newspaper account, he also "called on the female population to strive to take their 50 percent share in the country's educational programmes and institutions." The president also stressed that not only should women further their activities in all social fields but also that "even housewives should further their academic studies."[63]

One instance of a shift in gender ideology guided by pragmatic consideration is on the question of women and law. As mentioned previously, women in law, notably all judges, were purged from their positions immediately after the revolution. Women were discouraged from studying law because they are deemed to be by nature too emotional. However, as stated above, women continued to study law. Toward the end of the 1980s, the field of law became more open to women. Unless they were designated antirevolutionary, even those women who had been purged in the early 1980s were asked to come back to work, though not necessarily to their previous positions. Former judges could now work as inspectors in the equivalent of a district attorney's office.[64] Thus, after a decade of barring women from law, the Iranian state reversed itself and deemed it advantageous to draw on women with legal experience and education, including those who had acquired their expertise in the period before the revolution. The head of the Iranian judiciary, Ayatollah Mohammad Yazdi, asserts, "There is no law barring the way to female employment. . . . There is no discrimination against women in law or in practice. In practice women do get jobs."[65] Yazdi may have overstated the case. But even more startling is the attitude of Majlis speaker Hojatoleslam Mehdi Karrubi, who in September 1991 called on women to compete for key posts in the government and to enter the Majlis in greater numbers. In an address to a group of Islamist women, Karrubi said that women must find their way into the cabinet and take up posts such as vice-president.[66]

Another example of a shift in gender policy pertains to women and agriculture. As stated above, the 1986 Iranian census seriously undercounted rural women. Furthermore, there were hardly any female agricultural extension agents in postrevolutionary Iran. But by late 1991, the minister of agriculture, Issa Kalantari, announced that agricultural training centers for women would be established "to better utilize the female work force in the sector." The Ministry of Agriculture had apparently counted more women in agriculture than the Statistical Center of Iran had, for the minister said that 40 percent of the farm work in Iran is performed by women. According to a newspaper account, he "regretted that there still exist restrictions preventing women from enrolling in certain academic fields, and that there were certain difficulties in training female farmers." But he said that arrangements would be made to train women alongside men in agricultural fields. Interestingly, he also called on other government agencies to "further employ women and trust them with more key posts."[67]

These significant changes should be understood in the context of the government's new attention to economic issues, a shift from its earlier focus on cultural, political, and moral issues. The authorities are cognizant that economic growth and development cannot take place in a situation of unbridled population growth and the underutilization of the female resource base.

There will continue to be disputes over the "quantitative" versus "qualitative" approach to women's status and gender equality. A report on the social status of Iranian women before and after "the victory of the Islamist Revolution," authored by the Research Group for Muslim Women's Studies, evinces an approach rather more conservative than that of Rafsanjani, Karrubi, or Kalantari. It is worth quoting from the introduction *in extenso:*

> The social state of women like other strata has undergone various changes after the victory of the Islamic revolution, revealing the noble and true value of the Muslem women. Hence, the women who under the impact of foreign culture had lost their identity and had come to view freedom merely as a quantitative equality with men, as a consequence of the glorious Islamic revolution, opened their minds to their own supreme identity. Besides, under the enlightened acceptance of and following the commands of the Supreme Being, women gained independence of thought and true freedom, and realized that in an Islamic system a woman is no longer a mindless consuming agent of the foreign products and no longer is misused under the disguise of equality.
>
> The general policy of the capitalist West is based on shaking the foundation of the family institution and placing men and women in an apparently equal position in spite of their natural differences. In the teachings of Islam although men and women as human beings are considered equal, yet regarding human nature, they have been ascribed different tasks. In general, Islam has assigned real equal rights to all humanity, and the result of such equality in the view of social injustice in Islam is that everyone should come to realize his own true rights as well as divine rights.
>
> Islam regards men and women equal as far as their choice of securing their livelihood is concerned. Therefore, women, like men, can manage their lives independently, and keep the product of their own labor. Hence

men and women are equal in Islam, according to the verses of the Holy Quran, which is the voice of God. Mankind has accepted that these rights are divine in nature, rather than man-made.

Obviously, the apparent and quantitative equality is not the only goal of socio-cultural advancement of women. After the Islamic revolution in Iran, the attempt to obtain quantitative equality of women with men in educational centers, offices, and factories, in and of itself, is no longer the criterion of progress. That is why in so-called developed countries though Imperialist propaganda states that men and women are of equal proportion in most areas and occupations, the reality is that the rate of dissatisfaction of these women has increased due to lack of freedom and inequality, and their struggle for gaining equal rights is still continuing.

Iranian women and men, throughout the Islamic revolution and after its victory, have participated in many tasks. Their valuable contributions at home and behind the war fronts, cannot be evaluated by material standards. Therefore, the rate of their advancement or backwardness after the Islamic revolution and at the present situation, cannot be examined and judged by sheer international standards. A full knowledge of the social patterns and a reinterpretation of the concepts that represent the value system of the society are the essential prerequisites for such judgements.

Considering that the true role of women in the advancement of society after the revolution can only be appreciated with qualitative standards, it is not quite just to measure the social progress of women of different strata by mere quantitative standards, i.e., presenting the number of females in occupational, education, and professional categories. However, after the revolution, the Iranian women, adopting religious standards, have been able to gain a considerable amount of success, even quantitatively speaking, through participating in various social, educational, and professional activities, and hence regaining their true social status and esteem. The present paper is a part of change in statistics, showing the women's activities in social, cultural, educational and professional areas after the victory of revolution.

As the blessed founder of the Islamic Revolution puts it, "If women change, the society changes." With this in mind, let's hope that a day will come when the degree of true changes and the splendid rate of progress of the community of Iranian Muslim women will be known all over the world. So that the women in the Islamic Republic of Iran might be the example to be followed by all women in the Islamic nations.[68]

▲ Empowerment of Islamist Women

A more radical and critical approach to women's status in the Islamic Republic may be found in *Payam-e Hajar,* a periodical published by the well-known activist Azam Taleghani. One issue carried an article on family planning, calling it "a basic human right." Remarkably, the article stated that "the right of a woman to control her body and thus her own fertility is central to any discussion of human rights." A sidebar stated, "There is, I believe, great wisdom in the immortal words of Abdul Ibn Badis, the Algerian Muslim reformist, 'Educate a boy and you educate one person, educate a girl and you educate a nation.'" Another article examined the issue of women-in-development in the following way:

> The question that might be asked is why integration of Women in Development (WID) should be considered vital and if investment in this area is not made, what would actually happen. Women are at the heart of development. They control most of the non-money economy (subsistence agriculture, bearing and raising children, domestic labor) and take an important part in the money economy (trading, the "informal sector," wage employment). Everywhere in the world women have two jobs—in the home and outside it. Much of their work is unrecognized and unappreciated and those who do it can expect no support. Their health suffers, their work suffers, and their children suffer. Development itself is held back as a result of their suffering.

Payam-e Hajar also reported on a study by the research center of the Ministry of Agriculture on rural women's share in agricultural production and in handicrafts.[69]

It should be noted that educated middle-class women who supported the Islamic revolution attained a legitimacy that had been denied their Westernized (*gharbzadeh*) sisters. These educated and employed Islamist women must feel rather empowered, for they are not only speaking out on issues of women's rights but are also deferred to by Islamic Republic authorities. In early 1992, for the first time, a woman member of Parliament addressed the Friday Prayers. The debate on women's rights vis-à-vis divorce has reached the highest government leadership ranks. And in early 1992, a Bureau of Women's Affairs was set up at the presidential office, "with a primary aim of protecting women and ensuring their civil rights." A thirty-four-year-old biologist was named as adviser to the president.[70]

An example of an empowered Islamist woman is Maryam Behrouzi, a parliamentary member since 1980. Born in 1945 to a religious family in Tehran, Behrouzi studied theology in university and was involved in political campaigns against the Pahlavi state. Upon completing her studies in theology, philosophy, and law, she helped organize the Iranian Women's Islamic Association in over ten districts in Tehran. In 1975 she was prohibited from pursuing her political activities but continued to do so clandestinely. She was jailed in 1978 and released in early 1979. Behrouzi has said in a newspaper interview that she regards it as her role as a woman deputy to upgrade the status of women in Iran's Islamic society. Her tactics have included criticizing existing discriminatory laws against women, such as the law that prohibits unmarried women students from receiving government scholarships to study abroad. In the same interview she emphasized the importance of women's presence in the public and private sectors and pointed out that, unlike men, women also shoulder the responsibility of

child care and housework. Behrouzi has helped draft a bill to offer scholarship entitlements to unmarried women, another bill that would allow
women to retire with pensions after twenty years of employment irrespec-
tive of their age, and yet a third bill to ease restrictions on recruitment to
the Islamic Revolutionary Guards Corps. She is also in favor of marriage
reform to strengthen women's position in the family and before the law. In
the same interview, she noted that although Islam allows a man up to four
wives (in point of fact, when the Prophet Muhammad introduced this principle, the idea was to *reduce* the number of wives a man could take to no
more than four), in the Islamic Republic "marital status is based on monog-
amous rules." One bill on which she worked would provide a widow and
her children with some form of insurance.[71]

The legitimacy accorded to Islamist women and the consolidation of
the Islamic Republic have resulted in a relaxation of previously rigid gender codes. In particular, gender segregation is no longer the norm or the
policy in Iran. In some government agencies, such as the Ministry of
Justice, men and women employees share offices. In restaurants, men and
women sit at the same table. Although some buses have extensions
reserved for women, other buses do not have designated male or female
seating. There is certainly no gender segregation in Tehran's taxis, where a
driver will squeeze in up to five passengers. Although middle-class women
still don a headscarf and a *manteau* in public, there is more variety in colors
and styles. Children's dress is no longer strictly regulated. And in one of
the most interesting developments, stage and screen acting is now regarded
as a profession like any other—in part because the theater and cinema present serious and appropriate subject matter and in part because the new
generation of actresses is a product of the Islamic Republic. Unlike the
women deemed *gharbzadeh*, middle-class women in the Islamic Republic
have the correct "cultural capital."[72]

▲ Conclusions

In the first years of the Islamic Republic, the rhetoric and the policies were
intended to segregate the sexes and domesticate the women, based on the
notion of fundamental gender difference. Educated, Western-oriented,
upper-middle-class women bore the brunt of the regime's most retrograde
policies. Throughout the 1980s women in Iran operated under a set of formidable ideologies: the ideology of gender inequality, common to all societies, and the ideology of Islamic social relations, with its emphasis on gender differences, female domesticity, and the invidious notion of female
danger. Such a cultural/ideological milieu is unfavorable to women's economic independence, equality with men, and general social progress. That
women continued to participate in public life is all the more remarkable. It

suggests a certain resilience and resistance to domination. Certainly women's activities in Iran today exceed the parameters of the traditional, orthodox school of Islam.

In turn, women's continued participation in the public sphere has helped undermine the idea of a theocratic and male-dominated society. It subverts the notion of clearly defined gender roles and a rigid, gender-based social division of labor. Further educational attainment and employment of women could challenge patriarchal practices and authoritarian structures as a whole, with implications not only for women's economic independence and personal freedom but also for wider social change in Iran.

▲ 7
Women and Social Change
in Afghanistan

The December 1979 Soviet invasion of Afghanistan was one of the seminal events in the history of the Cold War. It represented the largest Soviet military operation since World War II and the first extension of the Brezhnev Doctrine outside Eastern Europe. The invasion was also decisively important for the United States. It was during the Afghan crisis that President Jimmy Carter shifted US policy from detente to Cold War confrontation. In addition to the hostage crisis in Iran, the Afghan crisis may have contributed to Carter's defeat in the 1980 election and the implementation of a much more aggressive foreign policy under Ronald Reagan. The invasion and nine-year-long military engagement became traumatic for the Soviet Union and may have contributed to Gorbachev's "new thinking": glasnost and perestroika internally, a new foreign policy externally.[1] And of course the conflict was especially important for the people of Afghanistan, who have seen their country devastated by war and experienced enormous suffering.

Events in Afghanistan have been studied almost exclusively in geopolitical terms. The study of Afghanistan has also been extremely ideologically charged, with many accounts explicitly partisan and largely pro-mujahidin and anti-Kabul. Geopolitical and partisan perspectives have precluded an understanding of the class, gender, and cultural dynamics of the battles within Afghanistan. In particular they have obscured the importance of the struggle over women's rights, a question that has long confronted modernizing elites but whose resolution has been consistently thwarted.

The issue of women's rights in Afghanistan has historically been constrained by two structural factors: (1) the patriarchal nature of gender and social relations, deeply embedded in tribal community, and (2) the existence of a weak central state, which since at least the beginning of the twentieth century has been unable to fully implement modernizing programs. The two are interconnected, for the state's weakness is correlated with a strong (if fragmented) society resistant to state bureaucratic expansion, civil authority, regulation, monopoly of the means of violence, and extraction—the business of modern states. In his study of causes and forms of collective action, Charles Tilly has noted a pattern of reactionary movements by declining or threatened social classes. Contenders who are in danger of losing their place in a polity are especially prone to "reactive" collective action, often taking communal forms.[2] Such reactions have occurred time and again in modern Afghan history. During the 1980s the Afghan state became stronger than it had been in the past, and some important steps were taken in the late 1970s and during the 1980s to improve the legal status and social positions of women. Yet war, the fundamentalist backlash, and a hostile international climate eventually defeated the goal of the emancipation of Afghan women and modernization of the society. In the late 1980s, the Afghan leadership shifted from social transformation to national reconciliation, postponing the emancipation of women until a more stable future. And in May 1992, the government of Afghanistan collapsed and the mujahidin assumed control.

This chapter surveys the struggle for women's rights in modern Afghan history, from the earliest reforms in the nineteenth century to 1989. Like modernization itself, efforts to improve the status of women have been constrained by a social structure characterized by patriarchal gender relations, tribal feudalism, and a weak central state.

▲ Afghan Social Structure and Its Implications for Women

Historically, the population of Afghanistan has been fragmented into myriad ethnic, linguistic, religious, kin-based, and regional groupings. The bases of the social structure are the *gawm* (communal group) and the *gabila* (tribe). These microlevel social and political affiliations based on primordial ties have been structural impediments to nation-building and economic development. In this social structure, which may be termed tribal feudalism, ethnic, religious, and tribal divisions have impeded class formation, maintained provincial patterns of local independence and hostility toward the central government, and perpetuated the use of violence in place of political negotiations. Afghanistan's rugged physical environment serves to isolate communities and create microenvironments. Members of the same ethnic group and tribe who reside in different locations must adapt to separate microenvironments, which may lead different kin-based groups within the same tribe and ethnic group to use different modes of production. For example, the Durrani Pushtuns that Tapper studied were primarily agriculturalists, while the Sheikhanzai Durrani Pushtuns, who were the subject of Tavakolian's research, were primarily pastoralists.[3]

The fragmented and stagnant Afghan economy has its origins in the periodic Turkish invasions of the medieval era, which weaked havoc on town and country alike. Later, when the country became involved in early international trade, it participated not as a producer of commodities but as a facilitator of transit trade. The early trade routes between China, Central Asia, the Arab states, and Turkey, as well as those between Europe, Russia, and India, cut across Afghan territory, giving rise to what are today the major Afghan cities—Kabul, Kbat, Kandahar, and Jalalabad—and to the emergence of an urban commercial sector geared to servicing caravans and organizing transportation of goods. In contrast to European cities, Afghan towns did not integrate markets, organizing the exchange of indigenously produced commodities among producers as well as between producers and consumers. Without such organization, a true national economy never evolved. In Afghanistan economic links between the towns were initially as undeveloped as their links with the surrounding rural areas. Competition from the Russians and the British in the nineteenth century inhibited further development. The reorientation of trade toward export production (of agricultural raw materials and carpets) at the end of the nineteenth century reinforced the stagnation of the national industrial sector. Other important factors in Afghanistan's economic and social underdevelopment are its rugged terrain, making transportation hazardous and costly, the absence of central authority and a taxation system, and the persistence of tribalism and pastoral nomadism.[4]

The development planning that began in the 1950s did not reduce the by-then deeply entrenched dichotomies between rural and urban areas and between foreign trade and domestic production. On the eve of the Saur Revolution, the bazaar controlled roughly 50 percent of financial transactions (including money-lending and foreign-exchange dealings), retail trade, and foreign trade. A public sector had been created, but investment remained low. Private sector investment was hindered by high interest rates: Bazaar interest rates were between 20 percent and 40 percent per annum. The Afghan government relied heavily on foreign aid—as much as 80 percent for its development expenditure.[5] Arable land was in short supply and patterns of ownership highly inequitable, with a few families (including families of some of the mujahidin leaders) owning vast acreages on which peasants sharecropped. Agricultural productivity was low, and the system of food distribution inefficient; thus, food shortages were common.[6]

Afghan nationalism, properly speaking, is incipient at best, as the concepts of nation-state and national identity are absent from much of the population; nationalism has been promoted primarily by modernizing elites since the nineteenth century.[7] During most of the country's recent history, the fragmented groupings have waged war on each other. Battles were fought principally over land and water, sometimes over women and honor, usually over sheer power. Interethnic hostility among Afghans has been widely discussed in the literature. Nancy Tapper describes ethnic identity in terms of claims of religiously privileged descent and superiority to all other ethnic groups. Durrani women, for example, are absolutely prohibited from marrying men of a "lower" ethnic status.[8]

One of the few commonalities in this diverse country is Islam. Yet Afghan Islam is a unique combination of practices and precepts from the Shari'a and tribal customs, particularly Pushtunwali, the dominant Afghan tribal culture. For example, the absence of inheritance rights for females is contrary to Islamic law but integral to the complex web of the tribal exchange system. The practice of usury, banned under Islamic law, has been widespread, and this has kept rural households in perpetual indebtedness. Exorbitant expenditure in marriages has also contributed to the rural household's debt accumulation. The Islamic dower, *mahr*, called *walwar* in Pushtu, has been abused in the Afghan tribal-patriarchal context. The *mahr*, a payment due from groom to bride, is an essential part of the Islamic marriage contract. In the Quran the *mahr* is a nominal fee. In many Muslim countries its purpose is to provide a kind of insurance for the wife in the event of divorce or widowhood. But in tribal Afghanistan, *walwar* is understood to be compensation to the bride's father for the loss of his daughter's labor in the household and is part of the groom's ownership claim over his wife. It is the price of a girl.[9]

In his study of reforms of family law in Afghanistan, Kamali explains that the link between Islam and tribalism stems from "the fundamental fact that Islam itself was revealed in a tribal society."[10] It is true that Islam challenged many of the pre-Islamic tribal traditions of the Arabs and introduced reforms that raised the sociolegal status of women to a level hitherto unattainable, given the patriarchal customs of the Arabs. Yet Islam nevertheless left many aspects of the prevailing tribal traditions unchanged; the religion was superimposed on a patriarchal society but did not radically change many of its institutions. Tribalism, therefore, survived under Islam, and tribal customs continued to exist—sometimes violating the laws of Islam itself. In Afghanistan, extravagant marriage ceremonies, child marriages, polygamy, divorce, and inheritance seem to be influenced more by tribal custom than by the Shari'a. As Roy explains:

> The tribal code and Muslim law are in opposition. Adultery (*zina*) should, according to the Shari'a, require four witnesses if it is to be proven; for the *pushtunwali*, hearsay (*peghor*) is sufficient, for what is at stake is honor (one's self-image) and not morality (defined by the Shari'at as what is permitted as opposed to what is not). Women in the tribes are not allowed to inherit property, for that would contradict the principle of strict patrilineage, which is the very basis of the tribal system; while the Qur'an grants to women half the share of the male. The dowry, a sign of prestige, frequently exceeds the limits set by the Shari'at, while, on the other hand, the repudiation of a wife by her husband, something which, according to the

Qur'an, presents no difficulties, is practically impossible in the tribes, for that would be an insult to the wife's family. Vengeance (*badal*) is commended within the tribal code, while the Shari'at attempts to limit the occasions on which it can take place.[11]

Audrey Shalinsky, who in 1976–1977 studied Uzbek and Tajik households in Kunduz, a provincial capital in northern Afghanistan, observed that Quranic rules about women's rights are more important in urban groups than they are in rural areas: "Thus, women could own property in their own right and they could, and did, retain their earnings or inheritance for their own use." She explains:

Many women sold dairy products such as milk, yogurt, or butter which they obtained from the few animals most households kept. It was not at all unusual for women to have this type of source of supplementary income and to spend their own money on household furnishings or clothing. Though the women were veiled outside the household, recently in this urbanised situation, it had become acceptable for women occasionally to go to the bazaar and buy things themselves while they were veiled.[12]

Afghanistan is one of the few remaining cases of classic patriarchy, a function of its tribal structure and economic underdevelopment. Afghan patriarchy is tied to the prevalence of such forms of subsistence as nomadic pastoralism, herding and farming, and settled agriculture, all organized along patrilineal lines. Historically, Afghan gender roles and women's status have been tied to property relations. Property includes livestock, land, and houses or tents. Women and children tend to be assimilated into the concept of property and to belong to a male. Among the Pushtuns studied by one anthropologist, a bride who shows signs of not being a virgin on the wedding night may be murdered by her father and/or brothers. (Such is not the case, however, with the Paghmanis and Absarinas, smaller ethnic groups studied by the same anthropologist.) A widow is often remarried to a cousin or a brother of the deceased husband (the custom of levirate).[13] Polygyny is not widespread because it is economically burdensome and has tended to be practiced more often by richer men. Yet among some groups polygyny makes economic sense and could indeed prove profitable in cases where the woman is skilled and able to earn additional income. According to Kamali, "This is often the case among the Turkomens of northern Afghanistan where polygamy is encountered most frequently because the income of a second wife through rug weaving tends to offset the cost of her support." Also, in a tribal context where strength is lauded and greater value attached to the proliferation of males, polygyny would function as a means of greater reproduction of potential warriors.

Gender segregation and female seclusion exist, though they vary by ethnic group, region, mode of subsistence, social class, and family. There are few accounts of how and to what degree women veil. Formally, women have the right to attend the mosque and participate in pilgrimages, but they seldom do so because of *purdah,* an institution widely enforced by the Afghans. *Purdah* (meaning curtain) prescribes that women keep out of the sight of men who are not part of their household. Men are kept away from women through veiling and through seclusion of women at home or in separate women's quarters. Similarly, in public areas, women screen themselves with the veil or turn their backs on male strangers. Among the Ghilzai, women veil or are secluded from men to whom they could be married. Men also avoid women who are potential mates. Shalinksy's description of the "women's community"—revolving around relational ties, household work, and life-cycle ceremonies—stresses the bonding and emotional support it provides. This is clearly a world separate from the world of men. Moreover, women revert to traditional veiling behavior when outside the household. In Afghanistan veiling takes the form of a *burqa,* a tentlike coverture with only a net before the eyes. As such it is far more confining than the modern Islamist hijab.

Writing in the mid-1960s, Griffiths asserted that "the most strikingly obvious divisions in Afghanistan are between the sexes." In the towns and cities, female seclusion involves the cooperation of men. Boys learn from early childhood to warn women relatives when men approach the compound walls, to respect the privacy of women, and not to enter a compound unless permission is granted. The control over *purdah* lies largely with the eldest male household member. Strictly speaking, it is he who decides whether a woman can leave the compound or not. He is also the major decisionmaker on female education and women's participation in training and employment.[14]

Griffiths has described a conversation with the governor of a district in Kunduz, who explained with some pride

> the way in which the region's beautiful hand-woven carpets were made; how five or six women might work together for four or five months to make a patterned carpet . . . and how a man would pay a very good brideprice for a girl who was an accomplished carpet weaver. When I asked him who got the money for the carpets, he looked at me in astonishment and replied: "Why the man of course, the woman belongs to the man." This is the attitude which is the chief obstacle facing the champions of women's emancipation in Afghanistan.[15]

In many parts of the Third World, the combination of preindustrial modes of production and men's social and political control over women's lives creates a cultural matrix in which men exchange women and control their productive and reproductive capacities within the family unit. This authority, which is based on patrilineal and kinship relationships, is not diminished by women's central role in agricultural production. Indeed, in some cases the participation of women in socially productive work may result in what Haleh Afshar calls their "enslavement rather than their liberation." What Afshar means is that in such a context, a woman's labor power is controlled and allocated by someone other than herself, the products of her labor are managed by others, and she receives no remuneration for work performed. The partial penetration of capital in rural areas, where, for example, carpet-making is a commercial enterprise, allows male kin to exploit women's labor without paying any wages. Here women's ability to contribute substantially to the family income leads directly to intensified subordination and intrahousehold inequality. In many such contexts, as Papanek has noted, women may be seen as "too valuable" to educate, and the money they earn may well finance the men's education. For both economic and ideological reasons, females may not get "release time" for education or labor market employment. In extended patriarchal, patrilineal households, collective (male) interests dictate strict control of female labor deployment throughout a woman's lifetime.[16] In most parts of Afghanistan, the husband or father of a woman decides whether she can engage in paid work outside the home, and women do not have the right to keep their wages. The money is considered to be at the disposal of the husband or father.

Another pattern of gender relations, apparently less patriarchal, has been described by anthropologist Bahram Tavakolian with respect to the Pushtu-speaking Sheikhanzai nomads of western Azerbaijan. The division of labor of these goat-herding pastoralists is described by the author as entailing complementary roles rather than gender hierarchy.[17] Tavakolian stresses "the considerable respect with which women and women's work are viewed by Sheikhanzai men and the appreciation and happiness shown when a girl is born."[18] He continues:

> A Sheikhanzai household is more hard-pressed economically if there is a shortage of women than if there is a shortage of men. While adolescent boys frequently provide daily labor services to other households, especially through overnight assistance to the shepherd, girls are usually far too valuable within their own household labor supply to be available for more than a few hours at a time. A further indication of the value of women is also to be found in the customary bride-price of 1 to 3 *laks* (ca. $3500–$7000) at the time of my field research. . . . Sheikhanzai men acknowledge that their pastoral economy would be impossible without the labors of their womenfolk.[19]

What is not explained, however, given the economic centrality of girls and women, is why Sheikhanzai men marry a second wife if their first wife bears only girls.[20] Tavakolian goes on argue that Sheikhanzai women have political power, which is expressed in two forms: (1) as power wielders within a household through their direct influence over their husbands, sons, brothers, and even their fathers, and (2) as power brokers through their influence over the relationships their male kin maintain with one another and with other men.[21] But he does report that "Sheikhanzai men still come out ahead of women in most aspects of official power and certainly with respect to public recognition of their power."[22]

Entrenched patriarchal relations in Afghanistan have been threatened several times by various modernizing initiatives. But these have invariably resulted in tribal rebellion against government authority. Gregorian describes opposition to the modernizing efforts, including education for girls, of Habibullah Khan (1901–1919) and Amanullah Khan (1919–1929). Persistent government difficulty in extending education to girls has been noted by other authors. In the section below, we turn our attention to the existence of a weak modern state in a predominantly patriarchal and tribal society, which has adverse implications for reform and development, as well as for the advancement of women.

▲ Afghanistan: Prototype of a Weak State

Max Weber defined the state as an organization enforcing regulations, at least in part through a monopoly of violence. States vary in the degree to which they actually approach such an ideal type. Badie and Birnbaum suggest:

> The progress of state-building can be measured by the degree of development of certain instrumentalities whose purpose is to make the action of the state effective: bureaucracy, courts, and the military, for example. Clearly, the more complex and highly developed these instrumentalities are, the greater the capacity of the state to act on its environment and to autonomously impose collective goals distinct from the private goals generated within the social system itself. In this situation, the state's autonomy corresponds to a tangible reality.[23]

But the autonomy and capacity of a state cannot be assumed, and not all states can impose their will on social groups. Neither can there be assured outcomes of state engagements with society. Political scientists and sociologists have distinguished between "strong states" and "weak states." Strong states are those with high capabilities to penetrate society, regulate social relationships, extract resources, and appropriate or use resources in determined ways. Weak states are on the low end of a spectrum of capabilities. Many states have encountered difficulties in effecting widespread changes in people's social behavior and overall transformations in social relations. In particular, they have had difficulties achieving their leaders' aims at the local level.[24]

Clearly Afghanistan is today, and has been throughout this century, a prototypical weak state, inasmuch as the central authorities have been unable to realize their goals, mainly in regulating social relations and using resources in determined ways. The Afghan state is not alone in these short-comings; many other Third World governments, especially those of poorer countries, have been stymied in their attempts to transform their environment. Even India, normally considered a strong state, has had persistent social and economic problems, suggesting that the extent of its control is not great. As one political scientist put it, "Three decades of democratically planned development have failed to alleviate India's rural poverty."[25] But the Afghan state's predicament is especially dire and exemplifies Huntington's observation twenty years ago that many "governments simply do not govern."[26] Although Afghanistan is not immune to the general process of social change enveloping the Middle East, it has seen less trans-formation than in neighboring countries. Gregorian explains:

> For most of the nineteenth century, Afghanistan remained culturally one of the most isolated and parochial regions of the Muslim world, almost totally cut off from the mainstream of European thought. It did not under-go any direct and intensive experience of European colonial rule; on the contrary, imperialism while impressing upon the Afghans the necessity of technological borrowing, contributed to Afghan political and cultural iso-lationism.[27]

British attempts to expand their sphere of influence outward from India led to two Anglo-Afghan wars (in 1839 and 1879), which contributed to the growth of a politicoreligious nationalism and xenophobia. Moreover, the struggle strengthened the position of the Afghan tribes and the monarchy's dependence on their military might and reinforced the position of the Afghan religious establishment. Gregorian states that in the absence of noteworthy learning institutions, a secular intelligentsia, or reformist move-ments among the Afghan *ulama,* the formulation and propagation of the aims of Afghan nationalism and modernism came late. The two causes were not linked until the first two decades of the twentieth century, when a small group of educated Afghans sought to broaden the base of support for political and economic reform by merging the two movements. Under the leadership of Amanullah Khan, these "Young Afghans," inspired by the Young Turks nearby, made ambitious plans for the modernization of the country, explicitly including the emancipation of women in their agenda (as was the case in Turkey). Their ultimate failure, Gregorian notes, deter-mined the course and nature of all future reforms and modernization pro-grams in Afghanistan. According to Urban, the record of Afghanistan's leaders until 1978 was a pitiful one: They had failed to give the country any of the attributes of the modern centralized state.[28]

One example of state failure is in education. The first secondary school (for boys only) was established in 1904 and was called Habibiyeh College after its patron, Habibullah Khan. In 1913 the Afghan Department of Education was founded. In 1922 Amanullah Khan established Amaniyeh School, later renamed Lycée Esteqlal, and founded Essmat (later renamed Malalai) School for girls, which was closed after his abdication. The foundations of Kabul University were laid in 1932 when its first faculty, the School of Medicine, was established. Malalai School was reopened in the 1930s under Nadir Shah, but according to Gregorian it was promoted as a special school for nurses and midwives so as to soften the opposition of the mullahs and the other traditionalists. It was to be some two decades before Malalai would become a true secondary school and produce its first graduates. As late as 1954, the total student enrollment in Afghanistan, excluding the students at Kabul University, was 114,266, or about 4.5 percent of the approximately 2.4 million school-age children. At that time there were only thirteen primary schools, one middle school, and two secondary schools for girls, most of them in Kabul, and only an estimated 8,625 girls were receiving any kind of education. There were reportedly no girls in the village schools.[29]

▲ Early Reforms Concerning Women

Since modernization began in the mid-nineteenth century, various governments and rulers have sought to discourage excessive expenditure not only on brideprice but also on marriage celebrations. The motivation was twofold: to improve the status of women and to reduce the rural population's indebtedness. Gregorian treats this subject in the most detail for the period 1860–1940. Reforms to improve the status of women began during the reign of Abdur Rahman Khan, who ascended the throne in 1880. He abolished a long-standing customary law that, in violation of Islamic law, bound a wife not only to her husband but to his entire family as well. Widows who wanted to remarry had to marry their husband's next of kin, often against their will. Abdur Rahman decreed that the moment a husband died his wife was to be set free. Unfortunately, there is no information on the extent to which this law was enforced, but it is likely that enforcement was weak. Among Abdur Rahman's other measures was a law requiring the registration of marriages (*sabt*). He also modified a law pertaining to child marriages, permitting a girl who had been given in marriage before she had reached the age of puberty to refuse or accept her marriage ties when she attained full age. Still another law allowed women to sue their husbands for alimony or divorce in cases involving cruelty or nonsupport.[30]

Mahmud Tarzi (1866–1935), royal adviser and editor of *Siraj al-Akhbar Afghaniyah,* a biweekly paper and forum for the Young Afghans, appealed for compulsory education of all children, including girls. According to Gregorian, he was the first Afghan to take a public positive stand on feminism, dedicating a series of articles to famous women in history that discussed the many abilities of women. A monogamist himself, Tarzi never explicitly attacked polygamy, but he did so implicitly by constantly casting a family in which there was one wife and a few children as the ideal family. In his view the health, welfare, and education of Afghan families was essential to Afghan progress, so he attacked the extravagant expenditures incurred in connection with multiple marriages, which often financially ruined families.

Habibullah Khan attempted to limit the burdensome expenses incurred in connection with marriage. Most Afghans had to borrow money to meet these expenses, at times paying as much as 75 percent interest on the loan. In 1922 Habibullah placed a ceiling on the amount that could be spent on marriages, urging his people to abandon the customary public celebrations in favor of private parties. The amounts he set varied according to class. Gregorian doubts that the law was strictly enforced but notes that on a few highly publicized occasions the royal family attempted to set an example for the rest of Afghan society in this connection. The emir himself also tried to set an example for the wealthy Afghans who exceeded the legal number of four wives. Officially banning the practice of keeping concubines and female slaves, Habibullah publicly divorced all but four of his wives in 1903. Habibullah also sought to broaden the educational system and established Habibiyeh College, the first secondary school (for boys only). The Department of Education's attempts to improve and standardize the curriculum were not totally successful, however. Gregorian writes that the mullahs, especially those outside Kabul, resented the government's control of education, the teacher-training center, and the teaching of English and modern subjects in general, and they vehemently resisted all further innovation.

Habibullah Khan was assassinated in 1919, and his son, Amanullah, had the enormous task of convincing the religious establishment that modern secular education and Islam were not incompatible and that the new schools he built did not threaten the sanctity or spiritual message of Islam in Afghanistan. His most audacious acts were to begin a study-abroad program for Afghan students and to open the first schools for girls. By 1928 there were about 800 girls attending schools in Kabul, and there were even some Afghan women studying abroad, notably in Turkey, France, and Switzerland. Gregorian notes that Amanullah had plans to build five more schools for girls and intended his planned compulsory education system to apply to girls as well as boys. But both efforts were dropped after his fall in 1929.

In the 1920s Amanullah set about to improve the status of Afghan women. His first step was the abolition of slavery early in 1920, which freed women from concubinage. Although slavery as an institution had been earlier abolished by Abdur Rahman, a number of female slaves, mostly Hazaras, were still held as concubines (*suratis*) by influential men in Kabul. The Decree of 1920 (*farman-i elgha-i ghulami*) put an end to this practice, giving upper-class males a choice between officially marrying their concubines or freeing them unconditionally.[31]

In examining Amanullah's reform program and the organized resistance to it, one discovers striking parallels with the experience of the PDPA government some fifty years later. The new family law promulgated in 1921 abolished forced marriage, child marriage, and the payment of bridal money. It also established restrictions on polygamy. Child marriages and intermarriage between close kin were outlawed as contrary to Islamic principles. In the new code Amanullah reiterated Abdur Rahman's ruling that a widow was to be free of the domination of her husband's family. He followed his father's example and placed tight restrictions on wedding expenses, including dowries, and granted wives the right to appeal to the courts if their husbands did not adhere to Quranic tenets regarding marriage. In the fall of 1924, Afghan girls were given the right to choose their husbands, a measure that incensed traditionalists.

These measures were introduced under the general rubric of *himaya-i niswan,* the protection of women's rights, which the government argued were in line with the principles of Islam and its interpretation of Islamic social justice. Reforms pertaining to the emancipation of women were based on the Muslim reformist ideas initiated by Jamal al-Din Afghani and Muhammad Abduh of Egypt in the last part of the nineteenth century and later championed by modernists in Egypt, Ottoman Turkey, India, and other Muslim countries. According to Gregorian, Amanullah's general program to improve the position of women was promoted by his wife, Queen Soraya (who founded the first women's magazine, *Ershad-e Niswan*), the reformer Mahmud Tarzi and his wife, the small intelligentsia, and the modernist and nationalist Young Afghans, who were impressed by developments in Turkey, Iran, and Egypt.

The presence in Kabul of a considerable number of unveiled women, especially Turkish women who had abandoned the veil and adopted modern dress, undoubtedly encouraged the efforts of the new Afghan feminists. However, their greatest support came from Amanullah himself. It was his belief that "the keystone of the future structure of new Afghanistan would be the emancipation of women." The Afghan press, including bulletins of the war office, took part in the emancipation campaign. In 1928, during the final months of his rule, Amanullah made a frontal assault against the institution of *purdah,* or veiling and seclusion, which "hid half the Afghan nation." Because of his efforts and the personal example of Queen Soraya, some 100 Afghan women had publicly discarded the veil by October 1928.

By this time Afghan legislation was among the most progressive in the Muslim world. No other country had yet addressed the sensitive issues of child marriage and polygamy. Afghan family law on these issues became the model for similar reforms in Soviet Central Asia in 1926.[32] It is not surprising that the family law of 1921 was a major cause of the uprising instigated by the clergy in 1924.

The first organized reaction against Amanullah reforms was directed against a controversial administrative code, the *Nizam-nameh,* that he passed in 1923. Among other things, the code attempted to liberalize the position of women and to permit the government to regulate the various family problems formerly dealt with by the local mullah. A few traditionalist mullahs inveighed against the new code, asserting that it was contrary to the precepts of Islamic law. Their cause was picked up in 1924 by the Mangal tribe of the Khost region and soon assumed dangerous proportions. By March armed warfare had broken out. The religious and tribal leaders of the revolt were particularly exercised over the sections of the code that deprived men of full authority over their wives and daughters, an authority that had been sanctioned by time-honored custom. They were further incensed at the opening of public schools for girls.

The Khost rebellion continued for more than nine months and dramatically illustrated the weakness of the Afghan army. Gregorian writes that Amanullah was forced to fall back on levies from certain tribes and proclaim a *jihad* before he was able to suppress the revolt. The rebels suffered enormous losses, as did the government side. The cost of the rebellion represented the government's total receipts for two years. As a result the king was forced to postpone various modernization projects and revoke or modify many important sections of the *Nizam-nameh*; the schooling of girls, for example, was limited to those under twelve. In 1928 the Loya Jirga, the traditional Afghan consultative body, rejected Amanullah's proposal to set an age limit on marriage, which the king suggested should be eighteen for girls and twenty for men. They also vehemently opposed modern, Western education for Afghan girls, either in Afghanistan or outside it.

In the fall of 1928, a group of female students was sent to Turkey for higher education, and the Association for the Protection of Women's Rights (*Anjoman-i Hemayat-i Neswan*) was established to help women fight domestic injustice and take a role in public life. The queen herself presided over several committees to strengthen the emancipation campaign. These unprecedented measures violated traditional norms and offended religious leaders and their following, especially in rural areas. Reaction against the campaign for women's emancipation was a major factor in the outbreak of violent disturbances in November and December 1928.

Amanullah's reform program threatened to upset the entire structure of patriarchal relations and property rights. When the king banned the practice of polygamy among government officials it caused an uproar among the religious establishment. A tribal revolt ensued, led by a bandit claiming Islamic credentials. As the political situation deteriorated, Amanullah was compelled to cancel most of his social reforms and suspend his controversial administrative measures. The Afghan girls studying in Constantinople were to be recalled, and the schools for girls were to be closed; women were not to go unveiled or cut their hair; the mullahs were no longer to be required to obtain teaching certificates; compulsory military recruitment was to be abandoned and the old tribal system reinstated. As a last, desperate concession, the unhappy emir agreed to the formation of a council of fifty notables, to be chosen from among "the most respected religious luminaries and tribal chieftains," and promised to abide by their advice and conform to Islamic law as interpreted by the orthodox religious leaders. Any measure the government proposed to enact was to be ratified by this council. But in the end, all of these concessions were to no avail. The rebels attacked Kabul, and Amanullah abdicated and left Afghanistan.

Not until the 1950s were reforms attempted again. The 1949 marriage law once again prohibited the practice of *walwar,* limiting payment to the Quranic *mahr,* and banned other ostentatious life-cycle ceremonies. It prohibited many of the expensive aspects of birth, circumcision, marriage, and burial rituals, but was difficult to enforce. The marriage law of 1971 was a further attempt to curb the indebtedness arising from the costs of marriage, which "are a burden for Afghan society as a whole." As Tapper explains, the heaviest expenses any household has to bear are concerned with marriage. The choice of bride, the agreed brideprice, and the time taken to complete a marriage may visibly confirm or indeed increase a household's poverty. The civil law of 1977 abolished child marriage and set sixteen as the age of majority for girls, removing the right of parents and guardians to wed a girl (for a brideprice) at the onset of puberty, as was customary. But in the absence of any specified sanctions for violators, the law remained weak and was ignored. Furthermore, the law left the husband's right to unilateral divorce basically untouched.[33]

The historical background presented above suggests the enormous difficulty faced by Afghan modernizers. The Afghan state had been too weak to implement reforms or undertake modernization in an effective way and was constantly confronted by strong religious-tribal forces seeking to prevent any change whatsoever, particularly in their power. In light of the historical record on modernization and social reforms, including reforms to improve the status of women, the revolutionary program the Taraki government announced in April 1978 was perhaps doomed. Faced with what Gregorian, writing in the late 1960s, frequently referred to as the "staggering socio-economic problems" of the country and the religious-traditionalist forces that have prevented resolution of these problems, the reformers of 1978 impatiently wished for change and betterment, assisted by their Soviet neighbors. But if Afghan history suggested anything, it was that social change could not come about rapidly and that direct foreign intervention in particular was highly unpopular. Moreover, the state—small and weak as it was—would be incapable of implementing its program in an effective way.

At the same time, all social and economic indicators proclaimed the need for change, especially in the areas of literacy, education, health, food production and distribution, infrastructural development, and the status of women.

▲ Characteristics of Afghan Patriarchy

Kamali notes that in Afghanistan, a man may acquire a wife in any one of the following four ways: He may inherit a widow, gain a bride in exchange marriage, gain a bride in compensation for a crime of which he or his relatives were the victim, or pay a brideprice. The last method is the most usual, the other three being variations of this form. *Walwar* is the sum of money (or commodity) paid by the groom or his family to the head of the bride's household. Wealthier men can more easily afford brides, and as wealthy men usually happen to be more advanced in age, the bride's parents often arrange the marriage of their young daughters to older men.[34] In a combination of pre-Islamic and Islamic customs, men exercise control over women in two crucial ways: by controlling marriage and property, and by barring land ownership for women (contrary to Islamic law and the actual practice in many other Muslim countries), especially among the Pushtuns.

The exchange of women in precapitalist agrarian societies organized around kinship structures has been extensively discussed in anthropological and feminist literature. The concept of honor in patriarchal societies has similarly been elaborated.[35] Both are important elements in Pushtunwali. Its elements are highly masculinist. Tapper reports that among the Durrani Pushtuns of north-central Afghanistan, "The members of the community discuss control of all resources—especially labor, land, and women—in terms of honor." *Purdah* is one important component of the honor code, honor being the most desired status symbol of Afghan society. It is an imperative component of the cultural codex and ascribed to the family or individual members by the outside world. Families in Afghanistan are nourished by the degree to which honor is bestowed upon the household, and women are crucial in this process. They are seen as the bearers of the honor of the family; the honor of a man is measured by others through the reputation and behavior of his wife and daughters. If they are seen to deviate from the norm by prominent figures in the community, the reputation of the entire household suffers, and the male is regarded as incompetent or unable to control his home affairs. Shame, the single most status-depriving social stigma, is then ascribed to the entire household.[36]

In Afghanistan, marriage, enforced or otherwise, has traditionally been a way of ending feuds, cementing a political alliance between families, or increasing a family's prestige. The exchange of women and the conception of women as pieces of property are integral to the social organization of Afghan tribal-feudalism. Women are given for brideprice or in compensation for blood to maintain a "status hierarchy" among households. In the exchange system, men are ranked in the first and highest sphere. Direct exchanges between them include the most honorable and manly of all activities, and these activities are prime expressions of status: vengeance and feud, political support and hospitality, and the practice of sanctuary. Women belong to the second sphere; they are often treated exclusively as reproducers and pawns in economic and political exchanges. There is only one proper conversion between the first two spheres: Two or more women can be given in compensation for the killing or injury of one man. Mobility and migration patterns also revolve around the brideprice. For example, men from one region will travel to another to find inexpensive brides, while other men will travel elsewhere because they can obtain a higher price for their daughters.[37]

Studies on Pushtunwali note that the code of Afghan behavior among the Pushtuns, who comprise over half the population, possesses three core elements: hospitality, refuge, and revenge. Other key values are equality, respect, pride, bravery, *purdah,* pursuit of romantic encounters, worship of God, and devoted love for a friend. These are, once again, male values. *Purdah* is a key element in protection of the family's pride and honor; Boesen has noted a Pushtun saying that "a woman is best either in the house or in the grave." This seclusion from the world outside the family walls is customarily justified by invoking Quranic prescription and by the notion that women are basically licentious and tempt men. Howard-Merriam explains that women are regarded as subordinates dependent on their husbands, a relationship exemplified by women's never asking men for their whereabouts or expecting marital fidelity. Women also are expected to give all the meat, choicest food, and best clothing to their husbands, as well as their personal wealth, if so demanded. Censuses and surveys undertaken in 1967, 1972–1974, and 1979 have revealed an unusually high ratio of males to females that exceeds even the expected underreporting of females in a conservative Islamic society. Statistical estimates showed that females constituted 48 percent of the whole population. This low figure is in part a result of a high rate of maternal mortality and probably in part reflects sex bias in the provision of food and health care to females.[38]

Since a woman's standing is maintained primarily through bearing sons to continue the family, she of course must marry; in the context of classic patriarchy, only through marriage can one's basic needs be legitimately fulfilled. The choice of husband is made by her family, with its own concerns for lineage maintenance and/or property gain. The best she can hope for is a handsome and kind cousin or close relative she has known and with whom she has grown up. The worst is an old man from another village whom she has never seen and who is unkind. In either case he is obliged to provide for her materially and, it is to be hoped, father her sons, who will endow her with status in her new home. If the husband treats her unbearably she does have the option of breaking out and returning to her own family or seeking refuge with another family. Howard-Merriam notes that this weapon is not used often, however, as a woman's natal family has given up rights to her through the brideprice at the time of marriage.[39]

Kamali sums up matrimonial problems in the following way:

> Extravagant marriage ceremonies and the payment of a huge brideprice . . . are included in the issues which have remained unresolved despite legislative efforts during the last sixty years. In a country where the annual per capita income is barely $150 a marriage can cost anything up to $20,000 or more. Marriage, as a result, has become the privilege of the wealthy which not only leads to intolerable discrimination against the poor but also seriously undermines the human dignity of women. Extravagant ceremonies also weaken the financial status of the family and tend to exacerbate poverty. They increase the dependence of the adults on the family resources thereby weakening their position regarding the exercise of their right of consent in marriage and their freedom of choice for a life partner. These excesses often bring about a wide disparity of age between the spouses and lead to resentment and frustration on the part of the married couple. And finally, such extravagant practices contribute to the continuation of the tradition-bound society and impede healthy social change.[40]

On the eve of the Saur Revolution, Afghanistan was among the poorest countries of the world, with low life expectancy, high child mortality, widespread illiteracy, malnutrition, and an unproductive agricultural system. Its economy was largely agricultural, although there was some light industry, mainly in textiles. Seventy-eight percent of the labor force was rural and agricultural. Infrastructure—especially paved roads, railways, and communications—was highly undeveloped. Along with high fertility rates, Afghanistan's infant mortality, under-five mortality, and maternal mortality rates were also very high. There was only one doctor for every 3,000 people, with medical facilities available only in the capital and a number of other cities. In 1979 medical services were poor and unevenly distributed; there was provision for only about 25 percent of the population, and facilities were concentrated in urban areas. Fifty percent of children died before the age of five.

Life expectancy was only about forty years for women and forty-two years for men, which made Afghanistan one of the few countries in the world with a higher life expectancy for men than for women. This may be explained in part by widespread cruelty toward women, noted by a number of observers. The estimated total fertility rate was seven births per woman. The infant mortality rate was about 190 of 1,000 live births—that is, almost one in five. Children died from infections, malnourishment, and poor

Table 7.1 Social Indicators, Afghanistan, 1965 and 1975

			1965	1975
AREA				
Total land area (thousands of sq. km)			647.5	647.5
Agricultural (percentage of total)			58.5	58.8
GNP PER CAPITA (current US dollars)			70	140
POPULATION AND VITAL STATISTICS				
Total population (thousands)			11,115	14,038
Urban population (percentage of total)			9	13
Population growth rate (in percent)		Total	n.a.	2.4
		Urban	n.a.	5.9
Life expectancy at birth (years)			35	37
Population density per sq. km of agricultural land			29	37
Population age structure (in percent)		0–14 years	43	45
		15–64 years	55	53
		65 and above	3	3
Crude birthrate (per 1,000)			54	54
Crude death rate (per 1,000)			29	29
Total fertility rate			8.0	8.0
Infant mortality rate (per 1,000)			n.a.	190
Child death rate (per 1,000)			39	35
FOOD, HEALTH, AND NUTRITION				
Index for food production per capita (1979–1981 = 100)			102	102
Per capita supply of				
Calories (per day)			2,203	2,206
Proteins (grams per day)			68	69
Population per physician (in thousands)			15.8	n.a.
Population per nurse (in thousands)			24.4	15.1
Population per hospital bed (in thousands)			n.a.	n.a.
Access to safe water (percentage of population):		Total	n.a.	6
		Urban	n.a.	20
		Rural	n.a.	3
LABOR FORCE				
Total labor force (in thousands)			3,733	4,569
Female (in percent)			6	7
Agriculture (in percent)			69	64
Industry (in percent)			11	13
Participation rate (in percent)		Total	31	30
		Male	56	54
		Female	4	4
Age dependency (in percent)			83.2	89.6
EDUCATION				
Enrollment rates	Primary	Total	16	26
		Male	26	44
		Female	5	8
	Secondary	Total	2	8
		Male	4	13
		Female	1	2
Pupil-teacher ratio	Primary		53	42
	Secondary		22	12
Pupils reaching grade six (in percent)			n.a.	50

Source: World Bank, *Social Indicators of Development 1988* (Baltimore: Johns Hopkins University Press, 1988), pp. 10–11.
   Note: n.a. = information not available

hygiene. The most frequent causes of infant death were respiratory infections, tuberculosis, diarrhea, malnutrition, and measles. In 1979 some 80 percent had not yet had any formal schooling, whereas religious education in Quranic schools held in the mosques was widespread. Formal educational facilities were mainly concentrated in urban areas, especially higher-level institutions. About 30 percent of the male population above five years of age was estimated to be literate, compared to only about 4 percent of the female population.[41] (See Table 7.1 for social indicators in 1965 and 1975.)

▲ The PDPA and Women's Rights

In 1965 a group from the small Afghan intelligentsia formed the People's Democratic Party of Afghanistan (PDPA). Invoking the Amanullah experiment, the PDPA envisaged a national democratic government to liberate Afghanistan from backwardness. Among its demands were primary education for all children in their mother tongue and the development of the different languages and cultures of the country. Its social demands included guarantees of the right to work, equal treatment for women, a forty-two-hour week, paid sick and maternity leave, and a ban on child labor.[42] That same year six women activists formed the Democratic Organization of Afghan Women (DOAW). DOAW's main objectives were to eliminate illiteracy among women, forced marriages, and the brideprice. From its inception, however, the DOAW encountered hostility from mullahs and other conservative elements. As a result of the activities of the DOAW and the PDPA, women won the right to vote, and in the 1970s four women from the DOAW were elected to Parliament. In the years before the Saur Revolution, the DOAW managed to win the legal right of women to study abroad. Another achievement was winning the right of women to work outside the home, previously the privilege of a few women from elite families. Both the PDPA and the DOAW were eager for more profound, extensive, and permanent changes.[43]

Among the most remarkable and influential of the DOAW activists was Anahita Ratebzad. In the 1950s she studied nursing in the United States, then returned to Kabul as director and instructor of nursing at the Women's Hospital. Nancy Dupree explains that when the faculty for women at Kabul University was established, Ratebzad entered the medical college and became a member of its teaching staff upon graduation in 1963. She joined the PDPA in 1965 and, along with three other women, ran as a candidate for Parliament. This was the first time liberals and leftists had openly appeared in the political arena, and they confronted a reaction against female visibility on the part of conservative members of Parliament. In 1968 the latter proposed to enact a law prohibiting young women from studying abroad. Hundreds of female students demonstrated in opposition.

In 1970 two reactionary mullahs protested such public evidence of female liberation as miniskirts, women teachers, and schoolgirls by shooting at the legs of women in Western dress and splashing them with acid. (Among those who joined in this action was Gulbeddin Hekmatyar, who went on to be a leading figure in the mujahidin, the "freedom fighters" hailed by President Reagan.) This time there was a protest demonstration of 5,000 girls.[44]

Modernization, however limited, had created a stratum of men and women eager for further and deeper social change. According to ILO data, Afghanistan in 1979 had a female population of 6.3 million, of whom 313,000 were considered economically active. Of that figure, 85 percent were production-related workers, employed mainly in textiles (clothing and carpets), where they typically did not receive a wage, a pattern also found in Iran and Turkey. The other major category of employed women was "professional, technical, and related workers": 13,000 women, or 4 percent of the economically active female population. These women were mostly teachers, nurses, government employees (all high-status occupations), secretaries, hairdressers, and entertainers (members of the salaried middle class). Two or three were parliamentarians. The salaried middle class, the modern working class, and the female labor force in Afghanistan were all small but a part of the social fabric nonetheless. (See Table 7.2 for data on the economically active population in 1979.)

In April 1978 the PDPA, after having seized power in the Saur (April) Revolution, introduced rapid reforms to change the political and social structure of Afghan society, including patterns of land tenure and gender relations. Three decrees—Nos. 6, 7, and 8—were the main planks of the program of social and economic reform. Decree No. 6 was intended to put an end to land mortgage and indebtedness; No. 7 was designed to stop the payment of brideprice and give women more freedom of choice in marriage; No. 8 consisted of rules and regulations for the confiscation and redistribution of land. The three decrees were complementary, particularly Decrees No. 6 and 7, for, as noted earlier in this chapter, extravagant expenditure on marriage added to or perpetuated rural households' indebtedness. Decree No. 7, however, seems to have been the most controversial, as it was meant to fundamentally change the institution of marriage. The Taraki government issued the decree with the explicit intention of ensuring equal rights for women and removing patriarchal and feudalistic ties between husband and wife. It was recognized that women were economically exploited in Afghan society, and the decree therefore outlawed traditional cultural practices that were economically significant. Putting a price on the bride was prohibited, and the woman's dowry was limited. Forced marriages and the practice of levirate were outlawed, along with marriage through subterfuge or coercion. A minimum age of marriage was set for both genders: sixteen years for women and eighteen years for men. In a

Table 7.2 Economically Active Population by Industry, Status, and Sex:
          Afghanistan, 1979

Industry (Major divisions)	Total	%	Males	Females
Afghanistan				
1 Agriculture, hunting, forestry & fishing	2,369,481	60.1	2,358,821	10,660
2 Mining & quarrying	59,339	1.5	57,492	1,847
3 Manufacturing	423,373	10.7	170,908	252,465
4 Electricity, gas & water	11,354	0.3	11,078	276
5 Construction	51,086	1.3	50,670	416
6 Wholesale/retail trade, restaurants & hotels	137,860	3.5	135,242	2,618
7 Transport, storage & communication	66,243	1.6	65,376	867
8–9 Major divisions 8 & 9	749,345	19.0	716,511	32,834
Unemployed persons not previously employed	77,510	2.0	66,057	11,453
Total	3,945,591	100.0	3,632,155	313,436

Source: ILO, *Yearbook of Labour Statistics 1945–1989: Retrospective Edition on Population Censuses* (Geneva: ILO, 1990).
  Note: Information from the June 1979 census. Major divisions 8 & 9 refer to business services and to community, social, and personal services.

speech on November 4, 1978, President Taraki declared: "Through the issuance of decrees No. 6 and 7, the hard-working peasants were freed from bonds of oppressors and money-lenders, ending the sale of girls for good as hereafter nobody would be entitled to sell any girl or woman in this country."[45]

The six articles of Decree No. 7 were as follows:

Article 1. No one shall engage a girl or give her in marriage in exchange for cash or commodities.

Article 2. No one shall compel the bridegroom or his guardians to give holiday presents to the girl or her family.

Article 3. The girl or her guardian shall not take cash or commodities in the name of dower in excess of ten *dirham* [Arabic coinage] according to Shari'at, which is not more than 300 afs. [about U.S. $10] on the basis of the bank rate of silver.

Article 4. Engagements and marriage shall take place with the full consent of the parties involved: (a) No one shall force marriage; (b) No one shall prevent the free marriage of a widow or force her into marriage because of family relationships [the levirate] or patriarchal ties; (c) No one shall prevent legal marriages on the pretext of engagement, forced engagement expenses, or by using force.

Article 5. Engagement and marriages for women under sixteen and men under eighteen are not permissible.

Article 6. (1) Violators shall be liable to imprisonment from six months to three years; (2) Cash or commodities accepted in violation of the provisions of this decree shall be confiscated.

Along with the promulgation of this audacious decree, the PDPA government embarked upon an aggressive literacy campaign led by the DOAW, whose task was to educate women, bring them out of seclusion, and initiate social programs. Literacy programs were expanded, with the objective of supplying all adult citizens with basic reading and writing skills within a year. Throughout the countryside, PDPA cadres established literacy classes for men, women, and children in villages; by August 1979 the government had established 600 new schools.[46] The PDPA's rationale for pursuing the rural literacy campaign with some zeal was that all previous reformers had made literacy a matter of choice; male guardians had chosen not to allow their females to be educated, and thus 99 percent of all Afghan women were illiterate. It was therefore decided not to allow literacy to remain a matter of (men's) choice but rather make it a matter of principle and law.

This was clearly a bold program for social change, one aimed at the rapid transformation of a patriarchal society and decentralized power structure based on tribal and landlord authority. Revolutionary change, state-building, and women's rights subsequently went hand in hand. The emphasis on women's rights on the part of the PDPA reflected (1) the party's socialist/Marxist ideology; (2) its modernizing and egalitarian outlook; (3) its social base and origins—urban middle-class professionals educated in the United States, USSR, India, and Western and Eastern Europe; and (4) the number and position of women within the PDPA, especially the outspoken and dynamic Anahita Ratebzad.

In 1976 Ratebzad had been elected to the central committee of the PDPA. Following the Saur Revolution, she was elected to the Revolutionary Council of the Democratic Republic of Afghanistan (DRA) and appointed minister of social affairs. Other influential PDPA women in the Taraki government (April 1978–September 1979) were Sultana Umayd, director of Kabul Girls' School; Soraya, president of the DOAW; Ruhafza Kamyar, principal of the DOAW's vocational high school; Firouza, director of the Afghan Red Crescent Society (Red Cross); Dilara Mahak, principal of the Amana Fidawa School; and Professor Mrs. R. S. Siddiqui (who was especially outspoken in her criticism of "feudalistic patriarchal relations"). In the Amin government (September–December 1979), the following women headed schools and the women's organization and sat on government subcommittees: Fawjiyah Shahsawari, Dr. Aziza, Shirin Afzal, and Alamat Tolqun. These were the women who were behind the program for women's rights. Their spirit was reflected in an editorial in the *Kabul Times* (May 25, 1978) that asserted: "Privileges which women, by right, must have are equal education, job security, health services, and free time to rear a healthy generation for building the future of this country. Educating and enlightening women is now the subject of close government scrutiny."[47] Their intention was to expand literacy, especially for girls and women, encourage income-generating projects and employment for women, provide health and legal services for women, and eliminate those aspects of Muslim family law that discriminate against women: unilateral male repudiation, father's exclusive rights to child custody, unequal inheritance, and male guardianship over women.

▲ Internationalized Civil Conflict

As mentioned above, the Saur Revolution was considered not a socialist revolution—which in any event was inconceivable in a tribal-feudalistic society—but a "national democratic revolution." President Taraki himself, in his first press conference on May 7, 1978, characterized the new regime as reformist, constructive, and tolerant of Islam. Taraki's conciliatory gestures, such as attendance at Friday congregational prayers and assurances that his government's policies would be consistent with Islamic principles, failed to prevent the mobilization of opposition. In response to the decree of July 1978 on agrarian reform, which reduced or cancelled all rural debts prior to 1984 and forbade lenders to collect usury in the future, many angry lenders murdered debtors who refused to pay.[48] There was also universal resistance to the new marriage regulations, which, coupled with compulsory education for girls, raised the threat of women refusing to obey and submit to family (male) authority. Believing that women should not appear at public gatherings, villagers often refused to attend literacy classes after the first day. PDPA cadres viewed this attitude as retrograde and thus resorted to different forms of persuasion, including physical force, to make the villagers return to literacy classes. Often PDPA cadres were either kicked out of the village or murdered. In the summer of 1978 refugees began pouring into Pakistan, giving as their major reason the forceful implementation of the literacy program among their women. In Kandahar three literacy workers from the women's organization were killed as symbols of the unwanted revolution. Nancy Dupree reports that two men killed all the women in their families to prevent them from "dishonor." According to another observer, the reforms "inevitably aroused the opposition of Afghan men, whose male chauvinism is as massive as the mountains of the Hindu Kush."[49]

The content of Decree No. 7 and the coercion of women into education were perceived by some as unbearable interference in domestic life. The prohibition of the brideprice also prevented the traditional transactions and ruined the economy of many households that had counted on brideprice as convertible capital for the future. Compulsory education was also disliked because the male householder could no longer be in control of the women and their external relations; if women were not in *purdah,* then the reputation of the household was at risk. These kinds of sentiments against the reforms are taken by many observers as the main reasons for the early resistance. Reaction was soon to follow. After the announcement of the decree, serious resistance against the PDPA regime was organized in Paktia and spread rapidly to other areas of eastern Afghanistan.[50]

Land reform, cancellation of peasants' debts, and marriage reform threatened vested rural interests and patriarchal structures. The large landowners, the religious establishment, and money lenders were especially appalled at the prospect of social structural transformation. An Islamist opposition began organizing and conducted several armed actions against the government in the spring of 1979. Thus, over a year prior to the Soviet military intervention, reaction developed to the government's program for land reform and women's rights. Internal battles within the PDPA (especially between its two wings, Parcham and Khalq) contributed to the government's difficulties. In September 1979 President Taraki was killed on the orders of his deputy, Hafizullah Amin, a ruthless and ambitious man who imprisoned and executed hundreds of his own comrades and further alienated the population. The Pakistani regime of Zia ul-Haq was opposed to having leftists next door and supported the armed uprising of the mujahidin. In December 1979 the Soviet army intervened. Amin was killed and succeeded by Babrak Karmal, who initiated what is called "the second phase" (*marhale-i dovvom*), predicated upon a more gradualist approach to change. Even so, the mujahidin continued their attacks, encouraged by Pakistan and the United States. In turn, Soviet aircraft carried out bomb raids that resulted in considerable destruction as well as further migration.

It should be noted that not everyone in the PDPA and the DOAW was in favor of the pace of the reforms. According to Soraya, many DOAW activists, including herself, were opposed to the pace and the compulsory nature of the program for land reform, women's education, and the new family law. As a result of her antagonism toward Hafizullah Amin, Soraya, like many members of the PDPA's Parcham wing, was imprisoned and even endured torture. She, along with the others, was released after the Soviet intervention, the death of Amin, and his replacement by Babrak Karmal.

In 1980 the PDPA slowed down its reform program and announced its intention to eliminate illiteracy in the cities in seven years and in the provinces in ten. In an interview that year Anahita Ratebzad conceded errors, "in particular the compulsory education of women," to which she added, "The reactionary elements immediately made use of these mistakes to spread discontent among the population."[51] Despite the slowing down of reforms (including concessions such as the restoration of Islamic family law),[52] the opposition movement spread, supported by Pakistan, the United States, China, the Islamic Republic of Iran, and Saudi Arabia. In contrast to the Iranian state next door, the Afghan state was unable to impose its will through an extensive administrative and military apparatus. As a result, the programs on land redistribution and women's rights faltered. The government's efforts to raise women's status by changing marriage laws were stymied by patriarchal structures highly resistant to change and by an extremely hostile international environment.

▲ From Revolution to Reconciliation

The DOAW was renamed the All-Afghan Women's Council in 1986 and underwent a shift in orientation: It became less radical and more of a service organization providing social and legal assistance to poor Afghan women. During the late 1980s the Women's Council was led by Massouma Esmaty Wardak, an early DOAW member and member of Parliament but not a PDPA member.[53] The PDPA's emphasis on the woman question subsided in favor of a concerted effort at "national reconciliation," which began in January 1987. In the constitution of November 1988, PDPA members and activists from the Women's Council tried to retain an article stipulating the equality of women with men. This measure, however, was opposed by the non-PDPA members of the assembly. A compromise was reached in the form of another article stating that all Afghan citizens, male and female, have equal rights and obligations before the law. According to a PDPA official, this compromise was reached after PDPA members and delegates from the Women's Council failed in their attempts to include an equal rights clause.[54]

Article 38 of the Constitution of the Republic of Afghanistan, ratified in November 1987, stated:

> Citizens of the Republic of Afghanistan, both men and women, have equal rights and duties before the law, irrespective of their national, racial, linguistic, tribal, educational and social status, religion, creed, political conviction, occupation, kinship, wealth, and residence. Designation of any illegal privilege of discrimination against rights and duties of citizens is forbidden.[55]

Mark Urban, a political journalist, was one of the few writers on Afghanistan to observe that "one genuine achievement of the revolution has been the emancipation of (mainly urban) women." He continued: "There is no doubt that thousands of women are committed to the regime, as their prominent participation in Revolutionary Defense Group militias shows. Eyewitnesses stated that militant militiawomen played a key role in defending the besieged town of Urgun in 1983. Four of the seven militia commanders appointed to the Revolutionary Council in January 1986 were women."[56]

Throughout the 1980s activist women continued to be engaged in formal politics. They continued to participate in the different ranks of the party and the government, although there were no women in the Council of Ministers. The Loya Jirga included women delegates, and in 1989 the National Assembly had seven female members. In 1989 women in prominent positions included Massouma Esmaty Wardak, president of the Women's Council; Shafiqeh Razmandeh, vice president of the Women's Council; Soraya, director in the late 1980s of the Afghan Red Crescent Society; Zahereh Dadmal, director of the Kabul Women's Club; and Dr. Soheila, chief surgeon of the military hospital, who also held the rank of general. The central committee of the PDPA had several women members, including Jamila Palwasha and Ruhafza Kamyar. Indeed, Mrs. Ruhafza's position exemplifies the sort of social mobility afforded women by the

Ruhafza Kamyar, foreman of the Kabul Construction Plant. Mrs. Ruhafza was also a "model worker," a party member, and a grandmother. Photo: Val Moghadam

PDPA. An alternate member of the central committee of the PDPA, she was also a working-class grandmother and "model worker" at the Kabul Construction Plant, where she did electrical wiring and supervised male workers.

In Kabul in January–February 1989, I saw women employees in all government agencies and social organizations visited. Ariana Airlines employed female as well as male flight attendants. An employee of the Peace, Solidarity and Friendship Organization remarked that he was thirty-seven and male, yet he had a supervisor who was ten years younger and female. There were female radio announcers, and the evening news (whether in Pushtu or Dari) was read by one male and one female announcer. The female announcer was neither veiled nor wearing a headscarf. There were women technicians and reporters working for radio and television stations, as well as newspapers and magazines. Women workers were present in the binding section of a printing house in Kabul, in the page-setting section of the Higher and Vocational Education press house, at the CREPCA state-run carpet company (where young women wove carpets and received a wage), and at the Kabul Construction Plant (which specializes in housing and prefabricated materials). Like their male counterparts, these women were members of the Central Trade Union. I also saw one woman employee (and several female volunteer soldiers) at Pol-e Charkhi Prison; she was assigned to the women's section, where she oversaw the six remaining female political prisoners, all charged with terrorist acts. I was told there were women soldiers and officers in the regular armed forces, as well as in the militia and Women's Self-Defense (Defense of the Revolution) units. There were women in security, intelligence, and the police agencies, women involved in logistics in the Ministry of Defense, women parachutists, even women veterinarians—the latter occupation is usually off-limits to women in Muslim countries. In 1989 all female members of the PDPA received military training and arms. These women were prominent at a party rally of some 50,000 held in early February 1989. As a concession to traditionalist elements, schools were now gender-segregated above the primary level, and middle school and secondary school girls could only be taught by female teachers. In offices and other workplaces, however, there was no segregation. Neither were buses divided into male and female sections.

In June 1990 the PDPA held a party congress and voted to change its name to Hezb-e Vatan (Homeland Party) and emphasize nationalism and reconciliation. One consequence of this political reorganization was the dismantling of a number of quasi-independent "social organizations" that had effectively functioned to increase female participation and visibility. Apart from the PDPA itself, they included the Council of Trade Unions, the Democratic Youth Organization, the Peace, Solidarity and Friendship Organization, the Women's Council, and the Red Crescent Society.[57]

▲ The Afghan Women's Council

The most important organization actively involved in women's rights and betterment was the Afghan Women's Council (AWC), a high-profile social organization that in 1989 was run by Massouma Esmaty Wardak and her staff of eight women. Mrs. Wardak (who in 1990 was appointed minister of education) was not a member of the PDPA, though some of her staff were. She is a graduate of the Academy of Sciences with a degree in sociology and an interest in literature and history. Among her published works is a book entitled *The Position and Role of Afghan Women in Afghan Society: From the Late 18th to the Late 19th Century;* she also wrote the introduction to a book on Mahmud Tarzi. Active in political and social affairs since the 1960s, she told me that she saw no contradiction between her activities and her religious beliefs: "Hekmatyar and some others think that only they are true Muslims. But I am a Muslim, too, and all those Afghan women working and studying in Kabul are also Muslims."[58]

Both Mrs. Wardak and Ms. Soraya (the latter president of the Red Crescent Society and a former president of the Women's Council) explained that the Women's Council was less political and more social and service-oriented than it had been in the past, especially when it was under the direction of Anahita Ratebzad. Soraya's view was that the reform program initiated by the Taraki government and the PDPA in 1978 had been ill-conceived, badly implemented, and too dramatic and hasty for the Afghan rural population. "We now have a gradualist approach," she said. The AWC provided social services to women, such as literacy and vocational training in such fields as secretarial work, hairdressing, and sewing (workshops were located in the complex); organized income-generating activities such as handicraft production (mainly rug- and carpet-weaving, as well as sewing); offered assistance to mothers and widows of "martyrs of the Revolution" in the form of pensions and coupons; and gave legal advice, mainly through a network of female lawyers. Some women had "outwork" arrangements with the AWC; as Mrs. Wardak explained, "They prefer to work at home; they bring their work to us and we pay them." During two trips to the Women's Council, I was able to observe dozens of women (many of them poor and veiled) entering the grounds to attend a class or to seek advice.

An example of the kind of cases and causes the AWC took up was the complaint by twenty-two-year-old Najiba, who had been abandoned by her husband for another woman because she could not give him a child. He had since remarried, but the AWC took up Najiba's case for maintenance rights

Massouma Esmaty-Wardak, director of the Afghan Women's Council, conducting a staff meeting in 1988. Photo: Ellen Ray

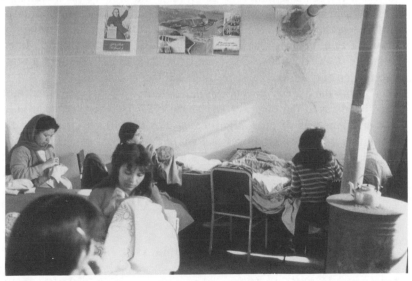

A sewing and embroidery workshop at the Kabul Women's Club. These women earned a salary. The club also offered literacy and other classes. Photo: Val Moghadam

in accordance with the law. According to Najiba: "Earlier a woman like me would have had no prospects. Today I am assured of my rights as an individual, and have also been given a job due to the efforts of the AWC."[59]

Mrs. Wardak told me the AWC had a membership of 150,000 with branches in all provinces except Wardak and Katawaz. The branches organized traditional festivals, which included awards for handicraft pieces, and "peace camps" that provided medical care and distributed garments and relief goods free of charge. The branches also assisted women in income-generating activities such as raising chickens, producing eggs and milk for sale, and sewing and craftwork. The work of the AWC continued to be supported by the government, which provided it with a generous budget. The principal objectives of the AWC were raising women's social consciousness, making them aware of their rights (particularly their right to literacy and work), and improving women's living conditions and professional skills. Mrs. Wardak stressed equal pay with men and workplace child care as two important achievements. As Decree No. 7 had been largely ignored by the population and the government had been unable to enforce it, there was an ongoing radio and TV campaign "against the buying and selling of girls." The AWC was also trying to change the laws on child custody, based on Muslim family law, that favor the father and his agnates.[60]

Like the AWC, the Kabul Women's Club was located on spacious grounds and held two-hour literacy classes every day. It also offered vocational training and employment workshops where women learned to weave rugs and carpets, sew uniforms, embroider, and produce handicrafts. The work was entirely waged, and child care and transportation were provided. Courses on house management, health, hairdressing, and typing were offered free of charge. The Women's Club also worked with the Ministry of Public Health on mother-and-child issues such as prevention of diseases, vaccination of children, breast-feeding, and family planning.[61]

During the 1980s women's organizations worked among and mobilized hundreds of thousands of Afghan women. This network of women's organizations was of great significance and could have played an even more important role in the lives and welfare of Afghan women, especially returning refugees. But by 1990 the state and party were neither able nor willing to risk further social division in pursuit of a broad program for women's rights. By 1992 the Kabul government had been driven out and an Islamic republic established.

▲ The Democratic Youth Organization

Established in 1975, the Democratic Youth Organization (DYO) was the youth wing of the PDPA. According to its director, Farid Mazdak, more than half of the members of the PDPA came out of the DYO.[62] Youth brigades were assigned to control traffic, dispense coupons and distribute goods at government stores, and ferret out food hoarders. Female DYO members were involved in all the above activities but were especially prominent in learning and dispensing first aid. The DYO also had economic activities, wherein members worked in productive units to help regular workers reach or exceed production targets. Some 12,000 DYO members worked in construction brigades in Kabul and three northern provinces. Mazdak said the construction brigades were the least successful of the DYO activities because—significantly—girls insisted that they take part. Their participation was culturally unacceptable. In the villages, DYO volunteers distributed eggs and chemical fertilizer and worked as assistants to government extension agents. Girls were involved in this kind of work, which, while culturally unacceptable, proved important: Female extension agents can talk to rural women, as well as address health and family-planning issues.

On the cultural front, the DYO was involved in the campaign against illiteracy and for the extension of teaching. Mazdak explained that, cognizant of "past mistakes," the campaign now used only female teachers for girls, even in Kabul. The country suffered from a serious lack of teachers, 2,000 of whom were killed during the war; others, notably those who were trained abroad, had left Afghanistan, while yet other teachers had become state ministers or assumed other government posts. As a result, DYO members were called up to construct schools (Mazdak said the DYO built twenty-six schools in Kabul alone) and serve as teachers. The DYO organized literary seminars, cultural festivals, and concerts featuring jazz and Afghan classical and folk music. The organization even put on fashion shows, not only to demonstrate folk and Western styles but also to suggest what is *not* acceptable. (Mazdak singled out leather and chains!)

The Young Pioneers organization, established in 1982, was part of the DYO. Mazdak explained that 100,000 youngsters between the ages of eight and fourteen were members and that its director was a woman. Patterned after the Soviet and Western scout models, the Afghan Young Pioneers attended camp, did artwork, and learned to play musical instruments at Young Pioneer Palaces.

The section below surveys women's access to health, literacy, and education services in Afghanistan during the 1980s, to provide a picture of the efforts of the Afghan government in a situation of poor resource endowment, weak state capabilities, and a civil war.

▲ Health

After 1981, health care and dental care became free for all citizens, and doctors in private practice could not charge above certain amounts.

According to Dr. Azizullah Saidali, in 1989 vice president of the Indira Gandhi Children's Hospital, a doctor could not charge more than "the price of an egg." The quality of medical care was not high and the quantity of services insufficient. In 1989, according to official sources, there was a total of 64 hospitals, 5,141 beds, and 98 clinics. Kabul had 14 hospitals and 5 clinics. Total medical personnel numbered 4,400, of which 2,379 were doctors. The monthly salary of the top administrators (both doctors) of a leading hospital in Kabul was afs. 5,000 in February 1989, the equivalent of $25.

Apart from the military hospital, Indira Gandhi Children's Hospital, built and equipped by India, was considered the nation's most modern hospital, but in 1989 it had an occupancy rate of 120 percent. It also suffered from a shortage of nurses, poor facilities (such as only one properly working ambulance), and chronic supply shortages. According to the hospital's president, Dr. Abdul Salaam Jalali, children frequently came in with malnutrition, infectious diseases, and war injuries. Blood donations came from the army, from members of the social organizations, and from medical personnel. The hospital relied on the army because parents and relatives were frequently unwilling to donate blood for superstitious reasons.[63] Dr. Jalali and Dr. Saidali explained that 60 percent of children under five suffered from malnutrition. Babies typically have low birthweight, generally a function of the poor health of mothers, who often suffer from anemia. The common diet of bread, tea, and some vegetables is not high in nutrition. Research on infant and under-five mortality suggests that vaccination, birth attendants, mother's literacy, poverty, and water supply are major determinants. Because of Afghanistan's poverty and underdevelopment, both infant mortality and maternal mortality are high.

In 1985 the Council of Ministers endorsed a national program called Protection of Mother and Child Health in Afghanistan. Mother-and-child health clinics were established in Kabul, offering, among other things, various birth control methods to limit family size. The government was not averse to family planning, but it did not have a specific program linking changes in family structure and size to broader socioeconomic achievements and changes. Nonetheless, in 1986 some 138,000 women adopted various birth control/family-planning techniques, and the birth control pill became the most popular form of contraception among women.[64] Although three maternity clinics were established in Kabul, most women preferred to deliver at home, and thus the training of midwives was also emphasized. It seemed clear that, given cultural concern about excessive male-female interaction, attention would have to be directed in a postwar future to the training of Afghan women in such fields as gynecology, obstetrics, and pediatrics. See Table 7.3 for population, health, and education data for Afghanistan in the mid-1980s.

Table 7.3 Social Indicators, Afghanistan, c. 1985

Population Statistics		Data on health		Literacy and Education	
Male	8,170,000	Births attended by trained health personnel (%)		Adult literacy (%)	
Female	7,700,000	1973	5	Male	39
Annual population		1987 estimate	5.5	Female	8
growth rate	2.6	Percent of population with		Primary enrollment rates (%)	
Urban growth rate	6.1	access to health services		Total	18
Sex ratio:		Total	29	Male	27
Females per 100 males	95	Urban	80	Female	14
Population age structure (%)		Rural	17	Secondary enrollment rates (%)	
0–4 years	46	Percent of population with		Total	8
15–64 years	52	access to safe water	21	Male	11
65+	2			Female	5
Life expectancy at birth		Daily calorie supply		Higher education	n.a.*
Male	37	(as % of requirements)	94	Dropout rate:	
Female	36	Population per physician	13,000	% of grade-one enrollment not	
Crude birth rate (per 1,000)	49	Population per nurse	9,000	completing primary school	37
Crude death rate (per 1,000)	26	Population per hospital bed	3,700	% pupils reaching grade six	25
Total fertility rate	7.4	One-year-olds fully immunized			
Age dependency (%)	93	against:			
		tuberculosis	20.5		
Under-5 mortality		diphteria/tetanus	18.2		
(per 1,000 live births)	300	polio	18.2		
		measles	19.3		
Maternal mortality rate					
(per 100,000 live births)	690			*n.a. = not available	

Sources: UNDP, *Human Development Report 1990;* World Bank, *Social Indicators of Development 1988;* World Bank, *World Development Report 1989, 1990;* UNICEF, *The State of the World's Children 1989;* Rasil Basu, "An Educational Profile of Afghan Women" (mimeo, 1989).

▲ Literacy Drives

There have been periodic literacy drives in Afghanistan since modernization began early this century, and that of Amanullah Khan was perhaps the
most vigorous. As we have seen, the education of girls has always been a
sensitive issue. A literacy campaign was established in 1968, but ten years
later only 5,000 persons had benefited from it. Following the Saur
Revolution, a more concerted effort was launched, but it was highly unpopular and subsequently abandoned, as described earlier in this chapter.

In the 1980s literacy drives were carried out in military units and in
factories. During the 1980s an average of 18,000 persons became literate
every year. The magazine *Afghanistan Today* reported in 1988 that in the
province of Badghis, "over 210 women are also acquiring literacy in 13 literacy courses conducted by members of the Provincial Women's Council."
In the province of Kabul, "over 250 housewives of Sorobi district are
admitted to 22 literacy courses, taught by volunteer teachers and preach-
ers." The literacy campaign annually convened professional seminars for
all the teachers involved in literacy programs. In 1985 Afghanistan was
cited by UNESCO for its literacy effort.[65]

Primary school enrollment rates for girls increased steadily—from 5
percent in 1965 to 8 percent in 1975 to 14 percent in 1987—but remained
very low. The rates for female attendance at secondary school increased
from 1 percent in 1965 to 2 percent in 1975 to 5 percent in 1987. (See
Tables 7.1 and 7.3.) Girls numbered less than half the primary school and
secondary school populations. School attendance has historically been low,
and during the 1980s the civil conflict made education even more precarious. This danger was the reason for the dispatch of students to the Soviet
Union—although Western anticommunists criticized this as "Sovietization"
and "brainwashing."[66]

To the extent that it could, the national educational system continued
to function. In 1985 a special program was worked out for rendering financial aid to outstanding students through a joint venture of Kabul University
and the Democratic Youth Organization. Students received a stipend of afs.
1,500 per month to facilitate their studies. Among these recipients of aid
were female students in the Faculty of Construction, again a field of study
usually off-limits to women in Muslim societies. Fully 65 percent of the
7,000 students at Kabul University were female. In 1988 a university was
established in Herat. As part of the government's nationalities policy,
Uzbeks and others could now learn in their own languages; textbooks in the
various languages were provided by the Ministry of Education. Some attention was also directed to vocational schools. With financial and technical
assistance from the United Nations, four schools were opened in 1988 to
train young people in carpentry, leather work, and tailoring.

According to an AWC survey conducted in 1988, there were 7,133

Adult literacy classes are one tool for improving the lot of disadvantaged women.
Photo: UN Photo 153540/John Isaac

women in institutions of higher education and 233,000 girls studying in schools. The total number of female professors and teachers was 190 and 22,000, respectively. It is instructive to contrast these figures with the educational situation in the refugee camps of Peshawar, where 104,600 boys are enrolled in schools, as against 7,800 girls. For boys there are 486 primary schools, 161 middle schools, and 4 high schools. For girls there are 76 primary schools, 2 middle schools, and no high schools.[67] A UNICEF study indicated that there are only 180 Afghan women with high school education in the camps. This is reflective of the highly patriarchal arrangements among the mujahidin and in Peshawar.

▲ Women in the Refugee Camps

At the end of 1989, the Afghan refugee population was estimated to comprise between 2.5 and 3 million people. Most of them had entered the country before 1981—that is, in the early years of the civil conflict. Some 350 camplike villages had been established and were administered by the government of Pakistan. There is some evidence that due to high casualties sustained by the mujahidin, the long-standing inverse sex ratio had been reversed and that women now outnumbered men. War casualties had also rendered thousands of women widows. In keeping with the Afghan tradition of the levirate, some widows were remarried to a cousin or a brother of the late husband. For those widows who could not be remarried, a controversial widows' camp was established, which was criticized as resembling a concentration camp.

In the refugee camps, the average family size was 8.5 members, as against 6.2 in Afghanistan.[68] One reason for the large families was improved health care; another was pressure on women to reproduce more mujahidin, the fetishization of reproduction. Although during the 1980s most adult male refugees developed sources of income through employment, most refugee women were barred from income-generating activities and remained secluded behind the compound walls. This was first noted by a 1982 UN report on Afghan refugees in Peshawar. In the section on family organization, the report noted

> the practice of female seclusion, belief in the defense of the honor of women, and a well-developed division of labor within the family on the basis of age and sex. The emphasis on manhood and its association with strength is pervasive and we were told in one camp that even old men were expected to remain out of sight along the women and children. . . . Men assume responsibility for relationships and tasks outside the family compound including purchase and sale of subsistence items from the market (i.e. monetary transactions), agricultural production, house construction, wage labor and maintaining social and political relationships outside

the immediate family (including attendance at educational and religious institutions). Where "contact with outsiders" is concerned, there are universal constraints on participation of women . . . puberty defines adulthood for women, and early marriage is common.[69]

The report also explained the difficulty of designing income-generating projects for women:

> The influence of both Islam and traditional codes is pervasive and has many ramifications and implications for our work. Likewise, the role and position of women and the division of work in the household among the different Afghan tribes, have defined the limits of what is feasible and acceptable for schemes for women refugees.[70]

It is not irrelevant to note that the refugee camps were set up during the Islamization campaign of Pakistan's President Zia ul-Haq. Having assumed power in a military coup and after executing the previous prime minister, Zulfikar Ali Bhutto, Zia ul-Haq and his Jama'at-i Islami Party imposed legislation to segregate the sexes, reinforce Islamic family law, and mete out harsh punishment for prostitution and adultery.[71] This political environment encouraged the intensification of patriarchal arrangements in the Peshawar refugee camps, including an extremely rigid and unequal gender division of labor. A study conducted for the United Nations Research Institute for Social Development described the very different lives led by men and by women and is worth quoting in some detail.

> With the exception of fetching water and washing clothes, all tasks outside the home are carried out by men or boys. On the other hand, the women participate in all domestic tasks, including house-building and repair work. The women clearly have the longest working day in most homes, working from five in the morning until nine in the evening, with a number of prayer periods and tea breaks in between. They start the day's work before dawn by making breakfast for the men who are going to work or to seek work, and then feed and milk the animals. It takes a couple of hours to make a dough and bake bread, washing clothes and bathing babies and infants. Midday dinner is then prepared. After the evening meal and the washing up, work continues on the handicrafts. The young women do the heavy housework. For example, they bake the bread, which is a particularly onerous task. They have to sit with their arms in an oven which is about 75 centimetres underground and burning hot. They bake bread on a raised site in the yard, mostly during the hottest time of the day. They also wash clothes and clean the compound and stable, and collect manure, which they dry in the sun and use for fuel. They also fetch water if they do not have big children to do this for them. Women walk either alone or in small groups of five to six to get water. Special pathways are followed to avoid being exposed to the attention of the adult male community.
> Men's working hours are usually from seven in the morning to four

in the afternoon. Their work in the household rarely takes more than a few hours each day unless they have gainful employment in the home. They spend most of their leisure time out in the local community among other men, with whom they discuss matters of common interest, the resistance work in Afghanistan and tribal affairs. The market belongs to the males. Bargains are made and loans arranged in the tea shops. News as well as rumours and personal affairs are discussed. Weapons are cleaned and tested, the *katcha* buildings under construction providing the targets for practice. Discussion about weapons takes up quite a lot of their energy. Guns and other firearms are bargained for at the bazaars or in individual compounds, especially when the *mujahids* return from Afghanistan. The new equipment and supplies are examined and tested out with absorbed attention. The time for the household is spent on shopping, collecting firewood, collecting aid rations and possibly herding animals. The identity of men is predominantly associated with public life. They obviously enjoy being with other men outside the private compounds, without questioning the inherent seclusion of women. Men also tend to take for granted that women and older girls should serve them at whatever time they may return home. Many apparently spend months away in search of employment or for bargaining purposes, without leaving word as to when they would expect to be back. Men and older boys ensure that *purdah* is observed, which means checking on who enters the compound and which of the younger women leave it for places other than nearby houses and the water source. If other men come visiting, they also ensure that women of childbearing age are hidden from the view of the guests. If a woman in *purdah* has to go the health centre, her husband escorts her there or finds someone else to go with her.[72]

In Peshawar, while women had to observe *purdah* at its strictest, refugee men enjoyed an unprecedented freedom of movement. Unlike most Southeast Asian camps, where refugees are contained by barbed wire, camps in Pakistan were not surrounded by a single fence. Refugees were free to move in and out of the camps at will. Many men found employment in the Pakistani labor market, others became small merchants in the adjacent villages, and still others crossed the border to fight with the resistance. Women, however, were rarely allowed to leave their uncomfortable and unsanitary environments. The only acceptable outing for a refugee woman was to visit a clinic, but not all were allowed to do even that. To some degree the situation for women was similar in prewar Afghanistan, but the restrictions in the camp setting served to isolate them more than ever. Traditional *maliks* expanded their role to control the lives of single women and widows and to be the guardians of *purdah*. They also took it upon themselves to prevent women from engaging in "unacceptable occupations," such as productive activities that could help them acquire some economic independence.[73]

Access to food was a persistent problem for single women and widows and infants. The traditional custom of feeding men and boys first continued. Since women did not fight in the so-called *jihad,* they were perceived as contributing less to the struggle and consequently in less need of suste-nance. According to one report, "When supplementary food is available, it is given to the boys and not girls." Women who had a male relative were not allowed to collect their own allocations. As a result, women heads of households often did not receive their fair share of food and had to rely on charity. Although the UN's World Food Program tried to correct this prob-lem, inequity in food distribution caused a high incidence of anemia among the adult female population.[74]

As women become excluded from productive activities, their role in human reproduction becomes exaggerated and fetishized. The control of women's fertility, sexuality, and even mobility becomes a matter of male honor. The honor/shame complex in Peshawar was thus not only a legacy of the traditional patriarchal social structure, but also a feature of the extreme privatization of the domestic sphere to which women had been rel-egated as a result of uprootedness and war.

The rather extreme nature of gender inequality notwithstanding, some authors have felt compelled to justify the invisibility and isolation of Afghan women as a functional requisite of the resistance. In one essay Howard-Merriam suggested that "the Mujahideen leaders recognize women's importance to the *jihad* (or holy war) with their exhortations to preserve women's honor through the continued practice of seclusion. The reinforcement of this tradition, most Westerners have failed to notice, serves to strengthen the men's will to resist." She continued to argue that "*purdah* provides the opportunity for preserving one's own identity and a certain stability in the face of external pressures. . . . Westerners who have been quick to impose their own ethnocentric perceptions should note the value of this seemingly anachronistic custom for a people under siege whose very survival is at stake."[75]

The UNRISD study by Christensen found that the inadequate food sit-uation and scarce incomes at the household level "hit the women directly," for they are the ones who manage these resources and see to it that there is food to eat every day. When they find it especially difficult to fulfill their crucial role as food preparers and household managers, they shortchange themselves, eating less than they should. This resulted in widespread ane-mia among the adult female population, something observed also by Howard-Merriam. Women's nutritional intake was reduced in another way. Because women did not go to the marketplace if there were a male relative in the extended household and because food rations distributed by aid workers or Pakistani authorities were also collected by men, there is evi-dence that women consequently did not receive their fair share. Unequal allocation of resources within households, mainly along gender lines, was widespread in Peshawar, as it is in many parts of South Asia.[76]

Observers repeatedly noted that Afghan refugee women suffered from depression and emotional imbalance. Feelings of loneliness, fear, and guilt over having left relatives and friends behind in Afghanistan were reportedly overwhelming psychological problems created by the refugee situation. According to Howard-Merriam, who conducted extensive interviews with women in the Peshawar refugee camps: "As beings set apart and excluded from the public, women are united in their hostility toward men as 'bad, ugly and cruel.'" Women's low level of expectation, the writer continued, stands in contrast to the "men's higher and often unrealistic ones of world conquest."[77]

Education for girls remained a contested terrain. According to Nancy Dupree, "Even the mere mention of education for girls was anathema and those who advocated it were branded as 'traitors' and 'communists.'"[78] Throughout the 1980s education for girls in the refugee camps in Peshawar, administered by the United Nations High Commissioner for Refugees (UNHCR), remained woefully inadequate. Surprisingly, UN officials acquiesced to Afghan male resistance to teaching girls; most of the UN's camp schools were for boys only. Boys went to school for as many years as possible, while girls left at the age of ten or eleven to weave carpets. In health care, too, the UNHCR initially encountered resistance to the extension of services to women. In Peshawar, Afghan men did not allow male medical workers to attend to women, and many were reluctant even to allow women to leave their houses or get treatment from female doctors or assistants. Because of the observance of *purdah,* many infants with developmental problems or disabilities were overlooked by relief workers and physicians. A French woman doctor once complained to a reporter, "We have to fight with the men to take women to a hospital when necessary."[79]

Unlike liberation, resistance, and guerrilla groups elsewhere, the Afghan mujahidin never encouraged the active participation of women. In Cuba, Algeria, Vietnam, China, Eritrea, Oman, Iran, Nicaragua, El Salvador, and Palestine, women were or are active in the front lines as well as in social services. We have seen in previous chapters that some Islamist movements, and certainly the Islamic Republic of Iran, not only have women supporters but also women activists, ideologues, spokespersons, and officials. Significantly, the mujahidin never had female spokespersons. Indeed, women in Peshawar who became too visible or vocal were threatened and sometimes killed. The group responsible for most of the intimidation of women is the fundamentalist Hizb-e Islami, led by Gulbeddin Hekmatyar, who received substantial military, political, and financial support from the United States, Pakistan, and Saudi Arabia.

The situation in the refugee camps was protested by a few Afghan women, notably an underground group of former Maoists who formed the Revolutionary Association of Afghan Women (RAWA). In the late 1980s they produced and distributed leaflets strongly criticizing the misogyny of the Hekmatyar group in particular. Other critics, such as longtime Afghanistan observer Nancy Depree, warned of reactionary attitudes on the part of the mujahidin leadership in Peshawar and among young men. When the mujahidin assumed control of Kabul in May 1992, their first step was to ban the sale and consumption of alcohol and to declare that all women would henceforth appear in public veiled. Two months later women television broadcasters were fired. By all accounts, in the summer of 1992 there were fewer women in the streets of Kabul than at any time in the previous decade.[80]

▲ Summary and Conclusion

In 1978 the government of the newly established Democratic Republic of Afghanistan, led by President Noor Mohammad Taraki, enacted legislation to raise women's status through changes in family law, reform of marriage customs, and new policies to encourage female education and employment. The Afghan state was motivated by a modernizing outlook and socialist ideology that linked Afghan backwardness to feudalism, widespread female illiteracy, and the exchange of girls. The leadership resolved that women's rights to education, employment, mobility, and choice of spouse would be major objectives of the national democratic revolution. In this connection the new leadership was simply continuing the tradition of reform and modernization. As in other modernizing and socialist experiments, the woman question constituted an essential part of the political project, as we have seen in Chapter 3. But the experiment failed, the victim of internal rivalries, tribal-Islamist opposition, and a hostile international climate.

This chapter has sought to explain the subordinate position of women, the resistance to female education, and the inability of the state to implement its reform program in terms of the persistence of patriarchal social structures and the existence of a weak state. Although Afghanistan is not the only patriarchal country in the world, it is an extreme case of classic patriarchy. A rugged terrain and armed tribes have made modernization and centralization a difficult, prolonged, and limited enterprise, with dire implications for the advancement of women. In a patriarchal context, constructions of gender fetishize women's reproductive roles, and there is resistance to a modernizing state's attempts to redefine or expand women's roles to include work and citizenship. Such a daunting project can only be carried out by a strong state and under favorable international circumstances. Neither of these two conditions was present in Afghanistan.

In the process of its struggles, concessions, and accommodations with the tribal-Islamist opposition, the Afghan state's goals and ideology underwent revision. The PDPA gradually toned down its early and fervent championship of women's rights. Following the PDPA party congress and change of name, the state stressed unity and reconciliation ("brotherhood") rather than social change and the advancement of women. And in May

1992 the Kabul government was replaced by a tribal-Islamist coalition, which bodes well for neither socioeconomic development nor women's emancipation.

This chapter has also sought to underscore the gender dimension of the long Afghan conflict. During periods of change or contestation, women become the sign or marker of political goals and of cultural identity; representations of women are deployed during processes of revolution and state-building and when power is being reproduced, linking women either to modernization and progress or to cultural rejuvenation and religious orthodoxy. In Afghanistan's case, the Soviet intervention and world attention to it obscured the very real conflicts between modernizers and traditionalists and between women's emancipation and patriarchy.

▲ 8
Conclusion: All That Is Solid Is Melting into Air

The visibility of women disturbs the patriarchal order and weakens men's position within society.—Doria Cherifati-Merabtine

The cultural revolution is happening right now, right before our eyes
—Fatima Mernissi

A spectre is haunting the Middle East—the spectre of modernity.

This book has analyzed the gender dynamics of some of the major social change processes in the Middle East, North Africa, and Afghanistan—economic development and the expansion of wage employment, political and social revolutions, the demographic transition, changes in family structure, the rise and expansion of Islamist movements, and civil war and political conflict. In so doing, I have tried to show that analyses of economic, political, and cultural developments within societies or regions are incomplete without attention to gender and its interaction with class, state, and the world system—they are systems of social relations that shape institutions, discourses, and movements, and they are structures that are subject to change as a result of certain economic, political, and cultural developments. This is as true of the Middle East as it is of any other region. The sex/gender system and all that it entails is undergoing profound change in Middle Eastern countries. This change in the position of women has been met with the politicization of gender and family law, the preoccupation of Islamist movements with women's appearance and behavior, shifting state policies, and cultural debates about authenticity and Westernization.

This book has been neither a catalogue of injustices and discrimination against women nor a celebration of the Middle Eastern woman. Rather, it has been an attempt to rectify the neglect of women as a subject of discourse and their exclusion as participants in the formation of systems of ideas and as actors in social change. My analysis of Afghanistan, in particular, has emphasized the centrality of gender and the power of women activists—a critical dimension that has been occluded in standard accounts. In this book I have placed the spotlight on middle-class women to bring into focus the rather pivotal role they have assumed—consciously and unconsciously, as secularists and as Islamists—in the social and political changes under way in the Middle East. I viewed these changes through a Marxist-feminist sociological lens.

Women are at the center of change and discourse about change in the Middle East. Whether they be socialist-feminists, women participating in political movements, the *chador*-clad pro-Khomeini women demonstrating against imperialism, prominent women such as the Palestinian Hanan Ashrawi and Egypt's audacious Nawal El-Saadawi, Fatima Mernissi and her regionwide network of antifundamentalist activists and intellectuals, or the growing silent minority of women at work in government agencies, universities, and factories—what is uncontestable is that middle-class women have come into their own in the latter half of the twentieth century. They are a product of socioeconomic development and change but are themselves spurring development and change. They are formulating ideas about women's rights, governance, and social justice, and ideas are being formulated with middle-class women as the reference point. They are the subject of intense debates among men—state managers, clerics, status-anxious petty bourgeois males—who are convinced that such women need to be put in their place. When complaints are voiced that the family is in danger, that cultural imperialism is taking place through "Westernized women," that women are assuming "inappropriate" forms of employment, that being a wife and mother is the most sacred obligation for a woman—these discourses refer to middle-class women with education and jobs. The fundamentalist backlash is directed at this stratum of women, who collectively symbolize social change in the Middle East.

As Fatima Mernissi points out, "It's these women, the teachers and others belonging to the petite bourgeoisie, who are in the process of changing the world around them, because their situation as it is is untenable. There are too many archaic aspects in marriage, in the relations between the sexes, in the work situation. These educated women were nourished with a desire for independence."[1] A Beirut-based Palestinian woman writer observes, "Here, the question of women lies at the bottom of things and cannot be touched without upsetting the whole order. Can the question of women be separated from religious arguments? Can it be separated from social or cultural ones?"[2] The answer is that it cannot. Accordingly, the 1986 report of the Arab Women's Solidarity Association tied the question of women to political, economic, social, and cultural issues. The preamble called on women "to unite, to close ranks and become a political and social force able to effect changes in prevailing systems, laws and legislation that will be beneficial not only for women but for all the people." A recommendation of the political committee was for the "release of general freedoms, particularly the freedoms of expression and organization; for respect of human rights for men and women; for a greater participation by women in political decision-making, and for an equal share with men in the authority exercised both in the state and the family."[3] Rights for women and overall civil rights are of a piece.

These are times of opportunity, risk, and challenge for women. If the economic crisis in the region continues, it could harm the progress made by women in the employment structure. If Islamist movements continue to apply pressure on governments, women could lose some of the basic rights they have gained over the years. As already noted in this book, the AWSA's headquarters in Cairo were closed down by government decree in June 1991. Can women stem the tide of reaction while also pushing for more legal rights, greater democratization, and societal development to benefit all women?

▲ Women's Movements in the Middle East

An important indicator of social change, modernity, and prospects for women is the rise and expansion of feminist groups throughout the region. In some countries, such as Algeria, feminist groups formed as a response to Islamist movements or state attempts to change family law. At two crucial points—in the early 1980s when the Algerian family code was being formulated, and in 1990 when the FIS was making political inroads—Algerian feminists were organized, militant, and audacious. Will they continue to organize themselves and mobilize support for women's rights, democratization, and modernization?

According to Algerian feminists, there is no choice but to carry on with the struggle, which they see as simultaneously democratic and feminist. They are critical of past practice, which subsumed the woman question under national liberation and the building of Algerian socialism. In Algeria the ideological and cultural divide between Islamist and non-Islamist women activists is enormous; feminists distinguish "women of the modernist trend" from the women of the Islamist movement. According to one such activist-theorist, the modernist women's movement is comprised mainly of older university women from the first postindependence generation of intellectuals. Cherifati-Merabtine observes that these women "have learned, at their expense, that no change is possible if the outlook on woman and her place within society does not evolve." And although these modernist women "carry generous ideas and an egalitarian project of society," their experience leads them to "put the recognition of the Woman-Individual on the agenda."[4] Consequently, as seen in Chapter 3, the rights of women and the identity and future of the Algerian nation-state are intimately connected.

Among Arab countries, Tunisia grants women a wider range of rights than do other Arab countries. This liberalism is usually attributed to the outlook and policies of the country's first president, Habib Bourguiba, but it should also be understood as part of Tunisia's tradition of reform. In the early twentieth century, Taher El Haddad, a male feminist leader, was even more daring than Egypt's Qasim Amin in his call for the emancipation of women. He condemned the veil, polygamy, sex segregation, the unilateral right of divorce, and unequal access to education. Although El Haddad was considered a renegade and his book, *Our Women in the Shari'a and in Society,* was condemned, his ideas persisted and found expression in the personal status code of 1956. As we have seen in earlier chapters, the Tunisian code abolished polygamy, forced marriage, and unilateral repudiation; it established civil marriage, divorce, and child custody rights for women, as well as a law for the adoption of children. In spite of these important reforms, Tunisian feminists emphasize the gap between legislation and implementation of laws. They also point out that women are still unequal in inheritance and that the law prohibits the marriage of a Muslim woman to a non-Muslim man while allowing a Muslim man to marry a Christian or Jewish woman.

Tunisian feminists have been equally concerned about the economic crisis and the rise of *intégrisme* in Tunisia and elsewhere in North Africa. During the 1980s the Taher El Haddad Club became a center for the discussion of social problems and women's rights. Other forums include the Women's Commission of the General Union of Tunisian Workers, the Tunisian Association of Women Democrats, the Tunisian Human Rights League, and, of course, the National Union of Tunisian Women. In 1985 a bilingual (Arabic and French) feminist magazine called *Nissa* (Woman) appeared, which, according to its opening editorial, would be "a place for personal testimony, information, reflection and debate, open to women and men alike . . . committed to respecting diverse points of view provided that . . . they aim to promote more harmonious and satisfying relations between the sexes and to establish the foundations of a more free and open society."[5] *Nissa*'s feature articles over the first year of publication included discussions of the problem of illegitimate children, the personal status laws of Tunisia and Egypt (both under attack that year), the Israeli bombing raid of the PLO headquarters in a suburb of Tunis, the pros and cons of sex-segregated activities, the risks of childbirth, and feminism. The magazine folded in 1987 mainly because of disagreements among its staff members, who then went on to join some of the associations mentioned above.[6]

In North Africa a series of books has been published under the editorial supervision of Fatima Mernissi that focuses on women and the law. The authors are lawyers, and they have written in a clear and simple style. Originally published in French, the books are in the process of being translated into Arabic for wider distribution across the Arab world. The titles are *La Femme et la Loi en Algérie,* by Saadi Nouredine, *La Femme et la Loi en Tunisie,* by Alya Chérif Chamari, and *La Femme et la Loi au Maroc,* by Abderrazak Moulay R'chid. As part of the same series, Khalida Said has authored *Women and Democracy in North Africa* (in Arabic). Several films and videos have also been produced. Touria Hadraoui and Myriam Monkachi have prepared *Etudes Feminines: Repertoire & Bibliographie,* which contains a directory of women's rights activists and scholars in Algeria, Morocco, and Tunisia, as well as a bibliography on women's studies.[7]

Activists are making women aware of their rights and criticizing restrictive laws throughout the region. Margot Badran explains that in the second half of the 1980s, several professional women in their forties and fifties came together to work on a legal literacy project. Calling themselves the Communication Group for the Enhancement of the Status of Women in Egypt, they produced a booklet in Arabic called *The Legal Rights of the Egyptian Woman in Theory and Practice.* An entire chapter was devoted to the Egyptian personal status code, and women were instructed how to write certain protective conditions into their marriage contracts. Other chapters dealt with labor law and conventions concerning work.

The Egyptian women's liberation movement has been in place since at least the early twentieth century. Apart from AWSA, there are a number of feminist groups that disseminate feminist views through their journals and have formed committees to deal with various everyday needs of ordinary women in areas such as health, legal literacy, and income generation. One such group, the New Woman Group, announced its stand in a communication in 1990: "The New Woman Group is a progressive and democratic feminist group of women who believe that while Egyptian and Arab women share with men the hardships brought about by backwardness, dependence and economic crisis, they have to carry a double burden and suffer from a variety of forms of subordination, oppression and suppression arising specifically from their position as women."[8]

In Turkey the women's movement was started by educated and professional women, products of the Kemalist reforms of the 1930s. Today the women's movement is divided among several factions: Islamist, Kemalist, and new-wave feminist. As seen in Chapter 5, the Islamist movement has its own forms of advocacy for women, particularly valuing domestic work and family attachment. Islamist and non-Islamist activists alike oppose commercial exploitation of women's sexuality but are divided over veiling and the introduction of Islamic legal codes. New feminists see the secularizing and capitalizing Kemalist agenda as having brought women into the public world of work without mitigating their domestic responsibilities or patriarchal domination at home. Daughters of the bureaucratic elite benefited, but Kemalists ignored the effect of class, which created differential recourse to services such as education, even as they ignored the effect of gender in the employment structure.

In the years immediately following the 1980 military coup, all leftist and radical thought and action were prohibited. At the same time, a law passed in 1982 mandated religious instruction in secondary schools, an anticommunist move that served to embolden Islamists. New-wave feminism emerged in this period.

Turkish new-wave feminists entered the political arena in the 1980s by waging colorful, sometimes quirky campaigns on women's issues—for example, protesting sexual harassment in the streets by selling large purple needles for women to use against harassers. In 1986 Ankara and Istanbul groups collaborated to launch a petition campaign and urge the government to implement the UN Convention on the Elimination of All Forms of Discrimination Against Women, which Turkey had signed in 1985. One year feminist groups organized a temporary Woman's Museum, where everyday utensils women used were displayed as tools that defined women's alienation. Since 1987 the centerpiece of the feminist movement has been a campaign against domestic battering.

The emphasis on questions of sexuality and home life has puzzled older, Kemalist feminists, who continue to connect feminist projects with other political agendas, such as nationalism or socialism. In the summer of 1989, a group of feminists demonstrated in support of prisoners who had gone on a hunger strike to protest the conditions in state prisons. Yet this was a singular event, for new feminists speak mainly to other women or address issues directly related to women. For this reason feminism in Turkey now appears diverse, with no single direction. But some Turkish feminist social scientists, such as Yesim Arat and Nükhet Sirman, argue that this polyphony is not necessarily a sign of disarray or leadership failure.[9] Arat concludes:

> The women's movement of the 1980s transformed the state feminism of the Kemalists at the same time that it upheld deep-seated Kemalist ideals. It brought dynamism to Turkish political life during a most repressive period in its history. It practiced liberalism, defended secularism, and sowed the seeds of pluralism at a period when governments that promised liberalism gradually resorted to conservative statism. . . . [The woman's movement] expanded the political space allotted to civil society. In the Turkish context, where the tradition of peaceful association against the strong state was weak, achievements of the women's movement were significant.[10]

As discussed in Chapter 5, Islamist movements draw considerable support from women, despite the fact that Islam, like all religions, relegates women to a secondary position in society and in the home. Why, then, do women join Islamist movements? Is it one way of defying the West? Is it due to the financial and moral support coming from such countries as Saudi Arabia and Iran? Is it a redefinition of an old identity? Is it defiance of state control of religion? The answer may be all of the above and more. Many of the women who have embraced the Islamic way of life are becoming more and more active. Some try to obtain a good education; others write in their own journals, go on protest marches, and take part in sit-down strikes. In a country such as Turkey, these actions are defended in terms of human rights and democracy, and some secularists have admitted that Islamists, too, have expanded civil society and opened up public space. Suna Kili writes that in the current context of dialogues and debates between Kemalists, Islamists, and feminists, "it is the Islamic women who have demonstrated a greater degree of openness to change, and a greater eagerness for dialogue than men."[11]

But what is also interesting is the effect of these forms of women's activism on the Islamist movement itself and on women's gender consciousness. As we have seen in the chapters on Islamist movements (Chapter 5) and on Iran (Chapter 6), some Islamist women question and criticize the secondary status of women in Muslim communities, and they blame men for oppressing women and limiting their activities. An unintended outcome of their participation in Islamist movements is that Islamist women become more participatory, more political, and more demanding of the men within their own movements. We have seen that in Iran, Islamist women are asserting their right to criticize gender discrimination and are using language similar to that used by women's rights activists in other countries. Such women are not only more open to change but more willing to engage in dialogue with persons outside their movements. As Kili writes regarding Islamist women in Turkey:

> Islam in Turkey needs a renaissance—a rebirth. It has to rethink its values and role and has to learn to be open to dialogue. It needs to reform itself and to define its role in a modern society. . . . Developments in recent years have amply demonstrated that Islamic women are becoming more and more aware of this responsibility. It is perhaps because these women have more to gain from such a renaissance than men.[12]

Economic development, universal schooling, mass communications, and legal reforms in Middle Eastern countries have produced a stratum of women whose very existence subverts the patriarchal order and accelerates the transition to modernity. Like the working class at other times and places, middle-class women in the Middle East are at the center of change—as participants, as beneficiaries, as winners, and as losers. In uncovering and explaining the class and gender dynamics of change processes in the region, it is hard to escape the conclusion that women are modernizing the Middle East.

▲
Notes

▲ Chapter 1

1. Daniel Chirot, *Social Change in the Modern Era* (San Diego: Harcourt Brace Jovanovich, 1983), p. 3. For an elaboration of the structuralist and Marxist approach, see Christopher Lloyd, *Explanation in Social History* (London: Basil Blackwell, 1986), especially Part III. On world system theory see Immanuel Wallerstein, *The Modern World-System*, Vol. III (San Diego: Academic Press, 1989), and Christopher Chase-Dunn, *Global Formation: Structures of the World-Economy* (Cambridge, UK: Basil Blackwell, 1989).

2. But see Sami G. Hajjar, ed., *The Middle East: From Transition to Development* (Leiden: E. J. Brill, 1985). Although the collection is uneven, especially useful are the introduction by Hajjar, the chapter on demography by Basheer Nijim, and the essay on education and political development in the Middle East by Nancy and Joseph Jabbra.

3. Nadia Youssef, "The Status and Fertility Patterns of Muslim Women," in Lois Beck and Nikki Keddie, eds., *Women in the Muslim World* (Cambridge, MA: Harvard University Press, 1978), pp. 69–99; John Weeks, "The Demography of Islamic Nations," *Population Bulletin* 43 (4) (December 1988); Fatima Mernissi, *Beyond the Veil: Male-Female Dynamics in Modern Muslim Society*, revised edition (Bloomington: Indiana University Press, 1987); Mai Ghoussoub, "Feminism—or the Eternal Masculine—in the Arab World," *New Left Review* 161 (January–February 1987):3–13; Ruth Leger Sivard, *Women . . . A World Survey* (Washington, D.C.: World Priorities, 1985); Julinda Abu Nasr, A. Khoury, and H. Azzam, eds., *Women, Employment, and Development in the Arab World* (The Hague: Mouton/ILO, 1985).

4. Sivard, *Women . . . A World Survey*, p. 13.

5. H. Azzam, J. Abu Nasr, and I. Lorfing, "An Overview of Arab Women in Population, Employment and Economic Development," p. 18; Mujahid, "Female Labour Force Participation in Jordan," p. 128. Both in Abu Nasr, et al., eds., *Women, Employment, and Development in the Arab World*.

6. Pnina Lahav, "Raising the Status of Women Through Law: The Case of Israel," in Wellesley Editorial Committee, ed., *Women and National Development: The Complexities of Change* (Chicago: University of Chicago Press, 1987), p. 199. See also Shulamit Aloni, "Up the Down Escalator," in Robin Morgan, ed., *Sisterhood Is Global* (New York: Anchor Books, 1984), pp. 360–364; Madeleine

Tress, "Halaka, Zionism, and Gender: The Case of Gush Emunim," paper prepared for the UNU/WIDER Roundtable on Identity Politics and Women, Helsinki (October 8–10, 1990).

7. Urvashi Boutalia, "Indian Women and the New Movement," *Women's Studies International Forum* 8 (2) (1985):131–133; Jean Dräze and Amartya Sen, *Hunger and Public Action* (Oxford: Clarendon Press, 1989), especially Chapter 4; Barbara Miller, *The Endangered Sex* (Ithaca: Cornell University Press, 1981). These points have also been made by Weeks, "The Demography of Islamic Nations."

8. See Vern Bullough, Brenda Shelton, and Sarah Slavin, *The Subordinated Sex: A History of Attitudes Toward Women* (Athens and London: University of Georgia Press, 1988).

9. Mernissi, *Beyond the Veil;* Fatna A. Sabbah, *Woman in the Muslim Unconscious* (New York: Pergamon Press, 1985); Azar Tabari, "Islam and the Struggle for Emancipation of Iranian Women," and Haleh Afshar, "Khomeini's Teachings and Their Implications for Iranian Women," both in Azar Tabari and Nahid Yeganeh, eds., *In the Shadow of Islam: The Women's Movement in Iran* (London: Zed Books, 1982). Freda Hussein distinguishes "authentic Islam" from "pseudo-Islam" and believes that the former is emancipatory. See her introduction in Freda Hussein, ed., *Muslim Women* (London: Croom Helm, 1984). Leila Ahmed once poignantly wrote, "One can perhaps appreciate how excruciating is the plight of the Middle-Eastern feminist caught between those opposing loyalites [sexual and cultural identities] forced almost to choose between betrayal and betrayal." See her essay in Hussein, ed., *Muslim Women.*

10. Yakin Ertürk, "Convergence and Divergence in the Status of Muslim Women: The Cases of Turkey and Saudi Arabia," *International Sociology* 6 (1) (September 1991):307–320. For critiques of the cultural relativist approach, see also Mona Abaza and Georg Stauth, "Occidental Reason, Orientalism, and Islamic Fundamentalism," *International Sociology* 3 (4) (December 1988):343–364; Val Moghadam, "Against Eurocentrism and Nativism: A Review Essay on Samir Amin's *Eurocentrism* and Other Texts," *Socialism and Democracy* 9 (Fall/Winter 1989):81–104; Val Moghadam, "The Critical and Sociological Approach in Middle East Studies," *Critical Sociology* 17 (1) (Spring 1990):111–124.

11. Abdelwahab Bouhdiba, *Sexuality in Islam* (London: Routledge and Kegan Paul, 1985).

12. See Division for the Advancement of Women, United Nations Office at Vienna, "International Standards of Equality and Religious Freedom: Implications for the Status of Women," paper prepared for the UNU/WIDER Roundtable on Identity Politics and Women, Helsinki (October 8–10, 1990).

13. Janet Z. Giele, "Introduction: The Status of Women in Comparative Perspective," in Janet Z. Giele and Audrey C. Smock, eds., *Women: Roles and Status in Eight Countries* (New York: John Wiley, 1977), pp. 3–31.

14. See Hisham Sharabi, *Neopatriarchy: A Theory of Distorted Change in the Arab World* (New York: Oxford University Press, 1988). Another useful discussion of the state is contained in Alan Richards and John Waterbury, *A Political Economy of the Middle East* (Boulder: Westview Press, 1990). And still relevant is Michael Hudson, *Arab Politics: The Search for Legitimacy* (New Haven: Yale University Press, 1977).

15. Doreen Ingrams, "The Position of Women in Middle Eastern Society," in Michael Adams, ed., *The Middle East* (New York: Facts-on-File Publications, 1988), pp. 808–813; Nermin Abadan-Unat, "Women in Turkish Society," *Social*

Economic and Political Studies of the Middle East (Leiden: E. J. Brill, 1981); Weeks, "The Demography of Islamic Nations," p. 26.

16. Theresa de Lauretis, *Technologies of Gender* (Bloomington: Indiana University Press, 1987), p. 5.

17. For a comparative study of changing family law in Western countries (from patriarchal to egalitarian), see Mary Ann Glendon, *State, Law and Family: Family Law in Transition in the United States and Western Europe* (Cambridge, MA: Harvard University Press, 1977), and *The Transformation of Family Law* (Chicago: University of Chicago Press, 1989).

18. Hanna Papanek, "Socialization for Inequality: Entitlements, the Value of Women, and Domestic Hierarchies," Center for Asian Studies, Boston University, 1989. See also Rae Lesser Blumberg, *Stratification: Socio-Economic and Sexual Inequality* (Dubuque, IA: W. C. Brown, 1978); Janet Saltzman Chafetz, *Sex and Advantage* (Totowa, NJ: Rowman and Allanheld, 1984).

19. Michael Mann, "A Crisis in Stratification Theory? Persons, Households/ Family/Lineages, Genders, Classes and Nations," in Rosemary Crompton and Michael Mann, eds., *Gender and Stratification* (Cambridge, UK: Polity Press, 1986), pp. 40–56. The quote by Papanek is from her paper "Socialization for Inequality." On patriarchy see Chapter 4.

20. Ralph Miliband, *Divided Societies: Class Struggle in Contemporary Capitalism* (Oxford: Clarendon Press, 1989), p. 25.

21. Constantina Safilios-Rothschild, "A Cross-cultural Examination of Women's Marital, Educational and Occupational Options," in M.T.S. Mednick, et al., eds., *Women and Achievement* (New York: John Wiley and Sons, 1971).

22. Margot Badran, "Women and Production in the Middle East and North Africa," *Trends in History* 2 (3) (1982):80.

23. Richards and Waterbury, *A Political Economy of the Middle East,* p. 49. See also Christian Palloix, *L'internationalisation du capital* (Paris: Maspero, 1977); F. Frobel, J. Heinrichs, and D. Kreye, *The New International Division of Labour* (Cambridge, UK: Cambridge University Press, 1989); Roger Southall, ed., *Trade Unions and the New Industrialization of the Third World* (London: Zed Books, 1988); Alain Lipietz, "Towards Global Fordism?" *New Left Review* 132 (March–April 1982):33–47.

24. Jean Pyle, "Export-Led Development and the Underdevelopment of Women: The Impact of Discriminatory Development Policy in the Republic of Ireland," in Kathryn Ward., ed., *Women Workers and Global Restructuring* (Ithaca: ILR Press, 1990), pp. 85–112.

25. Mary Chamie, *Women of the World: Near East and North Africa* (Washington, D.C.: U.S. Department of Commerce, Bureau of the Census, and U.S. Agency for International Development, Office of Women in Development, 1985); Azzam, Abu Nasr, and Lorfing, "An Overview of Arab Women in Population, Employment, and Economic Development," p. 11.

26. See J. S. Birks, I. J. Seccombe, and C. A. Sinclair, "Labor Migration and Labor Organization in the Arab World," in Michael Adams, ed., *The Middle East,* pp. 718–741.

27. The Iranian students abroad were organized in the Confederation of Iranian Students, one of the largest and best-organized student movements anywhere. See Afshin Matin Asgari, "The Iranian Student Abroad: The Confederation of Iranian Students, National Union," in Asghar Fathi, ed., *Iranian Refugees and Exiles Since Khomeini* (Costa Mesa, CA: Mazda Publishers, 1991), pp. 55–74. See also Val Moghadam, "Socialism or Anti-Imperialism? The Left and Revolution in Iran," *New Left Review* 166 (November–December 1987):5–28.

28. From *Women and the Family,* prepared by Helen O'Connell for the JUNIC/NGO Programme Group on Women and Development, March 1992, p. 160.

29. Mehdi Bozorgmehr and Georges Sabagh, "Iranian Exiles and Immigrants in Los Angeles," in Asghar Fathi, ed., *Iranian Refugees and Exiles Since Khomeini,* pp. 121–144. In the same volume, see also Janet Bauer, "A Long Way Home: Islam in the Adaptation of Iranian Women Refugees in Turkey and West Germany" (pp. 77–101), and Vida Nassehy-Behnam, "Iranian Immigrants in France" (pp. 102–119).

30. Bauer, "A Long Way Home," p. 93.

31. Samir al-Khalil, "Iraq and Its Future," *New York Review of Books,* April 11, 1991, p. 12. This does of course raise the question of the impact of the Gulf War and devastation of Iraq on women's status. Unfortunately, the paucity of information makes a serious study impossible at this time.

32. Ruth Milkman, *Gender at Work: The Dynamics of Job Segregation by Sex During World War II* (Chicago: University of Illinois Press, 1987); Karen Anderson, *Wartime Women: Sex Roles, Family Relations, and the Status of Women During World War II* (Westport, CT: Greenwood Press, 1981).

33. Aisha Harb Zureik, *The Effect of War on University Education,* project discussed in *Al-Raida* (Beirut University College) IX (52) (Winter 1991):4–5. See also Val Moghadam, "Women, Work and Ideology in the Islamic Republic," *International Journal of Middle East Studies* 20 (2) (May 1988):221–243.

34. Andrea W. Lorenz, "Ishtar Was a Woman," *Ms.* (May–June 1991), pp. 14-15.

35. See Khalil Nakhleh and Elia Zureik, eds., *The Sociology of the Palestinians* (New York: St. Martin's Press, 1980).

36. See Margot Badran and Miriam Cooke, eds., *Opening the Gates: A Century of Arab Feminist Writing* (Bloomington: Indiana University Press, 1990).

37. Miriam Cooke, *War's Other Voices: Women Writers on the Lebanese Civil War* (Cambridge, UK: Cambridge University Press, 1986). See also Margot Badran and Miriam Cooke, *Opening the Gates,* introduction.

38. On Palestinian women's political activism see Rosemary Sayigh and Julie Peteet, "Between Two Fires: Palestinian Women in Lebanon," in Rosemary Ridd and Helen Callaway, eds., *Women & Political Conflict: Portraits of Struggle in Times of Crisis* (New York: New York University Press, 1987), pp. 106–137; Rita Giacaman and Muna Odeh, "Palestinian Women's Movement in the Israeli-Occupied West Bank and Gaza Strip," and Mona Rishmawi, "The Legal Status of Palestinian Women in the Occupied Territories," both in Nahid Toubia, ed., *Women of the Arab World: The Coming Challenge* (London: Zed Books, 1988); Soraya Antonius, "Fighting on Two Fronts: Conversations with Palestinian Women," in Miranda Davies, ed., *Third World/Second Sex* (London: Zed Books, 1983), pp. 63–77; Nahla Abdo-Zubi, "On Nationalism and Feminism: Palestinian Women and the Intifada: No Going Back?" paper prepared for the UNU/WIDER Roundtable on Identity Politics and Women, Helsinki (October 8–10, 1990); Julie Peteet, "Women and National Politics in the Middle East," in Berch Berberoglu, ed., *Power and Stability in the Middle East* (London: Zed Books, 1989), pp. 136–156. For an especially critical view of Palestinian women's roles, see Fawzia Fawzia, "Palestine: Women and the Revolution," in Robin Morgan, ed., *Sisterhood Is Global,* pp. 540–545. A Marxist view is provided by Ehud Ein Gil and Aryeh Finkelstein, "Changes in Palestinian Society," and Magida Salman, "Arab Women," both in *Khamsin,* No. 6 (1978).

▲ Chapter 2

1. The following list is by no means complete, but it is representative of the WID and sociology-of-gender perspective, which puts a premium on women's integration into the paid labor force of the formal economy: Rae Lesser Blumberg, *Making the Case for the Gender Variable* (Washington, D.C.: Agency for International Development, Office of Women in Development, 1989); Valentina Bodrova and Richard Anker, eds., *Working Women in Socialist Countries: The Fertility Connection* (Geneva: ILO, 1985); Janet Saltzman Chafetz, *Sex and Advantage: A Comparative Macro-Structural Theory of Sex Stratification* (Totowa, NJ: Rowman & Allanheld, 1984); Daisy Dwyer and Judith Bruce, eds., *A Home Divided: Women and Income in the Third World* (Stanford: Stanford University Press, 1988); Barbara Finlay, *The Women of Azua: Work and Family in the Rural Dominican Republic* (New York: Praeger, 1989); Janet Giele, "Women's Status in Comparative Perspective," in Janet Giele and Audrey Smock, eds., *Women's Roles and Status in Eight Countries* (New York: John Wiley, 1977), pp. 1–32; Susan Joekes, *Women in the World Economy: An INSTRAW Study* (New York: Oxford University Press, 1987); Linda Lim, "Capitalism, Imperialism and Patriarchy," in June Nash and Maria Patricia Fernandez-Kelly, eds., *Women, Men and the International Division of Labor* (Albany: State Univesity of New York Press, 1983), pp. 70–92; Linda Lim, "Women's Work in Export Factories: The Politics of a Cause," in Irene Tinker, ed., *Persistent Inequalities* (New York: Oxford University Press, 1990), pp. 101–122; Val Moghadam, *Gender, Development and Policy: Toward Equity and Empowerment* (Helsinki: UNU/WIDER Research for Action Series, 1990).

2. For a good discussion of the debate, see Susan Tiano, "Gender, Work, and World Capitalism: Third World Women's Role in Development," in Beth Hess and Myra Marx Feree, eds., *Analyzing Gender* (Beverly Hills: Sage, 1987), pp. 216–243. For a more recent review, see Ruth Pearson, "Gender Issues in Industrialization," in T. Hewitt, H. Johnson, and D. Wield, eds., *Industrialization and Development* (Oxford, UK: Oxford University Press, 1992), pp. 222–247.

3. See, for example, Diane Elson and Ruth Pearson, "The Subordination of Women and the Internationalisation of Factory Production", in Kate Young, et al., eds., *Of Marriage and the Market: Women's Subordination in International Perspective* (London: CSE Books, 1981), pp. 144–166; Kathryn Ward, *Women in the World-System* (New York: Praeger, 1984); Nash and Fernandez-Kelly, eds., *Women, Men and the International Division of Labor;* Annette Fuentes and Barbara Ehrenreich, *Women in the Global Factory* (Boston: South End Press, 1983); and Gita Sen and Caren Grown, *Development, Crises and Alternative Visions: Third World Women's Perspectives* (New York: Monthly Review Press, 1987).

4. Ester Boserup, "Economic Change and the Roles of Women," in Irene Tinker, ed., *Persistent Inequalities*, pp. 14–26. Boserup's famous book is *Women's Role in Economic Development* (New York: St Martin's Press, 1970).

5. Boserup, "Economic Change and the Roles of Women," p. 24.

6. G.B.S. Mujahid, "Female Labour Force Participation in Jordan," in J. Abu Nasr, N. Khoury, and H. Azzam, eds., *Women, Employment and Development in the Arab World* (The Hague: Mouton/ILO, 1985), p. 114.

7. Ruth Leger Sivard, *Women . . . A World Survey* (Washington, D.C.: World Priorities, 1985), p. 13.

8. Cited in Blumberg, *Making the Case for the Gender Variable,* p. 91.

9. ILO/INSTRAW, *Women in Economic Activity: A Global Statistical Survey 1950–2000* (Santo Domingo: INSTRAW and Geneva: ILO, 1985).

10. See Susan Joekes, *Women in the World Economy;* Guy Standing, "Global Feminisation Through Flexible Labour," WEP Labour Market Analysis Working Paper No. 31 (Geneva: ILO, 1989). See also ILO/INSTRAW, *Women in Economic Activity,* p. 21.

11. ILO/INSTRAW, *Women in Economic Activity,* p. 35.

12. Mary Chamie, *Women of the World: Near East and North Africa* (Washington, D.C.: U.S. Department of Commerce and Agency for International Development, 1985), p. 3.

13. H. Azzam, J. Abu Nasr, and I. Lorfing, "An Overview of Arab Women in Population, Employment and Economic Development," in J. Abu Nasr, N. Khoury, and H. Azzam, eds., *Women, Employment and Development in the Arab World,* pp. 5–38. See also Doreen Tully, "Introduction," in Dennis Tully, ed., *Labor and Rainfed Agriculture in West Asia and North Africa* (Dortrecht, Boston, and London: Kluwer Academic Publishers, 1990), p. 84.

14. See ILO, *Women at Work* (Special Issue) (Geneva: ILO, 1985), and Anne-Marie Brocas, Anne-Marie Cailloux, and Virginie Oget, *Women and Social Security, Progress Towards Equality of Treatment* (Geneva: ILO, 1990).

15. Gulten Kazgan, "Labour Participation, Occupational Distribution, Educational Attainment and the Socio-Economic Status of Women in the Turkish Economy," in Nermin Abadan-Unat, ed., *Women in Turkish Society* (Leiden: E. J. Brill, 1981).

16. Constantina Safilios-Rothschild, "A Cross-Cultural Examination of Women's Marital, Educational and Occupational Options," in M.T.S. Mednick, et al., eds., *Women and Achievement* (New York: John Wiley and Sons, 1971).

17. Ayse Oncü, "Turkish Women in the Professions: Why So Many?" in Abadan-Unat, ed., *Women in Turkish Society,* p. 189.

18. ILO/INSTRAW, *Women in Economic Activity,* p. 36.

19. A very useful discussion of the methodological problems of Middle Eastern women's employment is by Kailas C. Doctor and Nabil F. Khoury, "Arab Women's Education and Employment Profiles and Prospects: An Overview," in Nabil F. Khoury and Kailas C. Doctor, eds., *Education and Employment Issues of Women in Development in the Middle East* (Nicosia: Imprinta Publishers, 1991), especially pp. 21–31.

20. Robert Mabro, "Industrialization," in Michael Adams, ed., *The Middle East* (New York: Facts-on-File Publications, 1988), p. 689; Alan Richards and John Waterbury, *A Political Economy of the Middle East: State, Class and Economic Development* (Boulder: Westview Press, 1990), pp. 78–79.

21. Rhys Jenkins, "The Political Economy of Industrialization: A Comparison of Latin American and East Asian Newly Industrializing Countries," *Development and Change* 22 (2) (April 1991):197–232. See also Nigel Harris, *The End of the Third World, Newly Industrializing Countries and the Decline of an Ideology* (Harmondsworth: Penguin, 1986).

22. Mabro, "Industrialization," p. 689; Richards and Waterbury, *A Political Economy of the Middle East,* pp. 25-33.

23. Mabro, p. 692.

24. Ibid., p. 692.

25. Susan Joekes and Roxanna Moayedi, *Women and Export Manufacturing: A Review of the Issues and AID Policy* (Washington, D.C.: International Center for Research on Women, July 1987), p. 21.

26. See F. J. Heinrichs Frobel and O. Kreye, *The New International Division of*

Labour (Cambridge, UK: Cambridge University Press, 1980), especially Appendix, Table III–17/18.

27. Mabro, "Industrialization," p. 692.

28. Richards and Waterbury, *A Political Economy of the Middle East*, pp. 70-73.

29. CERED, *Femmes et Condition Feminine au Maroc* (Rabat: Direction de la Statistique, 1989), pp. 103–104.

30. Mabro, "Industrialization," p. 695.

31. See Susan Joekes, "Female-Led Industrialization: Women's Jobs in Third World Export Manufacturing: The Case of the Clothing Industry in Morocco." Research Report No. 15, Institute of Development Studies, University of Sussex, 1982. See also ILO/INSTRAW, *Women in Economic Activity*, p. 35.

32. In a documentary film by the UNDP called *Arab Women at Work*, it was reported that one reason for the underrepresentation of working women in the national accounts is the existence of small private-sector enterprises that are not registered, do not pay taxes, and do not report a labor force. The women (and men) in such firms may be waged but do not receive benefits. In some cases this type of employment leads to official estimates rather than precise figures.

33. ILO/INSTRAW, *Women in Economic Activity*, p. 64.

34. Val Moghadam, "Industrial Development, Culture, and Working Class Politics: A Case Study of Tabriz Industrial Workers in the Iranian Revolution," *International Sociology* 2 (2) (June 1987):151–175. The proliferation of small establishments throughout the Middle East is noted also by Richards and Waterbury, *A Political Economy of the Middle East*, pp. 73–75.

35. By contrast, fully 76 percent of male production workers were salaried. But this changed after the revolution. By the 1986 census, self-employment among male industrial workers had doubled, while the proportion who were salaried declined to less than 40 percent. On changes in Iran, see ILO, *Yearbook of Labour Statistics, Retrospective Edition 1945–1989*, Table 2B, pp. 572–573. See also ILO/INSTRAW, *Women in Economic Activity*, p. 49. For details on Iran refer to Chapter 6 in this book.

36. Joekes, *Women in the World Economy*, p. 81; Standing, "Global Feminisation Through Flexible Labour," p. 25.

37. Mabro, "Industrialization," p. 696.

38. United Nations, *The World's Women: Trends and Statistics 1970–1990* (New York: United Nations Statistical Office, 1991), p. 84.

39. ILO/INSTRAW, *Women in Economic Activity*, p. 13.

40. Mujahid, "Female Labour Force Participation in Jordan," p. 115.

41. Patricia Higgins and Pirouz Shoar-Ghaffari, "Sex Role Socialization in Iranian Textbooks," Department of Anthropology, State University of New York–Plattsburgh, 1989.

42. United Nations Department of Public Information, *Economic Development: The Debt Crisis* (New York: UNDPI, 1989).

43. See Tim Niblock, "International and Domestic Factors in the Economic Liberalisation Process in Arab Countries," paper presented at the symposium on Economic Liberalisation and its Social and Economic Effects, University of Exeter (September 26–28, 1991); David Seddon, "Popular Protest, Austerity, and Economic Liberalisation in the Middle East and North Africa," discussion paper No. 221, School of Development Studies, University of East Anglia, Norwich, England, 1992; Said el-Naggar, ed., *Privatization and Structural Adjustment in the Arab Countries* (Washington, D.C.: International Monetary Fund, 1989); Ziya Önis, "The Evolution of Privatization in Turkey: The Institutional Context of Public-Enterprise Reform," *International Journal of Middle East Studies* 23 (2) (May

1991):163-176.

44. Nermin Abadan-Unat, "The Modernization of Turkish Women," *Middle East Journal* 32 (1978):303. See also June Starr, "The Legal and Social Transformation of Rural Women in Aegean Turkey," in Renée Hirschon, ed., *Women and Property—Women as Property* (New York: St. Martin's Press, 1984).

45. Caglar Keyder, "Social Structure and the Labour Market in Turkish Agriculture," *International Labour Review* 128 (6) (1989):731–744.

46. Brocas, Cailloux, and Oget, *Women and Social Security,* p. 26.

47. Yildiz Ecevit, "The Ideological Construction of Turkish Women Factory Workers," in Nanneke Redclift and M. Thea Sinclair, eds., *Working Women: International Perspectives on Labour and Gender Ideology* (London and New York: Routledge, 1991), pp. 56–78. The quote appears on p. 77.

48. International Labour Office, *World Labour Report 1989* (Geneva: ILO, 1990), p. 52.

49. Homa Hoodfar, "Return to the Veil: Personal Strategy and Public Participation in Egypt," in Redclift and Sinclair, eds., *Working Women,* p. 108.

50. Swedish International Development Authority, *Women in Developing Countries: Case Studies of Six Countries* (Stockholm: SIDA Research Division, 1974).

51. United Nations Fund for Population Activities/Ministère du Plan, *La Femme et La Famille Tunisienne a Travers Les Chiffres* (Tunis: United Nations Fund for Population Activities, and the Ministry of Planning, 1984); Union Nationale des Femmes Tunisiennes, *La Femme au Travail en Chiffres* (Tunis: UNFT, 1987).

52. *The Economist,* July 8, 1989, p. 48.

53. Richards and Waterbury, *A Political Economy of the Middle East,* p. 121.

54. ILO, *Women at Work,* p. 16. See also Ismail A. El Dulaimy, "Women, Human Resources and National Development in Iraq," in Khoury and Doctor, eds., *Education and Employment Issues of Women in Development in the Middle East,* pp. 91–105.

55. Andrea W. Lorenz, "Ishtar Was a Woman," *Ms.* (May/June 1991), pp. 14-15.

56. *Labour Law and Social Security of the Islamic Republic of Iran* (Tehran: Korshid Publications, 1369/1990), pp. 41–43 (in Persian). For an English translation, see *The Labor Law of Iran,* trans. Firouzeh Aminpour (Tehran: Ketab Sara Company, 1991).

57. See Peter Knauss, *The Persistence of Patriarchy: Class, Gender and Ideology in Twentieth Century Algeria* (New York: Praeger, 1987). See also Willy Jansen, "God Will Pay in Heaven: Women and Wages in Algeria," paper presented at the Middle East Studies Association annual meetings, Baltimore (November 1987).

58. Nouredine Saadi, *La Femme et La Loi en Algérie* (Casablanca: Editions Fennec for UNU/WIDER, 1991), p. 74. See also Institut National du Travail, *Revue Algérienne du Travail: L'Emploi en Algérie: Réalités et Perspectives* (Algiers: Institute National du Travail, 1987).

59. Nadia Hijab, *Womanpower: The Arab Debate on Women and Work* (Cambridge, UK: Cambridge University Press, 1988), p. 96.

60. Mujahid, "Female Labour Force Participation in Jordan," p. 105.

61. Ibid., p. 103. See also National Planning Council, Hashemite Kingdom of Jordan, *Five Year Plan for Economic and Social Development 1980–1985* (1981).

62. Hijab, *Womanpower,* p. 114.

63. Eugene B. Gallagher and C. Maureen Searle, "Health Services and the Political Culture of Saudi Arabia," *Social Science Medical (UK)* 21 (3) (1985):251–262.

64. Ghazy Mujahid, "Tradition, Women's Education and National Development in Saudi Arabia," in Khoury and Doctor, eds., *Education and Employment Issues*, pp. 75–89.

65. Youssef M. Ibrahim, "Saudis, Aroused by Iraqi Threat, Take Steps to Mobilize Population," *New York Times*, September 5, 1990, p. A1.

66. Within the United States, the public sector is most conducive to female advancement. The so-called glass ceiling blocking the advancement of women and minorities is more firmly in place in the private sector than in the public sector, where affirmative action goals are enforced. Guy Standing has recently pointed out that not only are women's wages and employment conditions better on average in the public sector than in private wage employment, but also wage differentials between men and women are smaller in the public sector. See Standing, "Global Feminisation Through Flexible Labour," p. 25.

67. Fatima Mernissi, "The Merchant's Daughter and the Son of the Sultan," in Robin Morgan, ed., *Sisterhood Is Global* (New York: Anchor Books, 1984), pp. 448–449.

68. See the sources in Note 3.

69. Amal Rassam, "Introduction: Arab Women: The Status of Research in the Social Sciences and the Status of Women," in *Social Science Research and Women in the Arab World* (London: Francis Pinter/UNESCO, 1984), pp. 1–3.

70. Fatima Mernissi, "The Degrading Effects of Capitalism on Female Labour," *Mediterranean People* 6 (January–March 1978); Fatima Mernissi, *Doing Daily Battle: Interviews with Moroccan Women*, trans. Mary Jo Lakeland (London: The Woman's Press, 1988).

71. See the following essays by Deniz Kandiyoti: "Sex Roles and Social Change: A Comparative Appraisal of Turkey's Women," in Wellesley Editorial Committee, ed., *Women and National Development* (Chicago: University of Chicago Press, 1977); "Urban Change and Women's Roles in Turkey: An Overview and Evaluation," in Cigdem Kagitcibasi, ed., *Sex Roles, Family and Community in Turkey* (Bloomington: Indiana University Press, 1982); "Bargaining with Patriarchy," *Gender & Society* 2 (3) (September 1988):274–289.

See also the following by Gunseli Berik: "From 'Enemy of the Spoon' to 'Factory': Women's Labor in the Carpet Weaving Industry in Rural Turkey," paper presented at the Middle East Studies Association annual meetings, New Orleans (November 22–26, 1985); *Women Carpet Weavers in Rural Turkey: Patterns of Employment, Earnings and Status* Women, Work and Development Series No. 15, (Geneva: ILO, 1987).

Also on Turkey see Mine Cinar, "Labor Opportunities for Adult Females and Home-Working Women in Istanbul, Turkey," working paper No. 2, G. E. von Grunebaum Center for Near Eastern Studies, UCLA, 1991; and Abadan-Unat, "The Modernization of Turkish Women," p. 127.

On Iran see Haleh Afshar, "The Position of Women in an Iranian Village," in Haleh Afshar, ed., *Women, Work and Ideology in the Third World* (London: Tavistock, 1985), pp. 63–82. On Afghanistan see Chapter 7.

72. Joakes and Moayedi, *Women and Export Manufacturing*.

73. Susan Tiano, "Maquiladora Women: A New Category of Workers?" in Ward, ed., *Women Workers and Global Restructuring*, pp. 193–223.

74. Mernissi, *Scheherezade*.

75. Interviews at Polymedic/Hoechst/Maroc, Route de Rabat, Casablanca,

December 3, 1990. I am grateful to the director-general, M. Abderrahim Chawki, for the opportunity to interview the women employees and especially grateful to M. Abdelhay Bouzoubaa of the national staff of UNDP for arranging the site visit and the interviews.

76. See International Labour Organisation and United Nations Centre on Transnational Corporations, *Economic and Social Effects of Multinational Enterprises in Export Processing Zones* (Geneva: ILO/UNCTC, 1988), especially Chapter 3.

▲ Chapter 3

1. See the collection of essays in Sonia Kruks, Rayna Rapp, and Marilyn Young, eds., *Promissory Notes: Women in the Transition to Socialism* (New York: Monthly Review Press, 1989). See also Val Moghadam, "Development and Women's Emancipation: Is There a Connection?" *Development and Change* 23 (3) (July 1992), pp. 215–256.

2. Kumari Jayawardena, *Feminism and Nationalism in the Third World* (London: Zed Books, 1986).

3. Janet Salzman Chafetz and Gary Dworkin, *Female Revolt: Women's Movements in World and Historial Perspective* (Totowa, NJ: Rowman and Allanheld, 1986), p. 191.

4. Mounira Charrad, *Women and the State: A Comparative Study of Politics, Law and the Family in Tunisia, Algeria and Morocco,* Ph.D. dissertation, Department of Sociology, Harvard University, 1980; Nira Yuval-Davis and Floya Anthias, eds., *Women-Nation-State* (London: Macmillan, 1989); Marie de Lepervanche, "Holding It All Together: Multiculturalism, Nationalism, Women and the State in Australia," paper presented at the XIIth World Congress of Sociology, Madrid (July 1990); Deniz Kandiyoti, ed., *Women, Islam and the State* (London: Macmillan, 1991).

5. On women and the French Revolution see Ruth Graham, "Loaves and Liberty: Women in the French Revolution," in Renate Bridenthal and Claudia Koonz, eds., *Becoming Visible: Women in European History* (Boston: Houghton Mifflin, 1977); Lynn Hunt, *Politics, Culture, and Class in the French Revolution* (Berkeley: University of California Press, 1984); Siân Reynolds, "Marianne's Citizens? Women, the Republic, and Universal Suffrage in France," in Siân Reynolds, ed., *Women, State and Revolution: Essays on Power and Gender in Europe Since 1789* (Amherst: University of Massachusetts Press, 1987), pp. 101–122; Jane Abray, "Feminism in the French Revolution," *American Historical Review* 80 (1975); Darline Gay Levy, Harriet Branson Applewhite, and Mary Durham Johnson, *Women in Revolutionary Paris 1789–1795* (Urbana: University of Illinois Press, 1979); Joan Landes, *Women and the Public Sphere in the Age of the French Revolution* (Ithaca: Cornell University Press, 1988).

6. Reynolds, "Introduction," in Reynolds, ed., *Women, State and Revolution,* p. xiv.

7. On women and revolutions in the twentieth century, see Guity Nashat, ed., *Women and Revolution in Iran* (Boulder: Westview Press, 1982); Judith Stacey, *Patriarchy and Socialist Revolution in China* (Berkeley: University of California Press, 1983); Sheila Rowbotham, *Women, Resistance, and Revolution* (London: Allen Lane, 1972); Maxine Molyneux, "Socialist Societies Old and New: Progress Toward Women's Emancipation?" *Monthly Review* 34 (3) (July–August

1982):56–100, and "Mobilization Without Emancipation? Women's Interests, State, and Revolution," in Richard Fagen, Carmen Diana Deere, and José Luis Corragio, eds., *Transition and Development: Problems of Third World Socialism* (New York: Monthly Review, 1986), pp. 280–302; Johnetta Cole, "Women in Cuba: The Revolution Within the Revolution," in J. Goldstone, ed., *Revolutions: Theoretical, Comparative, and Historical Studies* (San Diego: Harcourt Brace Jovanovich, 1986), pp. 307–318; Linda Lobao, "Women in Revolutionary Movements: Changing Patterns of Latin American Guerrilla Struggles," in Guida West and Rhoda Lois Blumberg, eds., *Women and Social Protest* (New York: Oxford University Press, 1990), pp. 180–204; and Kruks, et al., eds., *Promissory Notes*. Much of this scholarship is concerned with assessing the extent of female emancipation in socialist societies, or describing patterns of women's particpation in revolutionary movements, rather than theorizing the role of gender in revolutionary processes.

8. The most cited sociological studies of revolution are Theda Skocpol, *States and Social Revolutions: A Comparative Analysis of France, Russia, and China* (Cambridge, UK: Cambridge University Press, 1979); Charles Tilly, *From Mobilization to Revolution* (Reading, MA: Addison-Wesley, 1978); Ellen Kay Trimberger, *Revolution from Above: Military Bureaucrats and Development in Japan, Turkey, Egypt, and Peru* (New Brunswick, NJ: Transaction Books, 1978); Jeffrey Paige, *Agrarian Revolution: Social Movements and Export Agriculture in the Underdeveloped World* (New York: The Free Press, 1975). See also Jack Goldstone, ed., *Revolutions: Theoretical, Comparative, and Historical Studies* (Orlando: Harcourt Brace Jovanovich, 1986), and Terry Boswell, ed., *Revolution in the World-System* (Westport, CT: Greenwood Press, 1989).

I am grateful to John Foran for pointing out that gender is treated in Timothy Wickham-Crowley, *Guerrillas and Revolution in Latin America: A Comparative Study of Insurgents and Regimes Since 1956* (Princeton: Princeton University Press, 1992), which I had not seen at the time of this writing.

9. Samuel Huntington, *Political Order in Changing Societies* (New Haven: Yale University Press, 1968), p. 264; Theda Skocpol, *States and Social Revolutions*, p. 4; John Dunn, *Modern Revolutions* (New York: Cambridge University Press, 1972), p. 12.

10. Perez Zagorin, *Rebels and Rulers, Vol. 1* (Cambridge: Cambridge University Press, 1982), p. 17, cited in Michael S. Kimmel, *Revolution: A Sociological Interpretation* (Cambridge, UK: Polity Press, 1990), p. 6. Kimmel's synthesis of the structural and purposive dimensions of revolution accords well with the analysis in the present chapter.

11. Terry Boswell, "World Revolutions and Revolutions in the World-System," in Terry Boswell, ed., *Revolution in the World-System* (Westport, CT: Greenwood Press, 1989), pp. 1–18. Here I refer to twentieth-century revolutions. The contentious debate within the scholarship on the causes and outcomes of the French Revolution, initiated by Francois Furet's revisionist historiography, is somewhat separate. As regards the changes in Eastern Europe (the "1989 revolutions") and the former Soviet Union, whether or not these countries experienced a revolution in the sociological sense, and the nature of that revolution, remain a matter of debate and require further research. It is likely that our definition of revolution may need to be revised to account for the changes in the former state socialist societies, particularly with regard to the generally nonviolent nature of the collapse of the communist states. And although these societies were not "modernizing" societies, they seem to have been rather hard hit by the vagaries of the world system, which would suggest that class conflict and world-systemic imperatives may explain the

causes of the "1989 revolutions." But certainly what they have in common with earlier revolutions and with the discussion in this chapter is a gender dimension distinctly similar to the "Woman-in-the-Family" model of revolution.

12. See Kimmel, *Revolution: A Sociological Interpretation;* John Foran, "Theories of Revolution and the Case of Iran," paper presented at the annual meeting of the American Sociological Association, San Francisco (August 1989); Val Moghadam, "Populist Revolution and the Islamic State in Iran," in Boswell, ed., *Revolution in the World-System,* pp. 147–163. This proposition is equally valid in the case of the so-called 1989 revolutions in Eastern Europe and the transformation of the former Soviet Union.

13. Carol Pateman, *The Sexual Contract* (Cambridge, UK: Polity Press, 1988). See also Susan Okin, *Women in Western Political Thought* (Princeton: Princeton University Press, 1979).

14. Eric Hobsbawm called the woman question "the Achilles heel of the Enlightenment" in a personal communication, Helsinki, August 9, 1990.

15. Reynolds, "Marianne's Citizens?" p. 110.

16. Harriet B. Applewhite and Darlene G. Levy, "Introduction," in Applewhite and Levy, eds., *Women and Politics in the Age of the Democratic Revolution* (Ann Arbor: University of Michigan Press, 1990), p. 6.

17. Robert Darnton, "What Was Revolutionary About the French Revolution?" *New York Review of Books,* January 19, 1989, p. 4.

18. It is Rowbotham's contention that women's role in the French Revolution, and in particular left-wing women such as Claire Lacombe and the sansculottes women in the club and society, were the precursors of the socialist women of 1830–1848. See "Women in Movement: Feminism and Social Action," Manuscript, 1992, pp. 19–27.

19. Hunt, *Politics, Culture and Class,* pp. 31, 104, 109.

20. Quoted in Reynolds, "Marianne's Citizens?" p. 3.

21. Quoted in Linda Kelly, *Women of the French Revolution* (London: Hamish Hamilton, 1987), p. 127.

22. Quoted in Reynolds, "Marianne's Citizens?" p. 105.

23. Wendy Zeva Goldman, "Women, the Family, and the New Revolutionary Order in the Soviet Union," in Kruks, et al., *Promissory Notes,* pp. 59–81.

24. All three quotes by Lenin from *The Woman Question: Selections from the Writings of Karl Marx, Frederick Engels, V. I. Lenin, Clara Zetkin, Joseph Stalin* (New York: International Publishers, 1977), pp. 56, 59, 61.

25. Elizabeth Waters, "In the Shadow of the Comintern: The Communist Women's Movement, 1920–1943," in Kruks, et al., eds., *Promissory Notes,* pp. 29–56. As Engels himself put it in *Origin of the Family,* "The supremacy of the man in marriage is the simple consequence of his economic supremacy, and with the abolition of the latter will disappear of itself."

26. On Bolshevik strategies in Central Asia see Gregory Massell, *The Surrogate Proletariat* (Princeton: Princeton University Press, 1974).

27. Jayawardena, *Feminism and Nationalism in the Third World,* p. 25.

28. Bernard Lewis, *The Emergence of Modern Turkey* (Oxford: Oxford University Press, 1965), p. 105.

29. Jayawardena, *Feminism and Nationalism in the Third World,* p. 29.

30. Nermin Abadan-Unat, "Social Change and Turkish Women," in Abadan-Unat, ed., *Women in Turkish Society* (Leiden: E. J. Brill, 1981), p. 9.

31. Caglar Keyder, "The Political Economy of Turkish Democracy," *New Left Review* 115 (May–June 1979):9; Jayawardena, *Feminism and Nationalism in the Third World,* p. 34; Deniz Kandiyoti, "Women and the Turkish State: Political

Actors or Symbolic Pawns?" in Yuval-Davis and Anthias, eds., *Women-Nation-State*, p. 141.

32. Cited in Kandiyoti, ibid., p. 141.

33. Kandiyoti, ibid., p. 142.

34. Quoted in Jayawardena, *Feminism and Nationalism in the Third World*, p. 36.

35. Suna Kili, "Modernity and Tradition: Dilemma Concerning Women's Rights in Turkey," paper presented to the annual meeting of the International Society of Political Psychology, Helsinki, Finland (July 1–5, 1991), p. 7.

36. See Emel Dogramaci, *The Status of Women in Turkey* (Ankara: Meteksan Co., 1984), especially Chapter 3 on "The Status of Women as Reflected in the Works of Namik Kemal, Huseyin Rahmi Gürpinar, Halide Edip Adirar and Ziya Gökalp."

37. Dogramaci, ibid., p. 127.

38. Peter Knauss, *The Persistence of Patriarchy: Class, Gender and Ideology in 20th Century Algeria* (Boulder: Westview Press, 1987), p. 49.

39. Knauss, ibid., p. 75.

40. Doria Cherifati-Merabtine, "Algeria at a Crossroads: National Liberation, Islamization, and Women," forthcoming in Val Moghadam, ed., *Gender and National Identity: The Woman Question in Five Muslim Societies* (London: Zed Books).

41. Alya Baffoun, "Women and Social Change in the Muslim Arab World," *Women's Studies International Forum* 5 (2) (1982):234.

42. Knauss, *The Persistence of Patriachy*, p. 98.

43. Cherifa Bouatta and Doria Cherifati-Merabtine, "The Social Representation of Women in Algeria's Islamist Movement," paper prepared for the UNU/WIDER Roundtable on Identity Politics and Women, Helsinki (October 8–10, 1990).

44. Cherifa Bouatta, "Feminine Militancy: Algerian *Moudjahidates* During and After the War," forthcoming in Val Moghadam, ed., *Gender and National Identity*.

45. Quoted in Knauss, *The Persistence of Patriachy*, p. 99.

46. Baffoun, "Women and Social Change in the Muslim Arab World," p. 234.

47. Knauss, *The Persistence of Patriarchy*, p. xiii.

48. Doria Cherifati-Merabtine, "Algeria at a Crossroads."

49. Knauss, *The Persistence of Patriarchy*, p.111.

50. Maxine Molyneux, "Legal Reform and Socialist Revolution in Democratic Yemen: Women and the Family," *International Journal of Sociology of Law* 13 (1985):147–172.

51. Molyneux, ibid., pp. 161–162.

52. Molyneux, ibid., p. 157.

53. "Building A New Life for Women in South Yemen" (interviews with Aisha Moshen and Noor Ba'abad by Maxine Molyneux), in Miranda Davies, ed., *Third World/Second Sex* (London: Zed Books, 1987), pp. 135–142.

54. Nadia Hijab, *Womanpower: The Arab Debate on Women at Work* (Cambridge University Press, 1988), p. 24.

55. Noor Ba'abad, in Miranda Davies, ed., *Third World/Second Sex*, p. 142.

56. F. Sanatkar, "Feminism and Women Intellectuals" (in Persian), *Nazm-e Novin* 8 (Summer 1987):56–58; Nayereh Tohidi, *Women and Fundamentalists in Iran* (Los Angeles: Ketab Publishers, 1988; in Persian).

57. Murteza Mutahhari, *On the Islamic Hijab* (Tehran: Islamic Propagation Organization, 1987).

58. Kaveh Afrasiabi, *The State and Populism in Iran*, Ph.D. dissertation, Department of Political Science, Boston University, (1987), p. 307.

59. Afsaneh Najmabadi, "Power, Morality and the New Muslim Womanhood," paper prepared for the workshop on Women and the State in Afghanistan, Iran, and Pakistan, MIT Center for International Studies (March 1989).

60. Quoted in Nancy Tapper, "Causes and Consequences of the Abolition of Bride-Price in Afghanistan," in Nazif Shahrani and Robert Canfield, *Revolutions and Rebellions in Afghanistan* (Berkeley: University of California Press, Institute of International Studies Monograph Series, 1984), p. 292.

61. Cited in Tapper, p. 292. For full bibliographical details, see Chapter 7 in this book.

62. Richard Nyrop and Donald Seekins, eds., *Afghanistan: A Country Study* (Washington, D.C.: The American University, Foreign Area Studies, 1986), p. 128.

63. Thomas Hammond, *Red Flag Over Afghanistan* (Boulder: Westview Press, 1984), p. 71.

64. Hanna Papanek, "Why Do Regimes Raise the Woman Question Even When It Creates So Much Trouble?" Comments prepared for MIT seminar on the State and Restructuring of Society in Afghanistan, Iran, and Pakistan (March 20, 1989).

65. It should be noted that these comments apply equally well to the "1989 revolutions" in Eastern Europe and perestroika in the former Soviet Union, which demonstrate that a reactionary position on gender and on women's role within the society and the family in the late twentieth century is not limited to Muslim countries. For an elaboration, see Val Moghadam, ed., *Privatization and Democratization in Central and Eastern Europe and the Soviet Union: The Gender Dimension* (Helsinki: UNU/WIDER Research for Action Series, 1992), and forthcoming from Val Moghadam, ed., *Democratic Reform and the Position of Women in Transitional Economies* (Oxford: Clarendon Press, 1993).

▲ Chapter 4

1. On patriarchy in advanced industrialized society see Sylvia Walby, "Theorizing Patriarchy," *British Journal of Sociology* 23 (2) (1989):213–234. On patriarchy in the Middle East see Hisham Sharabi, *Neopatriarchy: A Theory of Distorted Change in Arab Society* (New York: Oxford University Press, 1988). My approach has been inspired by Deniz Kandiyoti, especially "Bargaining with Patriarchy," *Gender & Society* 2 (3) (September 1988):274–290; and "Islam and Patriarchy: A Comparative Perspective," in N.R. Keddie and B. Baron, eds., *Shifting Boundaries: Women and Gender in Middle Eastern History* (New Haven: Yale University Press, 1992).

2. Kingsley Davis, ed., *Contemporary Marriage* (New York: Basic Books, 1986).

3. Anastasia Posadskaya, "Changes in Gender Discourses and Policies," forthcoming in Val Moghadam, ed., *Democratic Reforms and the Position of Women in Transnational Economies* (Oxford: Clarendon, 1993).

4. Barbara Hanawalt, cited in John Boswell, *The Kindness of Strangers: The Abandonment of Children in Western Europe from Late Antiquity to the Renaissance* (London and New York: Penguin, 1988), p. 410.

5. David Levine, "Punctuated Equilibrium: The Modernization of the Proletarian Family in the Age of Ascendant Capitalism," *International Labor and Working-Class History* 39 (Spring 1991):3–20. See also James Vander Zanden, *Sociology—The Core* (St. Louis: McGraw-Hill, 1990), p. 254.

6. See, for example, Linda Gordon, *Heroes of Their Own Lives: The Politics and History of Family Violence* (London: Virago, 1989). See also John Boswell, *The Kindness of Strangers*. Boswell's study locates the phenomenon of child abandonment in *patria potestas*, the Roman-derived paternal authority. Gordon's study of wife and child abuses in Boston is highly critical of the patriarchal family and the prerogatives of the father. Needless to say, both studies recognize extra-family causes of abandonment and abuse, such as food scarcity, disease, poverty, and unemployment.

7. See John C. Caldwell, *Theory of Fertility Decline* (London: Academic Press, 1982), pp. 166–169. See also Teodor Shanin, "A Peasant Household: Russia at the Turn of the Century," in Teodor Shanin, ed., *Peasants and Peasant Societies* (London: Blackwell, 1987, 2nd ed.), pp. 21–34.

8. Amartya Sen, "Gender and Cooperative Conflicts," and Hanna Papanek, "To Each Less than She Needs, From Each More than She Can Do: Allocations, Entitlements, and Value," both in Irene Tinker, ed., *Persistent Inequalities: Women and World Development* (New York: Oxford University Press, 1990).

9. Barbara Einhorn, "Democratization and Women's Movements in Central and Eastern Europe: Concepts of Women's Rights," in Val Moghadam, ed., *Gender and Restructuring: Democratization, Economic Reform, and Women in Central and Eastern Europe and the Soviet Union* (forthcoming). See also Anastasia Posadskaya, "Changes in Gender Discourses and Policies"; Valentina Bodrova, "Women, Work, and Family in the Mirror of Public Opinion"; and Sharon Wolchik, "Women and the Politics of Transition in Central and Eastern Europe," in Val Moghadam (idem.).

10. Rebecca Klatch, "Coalition and Conflict Among Women of the New Right," *SIGNS* 4 (1988):671–694. The quotes appear on pp. 675–676.

11. Murteza Mutahhari, *Sexual Ethics in Islam and in the Western World*, trans. Muhammad Khurshid Ali (Tehran: Bonyad Be'that Foreign Department, 1982), pp. 7, 31, 58.

12. See Youssef M. Choueiri, *Islamic Fundamentalism* (London: Pinter Publishers, 1990), pp. 127–128.

13. Fereshteh Hashemi, "Women in an Islamic Versus Women in a Muslim View," *Zan-e Rouz* 22 (March 1981), translated and reprinted in Azar Tabari and Nahid Yeganeh, comp., *In the Shadow of Islam: The Women's Movement in Iran* (London: Zed Books, 1982), p. 180.

14. Research Group for Muslim Women's Studies, *The Social Status of Iranian Women Before and After the Victory of the Islamic Revolution* (Tehran: Cultural Studies and Research Institute, Ministry of Culture and Higher Education, 1990), p. 33.

15. See especially Eli Zaretsky, *Capitalism, the Family, and Personal Life* (New York: Harper, 1976), and Jane Humphries, "Class Struggle and the Persistence of the Working Class Family," *Cambridge Journal of Economics* 1 (1977):241–258. For a more critical view, see Wally Seccombe, "Patriarchy Stabilized: The Construction of the Male Breadwinner Wage Norm in Nineteenth-century Britain," *Social History* 11 (1) (1986).

16. This paragraph draws on Kandiyoti, "Bargaining with Patriarchy"; Ellen Meiksins Wood, "Capitalism and Human Emancipation," *New Left Review* 167 (January–February 1988):1–21; Gayle Rubin, "The Traffic in Women: Notes on a Political Economy of Sex," in Rayna Rapp, ed., *Toward an Anthropology of Women* (New York: Monthly Review, 1975), pp. 157–210; Raphael Patai, *Women in the Modern World* (New York: Free Press, 1967); Julian Pitt-Rivers, *The Fate of Shechem or the Politics of Sex: Essays in the Anthropology of the Mediterranean*

(Cambridge, UK: Cambridge University Press, 1977), especially Chapter 1; Germaine Tillion, *The Republic of Cousins: Women's Oppression in Mediterranean Society* (London: Al Saqi Books, 1983), especially Chapter 6; Renée Hirschon, "Introduction: Property, Power and Gender Relations," in Renée Hirschon, ed., *Women and Property—Women as Property* (New York: St. Martin's Press, 1984), pp. 1–22.

17. Michael Mann, "A Crisis in Stratification Theory?" in Rosemary Crompton and Michael Mann, eds., *Gender and Stratification* (Cambridge, UK: Polity Press, 1986), pp. 40–56.

18. Gerda Lerner, *The Creation of Patriarchy* (New York: Oxford University Press, 1986).

19. Boswell, *The Kindness of Strangers*, p. 106.

20. Ibid., p. 106. It was the discovery of this church document that roused Boswell's curiosity and led him to undertake the study of child abandonment in Europe. It is also worth pointing out that in his brief chapter on Islam, Muslim practices vis-à-vis children are found to be more humane than Roman-derived Christian practices.

21. Louise A. Tilly and Joan W. Scott, *Women, Work and Family* (New York and London: Routledge, 1978).

22. On the connection between modernity and the rise of women's rights and feminist movements, see Kumari Jayawardena, *Feminism and Nationalism in the Third World* (London: Zed Books, 1986); Janet S. Chafetz and Gary Dworkin, *Female Revolt: Women's Movements in World and Historical Perspective* (Totowa, NJ: Rowman and Allanheld, 1986); Marshall Berman, *All That Is Solid Melts into Air* (New York: Simon and Schuster, 1983); Nayereh Tohidi, "Identity Politics and the Woman Question in Iran: Retrospect and Prospects," paper prepared for UNU/WIDER Roundtable on Identity Politics and Women, Helsinki (October 8–10, 1990) (hereafter, UNU/WIDER Roundtable paper).

23. Judith Stacey, *Patriarchy and Socialist Revolution in China* (Berkeley: University of California Press, 1983).

24. There is evidence that "Muslim family law" is not uniquely Muslim but that elements were adopted from Christian and Roman law and customs. See Eleanor Doumato, "Hearing Other Voices: Christian Women and the Coming of Islam," *International Journal of Middle East Studies* 23 (2) (May 1991):177–199.

25. Jamal J. Nasir, *The Status of Women Under Islamic Law* (London: Graham & Trotman, 1990), pp. 122–126.

26. Alya Baffoun, "Women and Social Change in the Muslim Arab World," *Women's Studies International Forum* 5 (2) (1982):227–242.

27. Mounira Charrad, "State and Gender in the Maghrib," *Middle East Report* 163 (March–April 1990):19–24. The quotes appear on pages 20 and 21.

28. Nikki R. Keddie, "The Past and Present of Women in the Muslim World," *Journal of World History* 1 (1) (1990):77–108. The quotes are from pp. 81–82. In addition to the sources in Notes 1 and 16, see also Peter McDonald, "Social Organization and Nuptiality in Developing Societies," in John Cleland and John Hobcraft, eds., *Reproductive Change in Developing Countries: Insights from the World Fertility Survey* (New York: Oxford University Press, 1985), pp. 87–114; Hisham Sharabi, "The Dialectics of Patriarchy in Arab Society," in Samih K. Farsoun, ed., *Arab Society: Continuity and Change* (London: Croom Helm, 1985), pp. 83–104; Claude Lévi-Strauss, *Elementary Structures of Kinship* (Boston: Beacon Press, 1969); Jack Goody, *The Oriental, the Ancient and the Primitive: Systems of Marriage and the Family in the Pre-Industrial Societies of Eurasia*

(Cambridge, MA: Cambridge University Press, 1990). See also Dale F. Eickelman, *The Middle East: An Anthropological Approach* (Englewood Cliffs, NJ: Prentice Hall, 1989), p. 128. On family honor and *fitna* in the Middle East, see Fatna A. Sabbah, *Woman in the Muslim Unconscious,* trans. Mary Jo Lakeland (New York: Pergamon Press, 1984); Mai Ghoussoub, "Feminism—or the Eternal Masculine—in the Arab World," *New Left Review* 161 (January–February 1987):3–13; Fatima Mernissi, *Beyond the Veil: Male-Female Dynamics in Modern Muslim Society* (Bloomington: Indiana University Press, 1987).

29. David Mandelbaum, *Women's Seclusion and Men's Honor: Sex Roles in North India, Bangladesh and Pakistan* (Tucson: University of Arizona Press, 1988), p. 19; Naila Kabeer, "Subordination and Struggle: Women in Bangladesh," *New Left Review* 168 (March/April 1988), p. 95.

30. On South Asia, see especially Papanek, "To Each Less than She Needs"; Mead Cain, "The Material Consequences of Reproductive Failure in Rural South Asia," in Daisy Dwyer and Judith Bruce, eds., *A Home Divided: Women and Income in the Third World* (Stanford: Stanford University Press, 1988), pp. 20–38; Amartya Sen and Sunil Sengupta, "Malnutrition of Rural Children and the Sex Bias," *Economic and Political Weekly* 18 (1983):855–863; Jean Drèze and Amartya Sen, *Hunger and Public Action* (Oxford: Clarendon Press, 1989), especially Chapter 4: "Society, Class and Gender."

31. See, for example, Armelle Braun, "Slow Death for Turkish Patriarchalism," *Ceres/The FAO Review No. 117,* 20 (3) (May–June 1987):37–41. See also Deniz Kandiyoti, *Women in Rural Production Systems: Problems and Policies* (Paris: UNESCO, 1985).

32. Nahla Abdo-Zubi, *Family, Women and Social Change in the Middle East: The Palestinian Case* (Toronto: Canadian Scholars' Press, 1987), pp. 29–30.

33. John L. Esposito, *Women in Muslim Family Law* (Syracuse: Syracuse University Press, 1982), pp. 11, 15, 23. It should be noted that when Islam spread outward from Arabia, it grafted itself onto existing customs and rules—hence differences in family structure, law, and the mobility of women between Arab countries, Southeast Asia, and sub-Saharan Africa.

34. Nasir, *The Status of Women Under Islamic Law,* pp. 7–8.

35. Charrad, "State and Gender in the Maghrib," p. 20.

36. Charrad, ibid., p. 21.

37. Charrad, ibid.

38. Nouredine Saadi, *La Femme et La Loi en Algérie* (Casablanca: Editions le Fennec, 1991), p. 47; Peter Knauss, *The Persistence of Patriarchy: Class, Gender and Ideology in Twentieth Century Algeria* (Boulder: Westview Press, 1987); Nassera Merah, "Women and Fundamentalism in Algeria," UNU/WIDER Roundtable paper; see also the discussion on Algeria in Nadia Hijab, *Womanpower: The Arab Debate on Women and Work* (Cambridge, UK: Cambridge University Press, 1988), pp. 26–29. See also Mernissi, *Beyond the Veil,* and Abderrazak Moulay R'chid, *La Femme et La Loi au Maroc* (Casablanca: Editions le Fennec, 1991), pp. 53–54; and Alya Chérif Chamari, *La Femme et la Loi en Tunisie* (Casablanca: Editions le Fennec, 1991), pp. 39–41.

39. Sharabi, *Neopatriarchy,* p. 145.

40. Susan Marshall, "Politics and Female Status in North Africa: A Reconsideration of Development Theory," *Economic Development and Cultural Change* 32 (3) (1984):513.

41. Cain, "The Material Consequences of Reproductive Failure in Rural South Asia."

42. See Bina Agarwal, ed., *Structures of Patriarchy* (London: Zed Books,

1988); Val Moghadam, "Patriarchy and the Politics of Gender in Modernizing Societies: Afghanistan, Iran, Pakistan," *International Sociology* 7 (1) (March 1992):35–54.

43. Ghoussoub, "Feminism—or the Eternal Masculine"; Marie-Aimée Hélie-Lucas, "Women Facing Muslim Personal Laws as the Preferential Symbol for Islamic Identity," UNU/WIDER Roundtable paper; Sana al-Khayyat, *Honour and Shame: Women in Modern Iraq* (London: Saqi Books, 1990).

44. Gregory Massell, *The Surrogate Proletariat* (Princeton: Princeton University Press, 1974). See also Jayawardena, *Feminism and Nationalism in the Third World;* Maxine Molyneux, "Socialist Societies: Progress Toward Women's Emancipation?" *Monthly Review* 34 (3) (July–August 1982):56–100; Sonia Kruks, Rayna Rapp, and Marilyn Young, eds., *Promissory Notes: Women in the Transition to Socialism* (New York: Monthly Review, 1989); Val Moghadam, "Development and Women's Emancipation: Is There a Connection?" *Development and Change* 23 (3) (July 1992):215–255.

45. Deniz Kandiyoti, "Women, Islam and the State," *Middle East Report* 173 (November–December 1991), p. 11. See also Suad Joseph, "Elite Strategies for State-Building: Women, Family, Religion and the State in Iraq and Lebanon," in Deniz Kandiyoti, ed., *Women, Islam and the State* (London: Macmillan, 1991), pp. 176–200.

46. Sir Henry Main, quoted in June Starr, "The Legal and Social Transformation of Rural Women in Aegean Turkey," in Hirschon, ed., *Women and Property—Women as Property;* Caldwell, *Theory of Fertility Decline,* p. 220. This recalls Marx's comment at the beginning of his book *The Eighteenth Brumaire of Louis Bonaparte* that "the traditions of dead generations weigh like a nightmare on the brains of the living."

47. Caldwell, *Theory of Fertility Decline,* p. 162.

48. Goody, *The Oriental, the Ancient, and the Primitive,* p. 372. See also Carla Makhlouf Obermeyer, "Islam, Women, and Politics: The Demography of Arab Countries," *Population and Development Review* (March 1992).

49. Goody, ibid.; see also Kandiyoti, "Islam and Patriarchy," p. 14.

50. Goody, ibid., pp. 375–376.

51. Soheir A. Morsy, "Rural Women, Work and Gender Ideology: A Study in Egyptian Political Economic Transformation," in Seteney Shami, et al., *Women in Arab Society: Work Patterns and Gender Relations in Egypt, Jordan and Sudan* (Providence: Berg/UNESCO, 1990), pp. 87–159.

52. Ibid., p. 114.

53. Nancy Tapper, "Causes and Consequences of the Abolition of Brideprice in Afghanistan," in Nazif Shahrani and Robert Canfield, eds., *Revolutions and Rebellions in Afghanistan* (Berkeley: University of California International Studies Institute, 1984), pp. 291–305; Nyrop and Seekins, eds., *Afghanistan: A Country Study;* Goody, *The Oriental, the Ancient, and the Primitive,* p. 378; Nasir, *The Status of Women Under Islamic Law,* pp. 8–9.

54. Kandiyoti, *Women in Rural Production Systems,* p. 88. See also Nermin Abadan-Unat, "Social Change and Turkish Women," in Nermin Abadan-Unat, ed., *Women in Turkish Society* (Leiden: E. J. Brill, 1981), especially pp. 20–27.

55. Starr, "The Legal and Social Transformation of Rural Women in Aegean Turkey," p. 100.

56. Statistical Center of Iran, *National Census of Population and Housing 1986* (Total Country Summary) (Tehran: Plan and Budget Organization, 1987); John R. Weeks, "The Demography of Islamic Nations," *Population Bulletin* 43 (4) (December 1988). See also the chapter on Iran in this volume.

57. Levine, "Punctuated Equilibrium," p. 4. See also C. C. Harris, *The Family and Industrial Society* (London: George Allen & Unwin, 1983), especially Chapter 7.

58. Louise A. Tilly and Joan W. Scott, *Women, Work and Family*, pp. 89–90.

59. Caldwell, *Theory of Fertility Decline*, p. 176.

60. Ibid., p. 221.

61. Tilly and Scott, *Women, Work and Family*, pp. 91–93. Obviously age at marriage in rural England and France prior to the demographic transition was higher than it has been in rural Third World countries.

62. Carla Makhlouf Obermeyer, "Islam, Women, and Politics: The Demography of Arab Countries."

63. Basheer K. Nijim, "Spatial Aspects of Demographic Change in the Arab World," in Sami G. Hajjar, ed., *The Middle East: From Transition to Development* (Leiden: E. J. Brill, 1985), pp. 30–53.

64. Susan Greenhalgh, "Toward a Political Economy of Fertility: Anthropological Contributions," *Population and Development Review* 16 (1) (March 1990):85–106. The cost-of-children approach is offered by Kingsley Davis, "The World Demographic Transition," *Annals of the American Academy of Political and Social Science* 237 (1955):1–11; see also John C. Caldwell and Lado Ruzicka, "Demographic Levels and Trends," in John Cleland and Chris Scott, eds., *The World Fertility Survey: An Assessment* (New York: International Statistical Institute, Oxford University Press, 1987), pp. 742–772. The status-of-women approach may be found in Cain, "The Material Consequences of Reproductive Failure in Rural South Asia." See also Tim Dyson and Mick Moore, "On Kinship Structure, Female Anatomy and Demographic Behavior," *Population and Development Review* 9 (1) (1983):35–60.

65. Caldwell, *Theory of Fertility Decline*, p. 158.

66. Galal el Din 1977, cited in Caldwell, ibid., p. 364.

67. *World Fertility Survey: Major Findings and Implications* (Voorburg, Netherlands: International Statistical Institute, 1984), p. 49.

68. Nijim, "Spatial Aspects of Demographic Change in the Arab World," p. 48.

69. Starr, "The Legal and Social Transformation of Rural Women." See also Abadan-Unat, "Social Change and Turkish Women."

70. Caldwell, *Theory of Fertility Decline*, p. 219.

71. Ibid., p. 322.

72. Mernissi, *Beyond the Veil*, pp. xxiii–xxiv.

73. Hind A. Khattab and Syeda Greiss el-Daeiff, "Female Education in Egypt: Changing Attitudes Over a Span of 100 Years," in Freda Hussein, ed., *Muslim Women* (London: Croom Helm, 1984), pp. 169–197. The authors of the study found, however, that their respondents still distinguished between "suitable" and "unsuitable" jobs for women. Appropriate careers are teaching, social work, and, in medicine, pediatrics and gynecology (p. 183).

74. Mernissi's figure for Iran is 34.8, also the figure in the UN's *Compendium of Social Statistics and Indicators, 1988* (Table 10), but this refers to 1976. According to Table 20, on p. 54 in the Iranian National Census of Population and Housing of November 1986 (Total Country Summary), 18 percent of women below the age of twenty (for both urban and rural areas) are recorded as ever married. This may seem suspiciously low, but lower figures are recorded for Morocco and Tunisia in the *Compendium*. The average age at marriage (19.8 for women and 23.6 for men) is given in the *Statistical Yearbook 1367 [1988]* (Tehran: Statistical Center of Iran, Plan and Budget Organization, 1989), p. 52.

75. Mernissi, *Beyond the Veil*, p. xxiv.

76. *World Fertility Survey, The Egyptian Fertility Survey, 1980: A Summary of Findings,* No. 42, (November 1983), especially pp. 5, 14. Surveys for other Muslim countries include *The Turkish Fertility Survey, 1978* (WFS No. 28); *The Syrian Fertility Survey, 1978* (WFS No. 35); *The Sudan Fertility Survey, 1979* (WFS No. 36).

77. Mernissi, *Beyond the Veil,* p. xxv.

78. *World Fertility Survey: Major Findings and Implications,* p. 13; Caldwell and Ruzicka, "Demographic Levels and Trends," p. 749; McDonald, "Social Organization and Nuptiality in Developing Societies," p. 110.

79. *The World Fertility Survey,* p. 17; *The Syrian Fertility Survey,* pp. 5, 9, 12; *The Turkish Fertility Survey,* p. 7.

80. K. Mahedevan, Akbar Aghajanian, R. Jayasree, and G. S. Moni, "Status of Women and Population Dynamics: A Conceptual Model," in K. Mahdevan, ed., *Women and Population Dynamics: Asian Perspectives* (New Delhi: Sage, 1989), pp. 345–379. Another important effect on child mortality is the number of pregnancies of the mother. An Egyptian study found a positive relationship between the two variables, noting also that child mortality is higher in the rural areas, where female illiteracy is high, clean water is not always available, and a blood relationship between spouses is more frequent. See Hassan Y. Ali, "Egyptian Child Mortality: A Household, Proximate Determinants Approach," *The Journal of Developing Areas* 25 (July 1991):541–552.

81. Obermeyer, "Islam, Women, and Politics: The Demography of Arab Countries," citing P. Fargues on the decline of Arab fertility.

82. Chafetz and Dworkin, *Female Revolt.*

83. Mernissi, *Beyond the Veil,* p. xxvii.

84. Saad Eddin Ibrahim, "Anatomy of Egypt's Militant Islamic Groups," *International Journal of Middle East Studies* 12 (4) (1980):423–453.

85. Cited in Morsy, "Rural Women, Work and Gender Ideology," p. 138.

86. Mervat Hatem, "Women and Work in the Middle East: The Regional Impact of Migration to the Oil Producing States," paper presented at the Conference on Women and Work in the Third World, University of California, Berkeley (April 10–14, 1983), p. 1.

87. Quoted in Morsy, "Rural Women, Work and Gender Ideology," p. 141.

88. Hatem, "Women and Work in the Middle East," p. 1; Morsy, ibid., p. 142.

89. Esposito, *Women in Muslim Family Law,* p. 103.

90. Mann, "A Crisis in Stratification Theory?" p. 52.

91. Kingsley Davis and P. van Den Oever, cited in Levine, "Punctuated Equilibrium," p. 7.

▲ Chapter 5

1. See Margot Badran, "Independent Women: More than A Century of Feminism in Egypt," forthcoming in Judith Tucker, ed., *Old Boundaries, New Frontiers: Women in the Arab World* (Bloomington: Indiana University Press, 1993).

2. Eric Hobsbawm, *Primitive Rebels* (New York: W. W. Norton, 1959); Michael Walzer, *The Revolution of the Saints* (Cambridge, MA: Harvard University Press, 1965); Christopher Hill, *The World Turned Upside Down* (Harmondsworth: Penguin, 1975); Craig Calhoun, *The Question of Class Struggle: Social Foundations of Popular Radicalism During the Industrial Revolution* (Chicago: University of Chicago Press, 1982).

3. Yvonne Y. Haddad, "Islam, Women and Revolution in Twentieth Century Arab Thought," in Yvonne Y. Haddad and Elison Banks Finlay, eds., *Women, Religion and Social Change* (Albany: State University of New York Press, 1985), pp. 275–306; Division for the Advancement of Women, "Religious Standards of Equality and Religious Freedom: Implications for the Status of Women," paper prepared for the UNU/WIDER Roundtable on Identity Politics and Women, Helsinki (October 8–10, 1990). (Henceforth, this and other papers to be referred to as UNU/WIDER Roundtable paper.)

4. On "pseudo-modernism" and the weakness of an oil economy, see Homa Katouzian, *The Political Economy of Modern Iran 1926–1978* (New York: New York University Press, 1981).

5. Basheer K. Nijim, "Spatial Aspects of Demographic Change in the Arab World," in Sami G. Hajjar, ed., *The Middle East: From Transition to Development* (Leiden: E. J. Brill, 1985), p. 39.

6. R. Hrair Dekmejian, "Fundamentalist Islam: Theories, Typologies, and Trends," *Middle East Review* (Summer 1985):28–33, especially p. 30; Dilip Hiro, "The Islamic Wave Hits Turkey," *The Nation*, June 28, 1986, pp. 882–886.

7. Philip Hitti, *A History of the Arabs* (Princeton: Princeton University Press, 1971).

8. Asghar Ali Engineer, "Remaking Indian Muslim Identity," *Economic and Political Weekly*, April 20, 1991, pp. 1036–1038; Marie-Aimée Hélic-Lucas, "Women Facing Muslim Personal Laws as the Preferential Symbol for Islamic Identity," UNU/WIDER Roundtable paper. On the role of Saudi Arabia's support for fundamentalism, see also Georges Corm, *Fragmentation of the Middle East: The Last Thirty Years* (London: Hutchinson, 1988), especially p. 90.

9. I have elaborated this and similar terms in the Iranian Islamist lexicon in "Rhetorics and Rights of Identity in Islamic Movements," forthcoming in *Journal of World History* 4 (1993).

10. See various issues of *El Moudjahid* (Algiers), early 1992, on "la guerre aux bidonvilles," as well as articles in *Le Monde* (Paris).

11. Saad Eddin Ibrahim, "Anatomy of Egypt's Militant Islamic Groups," *International Journal of Middle East Studies* 12 (4) (1980):423–453; Sondra Hale, "Islamic and Secular Contradictions: Gender, Cultural Identity, and Political Mobilization in Sudan," UNU/WIDER Roundtable paper. On the educational background of Islamist intellectuals see also Yvonne Y. Haddad, "Middle East Area Studies: Current Concerns and Future Directions," Presidential Address 1990, *MESA Bulletin* 25 (1) (July 1991):1–12.

12. See John Entelis, *Culture and Counterculture in Moroccan Politics* (Boulder: Westview Press, 1989). At first glance, these class-based political affiliations appear the same as those of Germany in the 1930s. Many writers have suggested that Hitler's backers were mainly from the lower middle class, experiencing marginality, status anxiety, and downward mobility. In this analysis, the Nazis were the prime beneficiaries of all the evils associated with a modern society: uprootedness, excessive competition, rapid urbanization, breakdown of traditions, erosion of *Gemeinschaft*. All of these led to alienation, frustration, anxiety, and anomie, which ultimately could be resolved by casting a vote for the antimodern Nazis, led by a charismatic figure who promised to restore the bliss of a bygone era. However, Marxist theorists such as R. Palme Dutt have argued that the crucial support for the Nazis came from the German bourgeoisie and that fascism was a bourgeois solution to the capitalist crisis and the labor-capital contention. An empirical study of German voting patterns corroborates this view. In *Who Voted for Hitler?* (Princeton: Princeton University Press, 1982), Richard Hamilton shows that there

was a disproportionately favorable response to the Nazis among Germany's upper and upper-middle classes. Thus one must be careful not to stretch the analogy between Islamism and fascism. Certainly their respective social bases are different.

13. Robert Wuthnow, *Meaning and the Moral Order: Explorations in Cultural Analysis* (Princeton: Princeton University Press, 1987).

14. Carolyn Fleuhr-Lobban, "Arab-Islamic Women: Participants in Secular and Religious Movements," Dept. of Anthropology, Rhode Island College, March 1989 (photocopy).

15. Binnaz Toprak, "Women and Fundamentalism: The Case of Turkey," UNU/WIDER Roundtable paper.

16. Nayereh Tohidi, "Identity Politics and the Woman Question in Iran: Retrospect and Prospects," UNU/WIDER Roundtable paper. See also Afsaneh Najmabadi, "Hazards of Modernity and Morality: Women, State and Ideology in Contemporary Iran," in Kandiyoti, ed., *Women, Islam, and the State*, pp. 48-76.

17. Cherifa Bouatta and Doria Cherifati-Merabtine, "The Social Representation of Women in the Islamic Movement," UNU/WIDER Roundtable paper.

18. Some well-meaning Westerners have tried to argue that Islamist movements are legitimately concerned with cultural integrity, that they are not antidemocratic, and that they do not threaten Western interests. In so doing, these Westerners are naively echoing the arguments of Islamists themselves, who may be trying to garner international support in the wake of domestic state repression, especially in Algeria and Tunisia. (See, for example, the cover story of *Time* magazine, June 15, 1992.) The first claim is partially true, for Islamists are also concerned with power. The second claim is false. The third claim is true; Islamist movements do not threaten Western interests, especially economic ones. But it is important to focus on the Islamists' gender praxis. In the case of the Algerian FIS, for example, women have been harassed and intimidated by Islamist vigilantes. The many cases have been documented by the France-based international network Women Living Under Muslim Laws since 1990 and described in the UNU/WIDER Roundtable paper "Women, Equality, and Fundamentalism in Algeria" by Algerian activist Nassera Merah. For details on Islamist intimidation of women in Afghanistan, see Chapter 7.

19. Jamal J. Nasir, *The Status of Women Under Islamic Law* (London: Graham & Trotman, 1990).

20. See Nawal El-Saadawi, "The Political Challenges Facing Arab Women at the End of the 20th Century," in Nahid Toubia, ed., *Women of the Arab World* (London: Zed Books, 1988), p. 11.

21. See Chibli Mallat and Jane Connors, eds., *Islamic Family Law* (London: Graham & Trotman, 1990), especially Part II on Europe and Part III on South Asia, Southeast Asia, and China.

22. Marie-Aimée Hélie-Lucas, "Women Facing Muslim Personal Laws." See also various documents from the network Women Living Under Muslim Laws.

23. Benedict Anderson, *Imagined Communities* (London: Verso, 1983); Alya Baffoun, "Feminism and Fundamentalism: The Tunisian and Algerian Cases," UNU/WIDER Roundtable paper.

24. Quoted in Jean Bethke Elshtain, "The New Feminist Scholarship," *Salmagundi* 70–71 (Spring–Summer 1986), especially pp. 13–14; Cynthia Fuchs Epstein, *Deceptive Distinctions: Sex, Gender and the Social Order* (New Haven and London: Yale University Press and Russell Sage Foundation, 1988).

25. Feride Acar, "Women in the Ideology of Islamic Revivalism in Turkey: Three Islamic Women's Journals," paper presented at the workshop on Islam in Turkey, at the School of Oriental and African Studies, University of London (May 1988).

26. Debra Kaufman, "Paradoxical Politics: Gender Politics Among New Orthodox Jewish Women," and Rebecca E. Klatch, "Women of the New Right in the U.S.: Family, Feminism, and Politics," both UNU/WIDER Roundtable papers.

27. Val Moghadam, "Women, Work and Ideology in the Islamic Republic," *International Journal of Middle East Studies* 20 (2) (May 1988):221–243.

28. Deniz Kandiyoti, "Islam and Patriarchy: A Comparative Perspective," in Nikki R. Keddie and Beth Baron, eds., *Shifting Boundaries: Women and Gender in Middle Eastern History* (New Haven: Yale University Press, 1992), pp. 23–42; Fadwa El-Guindy, "Veiling *Intifah* with Muslim Ethic: Egypt's Contemporary Islamic Movement," *Social Problems* 8 (1981):465–485; Homa Hoodfar, "Return to the Veil: Personal Strategy and Public Participation in Egypt," in Nanneke Redclift and M. Thea Sinclair, eds., *Working Women: International Perspectives on Labour and Gender Ideology* (London and New York: Routledge, 1991), pp. 104–124; Arlene Elowe Macleod, *Accommodating Protest: Working Women, the New Veiling, and Change in Cairo* (New York: Columbia University Press, 1991).

29. Jim Coffman, "Choosing the Veil," *Mother Jones* (November/December 1991), pp. 23–24.

30. On North Africa's economic crisis, see David Seddon, "Popular Protest, Austerity and Economic Liberalisation in the Middle East and North Africa," discussion paper No. 221, School of Development Studies, University of East Anglia, Norwich, England (February 1992).

31. Pat Butcher, "Running on through the veil of tears," *The Guardian*, January 11, 1992, p. 15. This episode brings to mind a controversy in Israel in 1986, when Orthodox militants burned bus shelters displaying advertisements showing women in swimsuits. Secular Zionists countered by daubing swastikas on synagogues. See Thomas L. Friedman, "Israeli's Uneasy Mix of Religion and State," *New York Times*, June 22, 1986, p. E3.

32. Personal communication from Algiers, January 26, 1992.

33. This is indicative of Algeria's highly contradictory gender system, wherein women constitute under 10 percent of the measured labor force and were exhorted to accept the joys of domesticity, as we have seen in Chapters 2 and 3, and yet have women judges in the civil courts. In any event, Judge Ziani's decision was appealed. But in late April 1992, the Algerian Supreme Court rejected the appeal.

34. The discussion in this section is based on the UNU/WIDER Roundtable paper by Sondra Hale, "Islamic and Secular Contradictions."

35. Carolyn Fleuhr-Lobban, "Islamization in Sudan: A Critical Assessment," *The Middle East Journal* 44 (4) (Autumn 1990):610–623. See also *Tehran Times*, November 18, 1991, p. 1; *Ms.* (September/October 1991), p. 11.

36. Valerie Hoffman-Ladd, "Polemics on the Modesty and Segregation of Women in Contemporary Egypt," *International Journal of Middle East Studies* 19 (1) (February 1987):36.

37. The following discussion is based on Margot Badran, "Gender Activism: Feminists and Islamists in Egypt," UNU/WIDER Roundtable paper.

38. On the history of the Egyptian women's movement see Kumari Jayawardena, *Feminism and Nationalism in the Third World* (London: Zed Books, 1986), Chapter 3; Afaf Lutfi al-Sayyid Marsot, "The Revolutionary Gentlewomen in Egypt," in Lois Beck and Nikki R. Keddie, eds., *Women in the Muslim World* (Cambridge, MA: Harvard University Press, 1978); and Badran, "Independent Women: More than a Century of Feminism in Egypt."

39. For details, see "Egypt Moves to Dissolve Arab Women's Solidarity Association," *Association for Women in Development Newsletter* 6 (2) (April 1992), p. 1.

40. This section draws from Binnaz Toprak, "Women and Fundamentalism: The Case of Turkey," UNU/WIDER Roundtable paper.

41. References to the studies by Arat and Gole are from the paper by Binnaz Toprak. In discussions I had with Nilufer Gole (in Madrid, July 1990) and with Yesim Arat and Feride Acar (in Helsinki, July 1991), we compared the paradoxes and contradictions of Islamist movements in Iran and Turkey.

42. Acar, "Women in the Ideology of Islamic Revivalism in Turkey."

43. Yesim Arat, "Women's Movement and the Turkish State in the 1980–1990 Decade." Paper prepared for the International Society of Political Psychology Annual Meeting, Helsinki (July 1–5, 1991).

44. Both quotes from Sabra Chartrand, "The Veiled Look: It's Enforced with a Vengeance," *New York Times,* August 22, 1991.

45. *Tehran Times,* September 3, 1991, p. 15.

46. Quotes from Rema Hammami, "Women, the Hijab and the Intifada," *Middle East Report* (May–August 1990).

47. Nahla Abdo, "On Nationalism and Feminism, Palestinian Women and the Intifada: No Going Back?" UNU/WIDER Roundtable paper.

48. Rita Giacaman and Penny Johnson, "Mid-East Women Work Toward Democracy," *Ms.* (September/October 1991), p. 14.

49. *Women's International Network News* 18 (1) (Winter 1992):53.

50. Naila Minai, quoted in Hoffman-Ladd, "Polemics of the Modesty and Segregation of Women," p. 24; see also Nayereh Tohidi, "Identity Politics and the Woman Question in Iran," UNU/WIDER Roundtable paper.

51. Eliz Sanasarian, *The Women's Rights Movement in Iran: Mutiny, Appeasement and Repression from 1900 to Khomeini* (New York: Praeger, 1982); Guity Nashat, "Women in the Ideology of the Islamic Republic," in Guity Nashat, ed., *Women and Revolution in Iran* (Boulder: Westview Press, 1983), pp. 195–216; Haleh Afshar, "Women, State and Ideology in Iran," *Third World Quarterly* 7 (2) (April 1985):256–278.

52. Val Moghadam, "The Reproduction of Gender Inequality in the Islamic Republic: A Case Study of Iran in the 1980s," *World Development* 19 (10) (October 1991):1335–1350.

53. Tohidi, "Identity Politics and the Woman Question."

54. Shahin Gerami, "The Role, Place, and Power of Middle Class Women in the Islamic Republic," UNU/WIDER Roundtable paper.

55. Bassam Tibi, "The Renewed Role of Islam in the Political and Social Development of the Middle East," *The Middle East Journal* 37 (1) (Winter 1983):3–13, especially p. 13.

56. Hélie-Lucas, "Women Facing Muslim Personal Laws."

57. Nahid Yeganeh, "Women's Struggles in the Islamic Republic of Iran," in Azar Tabari and Nahid Yeganeh, eds., *In the Shadow of Islam: The Women's Movement in Iran* (London: Zed Books, 1982), pp. 26–74; Moghadam, "Women, Work and Ideology in the Islamic Republic," and "The Reproduction of Gender Inequality." Tohidi also shares this view.

58. Hisham Sharabi, *Neopatriarchy* (New York: Oxford University Press, 1988), p. 154.

▲ Chapter 6

1. Guity Nashat, "Women in the Ideology of the Islamic Republic," in Guity Nashat, ed., *Women and Revolution in Iran* (Boulder: Westview Press, 1983), p. 195.

2. Nashat, ibid.; see also Erika Friedl, "State Ideology and Village Women," in Nashat, ed., *Women and Revolution in Iran,* pp. 217–230; Mahnaz Afkhami, "Iran: A Future in the Past—The 'Prerevolutionary' Women's Movement," in Robin Morgan, ed., *Sisterhood Is Global* (New York: Anchor Books, 1984), pp. 330–338; Haleh Afshar, "Khomeini's Teachings and Their Implications for Iranian Women," in Azar Tabari and Nahid Yeganeh, eds., *In the Shadow of Islam: The Women's Movement in Iran* (London: Zed Books, 1982), pp. 75–90, and "Women, State and Ideology in Iran," *Third World Quarterly* 7 (2) (April 1985):256–278; Farah Azhari, *Women of Iran* (London: Ithaca Press, 1983); Adele Ferdows, "Women and the Islamic Revolution," *International Journal of Middle East Studies* 15 (2) (May 1983):283–298; Azar Tabari, "The Enigma of the Veiled Iranian Woman," *MERIP Reports* 12 (2) (February 1982):22–27; Eliz Sanassarian, "Political Activism and Islamic Identity in Iran," in Lynne B. Iglitzen and Ruth Ross, eds., *Women in the World: 1975–1985, The Women's Decade* (Santa Barbara: Clio Press, 1986), pp. 207–224.

3. Afshar, "Women, State and Ideology," p. 272.

4. Afshar refers to Ayatollah Ruhollah Khomeini, *A Clarification of Problems,* trans. Hamid Algar (Berkeley: Mizan Press, 1982). Mutahhari's critique of Western relations and his essentially functionalist arguments in favor of polygamy and temporary marriage were serialized in the popular women's magazine *Zan-e Rouz* in the years before the revolution. See also Murteza Mutahhari, *Sexual Ethics in Islam and in the Western World* (Tehran: Bonyad-e Be'that, Foreign Department, 1981).

5. Quoted in column by Jack Anderson and Dale Van Atta, *Washington Post,* December 21, 1988.

6. Ayatollah Yahya Nuri, *Hoquq va hodud-e zan dar Islam* (Tehran: n.d.), p. 55.

7. Quoted in Nashat, "Women in the Ideology of the Islamic Republic," p. 200.

8. Adele Ferdows, "Shariati and Khomeini on Women," in Nikkie Keddie and Eric Hooglund, eds., *The Iranian Revolution and the Islamic Republic* (Washington, D.C.: The Middle East Institute, 1982), p. 78.

9. Ibid.

10. Ayatollah Khomeini, "Address to a Group of Women in Qum," March 6, 1979, in *Islam and Revolution: Writings and Declarations of Imam Khomeini,* trans. and ed. Hamid Algar (Berkeley: Mizan Press, 1981). Ayatollah Khomeini was not as conservative as other religious leaders and interpreters of the Quran on the question of women. When Ayatollah Kho'i was in Najaf, both were asked whether women could meet with men to discuss political questions. Kho'i issued a *fatva* saying that under no circumstances, except for Friday prayers, could men and women who were not married gather together. Khomeini, on the other hand, permitted it in his *fatva.*

11. See Fatna A. Sabbah, *Woman in the Muslim Unconscious* (New York: Praeger, 1984). See also Afshar, "Women, State and Ideology in Iran."

12. Murteza Mutahhari, *On the Islamic Hijab* (Tehran: Islamic Propagation Organization, 1987), pp. 21–22.

13. The Constitution of the Islamic Republic of Iran, Tehran, 1984, pp. 14–15.

14. Ibid.

15. See Azar Tabari, "Islam and the Struggle for Emancipation of Iranian Women," in Tabari and Yeganeh, eds., *In the Shadow of Islam,* p. 15.

16. Nayereh Tohidi, "Identity Politics and the Woman Question in Iran: Retrospect and Prospects," paper prepared for UNU/WIDER Roundtable on Identity Politics and Women, Helsinki (October 8-10, 1990).

17. Fereshteh Hashemi, "Discrimination and the Imposition of the Veil," in Tabari and Yeganeh, eds., *In the Shadow of Islam*, p. 193.

18. Azam Taleghani, Shahin Tabatabai, et al., "Instead of Compulsory Veiling, Public Decency for All Should Be Compulsory," in *In the Shadow of Islam*, p. 194.

19. Fedayeen-Khalq (sic), "Women's Rights and Islamic Hijab," in *In the Shadow of Islam*, p. 136.

20. Nashat, "Women in the Ideology of the Islamic Republic," p. 197.

21. Many countries have similar laws, presumably to ease the burdens of mothers, but in practice to legitimize and strengthen gender roles. Collective bargaining contracts often provide for an earlier retirement age for women, while labor and social legislation assign the roles of postnatal care and child rearing to women, not to men. In more recent years, the example of the Islamic Republic has been followed by the new governments of "democratic" Eastern Europe as part of the transition to a market economy. In most countries, women have been explicitly encouraged to leave the labor market, which is becoming increasingly competitive. See Val Moghadam, ed., "Privatization and Democratization in Central and Eastern Europe and the Soviet Union: The Gender Dimension" (Helsinki: UNU/WIDER Research for Action Series, 1992).

22. Joan Scott, "Is Gender a Useful Category of Historical Analysis?" paper presented at the meetings of the American Historical Association (December 27, 1985). Scott's observations are made in the context of an analysis of the relationship between gender and power and the reorganization of inequality.

23. Afshar, "Women, the State, and Ideology," p. 277.

24. Patricia Higgins, "Women in the Islamic Republic of Iran: Legal, Social and Ideological Changes," *Signs* 10 (3) (Spring 1985):477-495.

25. World Bank, *World Development Report 1985*, Table 20, p. 213.

26. *Iran Times*, April 19, 1985, and May 17, 1985.

27. *Iran Times*, March 28, 1986, p. 5.

28. *Iran Times*, October 19, 1984.

29. Quoted in Haleh Afshar, "Women and Work: Ideology not Adjustment at Work in Iran," in Haleh Afshar, ed., *Structural Adjustment and Women* (London: Macmillan, 1991), p. 206.

30. Ibid., p. 215.

31. Patrick E. Tyler, "In Iran, Women's Fashion Ferment," *Washington Post*, February 2, 1989, p. B1.

32. Quoted in Afshar, "Women and Work: Ideology not Adjustment," p. 206.

33. Ibid.

34. Ibid., p. 214.

35. John R. Weeks, "The Demography of Islamic Nations," *Population Bulletin* 43 (4) (December 1988). In a personal communication (Helsinki, July 1991), Amartya Sen told me that nearly all Arab countries have an adverse sex ratio. An examination of demographic data compiled by the United Nations showed this to be true.

36. Interview with Dr. Azizullah Saidali, Indira Gandhi Children's Hospital, Kabul, February 9, 1989. See also *UN Statistical Yearbook 1983/4* (New York, 1986), Table 18, p. 65.

37. Barbara Harriss, "The Intrafamily Distribution of Hunger in South Asia," paper for WIDER Project on Hunger and Poverty, Seminar on Food Strategies (Helsinki: WIDER, 1986); Jean Drèze and Amartya Sen, *Hunger and Public Action* (Oxford: Clarendon, 1989), especially Chapter 4; Barbara Miller, *The Endangered Sex* (Ithaca: Cornell University Press, 1981); UNICEF, *The State of the World's Children* (New York: Oxford University Press, 1989).

38. UNICEF, *The State of the World's Children*, Table E, pp. 88–89; World Bank, *World Development Report 1984*, p. 166; *Selected Statistics* 5 (24) (Tehran: Central Statistical Office, Bahman 1368 [February 1990]), p. 14; UNICEF, *Situation Analysis of Women and Children in the Islamic Republic of Iran*, draft, Tehran (March 1992), p. 44.

39. Akbar Aghajanian, "Post-Revolutionary Demographic Trends in Iran," in Hooshang Amirahmadi and Manoucher Parvin, eds., *Post-Revolutionary Iran* (Boulder: Westview Press, 1988); *National Census of Population and Housing 1365* [1986] (Tehran: Central Statistical Office, 1988), p. 2. See also Yasmin Mossavar-Rahmani, "Family Planning in Post-Revolutionary Iran," in Nashat, ed., *Women and Revolution in Iran*, pp. 253–262; Afshar, "Women, State and Ideology."

40. See Hooshang Amirahmadi, *Revolution and Economic Transition: The Iranian Experience* (Albany: State University of New York Press, 1990), especially Chapter 3.

41. Scott Menard, "Fertility, Development, and Family Planning, 1970–80: An Analysis of Cases Weighted by Population," *Studies in Comparative International Development* 22 (3) (Fall 1987):103–127; World Bank, *Preventing the Tragedy of Maternal Deaths* (Nairobi: World Bank, 1987); Barbara Herz and Anthony Meacham, *The Safe Motherhood Initiative: Proposals for Action* (Washington, D.C.: World Bank Discussion Paper 9, 1987); James Trussell and Anne R. Pebley, "The Potential Impact of Changes in Fertility on Infant, Child and Maternal Mortality," *Studies in Family Planning* 15 (6) (November/December 1984). See also UNICEF, *State of the World's Children 1989*, Table 3, pp. 98–99.

42. The relevant literature includes Richard Anker, Mayra Buvinic, and Nadia Youssef, *Women's Roles and Population Trends in the Third World* (Geneva: ILO, 1982); Valentina Bodrova and Richard Anker, eds., *Working Women in Socialist Countries: The Fertility Connection* (Geneva: ILO, 1985); M. Concepcion, "Female Labor Force Participation and Fertility," *International Labour Review* 109 (5/6) (1974):503–518; Zeba Sathar, Nigel Crook, Christine Callum, and Shahnaz Kazi, "Women's Status and Fertility Change in Pakistan," *Population and Development Review* 14 (3) (September 1988):415–431. See also Barbara Finlay, *The Women of Azua: Work and Family in the Rural Dominican Republic* (New York: Praeger, 1989).

43. *National Census of Population and Housing*, November 1986 (Total Country) (Tehran: Central Statistical Office, 1989), Table 6.1, p. 86

44. Kaveh Mirani, "Social and Economy Change in the Role of Women, 1956–78," in Nashat, ed., *Women and Revolution in Iran*, pp. 69–86; Val Moghadam, "Women, Work and Ideology in the Islamic Republic," *International Journal of Middle East Studies* 20 (May 1988):221–243.

45. Patricia J. Higgins and Pirouz Shoar-Ghaffari, "Sex-Role Stratification in Iranian Textbooks," State University of New York–Plattsburg, Department of Communications, 1989); see also Golnar Mehran, "Socialization of Schoolchildren in the Islamic Republic of Iran," *Iranian Studies* 22 (1) (1989):35–50.

46. *Iran Yearbook 1988*, p. 627.

47. *Statistical Yearbook 1367* [1988], Table 5.46, p. 124.

48. Shahrzad Mojab, "The Islamic Government's Policy on Women's Access to Higher Education and Its Impact on the Socio-Economic Status of Women," Office of Women in International Development, Working Paper No. 156, Michigan State University, December 1987.

49. In the urban areas, women who are classified as "homemakers" may actually be economically engaged in the informal sector. Or they may be women whose domestic work and child care take up so much time there is no time left for work

outside the home. Other women may be bound by cultural or familial constraints, while yet others may choose to stay at home. Due to low prestige of certain occupations some women may identify themselves as housewives rather than workers.

50. *Iran Yearbook 1988*, p. 476.

51. *Statistics for Large Industrial Establishments 1984/85* (Tehran: Central Statistical Office, 1985), p. 263.

52. *Statistics for Large Industrial Establishments 1984/85*, p. 263.

53. *National Census of Population and Housing, 1976* (Tehran: Central Statistical Office, 1981) p. 87.

54. See Linda Y.C. Lim, "Capitalism, Imperialism and Patriarchy: the Dilemma of Third World Women Workers in Multinational Factories," in June Nash and Maria Patricia Fernandez-Kelly, eds., *Women, Men and the International Division of Labor* (Albany: State University of New York Press, 1983), pp. 70–91. A similar pattern of preference for male labor—the result of gender bias as well as the desire to avoid extra costs for child care and maternity leave—has been found for "privatizing" Eastern Europe. See Moghadam, ed., *Privatization and Democratization in Central Eastern Europe and the Soviet Union: The Gender Dimension* (1992).

55. *1986 Census*, Table 20, p. 140. See also ILO, *Yearbook of Labour Statistics 1991*, and the *Retrospective Edition on Population Censuses, 1945–1990*, Tables 2A and 2B.

56. On Turkey see Gunseli Berik, *Women Carpet Weavers in Rural Turkey: Patterns of Employment, Earnings and Status* (Geneva: ILO, 1987); Deniz Kandiyoti, "Rural Transformation in Turkey and Its Implications for Women's Status," in *Women on the Move* (Paris: UNESCO, 1984), pp. 17–30. On Afghanistan, see Chapter 7 in this volume. On Iran, see also Haleh Afshar, "The Position of Women in an Iranian Village," in Haleh Afshar, ed., *Women, Work and Ideology in the Third World* (London: Tavistock, 1985), pp. 66–82.

57. *1986 Census*, Table 21, p. 149.

58. Ibid., Table 22, pp. 160–161.

59. "New Plan to Check Population Growth," *Tehran Times*, July 15, 1991. See also *Tehran Times*, December 23, 1991, and January 5, 1992.

60. "Iran's Population Growth 0.7% Higher than Other Countries," *Tehran Times*, September 26, 1991, p. 1. See also H. Kalantari, "Population Explosion in Iran," *Kayhan International*, April 16, 1992, p. 8.

61. International Center for Research on Women [ICRW], *Keeping Women Out: A Structural Analysis of Women's Employment in Developing Countries* (Washington, D.C.: ICRW, April 1980). See also Elizabeth Jelin, "Women and the Urban Labour Market," in Anker, Buvinic, and Youssef, eds., *Women's Roles and Population Trends in the Third World*.

62. ICRW, *Keeping Women Out*, p. 92. According to *The World's Women: Trends and Statistics 1970–1990* (New York: United Nations, 1991), the figure for Iran around 1980 was 7 percent female-headed households. This seems to be a rather conservative figure, considering that Syria reported 13 percent, Tunisia and Turkey each 10 percent, and Morocco 17 percent female-headed households. See *The World's Women*, pp. 26–29.

63. *Tehran Times*, September 24, 1991, p. 1.

64. Shahin Gerami, personal communication, February 1991.

65. Quoted in Haleh Afshar, "Feminism and Fundamentalism in Iran," paper (n.d.).

66. "Majlis Speaker Says Women Should Aim Higher," *Tehran Times*, September 26, 1991, p. 3.

67. "Centers for Training of Women Will Be Set Up," *Tehran Times,* December 31, 1991, p. 3.

68. Research Group for Muslim Women's Studies, *The Social Status of Iranian Women Before and After the Victory of the Islamic Republic* (Tehran: Cultural Studies and Research Institute, Ministry of Culture and Higher Education, 1990), pp. 1–4.

69. *Payam-e Hajar* (Tehran) 1 (1) (Autumn 1370) [1991].

70. "Women Should Be More Fully Involved—President's Advisor," *Tehran Times,* January 1, 1992, p. 5; "Protection of Women's Right Goes up to the President's Office," *Tehran Times,* January 13, 1992, p. 5.

71. "Veteran Female Deputy Specializes on Women's Rights," *Tehran Times,* July 15, 1991, p. 5.

72. The description of male-female interaction is from a personal communication from the author's father, V. Mirza-Moghadam, April 24, 1992. He also pointed out that a Molière play he attended at Roudaki Hall in Tehran had performers in period costumes, not in hijab!

▲ **Chapter 7**

1. I am grateful to David N. Gibbs for these points.

2. Charles Tilly, "Revolutions and Collective Violence," in F. I. Greenstein and N. W. Polsby, eds., *Handbook of Political Science 3: Macropolitical Theory* (Reading, MA: Addison-Wesley, 1975).

3. Richard Nyrop and Donald Seekins, *Afghanistan: A Country Study* (Washington, D.C.: The American University, Foreign Area Studies, 1986), p. 105. See also Fred Halliday, "Revolution in Afghanistan," *New Left Review* 112 (November–December 1978):3–44; Olivier Roy, *Islam and Resistance in Afghanistan* (Cambridge, MA: Cambridge University Press, 1990).

4. Nyrop and Seekins, *Afghanistan: A Country Study,* pp. 140–185; David Gibbs, "The Peasant as Counterrevolutionary: The Rural Origins of the Afghan Insurgency," *Studies in Comparative International Development* 21 (1):36–95; Vartan Gregorian, *The Emergence of Modern Afghanistan* (Stanford: Stanford University Press, 1969), especially pp. 19–24; Yuri Gankovsky, *A History of Afghanistan* (Moscow: Progress Publishers, 1985), especially pp. 182–184.

5. John Griffiths, *Afghanistan* (Boulder: Westview Press, 1981), p. 136.

6. This is a matter of dispute among students of Afghanistan. Anthropologist Nazif Shahrani, for example, denies inequality in land ownership and therefore the need for land reform. See his "Introduction: Marxist 'Revolution' and Islamic Resistance in Afghanistan," in M. Nazif Shahrani and Robert L. Canfield, eds., *Revolutions and Rebellions in Afghanistan* (Berkeley: University of California International Studies Institute, 1984), especially pp. 10–24.

7. On this issue, see, inter alia, Gregorian, *The Emergence of Modern Afghanistan;* Robert Canfield, "Afghanistan: The Trajectory of Internal Alignments," *Middle East Journal* 42 (4) (Autumn 1989):635–648; Nyrop and Seekins, *Afghanistan: A Country Study,* pp. 112–113; and Ralph Magnus, "The PDPA Regime in Afghanistan: A Soviet Model for the Future of the Middle East?" in Peter Chelkowski and Robert Pranger, eds., *Ideology and Power in the Middle East* (Durham and London: Duke University Press, 1988).

8. See Nancy Tapper, "Causes and Consequences of the Abolition of Brideprice in Afghanistan," in Nazif Shahrani and Robert Canfield, eds., *Revolutions and Rebellions in Afghanistan,* p. 304.

9. On the meaning and function of the brideprice, see Nancy Tapper, "Causes and Consequences." My view of the brideprice is more critical.

10. Mohammad Hashim Kamali, *Law in Afghanistan: A Study of the Constitutions, Matrimonial Law and the Judiciary* (Leiden: E. J. Brill, 1985), p. 8. Kamali argues for the need for Shari'at law reform as well.

11. Olivier Roy, *Islam and Resistance in Afghanistan*, pp. 35–36. On Pushtunwali and its disagreement with Islam, see also Griffiths, *Afghanistan*, pp. 111–112, 122; Beverly Male, *Revolutionary Afghanistan* (New York: St. Martin's Press, 1982); Thomas Hammond, *Red Flag Over Afghanistan* (Boulder: Westview Press, 1984), p. 71; Raja Anwar, *The Tragedy of Afghanistan* (London: Verso, 1988), especially Chapter 11; Mark Urban, *War in Afghanistan* (New York: St. Martin's Press, 1988); Kathleen Howard-Merriam, "Afghan Refugee Women and Their Struggle for Survival," in Grant Farr and John Merrian, eds., *Afghan Resistance: The Politics of Survival* (Boulder: Westview Press, 1987), pp. 103–105; Inger Boesen, "Conflicts of Solidarity in Pushtun Women's Lives," in Bo Utas, ed., *Women in Islamic Society* (Copenhagen: Scandinavian Institute of Asian Studies, 1983), pp. 104–125.

12. Audrey Shalinsky, "Women's Relationships in Traditional Northern Afghanistan," *Central Asian Survey* 8 (1) (1989): 117–129. The quote appears on p. 127.

13. Simone Bailleau Lajoinie, *Conditions de femmes en Afghanistan* (Paris: Notre Temps/Monde, 1980); Anwar, *The Tragedy of Afghanistan;* Male, *Revolutionary Afghanistan;* Nyrop and Seekins, *Afghanistan: A Country Study;* Tapper, "Causes and Consequences"; Kamali, *Law in Afghanistan*, pp. 142–143.

14. Hanne Christensen, *The Reconstruction of Afghanistan: A Chance for Rural Afghan Women* (Geneva: United Nations Research Institute for Social Development, 1990), pp. 4–9.

15. John Griffiths, *Afghanistan* (New York: Praeger, 1967), p. 78.

16. Haleh Afshar, "The Position of Women in an Iranian Village," in Haleh Afshar, ed., *Women, Work and Ideology in the Third World* (London: Tavistock, 1985), p. 67; Hanna Papanek, "Class and Gender in Education-Employment Linkages," *Comparative Education Review* 29 (3) (1985):317–346; Christensen, *The Reconstruction of Afghanistan*, p. 5.

17. Bahram Tavakolian, "Women and Socioeconomic Change Among Sheikhanzai Nomads of Western Afghanistan," *The Middle East Journal* 38 (3) (Summer 1984):433–453.

18. Ibid., pp. 439–440.

19. Ibid., p. 440.

20. Ibid., p. 445.

21. Ibid., p. 440.

22. Ibid., p. 449.

23. Bertrand Badie and Pierre Birnbaum, *The Sociology of the State* (Chicago: University of Chicago Press, 1983), p. 35.

24. Joel Migdal, *Strong Societies and Weak States: State-Society Relations and State Capabilities in the Third World* (Princeton: Princeton University Press, 1988), p. 8. See also Peter Evans, Dietrich Rueschemeyer, and Theda Skocpol, eds., *Bringing the State Back In* (New York: Cambridge University Press, 1985); they, however, tend to emphasize state strength.

25. Quoted in Migdal, *Strong Societies and Weak States*, p. 8. Urban, in *War in Afghanistan*, also notes the historical incapacity of the Afghan state (p. 4).

26. Samuel Huntington, *Political Order in Changing Societies* (New Haven: Yale University Press, 1968), p. 2.

27. Gregorian, *The Emergence of Modern Afghanistan*, p. 3.

28. Urban, *War in Afghanistan*, p. 204; Gregorian, *The Emergence of Modern Afghanistan*, p. 7.

29. Gregorian, ibid., pp. 309–356.

30. Gregorian, ibid., pp. 138–139; Lajoinie, *Conditions des femmes en Afghanistan*, p. 61. The discussion that follows draws from Gregorian, pp. 138–264, and from Kamali, *Law in Afghanistan*, pp. 111–112.

31. Rhea Tally Stewart, *Fire in Afghanistan, 1914–1929* (New York: Doubleday, 1973), p. 370. See also Senzil Nawid, "Comparing the Regimes of Amanullah (1919–1929) and the Afghan Marxists (1978–1990): Similarities and Differences." Near Eastern Studies, University of Arizona (1991).

32. Gregory J. Massel, *The Surrogate Proletariat: Muslim Women and Revolutionary Strategies in Soviet Central Asia, 1919–1929* (Princeton: Princeton University Press, 1974), p. 219. See also Nawid, "Comparing the Regimes."

33. Tapper, "Causes and Consequences of the Abolition of Brideprice in Afghanistan"; Kamali, *Law in Afghanistan*, pp. 86–87, 196.

34. Kamali, ibid., pp. 84–85.

35. On the exchange of women, see Claude Lévi-Strauss, *The Elementary Structures of Kinship* (Boston: Beacon Press, 1969); Gayle Rubin, "The Traffic in Women: Notes on a Political Economy of Sex," in Rayna Rapp, ed., *Toward An Anthropology of Women* (New York: Monthly Review Press, 1976); Gerda Lerner, *The Creation of Patriarchy* (New York: Oxford University Press, 1986). On the honor-shame complex, see Pierre Bourdieu, "The Sentiment of Honor in Kabyle Society," in J. G. Peristiany, ed., *Honor and Shame* (Chicago: University of Chicago Press, 1965); Julian Pitt-Rivers, *The Fate of Shechem* (Cambridge University Press, 1977); Juliette Minces, *The House of Obedience* (London: Zed Books, 1982); Lila Abu-Lughod, *Veiled Sentiments: Honor and Poetry in a Bedouin Society* (Berkeley: University of California Press, 1986); Peter Knauss, *The Persistence of Patriarchy; Class, Gender and Ideology in Twentieth Century Algeria* (Boulder: Westview Press, 1987). See also Chapter 4 in this volume.

36. Tapper, "Causes and Consequences of the Abolition of Brideprice in Afghanistan," p. 304; Christensen, *The Reconstruction of Afghanistan*, pp. 5–6. See also Inger Boesen, "Conflicts of Solidarity in Pushtun Women's Lives," in Utas, ed., *Women in Islamic Society*, pp. 104–125; Nyrop and Seekins, *Afghanistan: A Country Study*, pp. 126–128.

37. Tapper, "Causes and Consequences of the Abolition of Brideprice in Afghanistan," p. 304.

38. Nyrop and Seekins, "Afghanistan: A Country Study," p. 86; Howard-Merriam, "Afghan Refugee Women," p. 114; Kamali, *Law in Afghanistan*, p. 141. The inverse sex ratio, high rates of maternal mortality, and widespread anemia among women were confirmed to me in interviews with Dr. Saidali Jalali and Dr. Azizullah Saidi at Indira Gandhi Hospital in Kabul, February 11, 1989.

39. Howard-Merriam, "Afghan Women and Their Struggle for Survival," p. 106.

40. Kamali, *Law in Afghanistan*, p. 142.

41. Christensen, "The Reconstruction of Afghanistan," pp. 7–8. Statistics by the Government of the Democratic Republic of Afghanistan were provided to me in October 1986 by the Office of the Permanent Mission to the UN in New York. See also The Economist, *The World in Figures 1981.*

42. Halliday, "Revolution in Afghanistan," p. 30.

43. Interviews with Soraya, DOAW founding member and past president, Kabul, February 6, 1989, and Helsinki, October 8, 1990. Soraya identified three of

the four women parliamentarians: Anahita Ratebzad, Massouma Esmaty Wardak, and Mrs Saljugi.

44. Nancy Hatch Dupree, "Revolutionary Rhetoric and Afghan Women," in Nazif Shahrani and Robert Canfield, eds., *Revolutions and Rebellions in Afghanistan* (Berkeley: University of California International Studies Institute), p. 310.

45. Quoted in Tapper, "Causes and Consequences of the Abolition of Brideprice in Afghanistan," p. 291. On Decrees No. 6 and 7, see also Mansoor Akbar, "Revolutionary Changes and Social Resistance in Afghanistan," *Asian Profile* 17 (3) (June 1989):271–281; Dupree, "Revolutionary Rhetoric and Afghan Women," especially pp. 322–325; and Hugh Beattie, "Effects of the Saur Revolution in Nahrin," in Shahrani and Canfield, eds., *Revolutions and Rebellions in Afghanistan*, p. 186.

46. Suzanne Jolicoeur Katsikas, *The Arc of Socialist Revolution: Angola to Afghanistan* (Cambridge, MA: Schenkman Publishing Co., 1982), p. 231.

47. Quoted in Dupree, "Revolutionary Rhetoric and Afghan Women," p. 316.

48. Henry Bradsher, *Afghanistan and the Soviet Union* (Durham: Duke University Press), p. 93. See also Kamali, *Law in Afghanistan*, p. 32.

49. Thomas Hammond, *Red Flag Over Afghanistan* (Boulder: Westview Press, 1984), p. 71. See also Dupree, "Revolutionary Rhetoric and Afghan Women," p. 321, and Katzikas, *The Arc of Socialist Revolution*, p. 231.

50. Christensen, *The Reconstruction of Afghanistan*, p. 9. See also Hugh Beattie, "Effects of the Saur Revolution in Nahrin." The brief account of the reform of the "dowry system" by Olivier Roy (*Islam and Resistance in Afghanistan*, pp. 94–95) is incorrect on several counts: It was not dowry but brideprice (or dower) that was being reformed; Decree No. 7 was not, strictly speaking, an affront to Islamic law but rather to customary law; Decree No. 7 provided for not only a ceiling on the brideprice but an end to the levirate, a minimum age of consent, and so on. The reaction to the decree was, as we have seen, far stronger than Roy suggests in his brief commentary.

51. Dupree, "Revolutionary Rhetoric and Afghan Women," p. 330.

52. The formal reinstatement of Muslim family law did not apply to party members. Interview with a PDPA official, New York, October 28, 1986.

53. Interview with Massouma Esmaty Wardak, Kabul, February 1, 1989.

54. Interview with Farid Mazdak, PDPA official, Kabul, February 9, 1989.

55. Constitution of the Republic of Afghanistan, Kabul, 1988.

56. Urban, *War in Afghanistan*, p. 209.

57. The Women's Council was not among the social organizations dismantled in 1990–1991.

58. Interview with Massouma Esmaty Wardak, Kabul, January 24, 1989.

59. *Afghanistan Today* 5 (September–October 1988), p. 22.

60. Interview with Massouma Esmaty Wardak, Kabul, January 24, 1989. Interviews with Soraya, Kabul, February 6, 1989, and Helsinki, October 8, 1990.

61. Interview with Zahereh Dadmal, director of the Kabul Women's Club, Kabul, February 8, 1989.

62. Interview with Farid Mazdak, Kabul, February 9, 1989. The Democratic Youth Organization was dismantled in 1990. Farid Mazdak himself was elected one of the four vice-chairs of the newly formed Hezb-e Vatan. The party chair was the president of Afghanistan, Dr. Najibullah.

63. Interview with Dr. Abdul Salaam Jalali and Dr. Azizullah Saidali, Indira Gandhi Children's Hospital, Kabul, February 11, 1989. This attitude is not uncommon in many developing countries.

64. *Afghanistan Today* 2 (March–April 1988), pp. 20–21.

65. Information from *Afghanistan Today* 1 (January–February 1988), p. 15; *Kabul Times*, September 22, 1988; *Afghanistan Today* 5 (September–October 1988).

66. This view is expressed in the Helsinki Watch Report of 1984 written by Jeri Laber and Barnett Rubin. The education provided to boys in the mujahidin camps in Peshawar (girls hardly received any education at all) emphasizes religion and mujahidin values and has not been criticized by Laber and Rubin.

67. See Henry Kamm, "Afghan Refugee Women Suffering from Isolation Under Islamic Custom," *New York Times*, March 27, 1988, p. A1, and "Aid to Afghan Refugees: Donors Bend the Rules," *New York Times*, April 2, 1988, p. A2.

68. Christensen, *The Reconstruction of Afghanistan*, p. 17.

69. ILO and UN High Commissioner for Refugees, *Tradition and Dynamism Among Afghan Refugees* (Geneva: ILO, 1983), p. 19.

70. Ibid., p. 3.

71. See Khawar Mumtaz and Farida Shaheed, *Women of Pakistan: Two Steps Forward, One Step Back?* (London: Zed Books, 1987).

72. Christensen, *The Reconstruction of Afghanistan*, pp. 50–53.

73. See Doris Lessing, "A Reporter at Large: The Catastrophe," *The New Yorker*, March 16, 1987.

74. "Issues and Options for Refugee Women in Developing Countries" (Washington D.C.: Refugee Policy Group, 1986).

75. Howard-Merriam, "Afghan Refugee Women," pp. 104, 114.

76. See Jean Drèze and Amartya Sen, *Hunger and Public Action* (Oxford: Clarendon Press, 1989), especially Chapter 4. On women's anemia, see Howard-Merriam, "Afghan Refugee Women," p. 116.

77. Howard-Merriam, "Afghan Refugee Women," p. 106.

78. Nancy Hatch Dupree, *Women in Afghanistan: Preliminary Needs Assessment* (New York: UNIFEM, 1989).

79. Henry Kamm, "Afghan Refugee Women Suffering from Isolation Under Islamic Customs," *New York Times*, March 27, 1988, and "Aid to Afghan Refugees: Donors Bend the Rules," *New York Times*, April 2, 1988. See also Christensen, *The Reconstruction of Afghanistan*, pp. 17–19. For a critique of the work of nongovernmental organizations in Peshawar, see Helga Baitenmann, "NGOs and the Afghan War: The Politicization of Humanitarian Aid," *Third World Quarterly* 12 (1) (January 1990).

80. See, for example, Derek Brown, "New Afghanistan Carries on Grisly Game of the Old," *The Guardian*, May 4, 1992, p. 7, and "Afghan TV Pulls Plug on Women," *The Guardian*, July 29, 1992, p. 6.

▲ Chapter 8

The first quote in the Chapter 8 epigraph is from Doria Cherifati-Merabtine, "Algeria at a Crossroads: National Liberation, Islamization, and Women," forthcoming in Val Moghadam, ed., *Gender and National Identity: The Woman Question in Five Muslim Societies*. Fatima Mernissi is the source of the second quote, in Kevin Dwyer, *Arab Voices: The Human Rights Debate in the Middle East* (Berkeley: University of California Press, 1991), p. 184. The third quote is my variation on a theme by Marx and Engels, the opening lines of *The Communist Manifesto*, and by Marshall Berman, *All that Is Solid Melts into Air: The Experience of Modernity* (New York: Simon and Schuster, 1982).

1. Fatima Mernissi, quoted in Dwyer, *Arab Voices*, pp. 182–183.

2. Jean Said Makdisi, *Beirut Fragments: A War Memoir* (1990).

3. The AWSA Final Report and Recommendations is reprinted in Nahid Toubia, ed., *Women of the Arab World: The Coming Challenge* (London: Zed Books, 1988), pp. 148–153.

4. Cherifati-Merabtine, "Algeria at a Crossroads."

5. Dwyer, *Arab Voices*, p. 145. See also various issues of *Al Raida*, publication of the Institute for Women's Studies in the Arab World, Beirut University College (in English), especially the Spring 1992 issue, which includes a discussion of "The Women of the Maghreb" by Rose Ghurayyib.

6. Dwyer, *Arab Voices*, p. 145.

7. These publications were produced under the direction of Fatima Mernissi as part of the *Femmes Maghreb Horizon 2000* project, supported by the United Nations University.

8. Margot Badran, "Independent Women: More Than a Century of Feminism in Egypt," forthcoming in Judith Tucker, ed., *Old Boundaries, New Frontiers: Women in the Arab World* (Bloomington: Indiana University Press, 1993).

9. Nükhet Sirman, "Feminism in Turkey: Which Feminism?" paper prepared for the New Voices in Turkish Women's Studies conference, Middle East Center, University of Pennsylvania, April 1991.

10. Yesim Arat, "Woman's Movement and the Turkish State in the 1980-1990 Decade," paper prepared for the annual meeting of the International Society for Political Psychology, Helsinki (July 1991), p. 10. In a personal communication to the author (October 14, 1992), Yesim Arat said she felt that there was indeed some disarray and leadership failure in the women's movement, although evidence of its resilience could be found in the Women's Library and in the campaign against wife-beating.

11. Suna Kili, "Modernity and Tradition: Dilemmas Concerning Women's Rights in Turkey," paper prepared for the annual meeting of the International Society for Political Psychology, Helsinki (July 1991).

12. Ibid, p. 15.

▲
Selected Bibliography

Abadan-Unat, Nermin. 1981. "Social Changes and Turkish Women." In Nermin Abadan-Unat, ed., *Women in Turkish Society*. Leiden: E. J. Brill.

Abdo-Zubi, Nahla. 1987. *Family, Women and Social Change in the Middle East: The Palestinian Case*. Toronto: Canadian Scholars' Press.

Abu Nasr, Julinda, A. Khoury, and H. Azzam, eds. 1985. *Women, Employment, and Development in the Arab World*. The Hague: Mouton/ILO.

Acar, Feride. 1988. "Women in the Ideology of Islamic Revivalism in Turkey: Three Islamic Women's Journals." Paper presented at the Workshop on Islam in Turkey, at the School of Oriental and African Studies, University of London (May).

Adams, Michael, ed. 1988. *The Middle East*. New York: Facts-on-File Publications.

Afshar, Haleh, ed. 1987. *Women, State and Ideology in the Third World*. London: Macmillan.

———, ed. 1985. *Women, Work and Ideology in the Third World*. London: Tavistock.

———, ed. 1991. *Women, Development and Survival in the Third World*. London and New York: Longman.

Agarwal, Bina, ed. 1988. *Structures of Patriarchy*. London: Zed Books.

Akbar, Mansoor. 1989. "Revolutionary Changes and Social Resistance in Afghanistan." *Asian Profile* 17 (3) (June):271–281.

Amirahmadi, Hooshang and Manoucher Parvin, eds. 1988. *Post-Revolutionary Iran*. Boulder: Westview Press.

Amirahmadi, Hooshang. 1990. *Revolution and Economic Transition: The Iranian Experience*. Albany: State University of New York Press.

Arat, Yesim. 1989. *The Patriarchal Paradox: Women Politicians in Turkey*. Rutherford, N.J.: Fairleigh Dickinson University Press.

Baffoun, Alya. 1982. "Women and Social Change in the Muslim Arab World." *Women's Studies International Forum* 5 (2):227–242.

Beck, Lois and Nikki R. Keddie, eds. 1978. *Women in the Muslim World*. Cambridge, MA: Harvard University Press.

Beckford, James A. 1986. *New Religious Movements and Rapid Social Change*. Beverly Hills: Sage; and Paris: UNESCO.

Berberoglu, Berch, ed. 1989. *Power and Stability in the Middle East*. London: Zed Books.

Berik, Gunseli. 1987. *Women Carpet Weavers in Rural Turkey: Patterns of Employment, Earnings and Status*. Geneva: ILO, Women, Work and Development Series No. 15.

Bodrova, Valentina and Richard Anker, eds. 1985. *Working Women in Socialist Countries: The Fertility Connection.* Geneva: ILO.

Boswell, Terry, ed. 1989. *Revolution in the World-System.* Westport, CT: Greenwood Press.

Bouatta, Cherifa and Doria Cherifati-Merabtine. 1990. "Social Representations of Women in Islamist Discourse." Paper prepared for the UNU/WIDER Roundtable on Identity Politics and Women, Helsinki (October 8–10).

Çagatay, Nilufer, and Günseli Berik, 1990. "Transition to Export-Led Growth in Turkey: Is There a Feminization of Employment?" *Review of Radical Political Economics* 22 (1):115–134.

Caldwell, John. 1982. *Theory of Fertility Decline.* London and New York: Academic Press.

Chafetz, Janet Saltzman. 1990. *Gender Equity: An Integrated Theory of Stability and Change.* Newbury Park, CA: Sage Publications.

———— and Gary Dworkin. 1986. *Female Revolt: Women's Movements in World and Historical Perspective.* Totowa, NJ: Rowman and Allanheld.

Charlton, Sue Ellen. 1984. *Women in Third World Development.* Boulder: Westview Press.

Charrad, Mounira. 1993. *States and Women's Rights: A Comparison of Tunisia, Algeria and Morocco.* Berkeley: University of California Press (forthcoming).

Chirot, Daniel. 1983. *Social Change in the Modern Era.* San Diego: Harcourt Brace Jovanovich.

Cleland, John and John Hobcraft, eds. 1985. *Reproductive Change in Developing Countries: Insights from the World Fertility Survey.* New York: Oxford University Press.

Cleland, John and Chris Scott, eds. 1987. *The World Fertility Survey: An Assessment.* New York: International Statistical Institute and Oxford University Press.

Concepcion, M. 1974. "Female Labor Force Participation and Fertility." *International Labor Review* 109 (5/6):503–518.

Crompton, Rosemary and Michael Mann, eds. 1986. *Gender and Stratification.* Cambridge, UK: Polity Press.

Drèze, Jean and Amartya Sen. 1989. *Hunger and Public Action.* Oxford: Clarendon Press.

Dwyer, Daisy and Judith Bruce, eds. 1988. *A Home Divided: Women and Income in the Third World.* Stanford: Stanford University Press.

Dyson, Tim and Mick Moore. 1983. "On Kinship Structure, Female Autonomy and Demographic Behavior." *Population and Development Review* 9 (1):35–60.

Eickelman, Dale F. 1989. *The Middle East: An Anthropological Approach.* New York: Prentice Hall.

El-Guindy, Fadwa. 1981. "Veiling Intifah with Muslim Ethic: Egypt's Contemporary Islamic Movement." *Social Problems* 8:465–485.

El-Naggar, Said, ed. 1989. *Privatization and Structural Adjustment in the Arab Countries.* Washington, D.C.: International Monetary Fund.

El-Sanabary, Nagat. 1989. *Determinants of Women's Education in the Middle East and North Africa: Illustrations from Seven Countries.* PHREE Background Paper Series. Washington, D.C.: The World Bank.

Engels, Frederick. 1972 [1884]. *The Origin of the Family, Private Property and the State.* Introduction by Evelyn Reed. New York: Pathfinder Press.

Engineer, Asghar Ali. 1991. "Remaking Indian Muslim Identity." *Economic and Political Weekly* 20 (April):1036–1038.

Epstein, Cynthia Fuchs. 1988. *Deceptive Distinctions: Sex, Gender and the Social*

Order. New Haven and London: Yale University Press and Russell Sage Foundation.

Esposito, John L. 1982. *Women in Muslim Family Law*. Syracuse: Syracuse University Press.

Evans, Peter, Dietrich Rueschemeyer, and Theda Skocpol, eds. 1985. *Bringing the State Back In*. New York: Cambridge University Press.

Farley, Jennie, ed. 1985. *Working Women in Fifteen Countries*. Ithaca: Cornell University Press.

Fathi, Asghar, ed. 1991. *Iranian Refugees and Exiles Since Khomeini*. Costa Mesa, CA: Mazda Publishers.

Ferdows, Adele. 1983. "Women and the Islamic Revolution." *International Journal of Middle East Studies* 15 (2) (May):283–298.

Fernandez-Kelly, Maria Patricia. 1989. "Broadening the Scope: Gender and International Economic Development." *Sociological Forum* 4 (4) (December):611–636.

Ghoussoub, Mai. 1987. "Feminism—or the Eternal Masculine—in the Arab World." *New Left Review* 161 (January–February):3–13.

Giele, Janet and Audrey Smock, eds. 1977. *Women's Roles and Status in Eight Countries*. New York: John Wiley.

Goody, Jack. 1990. *The Oriental, the Ancient and the Primitive: Systems of Marriage and the Family in the Pre-Industrial Societies of Eurasia*. Cambridge, MA: Cambridge University Press.

Greenhalgh, Susan. 1990. "Toward a Political Economy of Fertility: Anthropological Contributions." *Population and Development Review* 16 (1) (March):85–106.

Gregorian, Vartan. 1969. *The Emergence of Modern Afghanistan*. Stanford: Stanford University Press.

Hess, Beth and Myra Marx Ferree, eds. 1987. *Analyzing Gender*. Beverly Hills: Sage.

Higgins, Patricia. 1985. "Women in the Islamic Republic of Iran: Legal, Social and Ideological Changes." *Signs* 10 (3) (Spring):477–495.

Hijab, Nadia. 1988. *Womenpower: The Arab Debate on Women and Work*. Cambridge, UK: Cambridge University Press.

Hirschon, Renée, ed. 1984. *Women and Property—Women as Property*. New York: St. Martin's Press.

Hitti, Philip. 1971. *A History of the Arabs*. Princeton: Princeton University Press.

Hoffman-Ladd, Valerie. 1987. "Polemics on the Modesty and Segregation of Women in Contemporary Egypt." *International Journal of Middle East Studies* 19 (1):23–50.

Ibrahim, Saad Eddin. 1980. "Anatomy of Egypt's Militant Islamic Groups." *International Journal of Middle East Studies* 12 (4):423–453.

———. 1982. "Islamic Militancy as a Social Movement: The Case of Two Groups in Egypt." In Ali E. Hillal Dessouki, ed., *Islamic Resurgence in the Arab World*. New York: Praeger.

International Labour Office (ILO) and UN Research and Training Institute for the Advancement of Women (INSTRAW). 1985. *Women in Economic Activity: A Global Statistical Survey (1950–2000)*. Geneva: ILO; Santo Domingo: INSTRAW.

International Labour Office and UN High Commissioner for Refugees. 1983. *Tradition and Dynamism Among Afghan Refugees*. Geneva: ILO and UNHCR.

International Labour Office. 1989. *Yearbook of Labour Statistics, Retrospective Edition, 1945–1989*. Geneva: ILO.

Iran Yearbook 1988. 1988. Bonn: Moini-Biontino Verlagsgesellschaft.

Islamic Republic of Iran. 1987. *National Census of Population and Housing 1365* [1986]. Tehran: Central Statistical Office, Plan and Budget Organization.

Jayawardena, Kumari. 1986. *Feminism and Nationalism in the Third World.* London: Zed Books.

Joekes, Susan. 1987. *Women in the World Economy: An INSTRAW Study.* New York: Oxford University Press.

Kagitcibasi, Cigdem, ed. 1982. *Sex Roles, Family and Community in Turkey.* Bloomington: Indiana University Press.

Kahne, Hilda and Janet Giele, eds. 1992. *Women's Work and Women's Lives: The Continuing Struggle Worldwide.* Boulder: Westview Press.

Kamali, Mohammad Hashim. 1985. *Law in Afghanistan: A Study of the Constitutions, Matrimonial Law and the Judiciary.* Leiden: E. J. Brill.

Kandiyoti, Deniz. 1977. "Sex Roles and Social Change: A Comparative Appraisal of Turkey's Women." In Wellesley Editorial Committee, ed., *Women and National Development.* Chicago: University of Chicago Press.

———. 1984. "Rural Transformation in Turkey and Its Implications for Women's Status." In UNESCO, ed., *Women on the Move.* Paris: UNESCO.

———. 1988. "Bargaining with Patriarchy." *Gender & Society* 2 (3) (September):274–289.

Kandiyoti, Deniz, ed. 1991. *Women, Islam and the State.* London: Macmillan.

Keddie, Nikki R. 1990. "The Past and Present of Women in the Muslim World." *Journal of World History* 1 (1):77–108.

Khomeini, Ayatollah. 1981. *Islam and Revolution: Writings and Declarations of Imam Khomeini.* Trans. Hamid Algar. Berkeley: Mizan Press.

Kimmel, Michael. 1990. *Revolution: A Sociological Interpretation.* Cambridge, UK: Polity Press.

Knauss, Peter. 1987. *The Persistence of Patriarchy: Class, Gender and Ideology in Twentieth Century Algeria.* New York: Praeger.

Kruks, Sonia, Rayna Rapp, and Marilyn Young, eds. 1989. *Promissory Notes: Women in the Transition to Socialism.* New York: Monthly Review Press.

Lajoinie, Simone Bailleau. 1980. *Conditions des femmes en Afghanistan.* Paris: Notre Temps/Monde.

Leahy, Margaret E. 1986. *Development Strategies and the Status of Women: A Comparative Study of the United States, Mexico, the Soviet Union, and Cuba.* Boulder: Lynne Rienner.

Lerner, Gerda. 1986. *The Creation of Patriarchy.* New York: Oxford University Press.

Mahedevan, K., Akbar Aghajanian, R. Jayasree, and G. S. Moni. 1989. "Status of Women and Population Dynamics: A Conceptual Model." In K. Mahdevan, ed., *Women and Population Dynamics: Asian Perspectives.* New Delhi: Sage.

Male, Beverly. 1982. *Revolutionary Afghanistan.* New York: St. Martin's Press.

Mandelbaum, David. 1988. *Women's Seclusion and Men's Honor.* Tucson: University of Arizona Press.

Marshall, Susan. 1984. "Politics and Female Status in North Africa: A Reconsideration of Development Theory." *Economic Development and Cultural Change* 32 (3): 499–524.

McDonald, Peter. 1985. "Social Organization and Nuptiality in Developing Societies." In John Cleland and John Hobcraft, eds., *Reproductive Change in Developing Countries: Insights from the World Fertility Survey.* Oxford: Oxford University Press.

Mehran, Golnar. 1989. "Socialization of Schoolchildren in the Islamic Republic of Iran." *Iranian Studies* 22 (1):35–50.

Mernissi, Fatima. 1987. *Beyond the Veil: Male-Female Dynamics in Modern Muslim Society.* (Revised Edition.) Bloomington: Indiana University Press.
———. 1988. *Doing Daily Battle: Interviews with Moroccan Women.* Trans. Mary Jo Lakeland. London: The Women's Press.
Minces, Juliette. 1982. *The House of Obedience.* London: Zed Books.
Moghadam, V. M. 1988. "Women, Work and Ideology in the Islamic Republic." *International Journal of Middle East Studies* 20 (2) (May):221–243.
———. 1990. *Gender, Development and Policy: Toward Equity and Empowerment.* UNU/WIDER Research for Action Series (November).
———. 1992. "Patriarchy and the Politics of Gender in Modernizing Societies: Afghanistan, Iran, Pakistan." *International Sociology* 7 (1) (March):35–53.
Mojab, Shahrzad. 1987. "The Islamic Government's Policy on Women's Access to Higher Education and Its Impact on the Socio-Economic Status of Women." Michigan State University, Office of Women in International Development, Working Paper No. 156.
Molyneux, Maxine. 1985. "Legal Reform and Socialist Revolution in Democratic Yemen: Women and the Family." *International Journal of Sociology of Law* 13:147–172.
Morgan, Robin, ed. 1984. *Sisterhood Is Global.* New York: Anchor Books.
Mutahhari, Murteza. 1987. *On the Islamic Hijab.* Tehran: Islamic Propagation Organization.
Nashat, Guity, ed. 1983. *Women and Revolution in Iran.* Boulder: Westview Press.
Nasir, Jamal J. 1990. *The Status of Women Under Islamic Law.* London: Graham & Trotman.
Niblock, Tim. 1991. "International and Domestic Factors in the Economic Liberalisation Process in Arab Countries." Paper prepared for the Symposium on Economic Liberalisation and Its Social and Political Effects, University of Essex (September).
Nyrop, Richard and Donald Seekins. 1986. *Afghanistan: A Country Study.* Washington, D.C.: The American University, Foreign Area Studies.
Papanek, Hanna. 1985. "Class and Gender in Education-Employment Linkages." *Comparative Education Review* 29 (3) (August):317–346.
Parpart, Jane L. and Kathleen A. Staudt, eds. 1989. *Women and the State in Africa.* Boulder: Lynne Rienner.
Pitt-Rivers, Julian. 1977. *The Fate of Shechem or the Politics of Sex: Essays in the Anthropology of the Mediterranean.* Cambridge, UK: Cambridge University Press.
Qahreman, Shirin. 1988. "The Islamic Regime's Policy on Women's Access to Higher Education." *Nimeye Digar* 7 (Summer):16–31 (in Persian).
Redclift, Nanneke and M. Thea Sinclair, eds. 1991. *Working Women: International Perspectives on Labour and Gender Ideology.* London and New York: Routledge.
Reynolds, Sîan. 1987. "Marianne's Citizens? Women, the Republic and Universal Suffrage in France." In Sîan Reynolds, ed., *Woman, State and Revolution: Essays on Power and Gender in Europe Since 1789.* Amherst: University of Massachussetts Press.
Richards, Alan and John Waterbury. 1990. *A Political Economy of the Middle East: State, Class and Economic Development.* Boulder: Westview Press.
Roy, Olivier. 1986. *Islam and Resistance in Afghanistan.* Cambridge, MA: Cambridge University Press.
Saadi, Nouredine. 1991. *La Femme et La Loi en Algérie.* Casablanca: Editions Fennec for UNU/WIDER.

Sabbah, Fatna A. 1984. *Woman in the Muslim Unconscious.* Trans. Mary Jo Lakeland. New York: Pergamon Press.

Seddon, David. 1992. "Popular Protest, Austerity and Economic Liberalisation in the Middle East and North Africa." Discussion Paper No. 221, School of Development Studies, University of East Anglia.

Shahrani, Nazif and Robert Canfield, eds. 1984. *Revolutions and Rebellions in Afghanistan.* Berkeley: University of California International Studies Institute.

Shami, Seteney, L. Taminian, S. Morsy, Z. B. El Bakri, and E. Kameir. 1990. *Women in Arab Society: Work Patterns and Gender Relations in Egypt, Jordan and Sudan.* Providence: Berg/UNESCO.

Sharabi, Hisham. 1988. *Neopatriarchy: A Theory of Distorted Change in Arab Society.* New York: Oxford University Press.

Sivan, Emmanuel. 1985. *Radical Islam.* New Haven: Yale University Press.

Sivard, Ruth Leger. 1985. *Women . . . A World Survey.* Washington, D.C.: Global Priorities.

Standing, Guy. 1987. "Vulnerable Groups in Urban Labour Processes." WEP Labour Market Analysis Working Paper No. 31. Geneva: ILO.

———. 1989. "Global Feminisation Through Flexible Labour." WEP Labour Market Analysis Working Paper No. 31. Geneva: ILO. [Shorter version in *World Development* 17 (7):1077–1096.]

Statistical Center of Iran. 1987. *National Census of Population and Housing 1986* (Total Country Summary). Tehran: Plan and Budget Organization.

Statistical Yearbook 1367 (1988). 1989. Tehran: Statistical Center of Iran, Plan and Budget Organization.

Stichter, Sharon and Jane L. Parpart, eds. 1990. *Women, Employment, and the Family in the International Division of Labour.* London: Macmillan.

Stowasser, Barbara F. 1987. "Liberated Equal or Protected Dependent: Contemporary Religious Paradigms on Women's Status in Islam." *Arab Studies Quarterly* 9:260–283.

Tabari, Azar and Nahid Yeganeh, eds. 1982. *In the Shadow of Islam: The Women's Movement in Iran.* London: Zed Books.

Tillion, Germaine. 1983. *The Republic of Cousins.* London: Al-Saqi Books.

Tinker, Irene, ed. 1990. *Persistent Inequalities: Women and World Development.* New York: Oxford University Press.

Toubia, Nahid, ed. 1988. *Women of the Arab World: The Coming Challenge.* London: Zed Books.

United Nations. 1991. *The World's Women: Trends and Statistics 1970–1990.* New York: United Nations.

United Nations Development Programme. 1990. *Human Development Report 1989.* New York: Oxford University Press.

UNESCO. 1984. *Social Science Research and Women in the Arab World.* London: Francis Pinter.

United Nations Fund for Population Activities/Ministère du Plan (Ministry of Planning). *La Femme et La Famille Tunisienne a Travers Les Chiffres.* Tunis, 1984.

United Nations Children's Fund. 1987. *Adjustment with a Human Face.* Edited by G. Cornia, R. Jolly, and F. Stewart. Oxford and New York: Clarendon Press.

———. 1989. *The State of the World's Children 1989.* New York: Oxford University Press.

United Nations Division for the Advancement of Women. 1985. *United Nations Convention on the Elimination of All Forms of Discrimination Against Women.* Vienna: United Nations Office in Vienna.

————. 1990. "International Standards of Equality and Religious Freedom: Implications for the Status of Women." Paper prepared for the UNU/WIDER Roundtable on Identity Politics and Women, Helsinki (October 8–10).

Urban, Mark. 1988. *War in Afghanistan.* New York: St. Martin's Press.

Utas, Bo, ed. 1983. *Women in Islamic Society.* Copenhagen: Scandinavian Institute of Asian Studies.

Walby, Sylvia. 1989. "Theorising Patriarchy." *Sociology* 23 (2):213–34.

Ward, Kathryn. 1984. *Women in the World-System: Its Impact on Status and Fertility.* New York: Praeger.

————, ed. 1990. *Women Workers and Global Restructuring.* Ithaca: ILR Press.

Weeks, John. 1988. "The Demography of Islamic Nations." *Population Bulletin* 43 (4) (December).

Weiss, Anita M. 1993. "The Consequences of State Policy for Women in Pakistan." In Myron Weiner and Ali Banuazizi, eds., *Transformation in Afghanistan, Iran, and Pakistan.* Syracuse: Syracuse University Press (forthcoming).

Wolf, Diane L. 1990. "Daughters, Decisions and Domination: An Empirical and Conceptual Critique of Houschold Strategies." *Development and Change* 21 (1) (January):43–74.

Wood, Ellen Meiksins. 1988. "Capitalism and Human Emancipation." *New Left Review* 167 (January–February):1–21.

World Bank. Various years. *World Development Report.* New York: Oxford University Press.

Worsley, Peter. 1986. *The Three Worlds: Culture and World Development.* Chicago: University of Chicago Press.

Yuval-Davis, Nira and Floya Anthias, eds. 1989. *Woman-Nation-State.* London: Macmillan.

▲
Index

▲
About the Book and Author

Exploring the impact of social change in the Middle East on women's status and roles, as well as women's varied responses, this book focuses on the gender dynamics of some of the major social processes in the region: economic development and women's employment, reforms and revolutions, the changing family, and Islamist movements. In doing so, it reveals that middle-class women are at the center of change and discourses about change in the region.

Moghadam crafts a conceptual framework based on the role of the state, development strategies, class, and culture in the shaping of women's lives. Writing from a Marxist-feminist perspective, she looks at the salience of the "woman question" and constructions of gender in the midst of social and political change. Data from a number of countries are presented, including in-depth case studies of Afghanistan and Iran.

Valentine M. Moghadam is senior research fellow at the United Nations University's World Institute for Development Economics Research in Helsinki.